PERGAMON GENERAL PSYCHOLOGY SERIES

Editors: Arnold P. Goldstein, *Syracuse University*
Leonard Krasner, *SUNY, Stony Brook*

The Practice of Behavior Therapy

PGPS-1

Second Edition

.... It is the business of epistemology to arrange the propositions which constitute our knowledge in a certain logical order, in which the later propositions are accepted because of their logical relation to those that come before them. It is not necessary that the later propositions should be logically deducible from the earlier ones; what is necessary is that the earlier ones should supply whatever grounds exist for thinking it likely that the later ones are true.

Bertrand Russell
An Inquiry into Meaning and Truth

The Practice of Behavior Therapy

JOSEPH WOLPE, M.D.

*Professor of Psychiatry, Temple University
School of Medicine and Eastern Pennsylvania
Psychiatric Institute
Philadelphia, Pennsylvania*

Second Edition

PERGAMON PRESS INC.

New York · Toronto · Oxford · Sydney

PERGAMON PRESS INC.
Maxwell House, Fairview Park, Elmsford, N.Y. 10523

PERGAMON OF CANADA LTD.
207 Queen's Quay West, Toronto 117, Ontario

PERGAMON PRESS LTD.
Headington Hill Hall, Oxford

PERGAMON PRESS (AUST.) PTY. LTD.
Rushcutters Bay, Sydney, N.S.W.

Copyright© 1973, Pergamon Press Inc.

Library of Congress Cataloging in Publication Data

Wolpe, Joseph.
    The practice of behavior therapy.

    (Pergamon general psychology series, PGPS-1)
    Bibliography: p.
    1. Behavior therapy. I. Title. [DNLM: 1. Be-
havior therapy. WM 420 W866pa 1973]
RC489. B4W6   1973   616.8'91   72-11653
ISBN 0-08-017089-7
ISBN 0-08-017090-0 (pbk)

Second Printing

Printed in the United States of America

To Allan and David

Contents

From the Preface to the First Edition

Behavior therapy, or conditioning therapy, is the use of experimentally established principles of learning for the purpose of changing unadaptive behavior. Unadaptive habits are weakened and eliminated; adaptive habits are initiated and strengthened. The now popular term, *behavior therapy*, introduced by Skinner and Lindsley (1954), owes its wide promulgation and acceptance to Eysenck (1959, 1960, 1965).

Before the advent of behavior therapy, psychological medicine was a medley of speculative systems and intuitive methods. Behavior therapy is an applied science, in every way parallel to other modern technologies, and in particular those that constitute modern medical therapeutics. Therapeutic possibilities radiate from the uncovering of the lawful relations of organismal processes. Since learning is the organismal process most relevant to psychological medicine, the establishment of lawful relations relevant to the learning process is the main road to therapeutic power in this field.

However, the scientifically-minded behavior therapist need not confine himself to methods derived from principles. For the welfare of his patients, he employs, whenever necessary, methods that have been *empirically* shown to be effective. Colchicum was a well-authenticated and widely-used remedy for attacks of gout long before colchicine was isolated or the metabolism of gout understood (Stetten, 1968). In the same way, in present-day behavior therapy, we use mixtures of carbon dioxide and oxygen to alleviate pervasive anxiety without knowing the mechanism of their action. The criterion is the existence of compelling evidence of a relationship between the administration of the agent and clinical change.

But whereas in other fields of medicine empirical effectiveness is often quite easy to establish – as, for example, when a medicament consistently clears up a chronic skin infection in a few days – in psychotherapy unusual care is needed to ensure specification of the technique. For example, if interpretation is claimed to be an effective technique, the character and conditions of the interpretations need to be specified.

A very special difficulty in evaluating how much a psychotherapeutic technique *per se* contributes to change resides in the fact that almost any form of psychotherapy produces substantial benefit in about fifty percent of cases, apparently because of anxiety-inhibiting emotional reactions that therapists evoke in patients (Wolpe, 1958). Therefore, a particular technique must be, *prima facie* at least, effective beyond that level if it is to be even provisionally recommended on empirical grounds. Failure to observe this rule can lead to the gullible acceptance of almost anything that is touted, and back to the pre-scientific chaos of recipes from which modern technological principles have extricated us.

Two themes have recently been prominent among the criticisms voiced by opponents of behavior therapy. One is that it is 'mechanistic and non-humanistic.' The two adjectives are usually combined as though they belonged together like face and beard. Insofar as behavior therapy leans on mechanisms it is indeed mechanistic. But nobody can fairly call it non-humanistic. No basis exists for the idea that others have more compassion than the behavioristic psychotherapist. Internal medicine is not dehumanized when penicillin replaces bloodletting as a treatment for infections; and no more is psychotherapy when conditioning replaces free association. The therapist's concern for his patients and his sympathy with their sufferings is not diminished by his having at his command methods that are based on knowledge of mechanisms.

The other theme of criticism is that there is a narrowness of vision involved in the attempt to apply a 'simple' model to the complexities of the human personality (see for example, Breger and McGaugh, 1965). There are at least two answers. First, the stimulus-response model is not simple. Second, the methods that this model has generated are evidently more effective in changing the neurotic personality than the more in-volved frameworks that these critics favor. How can these other frame-works be 'better' without the validation of experimental testing which none of them have?

This volume, *The Practice of Behavior Therapy*, has grown out of my personal contribution to an earlier co-authored book, *Behavior Therapy Techniques* (Pergamon Press, 1966). In this new volume I have included additional material not formerly available. The main source of new techniques continues to be the experimental paradigms described in my original monograph, *Psychotherapy by Reciprocal Inhibition* (Stanford University Press, 1958). The emphasis is very much on the treatment of *neuroses*. There are augmented accounts of the variants of systematic desensitization, the treatment of frigidity, aversion therapy, 'flooding' techniques, the use of drugs, and a chapter on operant conditioning. The many illustrative cases include four complex ones given at length.

I am grateful to those who have helped in the literary side of the book's production—Mrs. Barbara Srinivasan, Mrs. Aviva Wanderer, and my wife; and to my old friend and colleague, Dr. L. J. Reyna, who, as so often in the past, has been a fount of information and ideas.

Preface to the Second Edition

In the three years that have passed since the publication of the first edition of this book, behavior therapy has continued to advance impressively on all fronts. Research activity has multiplied so that two new journals have arisen to contain it – the *Journal of Behavior Therapy and Experimental Psychiatry* and *Behavior Therapy*; and there has been a considerable increase in the educational offerings of university psychiatric departments and divisions of clinical psychology. Nevertheless, the amount of systematic practical training available is far short of the demand and textbooks continue to have an unusually large pedagogic role.

Research endeavor has been massive. In preparing a review of behavior therapy, Krasner (1971) found 4,000 titles to draw on. The findings of this research have by and large continued to confirm the efficacy of the practices of behavior therapy, demonstrating increasingly, both directly and indirectly, the relevance and power of its underlying principles, originally stated in B. F. Skinner's *Science and Human Behavior* and my own *Psychotherapy by Reciprocal Inhibition*. There have been important analyses of the constituents of the therapeutic procedures (e.g. Paul, 1966; Lang, Melamed, and Hart, 1970) and of the mechanisms by which change is presumed to occur (e.g. Lader and Mathews, 1969; Van Egeren, Feather, and Hein, 1971).

This edition is markedly different from the first. Those parts of the text that have been retained have been extensively revised. Some sections of the early chapters have been rearranged to improve their logical order, and others have been recast and extended in the interests of clarity. New case material has been added to all clinical chapters. Many new techniques are described, and a few older ones have been superseded.

Changes that deserve special mention are a much more thorough exposition of assertive training, a modernized account of systematic desensitization, the addition of several new variants of desensitization, a description of recent research on flooding and new indications for it, an extended treatment of operant conditioning methods, a greatly clarified description of aversion therapy, and a new chapter giving consideration to special syndromes such as homosexuality, character neurosis, and reactive depression.

I thank Dr. David A. Soskis for his incisive comments that led to many beneficial changes in this edition, my research assistant, Mrs. Barbara Srinivasan, for her skilful handling of the jigsaw of old and new pieces, and my secretary, Mrs. Betty Jean Smith, for her infallibly correct and beautiful typing.

J. WOLPE, M. D.

CHAPTER 1

Introduction

A habit is a consistent way of responding to defined stimulus conditions. Ordinarily a habit declines — undergoes extinction — when its consequences become unadaptive, i.e. when it fails either to subserve the needs of the organism or to avoid injury, pain, or fatigue. Some unadaptive habits, for various reasons, fail to extinguish; and it is these that become therapeutic problems. Behavior therapy consists of applying experimentally established principles to overcoming these persistent unadaptive habits, scanning the whole range of the behavioral sciences, if need be, to obtain relevant principles.

HISTORICAL PERSPECTIVE

While the modern behavior therapist deliberately applies principles of learning to his operations, therapeutic prescriptions involving behavior are probably as old as civilization — if we consider civilization as having begun when man first did things to further the well-being of other men. From the time that this became a feature of human life there must have been occasions when a man complained of his ills to another who advised or persuaded him on a course of action. This could be regarded as a behavioral therapy whenever the behavior itself was conceived as the therapeutic agent.

Ancient writings contain innumerable examples of therapeutic advice which would constitute behavioral therapy in this sense, even if they were ineffective. But we can hardly doubt that not infrequently some of the therapy did work, if not always in the way the counsellor believed.

Often, surely, there were 'suggestion' effects or 'placebo' effects, by virtue of the responses to which words or things had previously been conditioned; and sometimes the instigated changes in behavior would have led to reconditioning, with beneficial consequences for emotionally disturbed states.

Despite the derogation he usually receives, Mesmer (1779) deserves our salutation as evidently the first therapist to base his efforts at behavior change on a general behavioral principle. Though that principle did not stand up to scientific testing it generated procedures that *were* often successful. Their essential elements were subsequently elucidated by the researches of de Puysegur, Bernheim, and later investigators, and were the fountainhead of later techniques of suggestion and hypnosis (and other forms of verbal control of behavior) which have continued to play a part in behavior therapy — and probably always will.

The classical forms of suggestion are designed to substitute desirable for undesirable behavior by direct verbal prescription. As it now seems, when this works it is because the new response competes with the old, and, if it dominates, inhibits the latter. Whenever, either immediately or after repetition, this is followed by lasting diminution (or elimination) of the old response we have an instance of conditioned inhibition based on reciprocal inhibition (see below). If standard practices of hypnotherapy have not been impressive in their long-term results, it is probably because they have not brought the suggested responses into effective apposition with those it has been necessary to eliminate.

An early example of a less direct use of competing responses that is remarkably close to some modern practices was recently unearthed by Stewart (1961) from a book by Leuret (1846). The patient was a thirty-year-old wine merchant with a ten-year history of obsessional thoughts which had become so insistent that he had ceased to be able to carry on his business. Having admitted the patient to hospital, Leuret ordered him to read and learn songs which he could recite the next day. The patient's food ration depended upon how much he had learnt. This regime continued for about six weeks during which the patient's recitals steadily improved. Meanwhile his obsessional thoughts were interfering less and less, and at the end of the six weeks he told Leuret that he had not had the thoughts for several days and that he felt much better. Leuret found him work as a nurse, and a year later noted that he was still well and a very successful nurse. Further examples of the clinical operations of this forerunner of modern behavior therapy have recently been published (Gourevitch, 1968; Wolpe and Theriault, 1971).

The 19th century therapist had some empirical guidelines for his techniques, but each therapeutic foray was an experiment whose outcome could not be predicted. The writings of Sigmund Freud introduced a new system of therapeutic methods that were based on detailed and coherent theoretical principles. Strange as it may seem to some in the present context, this system was truly a more comprehensive kind of behavioral therapy than had ever before been available; for, no matter what may be said of the theory, it was through behavior, and that alone, that Freud set out to bring therapeutic change. The techniques did not, in fact, afford the hoped for increase in favorable and predictable outcomes, but the remarkably ingenious and colorful theoretical framework upon which Freud based them, and his uncanny persuasiveness in the exposition of his views brought an excitement into the field that made the topic more widely attractive than it had ever seemed before.

Nevertheless, during the first half of the 20th century, in terms of scientific advancement, no other field of knowledge lay more stagnant than behavioral therapeutics. No hypotheses were being put to the test; no lawful relations were being established; and no reliable rules existed for procuring therapeutic change. The explanation for this is that modern therapy is applied science; and behavior therapy could not enter the world of science before there was a sufficient foundation for it in data from the experimental laboratory.

THE DEVELOPMENT OF SCIENTIFIC BEHAVIOR THERAPY

Eventually, as studies of normal behavior, largely in the laboratory, revealed more and more about the factors determining the acquisition, elicitation, maintenance, and decline of habits, some of this knowledge lent itself to the construction of hypotheses to account for the special characteristics of certain types of abnormal behavior. Certain of these hypotheses subsequently withstood testing by observation, and thereby acquired scientific standing.

Behavior therapy had its conceptual origin in 1920 in Watson and Rayner's famous experiment on Little Albert. When the child had been conditioned to fear a white rat, and, by generalization, other furry objects, the experimenters proposed that the conditioning might be overcome in four possible ways—by experimental extinction, by 'constructive' activities around the feared object, by 'reconditioning' through feeding the child candy in the presence of the feared object, or by procuring competition with fear by stimulating erogenous zones in the presence of the feared object. The last three of these suggestions are all on the counter-conditioning model, but none of them were attempted because Albert left the hospital.

A few years later, one of Watson and Rayner's suggestions was adopted by Mary Cover Jones (1924) in connection with children's phobias. She described the method she employed as follows:

> During a period of craving for food, the child is placed in a high chair and given some-thing to eat. The feared object is brought in, starting a negative response. It is then moved away gradually until it is at a sufficient distance not to interfere with the child's eating. The relative strength of the fear impulse and the hunger impulse may be gauged by the distance to which it is necessary to remove the feared object. While the child is eating, the object is slowly brought nearer to the table, then placed upon the table and, finally, as the tolerance increases, it is brought close enough to be touched. Since we could not interfere with the regular schedule of meals, we chose the time of the mid-morning lunch for the experiment. This usually assured some degree of interest in the food and corresponding success in our treatment.

Jones (1924a) illustrated the use of this method in detail in a description of the now classic case of the boy Peter—"one of our most serious problem cases," who recovered after daily treatment over a period of two months. Jones was clearly aware of the role of hunger in the overcoming of the fear habit, noting that the effectiveness of the method increased as hunger was greater, and that "the repeated presentation of a feared object, with no auxiliary attempt to eliminate the fear, is more likely to produce a summation effect than an adaptation."

Such observations, indicating the lawful relations between the phenomena at issue, give her work an honored place in the history of the development of techniques of this kind. At about the same time, Burnham (1924), starting from a different orientation, was also proposing the use of counteractive behavior as an agent of habit change. Awareness of the relevant factors was not shared years later by Herzberg (1941) and Ter-hune (1948) who also made use of graduated tasks in the therapy of neurotic patients.

In the meantime, the most studied habit-eliminating process was—and has continued to be—experimental extinction—the gradual decrement in strength and frequency of responses associated with their unreinforced evocation. Dunlap (1932) probed the therapeutic possibilities of this process, and evolved the technique called 'negative practice,' whereby undesirable motor habits are overcome as a result of their repeated evocation. About the same time, Guthrie (1935) had noticed the general therapeutic applicability of the counterconditioning method that Jones had demonstrated, and concluded that the simplest rule for breaking a habit is "to find the cues that initiate the action and to practice another response to these cues" (Guthrie, 1935, p. 138). He stressed the need to control the situation so that the cue to the original response is present while "other behavior prevails."

The next step forward occurred when Guthrie's principle was applied to the experimental neuroses. These syndromes were first produced in Pavlov's laboratories early in the 20th century, and in many other places subsequently.

Because the behavior of neurotic animals is strikingly different from normal, and is moreover exceedingly persistent, all the earlier experimenters shared the opinion that some kind of lesion or physiopathology was the basis of these neuroses. The Russian workers believed this opinion to be supported by the finding that in certain instances the neuroses were overcome by giving the animals depressant or excitant drugs. However, in 1943, grounds for disagreement with this view emerged. Masserman, in the course of an imaginative series of experiments on cats that had been made neurotic by being shocked in a small cage, observed that the neuroses could be overcome when the animals were induced to feed in that cage by being forced towards the food. The fact that the mere evocation of the eating patterns of behavior could 'cure' the neuroses spoke against a lesion theory, and the fact that in order to procure the change the behavior had to be evoked in the experimental cage (in contrast to the living cage) strongly suggested that learning was at play. It must be said that these were not the conclusions reached by Masserman who, accustomed to 'psychodynamic' thinking, interpreted the facts in terms of "breaking through the motivational conflict"—an interpretation whose inadequacy was first pointed out several years later (Wolpe, 1956).

The next requirement was to devise tests for the learning hypothesis. To begin with, it was necessary to define 'learning' rather clearly. The following definition was adopted:

Learning may be said to have occurred if a response has been evoked in temporal contiguity with a given sensory stimulus and it is subsequently found that the stimulus can evoke the response although it could not have done so before. If the stimulus could have evoked the response before but subsequently evokes it more strongly, then, too, learning may be said to have occurred (Wolpe, 1952a).

Several predictions were then made that would necessarily be fulfilled if the neurotic behavior were indeed learned. If they were not fulfilled, the learning hypothesis would have to be abandoned. They were:

1. The behavior manifested in an experimental neurosis must be essentially the same as that elicited by the stimulus situation that precipitates the neurosis.
2. The neurotic behavior must be at greatest intensity when the animal is exposed to stimuli most like those in whose presence the neurosis was precipitated, and the intensity must decrease as a direct function of diminishing resemblance (according to the principle of primary stimulus generalization).
3. Unlearning of neurotic behavior should occur in circumstances like those that produce unlearning in other contexts, i.e. extinction and/ or counterconditioning.

Each of these predictions was submitted to experimental test[1] in 1947 (Wolpe, 1952, 1958) in cat neuroses produced by high-voltage low-amperage shocks in an experimental cage similar to that used by Masserman, and each prediction was sustained. In every animal the features of the reactions to shock were duplicated in the reactions of the neurosis; the intensity of neurotic response decreased as the environment to which the neurotic animal was exposed was less similar to that of the experimental cage; and while the reactions could not be overcome by the extinction process — partly, it seems, because of the small amount of reactive inhibition evoked by autonomic responses (Wolpe, 1958), it was possible to eliminate them through the reciprocal inhibition of weak anxiety responses by feeding. The animals would first be fed in a place where only slight anxiety was aroused — by stimuli remote on a generalization continuum — and when the anxiety was no longer noticeable in that place, we would advance along the continuum.

The foregoing having provided some assurance that experimental neuroses were learned, the next proposition that called for testing was that *human* neuroses are parallel to experimental neuroses in respect of the three features at issue: acquisition by learning, primary stimulus generalization, and elimination by unlearning.

[1]Generous laboratory facilities and technical assistance were provided by Dr. James M. Watt, Professor of Pharmacology at the University of Witwatersrand Medical School. It was also fortunate that just at that time Dr. Leo J. Reyna had taken up an appointment in the Psychology Department of the University. He was enormously helpful in the working out of the conceptual and practical problems involved in the experiments.

With regard to the first, a study was made of the historical antecedents of the 'symptoms' in clinical cases of neurosis. In a large proportion of them a clear history of the time of onset of particular reactions was obtained. In these instances, the patient recalled either a particular occasion of great distress or else the repeated arousal of anxiety in a recurrent situation involving, for example, a threatening parent or a hostile school-teacher. It was invariably found that neurotic reactions whose origin could be dated to such experiences had come to be evocable by stimuli similar to those that were to the forefront in the precipitating situations (although other stimuli later became effective in many cases, through second-order conditioning (see Wolpe, 1958)).

It was also evident that human neurotic reactions obey the principle of primary stimulus generalization (Wolpe, 1958, 1961a). As in the animal neuroses, their intensity is determined by the degree of similarity of the evoking stimulus to a zenithal stimulus that is often identical with the original conditioned stimulus. In a particular case, there may be several physically unrelated classes of anxiety-arousing stimuli, each of which is found on examination to have a zenith and a generalization gradient. The ranked members of a gradient constitute a 'hierarchy.' In man there are often hierarchies based upon similarities of internal effects (secondary generalization) – Osgood's 'mediated generalization.' For example, physically dissimilar situations may have the theme of rejection in common, and insofar as the patient is disturbed by rejection the hierarchical order of the situations is determined by the relative strength of the reactions they evoke. To take a particular instance in another area (Wolpe, 1961), a patient with claustrophobia also had claustrophobic reactions in situations that had the mere 'feel' of enclosement, e.g. a tight zipper, or wanting to remove nailpolish while having no access to polish remover (see Chapter 7).

As regards the third question – the role of learning in recovery from human neuroses – the following may be said. Like animal neuroses, human neuroses are not usually extinguishable by repeated evocation of the neurotic responses. The first evidence that they may be overcome by graduated counterconditioning came from Mary Cover Jones' treatment of children's phobias cited above (p. 4), whose technique was almost identical with that used to overcome animal neuroses. In recent years, adult human neuroses have been treated by methods that employ responses other than feeding for the reciprocal inhibition and counterconditioning of anxiety (Wolpe, 1958; Eysenck, 1960); and these are the main subject-matter of this book.

The facts pointing to the role of learning in human neuroses have been essentially 'clinical,' but insofar as the observations have been consistent and have been confirmed by independent observers, it may be said that the learning hypothesis of neurosis has cleared its first hurdles and qualified as a scientific hypothesis.

However, properly controlled experimental observations are necessary. Many tasks lie ahead, but data is already available, and all of it accords with the clinical findings. Experiments on the *production* of human neuroses are naturally considered with hesitation, if not trepidation, so that it is not surprising that only three can be cited. One is the previously mentioned Watson and Rayner experiment (1920). The second is Krasnogorski's (1925) induction of experimental neuroses in children by exposing them to ambivalent stimuli in relation to the conditioning of alimentary responses – a procedure very similar to a common technique for producing experimental neuroses in Pavlov's laboratories (Pavlov, 1927). Thirdly, Campbell, Sanderson, and Laverty (1964) have demonstrated (though not in a context of *neurosis-production*) that marked anxiety reactions can be conditioned by a single severe stress due to respiratory paralysis, and, furthermore, that later evocation of the conditioned response in the absence of the stress is associated with *increased* strength instead of the weakening that is usually seen in such circumstances. Their observation accords with a common clinical experience with neuroses (Wolpe, 1958, p. 99).

It is much more congenial to perform *therapeutic* experiments, and there is a growing output of studies of the therapeutic process. For example, Lang and Lazovik (1963), Lang (1964), and Lang, Lazovik, and Reynolds (1965), in controlled studies of the desensitization of snake phobias, have found therapeutic change to be correlated with the conditioning procedure, and not to be attributed to suggestion, rapport ('transference'), or muscle relaxation; and Rachman (1965) and Davison (1965) have both shown that the whole desensitization procedure is significantly more effective than either of its elements – scene presentation or relaxation. In the field of therapy employing operant conditioning, process studies are already numerous. A considerable number of them have been collected in volumes edited by Krasner and Ullmann (1965), Franks (1965), Eysenck (1964), and Ulrich, Stachnik, and Mabry (1966, 1970).

WHY BEHAVIOR THERAPY?

The most enviable feature of behavior therapy is in the command it gives to the therapist, both in general planning of his therapeutic campaign and in modifying its details as he goes along. When a particular maneuver fails to accomplish change, another will be tried that, like its predecessor, is logically deductible from an experimentally established principle — sometimes the same principle, sometimes another. When there are signs that a maneuver is inhibiting the anxiety responses to given stimuli, that maneuver is systematically used to break down the anxiety-evoking potential of these stimuli. The specificity of the effects obtained is often extremely clear, as demonstrated in the experimental case study of a multi-faceted automobile phobia described in Chapter 14. In classical phobias treated by desensitization therapy, there is a mathematical relationship between the number of scene presentations and the degree of recovery procured (see Chapter 6).

The power to intervene rationally and predictably makes a striking contrast to the uncertainty of the conventional therapist's position. Since the latter directs his procedures at an 'inner process' which he regards as responsible for the unadaptive behavior, instead of working on the behavior itself, he can only stand aside passively and hope for favorable behavioral effects to follow his efforts.

This being the case, it is not surprising that the literature on conventional psychotherapy gives so much weight to the patient-therapist relationship, and encourages the belief that the quality of that relationship is more relevant to the production of beneficial effects than any specific methods that the therapist employs. This is probably true of the conventional therapies. As Frank (1961) has shown, a relationship in which the therapist is able to mobilize the patient's expectation of help and hope of relief is in and of itself a powerful therapeutic instrument. It is probably because the conventional therapies all depend practically entirely upon the relationship that they all achieve much the same results (Eysenck, 1952). The procedures of behavior therapy have effects additional to these relational effects that are common to all forms of psychotherapy. The practice of behavior therapy may thus be viewed as a 'double-barrelled' means of alleviating neurotic distress (see Chapter 15).

Statistical studies of the effects of behavior therapy by competent therapists have shown that almost 90 percent recovery or marked improvement may be expected among patients who have had a reasonable amount of exposure to behavioral methods. These studies are summarized in Chapter 15, where they are also compared with statistics from other therapies. The comparisons are clearly favorable to behavior therapy, but vulnerable to the criticism of lack of control. The results of some well-controlled outcome studies, however, also emerge decisively on the side of behavior therapy. A point that must be given emphasis is that *behavior therapy is effective in all neuroses* and not only in unitary phobias.

All in all, there is reason for confidence in the practice of behavior therapy. It is founded in biology and its principles and practices are determined by the rules of science. Its clinical results are encouraging. And it is still in its infancy. The methods in use today will look very rough-hewn a decade or two from now. We may anticipate the fulfillment of Reyna's (1964) expectation that "more rigorous applications of the laws of learning will render conditioning therapies even more effective; and will extend their use to a broader range of behavior problems."

The *raison d'être* of psychotherapy is the presumption that it can overcome certain classes of human suffering. It is most frequently for neurotic symptoms and related disabilities that patients seek psychiatric help. The distress that the neurotic patient brings to the therapist for resolution is just as real and poignant as if it had been due to an organic illness. The most important criterion of therapeutic success is the lasting alleviation of this disturbance. It is of small comfort to a patient whose neurotic anxieties remain undiminished after treatment to tell him that he is cured because his personality has matured.

One consequence of the realization that neurotic behavior is learned is that it places the responsibility for the patient's recovery unequivocally in the hands of the therapist—in contrast to the view that emanates from the psychoanalytic mystique that the patient is responsible for failures of his treatment (the presumption being that the therapist would not fail but for the patient's invidious resistance!). The fact is that if a patient fails to improve despite his diligent cooperation in the treatment programs that have been applied to him there must be technical reasons for this. There may have been a faulty stimulus-response analysis of his case, or the techniques may have been inappropriately applied, or the techniques that are available may simply not be adequate to his particular problem.

When a behavior therapist finds himself without an effective strategy, he should frankly admit this to the patient, though he may often continue to 'support' also the hope that time and new knowledge may bring a solution to hand. There have been several cases with whom I have maintained contact after having for the time-being shot my bolt, and to whom I have later applied new methods as they have emerged, usually with a successful outcome sooner or later.

Some important consequences flow from the behavior therapist's acceptance of responsibility when treatment fails. It frees the patient from the agony of being blamed for 'resisting' recovery in the various ways that the psychoanalyst has popularized. Another consequence is that the behavior therapist does not insistently tug away at a particular technique because he 'knows' it is right and 'must' succeed if only the patient would allow it to. Only when he has evidence of change does the behavior therapist feel justified in dealing out 'more of the same.'

Quite often, moral issues are brought up by patients. Some question the morality of assertive behavior. It is not often difficult to satisfy them of its morality under the conditions in which it is advocated (see Chapter 5). One good strategy starts by pointing out that there are three possible broad approaches to the conduct of interpersonal relations. The first is to consider one's self only and drive roughshod over others whenever necessary to get what one wants. A psychopathic personality is the extreme expression of this basic attitude. He behaves in an asocial way because, apparently, he has not been conditioned to feel guilty or otherwise anxious in situations in which most people do. The result is that he often falls foul of society. The second basic approach to interpersonal relations is always to put others before oneself—the extreme opposite of a psychopathic pattern. People who follow this policy are frequently emotionally upset, their feelings fluctuating between guilt at falling short of their standards of selflessness and the lack of fulfillment that results from self-abnegation. No less than for the psychopath, though in a different way, their behavior has unhappy results. It is this kind of person whom the Talmudist had in mind when he wrote "If I am not for myself, who will be for me?" This statement accords with the biological truth that the welfare of the organism begins with its own integrity and leads to the third basic approach, the golden mean, dramatically expressed in this quotation from the Talmud: "If I am not for myself, who will be for me? But if I am for myself alone, what am I?" The individual puts himself first, but takes others into account. He conforms to the requirements of social living while acceding to the biological principle that the adaptations of the individual organism *primarily* serve its own needs, not those of others. This means that while he fulfills his obligations to humanity and to those of its subgroups to which he belongs, he claims and is prepared to defend what he believes to be his reasonable rights.

In the frame of this practical philosophy, to decide what behavior is suitable to particular circumstances is usually a simple matter. Most of the resultant behavior would be acceptable to people of many backgrounds and many religious beliefs, but there are inevitably prescriptions with which some would disagree. For example, if chronic unhappiness results from an unsatisfactory marriage and all efforts to rectify the situation have failed, it is reasonable and human to advise and aid the patient towards divorce, since the worth of a marriage should be weighed solely in terms of human happiness. Marriage is not a sacred entity to be preserved for its own sake. Similarly, it is justifiable to attack on rational grounds a patient's religious beliefs if they are a source of suffering. For example, finding that a patient (Case 12, Chapter 14) was greatly distressed by the stern view taken by his church of some of his behavior, the foundations of the church's judgment were questioned and the patient was lent a copy of Winwood Reade's splendid old book *The Martyrdom of Man* (1872). Though at first upset by its criticisms of religion, he later had a sense of relief. His more rational outlook was not only a good thing in itself but facilitated the psychotherapeutic procedures that eventually met with complete success.

In adopting this line of positive action, it is vital that the therapist does not confuse different aspects of it. He must be able to distinguish technical decisions from moral ones, and separate the tenets of his own moral requirements of the patient's situation. London (1964) summarizes the issues as follows in the course of an excellent and wide-ranging discussion:

> At the same level of abstraction, it is probably correct to declare that every aspect of psychotherapy presupposes some implicit moral doctrine, but it is not necessary to seek this level in order to say why it is important for therapists to recognize the moral concomitants of patients' problems and the implied moral position of some of their solutions. Some problems are inevitably moral ones from the perspective of either client or therapist, and some can be viewed as strategic or technical ones and treated without reference to particular value systems. In the one case, the therapist must fulfill a moral agency in order to function at all, whereas in the other he may restrict himself to the impartial helping or contractual function with which he is usually identified. But if he does not know the difference, then his own moral commitments may influence his technical functioning so that he willy-nilly strives to mold men to his own image, or his technical acts may imply moral positions which he might himself abhor.*

Our discussion of the moral aspects of psychotherapy cannot be concluded without reference to an objection to behavior therapy that is still

*London, P. (1964) *The Modes and Morals of Psychotherapy*. New York: Holt, Rinehart and Winston.

frequently heard. The complaint is that the behavior therapist assumes a kind of omnipotence by demanding the patient's complete acquiescence in his methods, which, it is felt, denudes the patient of human dignity. The truth is that the grade of acquiescence required is the same as in any other branch of medicine. Patients with pneumonia are ready to do what the medical man prescribes, because he is the expert. Why should the expectation be different when psychotherapy is the treatment?

CHAPTER 2

Foundations and Scope

STIMULI AND RESPONSES

The complex human behavior whose disorders and inadequacies are the concern of psychiatry is a matter of stimulus-response sequences mediated by the nervous system. A response is a behavioral event. A stimulus is the antecedent of a response. A sensory stimulus is an extrinsic source of energy that produces activation of an afferent nerve. Each member of a sequence of responses is a stimulus in relation to the responses that follow it. A movement is thus a response in relation to the nerve impulses that have led to it *and* to the sensory stimulus that may have been *their* stimulus. (For a fuller discussion, see Wolpe, 1958, pp. 3–6.)

For purposes of clarity of expression, it is frequently useful to depict behavioral sequences in terms of single chains of neurons and of discrete stimuli and responses. But even the simplest reflex involves the activation of thousands of neurons. Every sensory stimulus leads to a multiplicity of neuronal consequences that culminate in various combinations of motor, autonomic, and perceptual responses, and each response in turn has stimulus features that produce further responses — the response-produced stimuli of Hull (1943). Figure 1 purports to provide a general impression of the network of simultaneous and successive stimulus-response relations that go on incessantly during the active life of the organism. In the human being, an exteroceptive stimulus, whether it is the simple flash of light or the sight of a beautiful woman, produces a complex of perceptual, auto-

14

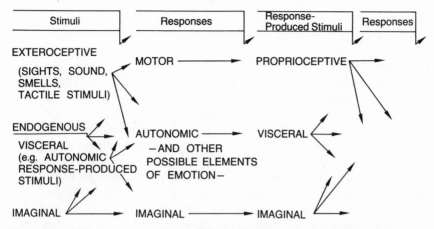

Fig. 1. A network of simultaneous and successive stimulus-response relations. (Courtesy of Graphic Communications, Eastern Pennsylvania Psychiatric Institute, Philadelphia.)

nomic, and motor responses. The motor response not only produces proprioceptive stimuli, but may, through changing the person's position in space, lead to the presentation of a different aspect of the object from which the visual stimulus originally came. The autonomic response also has effects that produce new interoceptive stimuli. Similarly, the image of the stimulus object leads to further imagery, and autonomic and motor responses, all according to what has been connected by previous learning. All responses taking place simultaneously interact with each other and are mutually modified.

Despite its complexity, there is a gross repeatability of the behavior of an organism to a particular stimulus situation within a certain range of physiological conditions. The empirical constancy of a stimulus-response relationship is what we call a habit. Habits are of many kinds, ranging from those consisting of simple movements in response to a stimulus to those resulting from the learning of sets (e.g. a set to listen or to look, or a set to imitate). Bandura (1969) has provided an excellent exposition of the intricacies involved in the development of many social habits. These habits we endeavor to change when we find that they do not further the welfare of the organism.

BASIC PRINCIPLES OF LEARNING

Since behavior therapy consists of applications of experimentally established principles of learning to the purpose of overcoming unadaptive habits, we shall survey the main principles that are used—counter-conditioning, reinforcement, and extinction.

1. Counterconditioning

Counterconditioning is the principle most extensively used in the treatment of human neuroses. Its potentialities became evident by its success in the treatment of experimental neuroses in animals.

An experimental neurosis can be produced by eliciting anxiety[1] at high intensity in an animal in a restricted environment. When repeatedly elicited, the anxiety comes to be strongly conditioned to the stimuli of that environment. Space restriction enables the conditioning to be confined to a relatively small number of stimuli instead of being diffused. To elicit the requisite high anxiety, one may use either strong noxious stimulation or else ambivalent stimulation—the simultaneous arousal of powerful opposing action tendencies, e.g. to eat and not to eat (Pavlov, 1927). The experiments referred to in Chapter 1 (Wolpe, 1952, 1958), utilized a cage 40 in. long by 20 in. wide and 20 in. high. For producing experimental neuroses in cats, an individual animal would be permitted to become accustomed to the cage, and then a highly disturbing, though physically harmless, electric pulse of about two seconds' duration would be passed into its feet through a grid on the floor of the cage. The animal scrambled about the cage, howled, and displayed such autonomic responses as pupillary dilatation, pilo-erection, and rapid respiration. The whole response complex subsided at the termination of the shock. But when the shock was repeated several times, the response complex persisted at increasing strength between shocks. The environmental stimuli had acquired the power to evoke the responses of the shock. From then onwards, the same agitated behavior appeared whenever the animal was placed in the experimental cage. It showed no tendency to extinction, whether the cat was put in the cage day after day, or kept away from it for weeks or months. At the same time, there were striking inhibitions of adaptive function. If the cat were starved for 48 hours and placed in the experimental cage on whose floor pellets of fresh meat were liberally strewn, it would not eat this meat if left there for many hours. There was also stimulus generalization. The animal was quite anxious on the floor of the experimental laboratory, and less so in other rooms, according to their resemblance to the laboratory.

[1]Anxiety is defined as an individual organism's characteristic pattern of autonomic responses to noxious stimulation. As a result of conditioning, a great many cues to conditioned anxiety are established.

We may note, in passing, some resemblances between the experimental and human neuroses. The latter, too, are persistent, and exhibit generalization; and while severe inhibition of eating is only occasionally seen, interferences with other adaptive functions are extremely common. A person will be unable to work if agoraphobia keeps him at home, of if claustrophobia makes his office unbearable. Fears of people may impair his social life; and anxieties related to sexual stimuli may cause sexual inadequacies — impotence or frigidity.

Because anxiety so decisively inhibited feeding in the neurotic cats, it seemed reasonable to think that if food were made available in circumstances in which anxiety was much weaker, feeding might occur and the anxiety be inhibited. It was possible to experiment with this idea in the various rooms mentioned above to which anxiety had generalized. The animal was offered food in them in descending order of similarity to the experimental laboratory. A room could always be found where the animal would eat despite showing some anxiety. In the course of eating a number of pellets of meat there, its anxiety in that room would subside entirely, and it would then accept food in a room more like the experimental laboratory. Proceeding systematically from room to room, it became possible to get the animal to eat in the experimental cage, and eventually entirely to overcome the anxiety responses that previously had been so powerfully aroused there.

These experiments led to the formulation of the reciprocal inhibition principle: *If a response inhibiting anxiety can be made to occur in the presence of anxiety-evoking stimuli, it will weaken the bond between these stimuli and the anxiety.*

In human neuroses, a considerable number of anxiety-inhibiting responses have been successfully used to overcome neurotic anxiety-response habits as well as other neurotic habits. For example, assertive responses (Chapter 5) are used to overcome neurotic anxieties that inhibit effective action towards those persons with whom the patient has to interact. The essence of the therapist's role is to encourage the outward expression, under all reasonable circumstances, of the feelings and action tendencies previously inhibited by anxiety. Each act of assertion to some extent reciprocally inhibits the concurrent anxiety and slightly weakens the anxiety-response habit. Similarly, relaxation responses can be employed to bring about systematic decrements of anxiety-response patterns to many classes of stimuli (Chapter 7).

There are a number of ways of bringing about inhibition of anxiety in which it is not obvious that the activity concerned is reciprocally inhibitory of anxiety. In one such process, one makes use of the consistent reinforcement of the motor responses to inhibit an accompanying anxiety – intra-response reciprocal inhibition. Another possibility is to employ a mild electrical stimulus as an anxiety inhibitor – apparently as a function of external inhibition (Pavlov, 1927). Then, it is possible to condition a neutral stimulus to counter-anxiety activity by repeatedly presenting that stimulus at the moment of cessation of a strong electrical stimulus; and subsequently, the counter-anxiety effect of that stimulus can be used to inhibit anxiety from various sources.

Finally, it seems likely that anxiety can sometimes be inhibited as a kind of 'protective' reaction to its own strong and sustained evocation – transmarginal inhibition (Pavlov, 1927; Teplov, 1959). This process may well be the basis of the effects of 'flooding.'

The reciprocal inhibition principle also comes into play in overcoming responses other than anxiety. It has a vital role in verbal and conceptual (cognitive) relearning. The reciprocal inhibition of a previously learned verbal response by a newly evoked one is the basis of 'retroactive' inhibition – the weakening of the original response (Osgood, 1946). Reciprocal inhibition is also the basis of the conditioned inhibition of obsessional and compulsive habits by aversive therapy (Chapter 11). A painful faradic shock, or other strong stimulus, inhibits the undesirable behavior, with the result that a measure of conditioned inhibition of the latter is established. Again, in the process of replacing an established motor habit by a new one, the evocation of the new motor response involves an inhibition of the old. For example, when assertive behavior is being instigated, at the same time that the expression of 'positive' feelings reciprocally inhibits anxiety, the new motor action inhibits the pre-existing motor response tendency. To take a simpler example, if one is being taught to play a backhand tennis stroke by rotating on the right foot, one inevitably inhibits one's tendency to play off the left foot.

2. Positive Reconditioning

The conditioning of new motor habits or ways of thinking may accompany elimination of unadaptive autonomic responses, as in the example of assertive training just given. But frequently new habits of action or of thought are induced in contexts that do not involve anxiety. An instance of this is the conditioning treatment of enuresis nocturna. By arranging for the patient to be awakened by an alarm as soon as the first drop of urine is excreted during sleep, the waking reaction is conditioned to the imminence of urination, and this subsequently leads to the development of an inhibition of the tendency to urinate in response to bladder stimulation during sleep (Jones, 1960; Lovibond, 1963). Another example is the conditioning of effective study behavior in individuals who have unproductive habits or fritter away their time when they should be working.

Successful conditioning of new habits always involves the use of 'reward' of one kind or another. It sometimes suffices to supply these on an *ad hoc* basis, but in recent years there has been increasing formal use of Skinner's (1953) operant conditioning principles to remove and replace undesirable habits. In order to establish a new behavior pattern in a particular situation, the desired response has to be elicited and frequently rewarded, while the undesired behavior is consistently not rewarded and even punished. For example, anorexia nervosa has been successfully treated by making social rewards such as the use of a radio or the granting of companionship contingent on eating, withdrawing these rewards when the patient fails to eat (Bachrach, Erwin, and Mohr, 1965). Various types of behavior in schizophrenics have been treated on the same principle (Lindsley, 1956; Williams, 1959; Ayllon, 1963; Davison, 1964) and major and lasting changes of behavior have been procured, even in patients who had been hospitalized for years.

3. Experimental Extinction

This is the progressive weakening of a habit through the repeated evocation without reinforcement of the responses that manifest it. Thus, behavior that has usually been followed by food reinforcement becomes progressively weaker if its elicitations cease to be followed by food. Similarly, avoidance behavior usually diminishes if it is not at least sometimes reinforced by a noxious event such as shock. The performance of a motor response has consequences that weaken its habit unless their effects are counteracted by the effects of reinforcement. The exact mechanism of experimental extinction has not been unequivocally established, but it is likely that it depends at least partly on the fatigue-associated reactive inhibition mechanism proposed by Hull (1943). I have elsewhere proposed a possible neurophysiological mechanism for the extinction process thus conceived (Wolpe, 1958, p. 27).

Therapeutic techniques based on the extinction mechanism, introduced a quarter of a century ago by Dunlap (1932) under the name 'negative practice,' have in recent years again been employed in the treatment of such motor habits as tics (Yates, 1958). In correlation with very large numbers of deliberate evocations of a tic, spontaneous evocations of the undesired movement may be progressively lessened.

THE SCOPE OF BEHAVIOR THERAPY

The province of behavior therapy is unadaptive (maladaptive) human habits. The therapist seeks to replace such habits by adaptive ones. Behavior is adaptive when its consequences satisfy the individual's needs, bring him relief from pain, discomfort, or danger, or avoid undue expenditure of energy (Wolpe, 1958, p. 32). Individual unadaptive acts are the normal order of everybody's day. It is only when particular unadaptive acts are habitual that a need for treatment arises. When an unadaptive habit is rooted in an organic state of affairs, such as a cerebral lesion, treatment entails dealing with that organic state. When the habit is based on learning, the learning process should provide the key to change. Unadaptive habits that are based upon learning are the domain of behavior therapy. They fall into five categories.

1. Neuroses

Persistent unadaptive habits that have been acquired in anxiety-generating situations and in which anxiety responses are almost invariably a central feature (Wolpe, 1958).

2. Other 'Pure' Learned Unadaptive Habits

These are unadaptive habits without the anxiety features that characterize neuroses. Examples are some tantrums, nailbiting, and enuresis nocturna.

3. Learned Unadaptive Behavior of Schizophrenics

Although schizophrenia, it is now clear, is at bottom a biological illness (Wolpe, 1970), many of the unadaptive habits that the patients display are due to learning.

4. Psychopathic Personality

This diagnosis is applied to people who habitually perform asocial or anti-social behavior regarding which they feel no guilt or other anxiety, so that the rebukes and chastisements of society have little restraining influence. While, quite possibly, a biological factor predisposes to the development of psychopathic behavior, the particular habits are presumably learned and should be subject to unlearning. However, very little therapeutic work has been done to date.

5. Drug Addictions

A person may habitually take a drug to relieve pain, anxiety, or other stress. If the drug-taking habit continues after the cessation of the stress, we have a drug addiction. Addiction is characterized by 'cravings' that compel the person to seek the drug. Underlying a craving is a biological state whose nature is not known and which makes drug habits uniquely different from other categories of unadaptive habits. Because we know no better, behavior modification has until now generally been directed at diminishing the patient's attraction towards the drug (aversion therapy). This can only be regarded as a stopgap.

As Taylor (1959) has epitomized the matter: "If we knew the mechanisms of drug habits we would be able to restore the alcoholic to being able to take a drink like anybody else."

It is to the neuroses that behavior therapy techniques have been most extensively applied. Since anxiety is generally a central constituent of neurotic habits, the deconditioning of anxiety forms the core of their treatment. The centrality of anxiety is often obvious. Many patients present themselves as being anxious either continually or in response to particular situations. Others, however, make no initial reference to anxiety, but complain of impotence, frigidity, obsessions and compulsions, sexual deviations, stuttering, blushing, kleptomania, and voyeurism, and other things. But, investigation in the careful manner that is essential to good behavior therapy shows in almost every case that anxiety underlies these complaints; that impotence or frigidity results from conditioned fears of aspects of the sexual situation; that an obsession is based on a fear of germs or some other 'baneful' agent (see Case 34); that stuttering and blushing are the consequence of anxiety reactions evoked in social situations – and so forth. The therapeutic requirement is the deconditioning of anxiety no less than if anxiety had been prominent from the first.

CHAPTER 3

Investigating the Case:
Stimulus-Response Analysis

The first step in investigating a case for behavior therapy is the taking of a careful clinical history. This is broadly similar to the history that might be taken by almost any conscientious clinician; but the behavioristic orientation leads to differences in the direction and manner of questioning. The special features can be more effectively communicated to the reader by the transcripts given later in this chapter of the initial interviews of Cases 1 and 2 than by any description that might be attempted.

THE STIMULUS-RESPONSE RELATIONS OF THE PRESENTING COMPLAINTS

Having obtained from the patient such personal details as name, address, telephone number, age, and occupation, the therapist at once proceeds to explore the patient's neurotic reactions. The circumstances surrounding the onset of each one of these reactions are meticulously examined in the hope of obtaining a coherent picture of its original determinants. In the case of an anxiety-response habit, such as a fear of heights or of being the focus of attention, we try to establish both the circumstances in which it was conditioned and what later contingencies may have modified its form or led to its 'spread' to other stimuli by second-order conditioning.

22

The conditioning history of each anxiety habit is traced in the same essential way.

This historical information provides a background for subsequent steps. At the very least, it gives the therapist a perspective on the case; but it may also provide important clues to the stimulus-response relationships that are currently relevant. These *current* relationships will be the focus of therapy. Therefore, the most intensive scrutiny is given to them. If the patient is anxious in social situations, it is necessary to find out exactly what aspects of these situations upset him. Perhaps he has a conditioned anxiety reaction to being looked at. Then, with what factors does it vary? It may increase with the number of people looking at him, or depend on the degree of speaking-performance-demand that the situation seems to hold, or on a fearful feeling of not being able to get away. The correct identification of the stimulus antecedents of reactions, indispensable to effective behavior therapy, depends, in the main, on searching questioning (see Cases 1, 2 and 3).

The task of stimulus-response analysis is always more complicated when there is a presenting complaint other than anxiety—for example, a stutter, a compulsion, or an illness like asthma. In cases of asthma and other presumed 'psychosomatic' conditions there may be the preliminary question of a purely organic etiology. Apart from that kind of possibility, all of these presenting complaints are usually consequences of neurotic anxiety responses. Therefore, the question must be raised whether the patient *also* has neurotic anxiety. If we find that he has, as is extremely likely, we shall want to know how this anxiety is related to the stutter, compulsion, or asthmatic attack. Usually, the relationship is quite clear and straightforward. For example, a stutter may be found to increase as a function of intensity of felt anxiety, which in turn depends upon the identity, number, and attitudes of the people in the patient's presence. But, especially in some psychosomatic cases, the correlation may be difficult to detect. An example was a case of asthma I saw several years ago, in whom the fact that the attack regularly took place four hours after a stressful event only became apparent after the patient had kept an hour-by-hour diary for several weeks.

Table 1 sets forth some of the consequences of neurotic anxiety. The deconditioning of the underlying anxiety generally brings these consequences to an end. Except for the rather rare cases of classical hysteria with *la belle indifférence*, there are very few neuroses which can be overcome without eliminating anxiety (see Chapter 12).

Table 1. Consequences of neurotic anxiety.

Mechanism of Consequence	Manifestation
A. AUTONOMIC	
1. Hyperventilation	Transient Somatic Effects, e.g.
	a Dizziness
	b Fainting attacks
	c Headaches
	d Paresthesia
	e Tachycardia
2. Protective inhibition (hypothesized) when anxiety is very prolonged and intense	Depression
3. Autonomic discharges expecially channeled into one organ system	Psychosomatic Symptoms, e.g.
	a Neurodermatitis
	b Asthma
	c Vasomotor rhinitis
	d Peptic ulceration and peptic ulcer syndrome
	e Spastic colon
	f Frequency of micturition
	g Dysmenorrhea
	h Hypertension
	i Migraine
B. MOTOR	
1. Prominent muscle tension, general or localized	Motor Disturbances, e.g.
	a Tremor
	b Stuttering
	c 'Fibrositic' pain, e.g. backache
	d Ocular dyskinesia
2. Motor avoidance conditioning (may be conditioned either simultaneous with anxiety or secondary to it)	Avoidance of anxiety-evoking stimuli
3. Complex motor behavior conditioned by its anxiety-reducing consequences	1. Compulsions
	2. Character Neuroses, e.g.
	a Promiscuity
	b Aimlessness
	3. Sexual Deviations, e.g.
	a Homosexuality
	b Pedophilia
	c Exhibitionism
	d Voyeurism
	e Promiscuity

Table 1. (Contd.)

Mechanism of Consequence	Manifestation
4. Anxiety interfering with complex functioning	1. Inability to work or impaired work capacity 2. Impaired capacity for social interaction (anxiety in social contexts) 3. Impaired sexual function (impotence or frigidity)
C. COGNITIVE 1. Cognitive distraction by anxiety-response-produced stimuli	Amnesia due to 'non-registration' of extrinsic stimuli
2. Cognitive distortion	Paranoid and related behavior

Since, almost universally, anxiety is a prominent constituent of neurotic reactions, and since anxiety is served by a primitive (subcortical) level of neural organization, its unlearning can be procured only through processes that involve this primitive level. Neurotic anxiety cannot be overcome purely by intellectual action – logical argument, rational insight – except in the special case where the unadaptive anxiety depends on a misconception – a conceptual 'wrong equation.'

Consider a person who has a fear of harmless snakes. When a snake (S_1) comes into his line of vision, it produces the neural effects that yield a perception (image) of the snake (rS_1) within him (Taylor, 1962) and,

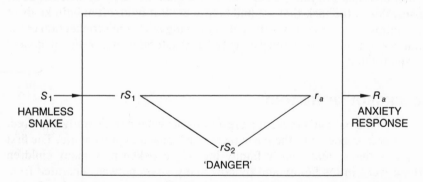

Fig. 2. The harmless snake (S_1) causes the perceptual response (rS_1) which may lead to the molecular responses for anxiety (r_a) either immediately or through the intermediary of the conditioned concept 'danger' (rS_2). (Courtesy of Graphic Communications, Eastern Pennsylvania Psychiatric Institute, Philadelphia.)

finally, the efferent processes shown as r_a lead to a pattern of anxiety and avoidance responses (R_a). There are two pathways through which this rS_1 may lead to R_a. The perception of the snake may evoke a secondary image of danger or death (rS_2) to which anxiety and avoidance responses have already been conditioned in almost everybody. The anxiety response habit would be eliminated by breaking the connection between rS_1 and rS_2. Here we would have the undoing of an association between two ideas — the breaking a 'cognitive' habit. This is technically what we do in 'correcting misconceptions' (Wolpe, 1958, p. 199).

To illustrate the foregoing with reference to a commonplace clinical case: a man reports anxiety whenever he feels a dull pain in the left side of his chest. The actual stimulus to this pain may be pressure on the diaphragm due to gaseous distension of the stomach or intestines. But the pain conjures up fear-evoking images conveying the message: "I am having a heart attack: I am going to die." Since it is not too unreasonable to be distressed at the thought of impending death, therapeutic action will not be directed at that emotional habit of response, but at breaking the erroneous and inappropriate association between the perception of chest pain and the thought of death.

The other possibility is that the perception (rS_1) immediately and without any cognitive intermediary evokes the anxiety response because it has been directly conditioned to do so. In that case, no operations on the 'cognitive' level will be of any avail in overcoming the fear of harmless snakes. It will be necessary to procure direct reconditioning of the emotional habit to that perception. In the great majority of cases of neuroses, this is the task that we find before us. But quite often both kinds of operations are necessary — the patient having *both* a misconception of the implications of the perceived object *and* an automatic non-rational anxiety response to it.

BACKGROUND HISTORY

When the patient's presenting reactions have been sufficiently explored, the therapist goes into the basic facts of his past and present life. The first topic is the patient's early family life. He is asked how many children there were in his family and by how many years he was separated from each sibling. What kind of person did his father seem to him to be? Did he show personal interest, did he punish, and if so did it seem just or not? Is the father still alive? If not, how did he die, and what was the effect of his death upon the patient? The same questions are asked about the mother. How well did the parents get on with each other? Were there any other important adults in the patient's early home life? Who were they and what was their influence upon the patient? How did he relate to his siblings? How important was his religious training, and how much of an influence upon him does religion retain? Were there any childhood fears or nervous habits?

The next group of questions relate to the patient's education. Did he enjoy school? If so, what did he like about it; if not, for what reason? How well did he do academically? Did he take part in athletics, and how good was he at them? Did he make friends and were any of the friendships intimate? Were there any people, either among teachers or students, whom he grew to fear or especially dislike? At what age did he leave school? Did he graduate from high school? What did he do next — embark on a life of leisure, go to work, or continue his studies at a university or other institution? How did he get on at the institution, academically and socially? Upon graduating, what work did he do, how did he function at it, and how satisfying did he find it? Have there been changes of employer, and if so for what reasons? How does he get on with employers, underlings, and peers?

The patient's sex life is then traced from his first awareness of sexual feelings. At what age and in what context was he first aware of sexual arousal? What were the experiences that followed? Did he masturbate, and was this associated with any feelings of fear or guilt? At what age did he commence dating? When did he have his first important relationship? What attracted him to the girl, and what brought the association to a close? The same questions are asked about subsequent associations. What attracted him to his wife? How did the courtship go? Were there obstacles from the families of either party? How have they got on together over the years? How has the sexual side of the marriage been? In general, as much attention is given to love and emotional warmth as to sexual behavior as such.

What are his present social relationships? Does he have difficulties with any of his friends? Does he have any particularly intimate friends? How does he get on with people with whom his association is casual?

After the anamnesis, the patient is given three inventories to fill out — the Willoughby Schedule (a short form of the Clark-Thurstone Inventory), a Fear Survey Schedule, and the Bernreuter Self-Sufficiency Scale. These inventories will be briefly discussed.

The Willoughby Schedule (Original form, Appendix 1) consists of 25 questions that are answered on a 5-point scale — (0–4). About half of the questions yield information about common areas of neurotic reactivity — mainly interpersonal, and the other half indicate degrees of general emotional sensitivity. This questionnaire is a highly significant indicator of neuroticism (Wolpe, 1958, p. 110). Decreases in the score are correlated with the patient's improvement (*ibid.* p. 221). But it is possible for a person to have a low Willoughby score and yet be highly neurotic in areas not covered by the Schedule. A revised Willoughby for self-administration is given in Appendix 2.

The Fear Survey Schedule (Appendix 3) Wolpe and Lang (1964) list a large number of stimulus situations to which fear is unadaptive. The patient indicates on a 5-point scale how disturbed he becomes in each situation. This schedule is an exceedingly useful clinical instrument frequently bringing to the therapist's attention neurotic sensitivities that he would not otherwise have suspected. A more recent list containing 108 items (Wolpe and Lang, 1969) is commercially available.*

The Bernreuter Self-Sufficiency Inventory (Appendix 4). This list of 60 questions is used less consistently than the two foregoing schedules. A normal score is generally between 24 and 42. A score of less than 20 shows marked lack of self-sufficiency. Low scores are found in cases of over-dependency, many of whom present themselves as agoraphobics. People low in self-sufficiency frequently find it difficult to carry out instructions for self-assertion.

When there is a question of psychopathic personality and when there are ambiguous manifestations of hysteria, the introversion-extraversion scale of the Maudsley Personality Inventory or of its derivative, the Eysenck Personality Inventory, often provides decisive information.

If there is the slightest suggestion that organic disease may be playing a part in the patient's illness, a medical investigation should be undertaken. One of the strongest indications for this is the presence of episodic anxiety attacks to which no constant stimulus antecedents can be attached. Common organic causes of anxiety are hypoglycemia, including relative hypoglycemia (Salzer, 1966), and hyperthyroidism. Among less common causes are limbic lobe seizures and pheochromocytoma.

When sufficient information has been obtained, the therapeutic goals and strategies are discussed with the patient. The therapist decides to

*Obtainable from Educational and Testing Materials, P.O. Box 7234, San Diego, California (92107).

which areas of disturbance to give priority. The degree to which a neurotic habit is detrimental to the life-economy of the patient is usually a prime consideration. Thus, in a particular case, agoraphobia was treated first because of its profoundly incapacitating consequences, even though other neurotic reactions had pre-existed it and, in a sense, spawned it.

SOME EXAMPLES OF INITIAL INTERVIEWS

Behavior therapy is always an individual program. However, a few general rules will be stated in order to make more comprehensible the examples of initial interviews given below: (1) The emotional climate is, as at all other times, a blend of objectivity and permissiveness. (2) The patient must be assured that his unpleasant reactions are reversible. Having been learned, they can be unlearned. The therapist can often illustrate the learning process from the patient's own history. (3) Misconceptions must be corrected as soon as possible. This applies both to socially conditioned misconceptions (e.g. "masturbation is dangerous") and iatrogenic misconceptions (e.g. "I need my symptoms"). How important this can be is illustrated in Case 3. (4) Assertive behavior (Chapter 5) should be instigated at an early stage whenever it is indicated unless there are severe phobic reactions to some aspect of it, e.g. to the patient's own 'aggression' (see Case 2).

The cases whose first interviews are given here are quite various. The first presented itself as a phobia for sharp objects, the second as a problem of interpersonal anxiety, and the third as one of inadequate sexual response. Yet the same central line of action is apparent in all three—a concentrated effort to secure the greatest possible definition in relating stimuli (situations) to the responses that constitute the complaints that have brought the patient to treatment.

Case 1:   First interview in a case of phobia for sharp objects (Mrs. P., age 32)

The interview with Mrs. P. was selected because the *apparent* unifocal phobia for knives led the therapist rapidly to uncover broad areas of the patient's history. The reader should attend to the manner and content of the questioning procedure. It should particularly be noted that the therapist goes out of his way to be permissive—condoning acts and attitudes that the patient seems to believe it natural to deplore; and that he tries to establish, with great precision, points that he thinks may be significant for therapeutic action. In this particular case, one benefit expected from therapy was obvious—the removal of the phobia.

An inexperienced therapist might have been tempted at once to proceed with systematic desensitization, but the *second* interview (not given here) led in another direction, and illustrated how unwise it is to plunge into the treatment of a case without adequate understanding of it. Exploration of factors currently controlling the fear of knives revealed that it became particularly strong when other people's children were unruly inside her house. It then emerged that she was extremely inhibited in almost all interpersonal situations, and habitually suppressed her anger for fear of disapproval. (Note that direct questioning failed to elicit the presence of suppressed anger during the first session). In keeping with all this, her Willoughby score was 66. The first therapeutic undertaking was, accordingly, *not desensitization, but assertive training.* It was postulated that by developing an ability freely and appropriately to express her feelings she would remove a major stimulus antecedent of her phobia. Assertive training was rapidly effective, but though the phobia then became less troublesome, desensitization eventually had to be carried out as expected.

THERAPIST: Dr. N. has written to me about you, but I want to approach your case as though I knew nothing about it at all.[1] Of what are you complaining?

MRS. P.: I'm afraid of sharp objects, especially knives. It's been very bad in the past month.

THERAPIST: How long have you had this fear?

MRS. P.: It began 6 years ago when I was in hospital after my first child was born. Two days later, my husband brought me some peaches and a sharp knife to cut them with. I began to have a fear that I might harm the baby with it.[2]

THERAPIST: How long had the knife been with you when it occurred to you that it might harm the baby?

MRS. P.: I don't believe I let him leave it overnight, that night; or else we left it that night and then the next day—I think you could say I told him to take it home. I can't remember exactly; I know I just didn't want

[1]It is always hazardous to rely upon the version of a case provided by a psychiatrist or psychologist whose orientation is not behavioristic, since a good deal of information that interests them does not interest us, and *vice versa.*

[2]One does not have to be a Freudian to suspect from this that the baby might have been a resented intrusion in her life—and, as will be seen, it was.

it around. From that day to this I don't mind using knives as long as I'm with someone, but when I'm alone with the children I just don't want them around.

THERAPIST: Can you remember in what way the thought first came into your mind that you might hurt the baby?

MRS. P.: I can't remember.[3]

THERAPIST: Now since that time, generally speaking, has this fear been the same all along, or has it got better or worse?

MRS. P.: Well, right after we moved to Richmond about 5 months ago I felt a little better about it. At first, when I got home from the hospital I made my husband take all the knives away from the house. I didn't want them around, so he took them to my mother's. I brought a couple back from her house when we moved to Richmond. But I couldn't—after I brought them—I couldn't use them. I couldn't keep them out where I could see them and might pick one up and, you know—use it sometime.

THERAPIST: So what do you say in general—that the fear has been much the same?

MRS. P.: It seems the same. In fact mostly I think it's gotten worse.[4]

THERAPIST: Is there anything—any situation—that you can associate with it getting worse?

MRS. P.: No. Only it just seems to be on my mind I guess. Ah—if you don't mind me going back to something that Dr. N. said that I just didn't want them around, that it was a habit, and I mean I guess I've just been thinking about that and—it's hard to admit—the children, I don't know why they make me nervous and I just am afraid that—that sometime it may get the better of me.

THERAPIST: Are the children making you more nervous—in the past month?

MRS. P.: Well, ah, you know in the summertime they stay outside; but in this kind of weather they can't get out, and, of course, they like to run and when they run in the house it does kind of get me.[5]

---

[3]It did not seem advisable to exert pressure on her memory at this early point when she was not yet comfortable with the therapist.

[4]It cannot be inferred from this that she continued to resent the child henceforth. Awareness of the destructive idea, by producing intense emotional disturbance, could have resulted in the conditioning of various stimuli to that disturbance and the associated idea.

[5]The worsening is thus apparently a result of increased seasonal stress.

THERAPIST: When you were in the hospital that time after your baby had been born, what was your general feeling about the situation?[6]

MRS. P.: Well, I wasn't too happy in the first place because we had just built a house. I had just started to work and was working about 6 months when I got pregnant and I wasn't too happy about the whole thing then, because I liked my job and, building a house, we wanted new furniture and all—Well, I guess we neither one of us were happy about it. And then just before the baby was born I said, if it's a girl, a dark-headed girl with brown eyes it will be fine, but it turned out that it was blonde and a boy, too. (*Laughs*)

THERAPIST: Was that important?

MRS. P.: That it was a girl or boy?

THERAPIST: Yes. Were you just joking?

MRS. P.: Well, no, I don't think I was joking, because I really didn't much want it to look like my husband and his side of the family, (*Laughs*) but it turned out to be the image of his Daddy.[7] But I think that was a selfish. . .

THERAPIST: Well, that's all right.

MRS. P.: . . . on my part. It's probably a selfish way to look at it. I wanted a dark-headed girl.

THERAPIST: Well, you were expressing how you felt about the child at that time. It was just your feeling, and there's no question of right or wrong. It was your true feeling[8]. . . Don't you like the way your husband's family looks?

MRS. P. (*Laughing*): I could never like their looks. I know they like me because of the way they act and . . . I wouldn't do anything against them.

THERAPIST: It is quite possible not to like the way some people look.

MRS. P.: I must have liked the way my husband looked or I wouldn't have married him.

THERAPIST: Then why was it important to you to have a child look like your family?

MRS. P.: Well, as I said, I think it was just selfish on my part.

[6]A return to the quest for information regarding the circumstances concerning the onset of the phobia.

[7]Not only had the pregnancy been unwelcome, but when the child arrived, it was physically displeasing.

[8]Note the matter-of-fact acceptance of her account and the strong rejection of the suggestion of moral turpitude implied in her use of the word 'selfish.'

THERAPIST: But you had a preference. It is not a matter of being selfish. You had a preference.[9]

MRS. P.: Well, I felt I had to go through having and caring for the baby and all and I felt like I sort of wanted it to look like me since I had to go through it all.

THERAPIST: Sort of reward for your trouble?

MRS. P.: That's right.

THERAPIST: Did you ever have this sort of feeling before this child was born?

MRS. P.: Never.

THERAPIST: Well, when I said that, I wasn't thinking only about this feeling about knives, but has it ever happened before that you had a feeling of wanting to smash up things, maybe, if you were cross about them?[10]

MRS. P.: I've always been sort of, you know, perfectionist, I guess you'd say, particular about my things. I had two younger sisters and I know if they meddled with any of my things it . . . I would get awfully mad about that . . . but I never wanted to hurt anybody.

THERAPIST: Would you ever want to hit them?

MRS. P.: I don't think so.

THERAPIST: Would you ever want to hit anybody who annoyed you? Or when situations worked out the way you didn't like?

MRS. P.: I don't think so. I can't remember it . . .

THERAPIST: Well, it doesn't have to be a matter of hurting anybody physically, but just a feeling of anger and expressing anger towards people. Well, now let's get your background. Where were you born?

MRS. P.: Norfolk.

THERAPIST: How many brothers and sisters?

MRS. P.: Four sisters and one brother.

THERAPIST: And where do you come?

MRS. P.: I'm in the middle. There's two sisters and a brother older and two sisters younger.

THERAPIST: Will you just tell me how much older than you your eldest sister is?

MRS. P.: She was 47 in October . . . and I've got one who will be 45 in

[9]The idea of selfishness is again combatted.

[10]This raised the question whether, in general, she had a tendency towards anger and aggression when thwarted. According to her following statements, this was not so.

January and my brother will be 43 in December, and then 18 months younger there's a sister, and one 2 years younger than her.

THERAPIST: Are your parents alive?

MRS. P.: Yes.

THERAPIST: What kind of person is your father, especially as you remember him in your childhood?

MRS. P.: Sweet and easy-going.

THERAPIST: Did you feel he was interested in you?

MRS. P.: You mean what I did at school and like that?

THERAPIST: Was your father interested in you personally and in what you were doing?

MRS. P.: Not too much.

THERAPIST: Did he ever punish you?

MRS. P.: No.

THERAPIST: And what about your mother?

MRS. P.: Well, I could say the same about her. They were both good — you know — provided. She ... well she was interested, did things like driving us to school. She didn't seem to be too interested in how we got along or what we did. And I failed and I made awful grades in school. She never talked to the teacher to find out if I could have done better, or anything like that. She never helped with homework or anything like that. Of course, I guess she always had too much else to do.[11]

THERAPIST: Aside from the fact that your parents were rather similar people would you say they sort of liked each other and also behaved towards you as though they liked you?

MRS. P.: Well, they tried to see that we did right and I can remember they always took us to Sunday School and to church.

THERAPIST: Did they get on well together?

MRS. P.: Well, yes. As far as I know. They had arguments.

THERAPIST: Did they have lots of arguments?

MRS. P.: Well, no; after all they lived together some forty years.

THERAPIST: Were there any other adults who played any important part in your early home life — like grandmothers, aunts, or nurses?

MRS. P.: No, I don't remember any grandmothers or aunts.

---

[11]Having had such uninvolved parents, it is hardly surprising that Mrs. P. was unenthusiastic about having children.

THERAPIST: How did you get on with your brother and sisters?

MRS. P.: Well, pretty good, I guess. Of course, when you are children I think you fuss and fight lots of times. Now I think we all get along good.

THERAPIST: Did you have any particular fears when you were a child?

MRS. P.: Well no, not that I know of. But when I was eight years old our house burned down. I was on my way home from school and the fire trucks passed us. It was in January and it was snowing like anything and somebody told us that our house was on fire. And there was a fear . . . it was. My parents lost almost everything they had. And I know they . . . oh, 5 or 6 years after that every time I would hear a fire engine I would get so nervous if I was in school I would have to get up and leave. I wouldn't leave the school, but I would have to get out of the class — but things like that don't bother me now.[12]

THERAPIST: Did you have any other such experiences, or any other fears at all when you were a child?

MRS. P.: No.

THERAPIST: Well, now, you said that you didn't get on very well at school. Apart from the fact that your studies were difficult, how did you like school?

MRS. P.: I liked it fine. I mean I just played right along.

THERAPIST: Well, did you always do badly at your classes?

MRS. P.: Yes.

THERAPIST: What about sports? How were you at them?

MRS. P.: I might have taken after father in sports. I did well.

THERAPIST: Did you make friends at school?

MRS. P.: Yes, I had plenty of friends at school.

THERAPIST: Did you have any close friends?

MRS. P.: Well, yes. There were about six or eight of us that always chummed around together, girls and . . .

THERAPIST: Were there any people at school you were afraid of? I mean either among the girls or teachers?

MRS. P.: No.

THERAPIST: How far did you go in school?

MRS. P.: I finished high school.

---

[12]It is usual for childhood phobias to be deconditioned by the experiences that life provides and without formal treatment.

THERAPIST: How old were you then?

MRS. P.: Eighteen.

THERAPIST: And then what did you do?

MRS. P.: I worked for a doctor for three years.

THERAPIST: As a receptionist?

MRS. P.: I did his lab work and typing, shorthand ... helped with his patients.

THERAPIST: Did you like that work?

MRS. P.: Yes, very much.

THERAPIST: And then what did you do?

MRS. P.: I worked for a power company for five years, as a clerk-stenographer. I liked that too.

THERAPIST: And then?

MRS. P.: Got married. I didn't work for about ten months. Then I worked for a plastic firm in Norfolk until the first child was born—as I told you.

THERAPIST: And since then?

MRS. P.: Housewife.

THERAPIST: How do you like being a housewife?

MRS. P.: Fine.

THERAPIST: Is there anything you don't like about it?

MRS. P.: That things don't stay clean when cleaned. (*Laughs*) No, I like it fine, I wouldn't go back into public work for anything. Unless I could work in a hospital, something like that. I should get something like that when my children are through school.

THERAPIST: How old were you when you first had any kind of sexual feelings?

MRS. P.: Well, I ... (*Desperate gesture*)

THERAPIST: Well, roughly—were you ten, or fifteen or twenty? More or less?

MRS. P.: Well, I can't remember. I have no idea.

THERAPIST: Well, then, was it before ten?

MRS. P.: I wouldn't think so.

THERAPIST: Was it before fifteen? .. Before twenty?

MRS. P.: Well I would think it was before twenty.

THERAPIST: Say about seventeen?

MRS. P.: Well, yes, maybe.[13]

THERAPIST: In what kind of a situation did you have your first sexual feeling? Was it out with boys, or at the movies, or what?

MRS. P.: Well, I never dated too much. And when I was in school, well, in my class in school there just wasn't any boy. And . . .

THERAPIST: So, you started to date when you were eighteen or so, after you left school?

MRS. P.: That's right.

THERAPIST: At that stage did you go out with lots of different boys or just one at a time? Did you go to parties? What was the pattern?

MRS. P.: Well, I went around with several. I belonged to the choir at church and whenever there were things like Sunday School parties we'd usually take somebody with us.

THERAPIST: Well . . . when did you first become especially interested in anybody?

MRS. P.: Well, let's see. I started going with my husband, Charles, I guess in July of '49. And after I started going with him I never did go out with anybody else.

THERAPIST: There has been nobody else ever in whom you have been really interested?

MRS. P.: Well, when I was working at my second job, there was a boy there, but he was married, and I never did go out with him.

THERAPIST: What did you like about him?

MRS. P.: Well, just everything. (*Laughs*) And, ah, well he showed me a lot of attention too. Then he quit and went to Richmond to work and I never did see him again.

THERAPIST: So you didn't have any kind of going out with him or any physical contact?

MRS. P.: I know a lot of people wouldn't believe this, but it's absolutely true.

THERAPIST: Well, then you began going out with Charles?

MRS. P.: No, I had already been going out with him previously, since the summer of '49, and I didn't stop work there until summer of '51.

THERAPIST: What did you like about him?

MRS. P.: My husband is just . . . the way he . . . well, just everything I

[13]Note the therapist's insistence on at least an approximate answer, and that, once it has been obtained, details are pursued.

guess. He was nice and the thing that impressed me with him most was the way he treated his mother. He was good to his mother. His father had been dead for a few years and he was good to her, and he always phoned her, and I felt like anybody who would be that good to his mother might be a good husband.[14]

THERAPIST: Well, when did you feel that you were ready to marry him?

MRS. P.: I don't know if I ever did feel like I was. I went with him for seven years.

THERAPIST: Well, was he interested in marrying you earlier?

MRS. P.: Uh-huh. Every time I would put it off. And I would say okay and then I would get nervous and upset and couldn't sleep and would say, well, I can't go through this again. So we would put it off again, until he got fed up with that. He was working, and when he got fed up he said he was going to quit his job and go to college. And he did.

THERAPIST: He went to college?

MRS. P.: Uh-huh. From January '53 to June '56. And then he went to Tennessee and got a job at ——. When he left, of course, it left me sitting at home by myself and I nearly died. I lost twenty pounds; I couldn't eat; I couldn't sleep.

THERAPIST: Well, can you tell me what the other man you mentioned had that Charles didn't have? What points were important as far as your feelings were concerned?

MRS. P.: Oh, he was good looking. But I was thinking of my husband's blonde hair and blue eyes. He had dark hair and dark eyes.[15]

THERAPIST: When you had the prospect of marriage to Charles before you, and you felt nervous, what did you feel nervous about? Was there any particular aspect of the relationship that made you feel nervous?

MRS. P.: The whole thing, I guess. I just wasn't ready to get married.

THERAPIST: In 1954 Charles went to study?

MRS. P.: January 1953. And he finished in '56.

THERAPIST: To do that he went out of town?

MRS. P.: Yeah, he went to Baltimore.

THERAPIST: So eventually you got married. When?

---

[14]Clearly, the choice of a husband was made on rational grounds, and not because of his emotional appeal — in contrast to the married man previously mentioned.

[15]Physical appearance is obviously of great emotional importance to her, accounting very largely for the strength of her negative reaction to her newborn child.

MRS. P.: In August of 1956.

THERAPIST: At that stage, were you satisfied about being married?

MRS. P.: Well, he first of all, he called me from Tennessee and said, "If you don't marry me now," he says, "we're through. I'm leaving the country." So it was then or never, so I said "Okay." So we got married the next Autumn.

THERAPIST: Well, how do you get along together?

MRS. P.: We get along fine. I knew I would never marry anybody else. Well, I guess I'm just the type of person, you know, someone sort of has to say well, we are going to do it now or never.

THERAPIST: How is the sexual side of your marriage?

MRS. P.: Fine; I hope he'd say the same (*Laughs*).

THERAPIST: At this moment I'm only interested in your side.[16] Do you have climaxes?

MRS. P.: Yes.

THERAPIST: Always?

MRS. P.: Well, no, I don't always, but I do at least part of the time.

THERAPIST: So you're quite happy in general about the marriage?

MRS. P.: Well, I wouldn't be any other way.

THERAPIST: What do you mean by that?

MRS. P.: Well, I mean I wouldn't be single again.

THERAPIST: But you have no complaints about the marriage?

MRS. P.: No.

THERAPIST: How many children have you now?

MRS. P.: I have two. The girl will be three on the 16th of this month.

THERAPIST: Do you like your children?

MRS. P.: Well, I should say I do.

THERAPIST: Except when they make a lot of noise and get on your nerves?

MRS. P.: Well, that's to be expected. I wonder sometimes what my mother did when there were six of us. Of course, we weren't all there at the same time.

THERAPIST: Your children are quite well?

MRS. P.: Yes.

[16]This statement expresses the central orientation of a behavioristic history. Everything has to be seen from the standpoint of the sufferer, for it is she who needs to be changed.

THERAPIST: Do you like living in Richmond?

MRS. P.: Better than I expected. I'd heard that the people were not too friendly, but I found out that they are.

THERAPIST: Is there anything you're not satisfied with?

MRS. P.: Well, I would like to have a new house. We had to buy an old house and there wasn't anything to rent or to buy right when we had to move so we bought this old house and it still needs a lot done to it.

THERAPIST: What's your religion?

MRS. P.: Methodist.

THERAPIST: Is religion important in your life?

MRS. P.: Yes, it is.

THERAPIST: Well, in what way?

MRS. P.: Well, I don't think you can get along without it.

THERAPIST: Do you spend a lot of time with church activities?

MRS. P.: Oh, no, no. I haven't been to church in Richmond. We have taken the children to Sunday School.

THERAPIST: Well, do you worry much about what God is thinking about what you're doing?

MRS. P.: I do the best I can.

THERAPIST: Well, I've got enough of the important background information. I will give you one or two questionnaires to do as homework and then next time you come here we'll talk of the treatment procedures.[17] We'll probably be doing a special kind of treatment, called desensitization. It involves deep muscle relaxation and other special procedures. That is all for now.

Case 2: First interview in a case of interpersonal anxiety (Miss G., age 21)

This is the transcript of the first of two interviews in a filmed demonstration of basic procedures in behavior therapy of neurosis.* The reader should note the therapist's insistent endeavors to define the stimulus

---

[17]Already, at this first interview, the patient is given the message that active therapy will begin very soon.

*A short which is technically excellent is available from Psychological Cinema Register, Penn State University, State College, Pa., under the title *Behavior Therapy Demonstration*. The viewer should, however, know that it is an approximate 35-minute condensation of almost two hours of interviewing, so that a misleading impression of cursoriness is at times given.

sources of the anxiety reactions that the patient reports in certain kinds of social situations. After some initial probing, he turns his attention to that patient's life history, but interrupts the chronicle repeatedly to follow clues that promise to throw further light on anxiety-eliciting stimuli. Towards the end of the interview, he turns away from the uncompleted life history to renew his investigation of these stimuli. Finally, he makes an examination of some situations in which self-assertive behavior (see Chapter 5) would be appropriate; but it emerges that the anxiety that Miss G. would have in response to the consequences of assertion is so great as to render futile any attempt at assertive training at this stage. It will first be necessary to desensitize her to being looked at and to disapproval.

THERAPIST: So your name is Carol Green? How old are you?

MISS G.: 21.

THERAPIST: What is your complaint?

MISS G.: I am very very nervous all the time.

THERAPIST: All the time?

MISS G.: Yes, all the time.[18]

THERAPIST: How long has this been so?

MISS G.: Since I was about fourteen.

THERAPIST: Can you remember what brought it on?

MISS G.: No, not really. I wish I could.

THERAPIST: But, are you not saying that before you were fourteen you were not nervous?

MISS G.: Well, I was, but not to this extreme. I remember being . . . especially in elementary school when I would have to read something in front of the class, then I would get very nervous about that — giving speeches or anything or answering in class. That would bother me.

THERAPIST: Well, that is a special situation.

MISS G.: Yes, but now all the time. When I go out of the house, or walk out the door.

THERAPIST: Well, let's try to build up a picture. You say in elementary school you were only nervous when you had to get up and speak in front of the class. Only then?

---

[18]It is important to establish the presence or absence of continuous anxiety. Its sources are various — the most common being ongoing conflicts, ruminations about possible catastrophes, and pervasive anxiety (see Chapter 9). Here, Miss G.'s statement about being always anxious turned out later to be incorrect.

MISS G.: Yes.

THERAPIST: And then in high school?

MISS G.: It got worse. When we would go out with boys I would be very nervous.

THERAPIST: Do you mean that you became more nervous in front of the class?

MISS G.: I wouldn't sleep for nights worrying about giving a speech in front of class or something like that.

THERAPIST: And you also said you became nervous about going out with boys.

MISS G.: Yes. You know, I was afraid, especially if I would have a blind date I would be scared to death.

THERAPIST: Well, isn't that to some extent natural?[19]

MISS G.: I guess so, but not to the extremes that I would go to.

THERAPIST: And if you went out with somebody you knew. What about that?

MISS G.: Well, after a while I would be a little calmer, but still nervous.

THERAPIST: And what about if you went out with girl friends?

MISS G.: Not as much. I wouldn't be quite as nervous, but still a little bit.

THERAPIST: Were there any other situations in which you developed nervousness while you were in high school?

MISS G.: No others that I can think of, just basically when I would walk out of the house everything would just bother me.

THERAPIST: Everything? Like what?

MISS G.: Well, you know I was afraid to take tests or things like that or make speeches like I said before. Just to be with people would scare me.

THERAPIST: Just being with any people?

MISS G.: Yes, it would bother me more if I was with people I didn't know too well.[20]

THERAPIST: What about at times of vacation?

MISS G.: Vacation? I don't understand what you mean.

[19]This was said to imply that her reaction was really not so 'far out.'

[20]This tells us that her interpersonal anxiety *varies* directly with the strangeness of other persons.

THERAPIST: Well, I mean you have to take tests and so on at school, but during vacation there are no tests. So would you still be nervous going out of the house?

MISS G.: A little bit. But not quite as much.[21] Because I wouldn't be thinking of that.

THERAPIST: What year did you graduate from school?

MISS G.: 1963.

THERAPIST: And what did you do then?

MISS G.: I went to school and became a technician.

THERAPIST: What kind of technician?

MISS G.: X-ray.

THERAPIST: Do you like this work?

MISS G.: Not really. It's just because I didn't know really what else to do. I thought it would be interesting and the only reason I went into it is because I thought it was interesting, but once I got there I was very nervous about everything. It would scare me to be with patients.

THERAPIST: Patients would scare you?

MISS G.: Well, especially the sick ones. If something would happen to them.

THERAPIST: You were scared that something might happen to them?

MISS G.: Yes, like they would have an attack or something.[22]

THERAPIST: Has this ever happened?

MISS G.: No, not really.

THERAPIST: Well, it is now about five years since you became a technician.

MISS G.: It is about four.

THERAPIST: During those four years, did you become more nervous or less nervous or stay the same?

MISS G.: Definitely more.[23]

THERAPIST: You have been getting gradually more nervous?

MISS G.: Yes.

THERAPIST: All the time?

MISS G.: Yes. My mouth tightens up all the time.

[21]When the threat of tests was present the general level of anxiety was increased.

[22]Here we have anxiety from an entirely different source.

[23]This makes it important to know in what directions reactivity has spread.

THERAPIST: I see. Now, are there any special things that make you nervous nowadays?

MISS G.: Special things?

THERAPIST: Well, let's start off by considering your work situation.

MISS G.: Yes?

THERAPIST: You said that sick patients make you more nervous.

MISS G.: And my boss.

THERAPIST: Yes?

MISS G.: He makes me extremely nervous. I am afraid of him.

THERAPIST: Why, is he very strict?

MISS G.: Um, yes, he gives that appearance.

THERAPIST: Does he carry on? Does he scream and so on?

MISS G.: Never at me. But I am always afraid that will happen.

THERAPIST: And what about nurses?

MISS G.: Not really. I am not in too much contact with them.

THERAPIST: And who else scares you?

MISS G.: Men.

THERAPIST: Men?

MISS G.: If I go out with them.

THERAPIST: Yes. What about men who come in where you are working, like medical students?

MISS G.: Yes, they scare me, too. They do.

THERAPIST: They scare you, how?

MISS G.: I am afraid to ... I don't know. I am not afraid of them really. I am just afraid of how I'll act ... that my nervousness will show through. And I think about it so much.

THERAPIST: Well, is it correct to say that you are sort of scared of being watched?[24]

MISS G.: Yes. I think everybody is always watching me.

THERAPIST: Now, that is at work. What other circumstances scare you when you are away from work?

MISS G.: Just going out. I am afraid, you know, that they'll see the way I am. I am afraid to pick something up, because I am afraid that I am

[24]Being watched by people means greater contact than when they are not watching.

going to shake, and my mouth is all tightened up. I am afraid to look at people directly in the eye.[25]

THERAPIST: Are you only afraid of looking at your escort in the eye, or afraid of anybody?

MISS G.: Anybody.

THERAPIST: So looking at a person face to face increases your nervousness?

MISS G.: Yes.

THERAPIST: Suppose that you were walking down the street and there was a bench across the road with some people waiting for a bus. Now those people would be sort of vaguely looking across the street. Would you be aware of their presence?

MISS G.: Yes, definitely.

THERAPIST: Even though they might not be particularly looking at you?

MISS G.: Yes.

THERAPIST: Now, supposing we take people away altogether. Suppose that you are just walking all by yourself, say in a park. There is no one else at all there. Are you then completely comfortable?

MISS G.: Yes.

THERAPIST: I must be quite certain of this.[26]

MISS G.: Yes.

THERAPIST: If you are completely by yourself, are you absolutely calm and comfortable?

MISS G.: Yes, I am. The same way I am at home. I feel alright.

THERAPIST: Well, that means there are some people who can look at you and not bother you.

MISS G.: Yes, at times. But I don't know why this happens.

THERAPIST: Well, what about your mother?

MISS G.: No, it doesn't bother me at home.

THERAPIST: Your mother can look at you as much as she likes?

MISS G.: Yes. It's silly but...

THERAPIST: Well, that's not silly.[27] I mean this is just the way things have developed.

[25]This maximizes the effect of the being-looked-at stimulus.

[26]Many patients will initially report moderate distress as 'completely comfortable.'

[27]The patient is to accept her reactions as matters of fact. They are neither 'wrong' nor 'stupid.'

MISS G.: I know.

THERAPIST: And who else can look at you without bothering you?

MISS G.: My whole family.

THERAPIST: Who is in your family?

MISS G.: My father, my mother, my sister, my grandmother.

THERAPIST: Besides these people, are there any others at all who can look at you without disturbing you?

MISS G.: No.

THERAPIST: What about a little baby?

MISS G.: No, that doesn't disturb me. And an older person who is senile or something — that doesn't bother me.

THERAPIST: What about a little boy of four?

MISS G.: No.

THERAPIST: Six?

MISS G.: No.

THERAPIST: Eight?

MISS G.: No. It's when they get older, I get nervous.

THERAPIST: Twelve?

MISS G.: Around in their teens.

THERAPIST: About twelve? They sort of begin to bother you?

MISS G.: Yes.

THERAPIST: I take it that a boy of twelve wouldn't be as bad as one of eighteen?

MISS G.: No.

THERAPIST: Let's go back to the street where you are walking and there are three people sitting on a bench across the road. Would it make any difference to you whether they were three men or three women?

MISS G.: No, it wouldn't. I would feel worse if I would see somebody very handsome.

THERAPIST: When you see him, even if he is not looking at you?

MISS G.: Yes, that's correct.[28]

THERAPIST: If you go to a movie and see a very handsome film star, does that bother you?

---

[28]At first glance this is an exception to her rule. But on the indications of the succeeding conversation, it seems clear that she is reacting to the anticipation of being looked at by this kind of very strongly anxiety-evoking figure.

MISS G.: No, not really, because I know he is not there looking at me.

THERAPIST: And if there is a handsome actor on the stage?

MISS G.: Yes, it would.

THERAPIST: It would bother you even though he was not looking at you?

MISS G.: Unless it is very dark and he could not see me.

THERAPIST: Well, then, it is only if he can see you that you feel afraid – because you think that he might see you.

MISS G.: I think he might.

THERAPIST: Besides looking at you, what else can people do to make you nervous? You have, I think, mentioned one thing. They can be critical of you. You are scared of your boss criticizing you.

MISS G.: Any criticism gets me upset even if I know that I am right. I can't talk back and tell them that I am right[29] in this case; I just get all choked up and feel like I am going to cry.

THERAPIST: Is there anything else that people do to upset you?

MISS. G.: Well, let them just tell me I'm wrong – if I am wrong or if I'm right, it still bothers me. It upsets me.

THERAPIST: That's a kind of criticism. Supposing people praise you?

MISS G.: That makes me feel good.

THERAPIST: It makes you feel good. Okay. Who is older, you or your sister?[30]

MISS G.: I am.

THERAPIST: By how much?

MISS G.: Three years.

THERAPIST: What sort of person is your father?

MISS G.: He's on the quiet side, and both of my parents are on the nervous side. My sister, too. The whole family really.

THERAPIST: Was your father kind to you when you were a little girl?

MISS G.: Yes.

THERAPIST: And your mother?

MISS G.: Yes, she's the stronger one. I'm more like my father and my sister is more like my mother.

THERAPIST: In what way is your mother stronger?

[29]Another major anxiety source.
[30]This begins the questioning about general background.

MISS G.: Well, things don't bother her, at least outwardly, as much as they do my father and me. She sort of makes decisions.

THERAPIST: What does your father do?

MISS G.: He sells insurance.

THERAPIST: Did either of your parents punish you when you were young?

MISS G.: They used to hit me once in a while. My mother did. My father hardly ever did.

THERAPIST: Did your mother hit you often?

MISS G.: Not that often.

THERAPIST: Well, did she do anything else to discipline you?

MISS G.: No, that's all. She would have little talks.

THERAPIST: Did you feel when your parents punished you that it was unreasonable?

MISS G.: Sometimes I did.

THERAPIST: Were there any other adults who played any important part in your home life — grandmothers, aunts, nurses?

MISS G.: Yes, my grandmother — she lives with us.

THERAPIST: Okay, well now — what about her? What kind of a person is she?

MISS G.: She is very good to me. I am her first grandchild, so she pays more attention to me than to my sister, but she doesn't understand a lot of things because she wasn't born in America and she did not have an education.

THERAPIST: How do you get along with your sister?

MISS G.: We used to fight an awful lot, but lately we have been getting along better than we used to, but we are not really close because she is completely different than I am.

THERAPIST: What is she like?

MISS G.: She's more talkative than I am — more outgoing. I'm on the quiet side.

THERAPIST: Did you go to school in Philadelphia, Carol?

MISS G.: Yes, I did.

THERAPIST: Did you like school?

MISS G.: Not really.

THERAPIST: What did you dislike about it?

MISS G.: I was afraid of getting up in front of the class.[31]

THERAPIST: Yes, is that all?

MISS G.: Yes.

THERAPIST: How well did you do?

MISS G.: I was a B average.

THERAPIST: Did you take part in sport?

MISS G.: No.

THERAPIST: Did you make friends?

MISS G.: Yes, I have a lot of friends.

THERAPIST: Any close friends?

MISS G.: Yes, one in particular.

THERAPIST: You say that you don't like being an X-ray technician. What would you like to be?

MISS G.: I would like to be a kindergarten teacher.

THERAPIST: A kindergarten teacher?

MISS G.: I like to be with children.

THERAPIST: Apart from this fear of getting up and speaking, did you have any other fears when you were small?

MISS G.: No.

THERAPIST: Like, maybe, insects, darkness?

MISS G.: I was afraid to take a shower because I had claustrophobia.

THERAPIST: When was that?

MISS G.: It was about 12 or 13. I was afraid to be closed in. Somebody locked me in a closet and I couldn't stand it. It scared me.

THERAPIST: How old were you when that happened?

MISS G.: I really don't remember. I guess about 10 or 11.

THERAPIST: After you were 12, that fear disappeared?

MISS G.: Well, I would still be afraid if someone would lock me in a closet. I am not afraid to take showers.

THERAPIST: Do you like going into elevators?

MISS G.: I used to be afraid; I am not anymore.[32]

THERAPIST: You're quite okay now?

[31]This has already been noted and partly explored. It will shortly be pursued further.

[32]Especially in childhood, many fears are overcome by life experiences. Miss G. still has some degree of claustrophobia (in closets), but it is not evidently related to her present serious neurosis.

Miss G.: Yes, I take it everyday.

THERAPIST: Do you remember any experience at all when you were at school that was particularly frightening in relationship to getting up and talking in class?

Miss G.: Yes, when I was in sixth grade I had to read something in front of the class. I was holding the paper and I started shaking. And the teacher said "What's the matter?", and I couldn't really talk.[33] And from then on if I had to read something I'd put it down on the desk and look at it. I would still be nervous.

THERAPIST: Before this happened were you already nervous?

Miss G.: Yes.

THERAPIST: And after this, you were much worse?

Miss G.: Yes.

THERAPIST: Let me ask you how you would react to certain everyday situations.[34] Supposing you were standing in line and somebody got in front of you, how would you feel and what would you do?

Miss G.: I wouldn't do anything, but I would feel I would be ready to explode because I would think it was wrong.

THERAPIST: Yes, certainly it would be wrong.

Miss G.: But I can't say anything about it. I can't get up the nerve to say anything.

THERAPIST: And does that apply to every situation of that type?

Miss G.: Yes. There's a man who gets on the same bus and he limps and he hasn't gotten in front of me, but he pushes and slides and nobody says anything to him and it really upsets me because everybody always complains, but nobody says anything.

THERAPIST: Well, why would you not say something to him?

Miss G.: I would be afraid to. He has a mean temper.

THERAPIST: Well, supposing it wasn't him? Supposing you were standing in line at the Academy of Music box office and somebody you don't know got in front of you?

Miss G.: I probably still wouldn't say anything.

THERAPIST: Why not?

[33]This might well have been a critical conditioning event, but the tremor of her hands indicates that there was a pre-existing anxiety conditioning.

[34]The answers to these questions throw light on interpersonal anxieties of the kind calling for assertive training (see Chapter 5).

MISS G.: Just because I'm afraid to. I'm afraid to open my mouth.

THERAPIST: Does this have anything to do with the idea that if you were to say something, people would start looking at you?

MISS G.: Maybe.

THERAPIST: Let me try to put the question in another way. I would like you to think very carefully before you answer. Supposing you didn't care if people looked at you, would you say something?

MISS G.: I really don't know. It's just that I can't get it out. The words just won't come out.

THERAPIST: Well, all right. You realize that if somebody does a thing like that, getting in front of you, he is doing you a wrong. One of the things you are going to learn to do when you are treated here is precisely to take action about that kind of thing — to stand up for yourself and not allow people to do you wrong.

MISS G.: How do you go about planning that?

THERAPIST: Essentially what you do is to express the annoyance that you rightly feel.[35] It is very hard at first, but if you make a special point of doing it, you find that it gets easier and easier.

MISS G.: I have tried but I can't; if the situation arises, the words just don't come out and I start stuttering.

THERAPIST: Well, I will help you. Later on, each time you come here, I will say, "Carol, did you have any situations of this sort last week?" You will say, maybe, "Yes," and I will want to know what you tried to do about it. But in the meantime, I know it is difficult for you because of the very special fear you have of being the center of attention. If you told someone to get back in line, he would look at you and other people would look at you. And that makes it more difficult.[36]

MISS G.: Yes.

THERAPIST: So one of the things we will have to do is to break down this fear that you have of being looked at. In order to do this, we need to know more about it. Let's use as a kind of basic situation the one we mentioned in which you are seen from a bench across the road.[37] Now, would it make any difference to you how wide the street was?

MISS G.: Yes — if they were closer to me I would feel worse.

THERAPIST: I see. Now I find it very useful to have some kind of

[35]A basic principle in assertive training (see Chapter 5).
[36]Assertive training is for the time being precluded by her reaction to being looked at.
[37]What follows is the beginning of a hierarchy construction (see Chapter 6).

quantitative way of expressing how much afraid a person would be. One way to do it is to ask you to think of the worst fear that you ever had and call that 100; and then you think of being absolutely calm, as when you are at home, and call that zero. Now, consider that the street is as wide as Broad Street (about 100 feet) and there is just one person sitting on that bench; how much anxiety would you feel? Would it be five, fifty, or twenty or what?

MISS G.: I guess around 50.

THERAPIST: Now, supposing that the street was twice as broad as Broad St. and there is just this one person?

MISS G.: I guess about 25.

THERAPIST: Now, if you see two persons, would it still be 25?

MISS G.: Yes.

THERAPIST: It doesn't matter how many?

MISS G.: No, well, if there is a whole group it's worse.

THERAPIST: Supposing that you are standing at one side of a football stadium that is twice as wide as Broad St., and there is one man sitting on one of the stands right across the other side; how much anxiety would that cause you?

MISS G.: Around 25.

THERAPIST: And if, instead of being a man, it was a boy of twelve?

MISS G.: It wouldn't be as large . . . 5, 10.

THERAPIST: Well, if when you were standing at one side of the stadium, there was one boy of 12 sitting in the stand at the other side, you said you would have 5 or 10 degrees of anxiety. If it is a man of 25 it would be 25 degrees. With a boy about 15, would it be in between?

MISS G.: Yes.

THERAPIST: I see. Well, I think we can take that as a basis for action. But before we can take any action we have to do something else. Let me explain something to you. You know well enough that you have anxiety where you shouldn't have it. In order to combat the anxiety, we have to use reactions inside of you which will fight the anxiety. One very convenient one is brought about by muscle relaxation. Now, you have probably never learned how to relax your muscles properly, have you?

MISS G.: No.

THERAPIST: Next time I will start to show you.

CHAPTER 4

Orientation and the Correction of Misconceptions

The objective non-judgmental attitude that characterizes the gathering of information as portrayed in the previous chapter permeates every phase of behavior therapy. It is an attitude that comes easily to the dyed-in-the-wool behaviorist, but is awkward for almost everybody else.

The behavior therapist takes it for granted that human behavior is subject to causal determination no less than the behavior of falling bodies or of growing plants. For example, a man pauses at crossroads, undecided along which of two routes to proceed. The route that he eventually takes is the inevitable one, being the resultant of a balancing out of conflicting action-tendencies. The strength of each action-tendency is essentially a function of the incipient reactions evoked by impinging stimuli, internal and external, whose effects depend primarily on the character of previously established neural interconnections — that is, on pre-existing habit structures.

The general attitude of the behavior therapist to his patients accords with this deterministic outlook. He regards the patient as the product of his physical endowment and the cumulative effects of the experiences he has undergone. Each environment, each exposure to stimulation, has modified, through learning, the patient's character as a responding organism to a greater or lesser extent. Attitudes, thoughts, verbal behavior, and emotional behavior have all been shaped in various ways and various degrees by the organism's previous interactions with his environments.

Since the patient has had no choice in becoming what he is, it is incongruous to blame him for having gone awry, or to disparage him for the

53

continuance of his unhappy state. The behavior therapist, therefore, does not moralize to his patient, but on the contrary goes out of his way to dislodge any self-blame that social conditioning may have engendered and that may have been magnified by statements made by friends, relations, and previous therapists. He explains to the patient that his unpleasant reactions are due to emotional habits that he cannot help and that have nothing to do with 'moral fiber' or an unwillingness to get well. To some sophisticated patients he describes how similar reactions are easily induced in animals, who remain neurotic for just as long as the experimenter chooses, and that he 'cures' them by methods that are determined by principles of learning, and that in a parallel way the overcoming of the human neurosis involves techniques quite similar to those used in the laboratory.[1]

The patient is now introduced to the practices of behavior therapy. This is done either by means of short didactic speeches, or else in the course of discussions between patient and therapist that may include other topics.

The central role of fear (anxiety) in the neurosis must be brought to the fore at an early stage. Most patients are quite aware of being hamstrung by fear. Not so many recognize it to be the essence of their disturbed reactions (as shown in Table 1); but most can accept it when the therapist points it out. The distinctive features of the origins of *neurotic* fears are brought out in statements on the following lines:

You have realized that fear figures excessively in your life. It is necessary to have some perspective about it. It is an emotion that plays a normal part in everybody's life whenever a situation involving a real threat arises – for example, walking alone and unarmed at night in an unsavory neighborhood, learning that one's firm is about to retrench its staff, or being confronted by a poisonous snake. Nobody would come for treatment because he experiences fear in such situations. It is a different matter when fear is aroused by experiences that contain no real threat – such as seeing an ambulance, entering a crowded room, or riding in a car – to take examples other than your own. To be fearful in such situations is obviously inappropriate, and can interfere

---

[1]It is particularly difficult for those who have previously been trained psychoanalytically to align themselves with this orientation. Even those who have become intellectually disenchanted with 'dynamic' theories and practices lapse through habit into teleological modes of thought and tend to make interpretative statements that sometimes have condemnatory overtones.

with daily functioning in a most distressing way. It is this that we call neurotic fear; and it is the task of therapy to detach it from the stimuli or situations that provoke it.

Let us consider how neurotic fears originate. The process is really what common sense would lead you to expect. Let me illustrate it by the old-fashioned example of the burnt child. The child places his hand on the big, black, hot coal stove. He quickly withdraws the painful hand, tearful and fearful. His mother comforts him, but later notes that he keeps away from the stove and seems afraid of it. Clearly, the child has developed a beneficial habit of fearing and avoiding an actually harmful object.

But in some cases the experience also has other and less favorable consequences. Suppose in the mother's bedroom there is a large black chest of drawers. The child may have become afraid of this too — purely on the basis of its *physical resemblance* to the stove — a phenomenon known in psychology as generalization. Fear of the chest of drawers is neurotic because there can be no harm in touching it. It can have several undesirable implications. In the first place, the very presence of an unpleasant emotion like fear, where it is not appropriate, is objectionable. Secondly, the child is now forced to make a detour if the chest of drawers is in his path; and thirdly, he no longer has easy access to any delectable contents of the drawers, such as candy. These features of the child's case are typical of all neurotic fear reactions.

Your own fears were likewise acquired in the course of unpleasant experiences, some of which we touched upon in your history. The unpleasant emotions you then had became conditioned, or connected, to aspects of the situation that made an imprint on you at the time. This means that subsequent similar experiences led to the arousal of these same unpleasant feelings. Now, just because these reactions could then be produced by particular stimulus-triggers as a result of the operation of a process of learning it is possible to eliminate them by the application of the principles of learning.

In animals, the treatment of a neurosis is a very straightforward matter, especially when the experimenter himself has induced the neurosis. In human subjects, it can be just as simple, but may be complicated by various factors in the more complex organism. However, endowed with language, we can unravel most webs and our very complexity gives to human behavior therapy the possibility of a large repertoire of techniques. For example, some boys who have had frightening experiences at the stoves might lose their fears of chests of drawers by verbal explanation and physical demonstration of the differences between the two kinds of objects – one kind of solution that is not available for the neuroses of animals.

Other kinds of orientating information are quite often needed. Although the patient can usually distinguish quite easily between those of his anxiety reactions that are adaptive and those that are not, there can be misapprehensions, and when they are apparent the therapist must spare no effort to remove them. It is scarcely possible to decondition anxiety from a situation that the patient believes, however wrongly, to embody real danger. No amount of desensitizing effort is likely to make a person indifferent to handling a snake he believes to be poisonous. Misapprehensions are particularly common in fears of the 'hypochondriacal' kind. Only when the patient with recurrent pains in his chest is both assured that the pains do not signify heart disease and also shown their *actual* source, can desensitizing operations be hopefully undertaken. Information alone can dispel fears based purely on misinformation (see p. 25).

Some other kinds of corrective statements that commonly need to be made are typified by the following:

1. *"You are not mentally ill and there is no chance of your going insane."* The bizarreness of their symptoms causes many patients to feel they are 'cracking up,' an impression that is 'confirmed' when other people, and particularly doctors, do not understand what they are talking about when they try to describe their symptoms. These misinterpretations are naturally even more strongly set up and correspondingly more damaging if psychiatrists have told them that they are, or may become, psychotic. It is often sufficient for the behavior therapist to correct this kind of misinformation in an authoritatively dogmatic way; but with educated patients a good deal of evidence may have to be provided. It may have to be argued that neuroses and psychoses are not on the same continuum, so that however bad a neurosis becomes it is still not a psychosis. Unusually sophisticated individuals may need to be given supporting facts: that psychoses show a clear inherited pattern not manifest in neuroses; that there is evidence of biochemical abnormality in the serum of psychotics while that of neurotics is indistinguishable from normal; and that in the course of World War II, while the incidence of neuroses gradually rose, that of psychoses remained stationary. They may also be told of Eysenck's (1958) finding that neuroses and psychoses are deviations in different dimensions, and of Rubin's (1970) pupillographic differentiation. For a fuller exposition of the evidence, see Wolpe (1970).

2. *"All your reactions are explicable."* Patients who from time to time are overtaken by panic states or depressions whose antecedents are not clear may come to feel chronically apprehensive: they do not know when the 'hidden forces' will strike. Careful examination of the circumstances of these severe reactions almost invariably reveals constancies; and knowing them gives great comfort to the patient — an example of insight removing a significant source of anxiety.

3. *"There is no virtue in confronting your fears."* Many patients, either on the basis of their moralistic training, or urged by friends or therapists, feel that they should benefit by 'facing up' to the situations that evoke anxiety in them. It is usually sufficient to refer to their own experience to convince them that this is futile and even aggravating. Their fortitude leads to penance unrewarded by blessings. They should be told that an emotional change depends on *controlled* exposures to disturbing stimuli.

*Case 3: A transcript exemplifying the correction of misconception**

A good many misconceptions can be corrected by a few authoritative statements. But sometimes a complex system of faulty thinking has been woven into the patient's life, and then a great deal of instruction and argumentation may be needed to decompose it. This is illustrated in the transcript below.

The patient, Lisa, was a very intelligent 35-year-old woman who had suffered greatly for more than 10 years from marked irritability, severe depressions, and frequent tantrums, sometimes violent. She had never had a coital orgasm; and had accepted the consensus of friends, relations, and doctors that she was somehow biologically incapable of normal sexual function — a view that was confirmed in her mind when almost 10 years of psychoanalysis failed to produce any change. This view of herself, coupled with an impression of disinterest on the part of her husband, Ed, filled her with despair, and caused the depressions and tantrums.

Intermingled with the history-taking in Lisa's early sessions was a concerted attack on the whole erroneous conceptual structure. She was shown that, in fact, she was a well-integrated person who had, through learning, picked up some unadaptive habits — most notably a fear of trusting people, particularly in the context of the most deeply felt sexual experience — the orgasm.

When she realized this, Lisa experienced tremendous emotional relief, and eagerly cooperated in the efforts that were then instituted to normalize

*The first of these transcribed interviews was published in the *Journal of Behavior Therapy and Experimental Psychiatry*, 2, xxx, 1971.

her sex life. She had for years been able to masturbate to orgasm by squeezing her thighs together, but only if quite alone in the house. The first target in the domain of sex was seen to be to overcome her fear of being observed at orgasm. Anxiety began to be felt at the idea of masturbating if her husband was 3 houses away, and increased as he came nearer. Accordingly, desensitization (Chapter 7) on a proximity dimension was planned. But when she was asked to close her eyes for the purpose of relaxing, she became very anxious—associated, as the transcript suggests, with a fear of trusting people. Through graduated periods of *in vivo* eye-closing, this fear was soon overcome; and then desensitization to the hierarchy of Ed's proximity during masturbation was rapidly accomplished.

As Lisa was now able to masturbate in Ed's presence, it was possible to organize a series of steps through which the masturbatory orgasm was integrated into coitus in a way that both of them found thoroughly satisfying. The jealousy reaction faded out as sexual progress continued. Five months later, Lisa wrote: "My days continue to be filled with sunshine and my evenings begin with a million stars." There had never been the shadow of recurrence of her previous symptoms.

The transcript consists of excerpts from Lisa's first three interviews. During the first half of the initial interview, Lisa was seen alone, and at several points I disputed that her disability was a 'sickness,' and that she was to blame for the marital trouble. Ed participated in the second half, to make it possible to correct Lisa's impression that he did not care for her. At the end, they were both given the Willoughby Schedule to fill in at home. A few days later, Ed called to say that Lisa was in a state of crisis and had taken 30 tablets of oxazepam the previous day. At a short emergency session, she stated that her Willoughby responses (a score of 51) in contrast to Ed's (16) had convinced her that she must be hopeless. As the excerpts from the session show, I persuaded her that the difference was purely a matter of conditioning. After this, she never looked back. The third session continued the emphasis on conceptual clarification. The excerpts from it include some of Lisa's background history.

First Session

Dr.: I gather from Ed, your husband, that there is a lack of harmony in certain ways between you.[2] The question is whether there is any practical

---

[2]The statement was deliberately phrased in these extremely general terms so that the patient could state without constraint the issues as she saw them.

possibility of straightening out your relationship and making it mutually desirable.

LISA: I think we're very different people. Of course, most people are different; but I think that I married my husband for very neurotic reasons, and I'm sure there had to be something like that on his side, too. I've spent ten years in therapy. You're the third doctor my husband has made me come to—not made me come to. I shouldn't phrase it that way.

Dr.: Well, sometimes it's not a matter of therapy.[3] Anyway, before we make any decisions, let's get some facts. When did you first meet him?

LISA: I guess I knew him casually when we were in our teen-age years. I was a freshman at college when he was a senior. I didn't start dating him until after my first marriage dissolved.

DR.: What did you like about Ed?

LISA: He was entirely opposite from my father.

DR.: How old were you when your first marriage dissolved?

LISA: 20.

DR.: You liked the fact that Ed was different from your father. Well, what was the difference?

LISA: He was quiet and more stable, certainly emotionally more balanced. He was the type of man that I've always been attracted to— protective, I guess.

DR.: Well, he was stable and elicited a feeling of protectiveness. Is that the essence of it?

LISA: I don't know. I never thought about it that way.

DR.: Did you feel very strongly attracted to Ed at that time?

LISA: Yeah.

DR.: How long after this did you get married?

LISA: Six months.

DR.: And how did you get along with him during those six months?

LISA: Ah—it was sort of a topsy-turvy relationship.

DR.: What do you mean?

LISA: Well, there were certain periods of stress and strain. It was never what I would call a quiet courtship period.

---

[3]Some marital incompatibilities are not resoluble by psychotherapy. This is true, for example, of intellectual differences and wide divergencies of interest. This idea was now introduced in order to suggest to the patient that she might, after all, not be 'sick,' as had always been assumed. As it turned out, this was the key move in the treatment of the case.

DR.: What were the causes of the stresses and strains?

LISA: Me, I guess. I was a very emotionally sick person at the time and I –

DR.: Something must have upset you.[4]

LISA: I don't know. I guess his background.

DR.: I'm not asking you in that sense. I'm not asking you what caused the upset. I'm just asking what upset you.[5]

LISA: Oh, I don't know. I guess I was demanding and insecure and jealous of the amount of time he spent with me. I never go along on an even keel; I'm always up or down or –

DR.: Still, what are the kinds of things that upset you?

LISA: When he gives attention to another woman, that upsets me.

DR.: Well that's clear enough. Was that the sort of thing that used to happen?

LISA: It's so long ago, I can't remember. I was in such a state of complete unreality when Ed and I were dating, I don't even remember what my behavior was like.

DR.: But you liked to be with him and you were happy with the relationship.

LISA: Yeah.

DR.: But there were just some things that upset you.

LISA: Yeah. Well, I was living at home with a small baby[6] – not exactly an ideal setup.

DR.: What was the sexual relationship[7] at that period?

LISA: I don't know. For me, there never has been any sexual satisfaction, but I guess I have tried very hard because I want to hold on to him.

DR.: So there wasn't any real sexual enjoyment for you?

LISA: There never has been with anyone.

DR.: You know some women will say they don't reach a climax, but they enjoy sex. You don't even enjoy it?

LISA: Oh, I guess I enjoy it. Yeah, to a point.

DR.: Yes?

[4]Further deflecting from the idea of 'sickness,' and suggesting accountable reactivity.

[5]Patients who have had psychoanalytically-informed therapy are characteristically more ready to provide causal hypotheses than facts.

[6]The offspring of her first marriage.

[7]It should be noted how noncommittally this crucial topic was introduced.

LISA: Yes, I guess I never really tore it apart like that.

DR.: Well, do you get stimulated up to a point and then feel left high and dry. Do you feel frustrated?

LISA: No, the anger has completely faded out of it for me. I'm no longer angry about it or demanding of it. I become very irritable and hostile toward Ed.

DR.: Well, that's what I mean.

LISA: But I don't feel that this is my fault because —

DR.: It's not important whose fault it is.[8]

LISA: No, but I mean, there isn't any sexual relationship — unless it comes from me, there isn't any.

DR.: I see. Anyway, going back to that time. At that time, you were having some sex with him?

LISA: Yeah.

DR.: And, you were enjoying it up to a point —

LISA: Oh, yeah.

DR.: And then you were left irritated afterwards?

LISA: Yeah.

DR.: So that tended to make you keep away from him because it was sort of punishing.

LISA: Well, I think eventually, yes. Especially after you're married and you're legally bound to one another, you're safer and you can turn it off, so to speak, emotionally. When I went to the first psychiatrist, and Ed found out there was a problem, he completely dropped sexual approaches. In the last ten years — if I didn't initiate it, there was nothing. Last year, we went the entire year without any sex at all. But I do feel that my therapy has been — it's been long, but it has served the purpose.

DR.: What purpose has it served?

LISA: Well, I have found out, I think, the reasons for my problems. I consider myself a controlled neurotic[9] now. I'm afraid to do anything.

DR.: You're afraid to do anything?

LISA: Right. I don't do anything — at all. If I know it's dangerous to my —

[8]The therapist seizes every opportunity to assuage guilt and diminish self-blame. It does not matter that in this instance the patient's next remark showed him to be off-target.

[9]By whatever route her therapy led to this conception, it boils down to an acceptance of permanent inferiority.

DR.: This is very important. Take this sexual situation. If you find that sex leaves you very upset and irritated, then it's reasonable to avoid it. It doesn't necessarily mean that your failure to respond sexually is itself neurotic. It may be; I don't know. But it may not be.[10]

LISA: Well, it's a different feeling now. But since I returned to Ed — I'm sure he explained to you — following the circumstances of last Fall,[11] he made an effort and I made an effort. But he has backed off and this makes me more irritable —

DR.: He has backed off in what way?

LISA: He doesn't make advances toward me anymore. He tried for a while — I never rejected him in this entire period; and I was cooperative and enjoyed it and —

DR.: So today you would like him to make advances?

LISA: But he doesn't. And this is when I started questioning him. I said, "Ed, I am not going to any more psychiatrists because it's a two way street." And I said, "I am tired of always being the aggressive one in our relationship." I can never be subordinate in my mind if I'm the only one who's aggressive.

DR.: In the beginning, you were the one to avoid intercourse and now he avoids it.

LISA: Well, he avoided it during the entire eight-year period. The doctors questioned about it.[12] They felt that Ed had dropped it much too quickly when he found out that I had a mental block concerning — well, they called it an oedipus complex, a father complex, you don't have the ability to have an orgasm.[13] It's so beyond me. A lot of girls adore their fathers — so what? After ten years of therapy, there certainly should have been some change.

DR.: I agree with you.[14]

LISA: Here we are in the same situation and, for some reason, these women are still very upsetting to me — his mother, his sister — it doesn't

[10]Like the referent of Footnote 3, a thrust in the direction of throwing doubt on the assumption of the patient's 'sickness.'

[11]The reference is to an affair with a student that Ed had described and that she later details.

[12]Without, however, dispelling doubt that the primary blame was Lisa's.

[13]This confident equation would inevitably preclude any exploration of the evolution of Lisa's sexual behavior.

[14]Reinforcing her questioning of the analytic theory, and augmenting the statements referred to in Footnotes 2 and 9.

make any difference; it's just women in general. My mother was my competitor, so any woman is my competitor.[15]

DR.: Well, do you think you would feel this as much if Ed were making advances to you?

LISA: No, I wouldn't. I would feel more secure.

DR.: That makes sense.

LISA: As it is now, I feel very insecure. I feel any woman is a threat to me. There are certain kinds of women that are very feminine women, who seem secure enough in their own life. They don't pose a threat. But then there are those that all of a sudden bleach their hair and are dissatisfied with their home situations. To me they are threatening.

DR.: But there's a basis for this. You realize that Ed is a person and has needs. If he doesn't come to you, maybe he feels these dissatisfied people are more accessible.

LISA: Well, if it's that, I've disguised it to myself. Perhaps that would be too horrible for me to face.

DR.: But you are acting as if you were feeling that way, aren't you?

LISA: I guess.

DR.: Apart from this sexual business, how do you get along?

LISA: Terribly. I'm constantly irritable — we're just like two people grating against each other.[16] I do love Ed and we have three of the loveliest children. They're very stable, healthy in body and spirit. It's amazing to me. I look at them and think, "With my mental condition, how could these children possibly be the way they are?" Ed has never been around for twelve years. I guess to escape me he throws himself into work. I don't know. I guess a lot of men do. Maybe it's just a pattern of behavior. It runs in his family. His own sister never stays home and she has four children; and she is constantly going. And his brother has been through three divorces at 38. I look at all these things and I think, "Is it all me?" I've said to Ed, "I'm through with the therapy. I feel like I've been placed under doctor's care so I couldn't make waves[17] so you could go on your merry way and enjoy life while I was trying to keep the lid on, plus raise the children." I guess you get to a certain point where you just don't care.

DR.: Have your thoughts ever turned to other men?

LISA: Last year, I went away with a college student for a few days. He

---

[15]The reason being, as it emerged, that no other woman suffered from her 'abnormality.'

[16]In the light of what has been said, it could scarcely be otherwise.

[17]While this was not the purpose of "doctor's care," it was certainly a consequence of it.

was unhappy with his personal life. His family are our neighbors. He came to speak to me and I got involved. Reality just seemed to leave me. I look at it now and I think it couldn't possibily have happened. But it did.

DR.: Was it an emotionally satisfying situation?

LISA: Emotionally satisfying, yes. It fulfilled a need. I guess I've been looking and looking for years, but I just didn't think it would be a boy of 20.

DR.: Well, that doesn't matter.[18] Did you have orgasms?

LISA: No.

DR.: Well, did you get close to it?

LISA: No.

DR.: What do you think is lacking—preventing you from having an orgasm?

LISA: Well, I've been told it's an oedipus complex.

DR.: Never mind that.[19] What do you think?

LISA: I just don't think that I feel adequate. I don't know.

DR.: Can you picture any circumstances that might enter into a relationship that would let you—

LISA: Oh—I feel that I have a fear of losing touch with reality.

DR.: Sort of a fear of letting go, is it?

LISA: This is what it is. I don't trust anyone enough.[20]

DR.: Of course, really, if you have an orgasm, you're not losing touch with reality. You are engrossing yourself very very much in reality.[21] I can see that you might feel the other way, though. We find people who are afraid even to relax.

LISA: Well, I never relax either. I don't mean just in sex, I mean in anything. And they tell me, "Don't be nervous." It's very fine to tell somebody, you know, don't be nervous, but—

DR.: Well, I would like to ask Ed to come in and see if we can get some further orientation.

---

[18]A few words to dispel any thought of censure.

[19]A further undermining of the 'sickness' diagnosis and suggestion of self-exploration.

[20]This remark opens a new direction of investigation. What does she mean by 'trust'? How did fear of it begin? What factors are involved?

[21]I reverted to this topic because, before anything else, I wanted the basic facts about sexual responding in general to be clear in her mind.

Ed is summoned and enters.

ED: Good morning, sir.

DR.: Do sit down. We've had a brief conspectus of the marital problem from Lisa's point of view and it seems to me that there are both general and situational factors. One situational factor that seems very important to me is that, according to her account, you don't make any sexual approaches to her. Can you comment on that?

ED: I'd say that generally it's true.

DR.: Uh-hum. Well, there must be a reason for it. What prevents you?[22]

ED: There's been a particularly bad spectacle, so to speak, between us over this thing. I was just turned off somewhere along the line.

DR.: Perhaps there has been some bad communication between you. Long ago,[23] Lisa became negative towards sex because she was irritable after not having orgasms. But her feeling is different now. She now looks for signs of affection from you and would respond to them. I guess that you're not aware of that.

ED: Well, she's told me that. Perhaps I have a block now, because of past bad experiences with her.

DR.: Well, do you like her?

ED: I love her.

DR.: Do you like to be close to her?

ED: Very much so.

DR.: Well, how do you get there without approaching her?

ED: I'm not following your question.

LISA: He means how to get to first base, honey, if you don't try.

ED: Oh, I see. Well, it's a good question, but I don't have an answer.

DR.: It's very understandable that you've become scared, like a child who has had his knuckles rapped quite a number of times. To be perfectly frank with you, a situation can become so powerfully aversive that the approach movement cannot be made.[24] There will then be a therapeutic problem. But, before trying therapeutic solutions, I want to see if

[22]This is a characteristically behavioristic question, seeking the antecedents of the behavior. It is to be contrasted with other kinds of therapist responses at a juncture like this — moralizing, directing, interpreting, 'reflecting,' etc.

[23]A thumbnail resumé of the history as background to discussing the present situation.

[24]By raising the possibility that emotional factors might render action impossible, I freed Ed from the burden of a moral imperative and thus probably made voluntary efforts easier.

I can persuade you to make approaches. The fact that the three of us have been discussing the matter openly may already have facilitated action, because you now know in advance, Ed, that you are going to be accepted. Would you welcome it, Lisa?

LISA: I think it would take some effort. I've become angry to the point that I just can't predict an answer. I mean, you can become so completely turned off that it would take a longer period of time to be aroused. But I'd welcome it, sure.

DR.: I think, Lisa, a lot depends on what we mean by an approach. An approach can take many forms. It can be just holding your hand. It can be walking into the kitchen and giving you a hug. At this stage, Ed is sort of hesitant and you are sort of resentful. But since affection is mutual, action should start.

LISA: I think that I would be very suspicious. I would feel that he was initiating it because you told him to.

DR.: Well, that's true, but he also wants it.

LISA: I'm not convinced of that.

DR.: Well, how can we find that out?

LISA: I don't know. I've spent ten years in therapy and I haven't found out.

DR.: I really don't see how that therapy could have helped you find this out. You said that you would be pleased if he were to approach you. If he didn't want you, he could just leave you, couldn't he?

LISA: Yeah. Sure.

DR.: What would be the point in his lying? Why should he pretend he wants you? Why should he endure the dissatisfaction, unless he really hopes that something will work out?

LISA: Well, I think this is true.[25]

DR.: Therefore, I think there's a primary reason for accepting him. There is what we might call ground for an experiment. I would like to see him making approaches, small approaches, many approaches. He would be uncertain at first, but you would reinforce him. Then it would become easier for him to do it.

LISA: I have been forthcoming since Christmas time, since I went back to Ed.

---

[25]The purpose (and evident result) of the foregoing argument was to break down Lisa's firmly-held conception of Ed's attitude towards her.

DR.: Yes, but I mean when he makes an approach.

LISA: I have.

DR.: But you said he never makes an approach.

LISA: He tried. He read this book by Masters and Johnson, and then he dropped it again.

DR.: Why did you drop it again, Ed? Did you feel unwelcome or what?

ED: Yes, to a great extent, I did. I felt that it was a failure, although at first we did have a good relationship on occasion. But then after that, if I did reach an orgasm — it was premature and Lisa said, "Why are you so fast?". Sometimes the act just was a failure.

DR.: What is foremost here is not sex, but love, of which the sexual act is an outward expression, but not the only one.[26] There are also many small things that happen between people — small approaches where sex needn't happen, and perhaps couldn't happen. If Ed will do these things and Lisa responds positively, a strong feeling of mutual assurance will build up, from which sex is a natural offshoot, though it will not necessarily be an enormous success from the beginning. Lisa's fear of letting go may make it impossible for her to have coital orgasms. But I'm pretty sure she will eventually have orgasms with you.

LISA: I don't think we accept each other as individuals.[27] Therefore, I don't see how we can possibly have a satisfactory sexual relationship.

DR.: Let's consider that. Sometimes people don't accept each other because they really are terribly different and incompatible. Sometimes they don't accept each other because of a succession of wrong messages. I don't really know what the situation between you is. Let's explore these things. I'll ask each of you some questions. Do you, Ed, feel attracted to Lisa physically?

ED: Yes.

DR.: Do you feel attracted to Ed physically?

LISA: Yes, definitely.

DR.: Do you have a substantial number of common interests?

ED: We have a number of them; we have golf, we have our children.

LISA: I took up golf to be with you.

DR.: But it's there now.

---

[26]The expression of affection solely in the context of sexual intercourse is amazingly common, and a major source of marital disaster.

[27]Now, though granting mutual goodwill, she expresses the idea that a fundamental incompatibility comes between them.

ED: It's there, yes.

LISA: We enjoy it.

DR.: What else are you interested in?

LISA: Not very much anymore.

DR.: What could you be interested in?

LISA: Creative things. Anything creative; I sew a lot. Things that Ed isn't interested in.

DR.: Well, you don't have to share everything.

LISA: Don't you have to share some things?

DR.: Some things.[28] You have golf and you have the children.

LISA: But golf only came about in the last four years.

DR.: That doesn't matter. It's here now. What about movies and books and so on?

LISA: We don't like the same movies at all.

DR.: I think the most important thing is a feeling of mutual participation in living itself. That is more important than movies and books, to the extent that you can feel yourselves capable of building a life together, in which your house and children are an important part. Do you have any such general feeling?

ED: Of being able to build a life together?

DR.: Yes.

ED: Oh, certainly I have.

LISA: I thought you said "participation."

DR.: Yes. I mean emotional participation in building a life together.

ED.: Well, I think that—I think we both really want that. I think this is—

DR.: All right, Lisa, what are the things that you would like that Ed doesn't provide?

LISA: Well, I think the most important thing is to be able to see somebody's needs.[29] And when they need you, you've got to be there.

DR.: I'll tell you what I'd like you to do. Would you each make a list of the things that you feel come between you? As many as you can. Then I would like you to give each other these lists and indicate whether you think that anything can be done to reconcile each particular objection. I

---

[28]There is quite enough mutual interest to build on.
[29]She regards Ed as lacking in this respect.

would also like each of you to fill in one of these Willoughby Question-naires.

Second Session

This was an emergency session that took place 3 days before the next one that had been scheduled. Ed telephoned that Lisa had been in a state of great emotional distress culminating in her having swallowed 30 tablets of oxazepam. I asked him to bring her to see me without delay. The following is the relevant part of the brief, but important, interview that followed.

DR.: You seemed rather hopeful at the end of the last session. Then there was a collapse. What happened?

LISA: Those Willoughby tests we did showed that I am the sick one and that Ed the normal one. My answer to practically every question is the opposite to his. He was right all along. His answers show stability and mine show instability. I feel hopeless.

DR.: That test measures social neuroticism. That means the extent to which there is excessive anxiety or nervousness in relation to other people. Your score of 51 in contrast to his of 16 shows that you are much more vulnerable than Ed is to people's statements and their attitudes toward you. But this anxious reactivity is not organic. It is not inherited. It was acquired by learning. It is a matter of emotional learning. What has been learned can be unlearned.

LISA: But how? All these years of psychotherapy!

DR.: Well, we have methods that are based on our knowledge of how learning takes place. Your previous therapists did not use such methods because they operated on the theory that your troubles are caused by emotional complexes deeply buried in your supposed unconscious mind. Since that theory, though very widely held, has no scientifically accep-table support, it is not surprising that their efforts have not helped you.

LISA: I never could understand how all the analyzing of my childhood was supposed to help. But what else would help?

DR.: If we take a laboratory animal and make him fearful by means of a mild electric shock in a particular room or in the presence of a particular sound, such as a gong, that room or that gong will become attached to the fear—associated with it. It acquires independent power to arouse fear. The fear reaction to the gong can last for years even if the animal is never again given a shock in its presence. But we can do things with him that we know will break that habit. I am sure that when we examine your history we will find that you have had experiences that led to your reacting fearfully to various social situations, including certain aspects of sex. Different kinds of experiences can be arranged here that can disconnect fear from these situations.

LISA: I get the idea.

DR.: We'll begin to develop that kind of program when you come here on Thursday as arranged. How do you feel now?

LISA: Happier. Very encouraged.

Third Session

DR.: How have you been feeling since we had our last session?

LISA: I felt very, very good. Better than I've felt in a long time. It's a strange feeling when somebody offers you a hug and you're ready to grab it.[30] I feel like I'm sort of halfway home.

DR.: Well, we have to proceed systematically now. What have your complaints been?[31]

LISA: All of them? You mean my complaints of my marriage or of my personality?

DR.: You had psychiatric treatment. What has been the trouble in that sense?

LISA: The fact that I haven't been able to produce since I was about thirteen years of age. My studies started to fail. I was a very bright student—bright enough to have skipped sixth grade. Then I started to slip. I became grossly overweight, and then I was sent to a fine girls' school, but it wasn't fine for me. I became heavier and my work failed. I was taken out and sent to public high school for the last year where I didn't produce either. I was accepted at the Philadelphia Museum School of Art, but I wasn't permitted to attend. I was sent to Penn State University. I still could not produce.

---

[30]The elucidation of the nature of her illness at the second interview had given her a feeling of complete acceptance by me and convinced her that her troubles were not only understood, but also remediable. The emotional crisis that preceded that interview was the last of its kind to date. She subsequently had 'normal' upsets to ordinary frustrations and difficulties, but not again the helpless distress that had previously been more or less omnipresent.

[31]It was necessary to pose this question anew because we had previously concentrated on the sexual problem and its repercussions.

DR.: Okay, you were unproductive. What do you think was the reason for this?

LISA: I refused to compete because I didn't want to fail. My father only has one measuring stick, and that's the top; there's no in-between. It's either A + or nothing. And I was tired of my mother as a competitor. I always came out second-best anyway.

DR.: Now, there was a time when you were doing very well.

LISA: Uh-hum.

DR.: And then you stopped doing very well. Something must have changed. What changed?

LISA: I don't know. Me. I had a sexual attitude, I guess. I don't know.

DR.: Why do you say a 'sexual attitude'?

LISA: I don't know. It must have been. Isn't that the age when you start to have — [32]

DR.: Maybe, but I want to know what actually happened to you.

LISA: Nothing. Not a thing.[33] It was just a period of — I started to change.

DR.: Well, there was a time when you did your work and a time when you didn't. What was it that prevented you from doing your work?

LISA: A lack of desire.

DR.: You lost interest in work?

LISA: It was a way of getting complete attention because I didn't do it.[34]

DR.: No, that's theory. Don't give me any theory. We have lots of theories.

LISA: I don't know. I can't tell you. It was so many years ago. I was so nervous. Maybe I couldn't concentrate.

DR.: What made you nervous? What were you nervous about?

LISA: Maybe of being accepted into a world I didn't want any part of. I don't know. I guess I had seen a bad relationship between my mother and father. Maybe I didn't wish to grow up.

DR.: You are full of psychoanalytic indoctrination, and when I ask

[32]The 'explanation' clearly derives from her psychoanalytic experience.

[33]This is not credible. Something *must* have happened. The patient may truly be unable to recall it. The therapist must do all he can to jog her memory — but gently, not derogatorily.

[34]She had either been told this or deduced it from standard psychoanalytic thinking, in which she was well versed.

you to tell me what happened, you give me theory. I don't want theory.

LISA: But I don't know what happened.

DR.: I'm just asking you what were the events. I don't want to know motives or things like that. I want you to give me a kind of story. The details will be yours. The kind of story I'm expecting from you now is this: "I was doing fine until the age of fifteen and then my grandmother began to live with us. There are things about her that I find disturbing and I got into a nervous state and I couldn't do my work." These would be facts; that's the kind of story I want.

LISA: There had been a great big Halloween Party in fourth grade and we had all run off in the woods.[35] And I can remember the boys starting to tease us and call us by dirty names, you know. And then in junior high school, boys who had also transferred from the other school continued to ride me.

DR.: They continued to ride you?

LISA: Yeah, about these episodes that had happened when we were in fourth grade. They kept calling me names. I can remember how tremendously upsetting it was. Some days I didn't even want to go to school.

DR.: You were very distressed by the attitude of these boys?

LISA: Mortified. Just absolutely horrified.[36]

DR.: This went on all through the seventh grade?

Lisa: Eighth grade and part of ninth.

DR.: Now you're telling me the kind of thing I want to know. Were you sensitive to other things that people might say?

LISA: Oh, yes. I had my nose straightened a few years ago. I had a pug nose, not large, but enough that I looked like my mother. They used to tease me about this nose and it upset me.

DR.: How would you defend yourself?

LISA: By retaliating or saying something harsh about some other person—which I didn't do.[37] I usually was so wounded that I never said anything. There was no doubt about my parents being critical of me. I mean it was a life of criticism: "Sit straight"—"Put your napkin on your lap."

[35]We get to first base.

[36]Possibly a key conditioning experience in the development of the 'fear of trusting' element in the inhibition of her sexual response.

[37]Patients are often aware that they should behave assertively, but usually cannot do so without help.

DR.: Are your parents alive?

LISA: Yes.

DR.: What sort of a person is your father?[38]

LISA: Brilliant—unfortunately. He's always a perfectionist.

DR.: How did he treat you when you were a little girl? Was he good to you?

LISA: Oh yes—yes, very good—very generous. He didn't have very much time, because of his business, to give to me, but he was very generous materially. He never doled out any punishment—my mother gave it all. He always wanted to be the good guy.

DR.: And he always wanted to see high standards from you?

LISA: Oh yes—completely. He gave me everything he lacked when he was raised in the semi-slums of Philadelphia.

DR.: What about your mother?

LISA: Possessive—critical—domineering—competitive—negative—but she tried to do everything for me. I mean I never lacked anything. She was always there to drive me or take me or pick me up.

DR.: Well, what was your general feeling towards her?

LISA: I didn't like her—I still to this day can't bear to have her near me or touch me. I didn't want either of them to touch me as a child.[39] It even distresses me to think about it—that's how hostile I was towards both of them.

DR.: Something must have happened to make it unpleasant.

LISA: She was just critical—it was just one constant criticism.

DR.: What in particular did she criticize?

LISA: I don't mean criticizing me as a person—I mean critical of my actions—if I didn't put my napkin on my lap at dinner time—corrective measures. It was just a constant sort of thing. My father had a very destructive side. He used to get me pets and if they didn't please him, then he would have them given away or destroyed, which was extremely upsetting to me as a child.[40]

DR.: That's extraordinary.

[38]This begins the formal background questioning. Topics previously covered will, of course, not be repeated.

[39]It is possible that this negative conditioning to touching was a factor in the development of her sexual inhibitions. However, she had always enjoyed erotic touching.

[40]It would be strange if this did not engender a fear of involvement.

LISA: It's a little cruel, isn't it? When I went away to school and wasn't a good student, when I came home for vacation my dog was gone. When I first got married, I had played the piano for fourteen years. I came back and my piano was gone. There were lots of little things like that. When I wouldn't divorce my first husband during a very rocky marriage, I was disowned. It's amazing to me that I've lasted twelve years with Ed. To me it's just incredible; that he's seen all of me and he still doesn't hate me.

DR.: Well, why should he?

LISA: I guess because maybe I hate myself and I'm sure everyone else will, too. I mean in total picture; oh, there are lots of things I don't desire to change at all.[41]

DR.: You mean you expect to be hated?

LISA: Maybe, yes — disliked.

DR.: But you might be quite wrong in thinking that you should be.[42]

LISA: I don't know.

DR.: Well, I rather think that's true. At what age did you have your first sexual feelings?

LISA: Towards boys — I guess about —

DR.: Did you have them towards girls?

LISA: No. I guess around nine — eight or nine.

DR.: Did you engage in masturbation?

LISA: Yes.

DR.: At what age?

LISA: About nine.

DR.: Did you have any feelings of guilt about it?

LISA: Yes.

DR.: What did you think would happen?

LISA: I was afraid someone would discover me.[43]

DR.: You didn't think it would do anything terrible to you?

LISA: I didn't know.

DR.: Well, some just enjoy themselves and don't care.

LISA: Oh, really?

---

[41]Another offshoot of 'dynamic' flak.

[42]Putting a spoke in the wheel of this belief.

[43]This early fear is the etiological hub of her present sexual difficulties. The source of fear is, of course, no longer her demanding parents.

DR.: And some have been given some sex instruction and they—

LISA: I was given none—ever about anything.

DR.: So you had a sort of fear of discovery. But did you have any fear that you might be doing harm? Did you think that God might punish you?

LISA: There wasn't any God in my life. I had never been taken into the Church.

DR.: When did you start dating and all that sort of thing?[44]

LISA: Well, I went to dancing class when I was about nine years of age —but dating—maybe twelve, thirteen—you know, little parties where your parents drove you, picked you up—stupid little tea dances.

DR.: Well, when did you become interested in any person?

LISA: I was interested very definitely in one boy when I was—from about the age of nine on till about twelve or thirteen maybe. I thought he was perfectly marvelous.

DR.: What did you think was marvelous about him?

LISA: He was just bright and blond and handsome and athletic.

DR.: Was there anyone important before your first husband?

LISA: No—none.

DR.: What was your first husband's name?

LISA: Sid.

DR.: What did you like about him?

LISA: He was blond and charming and quiet, pleasant and handsome— all the men in my life were quiet.

DR.: Well, what happened?

LISA: It was one constant harangue—one violent fight after another.

DR.: What were the causes?

LISA: I guess I was hostile and irritable. Sexually we weren't compatible—I knew something was wrong with me.

DR.: With you?

LISA: Yes—I mean I couldn't achieve orgasm and, of course, this started to disturb me greatly.

DR.: Was this the main thing that disturbed you?

LISA: Oh, I think so, yes.

DR.: This is terribly important. Are you telling me that if you had had orgasms no trouble would have arisen in this marriage?

[44]Further inquiries into her sexual history are now begun in a very open-ended way.

LISA: I think I would have been able to adapt. I really don't know. I mean if you're irritable and hostile because your sexual relations aren't right—how do you know how you'd react to everyday living?

DR.: Well, tell me, actually what used to happen?

LISA: It just was a tempestuous sort of relationship. I think he was a perennial sophomore college type and, of course, I was trying to do all the little things to make a marriage hold together. He wanted a playmate and I wasn't it.

DR.: Before you married did you get on well?

LISA: Oh, yes. I can never remember one bad fight that we ever had.[45]

DR.: Then, when you got married and there were attempts at sex, you would get roused and you wouldn't have an orgasm?

LISA: We had sex a few times before we were married and of course, when I didn't have any orgasm he said, "Well, that's all right because it's unnatural circumstances and you're not relaxed, etc." Of course, after you get married, you're supposed to be relaxed, aren't you?

DR.: Are you saying that not having orgasms had a very strong physiological disturbing affect?

LISA: Definitely it did. It was so disturbing I went to see a strange doctor down in Memphis, Tennessee. All he did was look at me and say, "Well, I'm sure it will right itself in time—don't worry about it."

DR.: Can you say why you didn't have orgasms? Could it have been anything to do with him?

LISA: No—it's me.

DR.: No, wait a minute—that's sort of—

LISA: An assumption—I shouldn't—

DR.: I'd just like to know why you say that—could it be that if he had handled you differently, you might have had orgasms?

LISA: No. There have been many men in my life since my first husband. It's me.

DR.: Has your pattern of response to each of them been the same?

LISA: Exactly.

DR.: What is that pattern of response?

LISA: Pleasure to a certain degree and wanting to be closer to somebody; and yet when it comes to the act of intercourse—nothing. You

---

[45]This strongly suggests that they might have 'made out' if there had been no sexual problem.

know I've always made a joke, saying I want somebody to hold my hand — period. Maybe I'm still waiting to go back to adolescence.[46]

DR.: That's rubbish.

LISA: Well, I don't know — may not be.

DR.: You say you get pleasure up to a degree. Tell me what the pattern is in detail?

LISA: I don't dislike it. I find the intimacy pleasurable and I like to be close to Ed, — but there's no sensation there at all. I become a little edgy about it — uncomfortable — it makes me feel bad — sad — melancholy — not irritable, as in the past, — I accept the pleasure that I do get to a certain degree, and accept the fact that there is nothing else. I have accepted this.

DR.: Well, what actually happens — first of all, there's petting, etc. Do you find that pleasurable?

LISA: Yes — I find everything pleasant.

DR.: Do you get excited?

LISA: Oh, yes.

DR.: Do you get really strongly excited?

LISA: Yes.

DR.: And then it's only during the actual act of intercourse that you get no sensation?

LISA: No sensation whatsoever.

DR.: What happens if your clitoris is stimulated?

LISA: Nothing.

DR.: Nothing at all?

LISA: No.

DR.: But you said to me at an earlier stage that you had masturbated.

LISA: Yes.

DR.: Does that mean that an orgasm can be induced by digital stimulation?

LISA: It hasn't so far — no.

DR.: And by you yourself?

LISA: No.

DR: When you were a child?

---

[46]Even if there were some evidence to support this proposition, it has no practical implications — suggests no direction of action for change.

LISA: No.

DR.: You never had an orgasm?

LISA: Yes I have, but I don't touch myself.

DR.: How do you have an orgasm?

LISA: By crossing my legs and applying pressure on my muscles.

DR.: Well, what does that stimulate?

LISA: I guess my clitoris, I don't know. I mean medically I don't know.

DR.: I'll try not to impose the answer on you.

LISA: Well, I don't know the answer.

DR.: But if it's compressed by hand, that doesn't have any effect?

LISA: No.

DR.: How often can you have an orgasm that way?

LISA: How often? What do you mean how often?

DR.: Well, can you do it every day?

LISA: Oh, certainly.

DR.: Can you do it repeatedly?

LISA: Four or five times in a row.

DR.: You regularly do that sort of thing?

LISA: Not every day – no, but when I do I can maybe four times in a row. So I'd say I'm a pretty healthy woman. But for some reason I cannot build up an intimacy with another person. And it's not just Ed. It's anybody.

DR.: Why do you say it that way? You say you can't build up an intimacy. Do you mean that in a general way or just in a physical sense.

LISA: I mean in any way.

DR.: You spoke of this kind of thing happening when you were at school. There was sort of a fearfulness about persons. Do you still have the feeling that way?

LISA: Yes.

DR.: Well, that might be the clue. Let me just pursue it one step further. Suppose you have been stimulated sexually and you haven't had an orgasm in the usual way, can you or do you then go ahead and give yourself one by compressing your thighs?

LISA: No.

DR.: Now, why is that?

LISA: Because Ed is there.[47]

DR.: Oh, I see.

LISA: I told you it was an embarrassing thing with me when I was a child and it still is. I guess it became a personal withdrawn sort of action.

DR.: How terribly interesting. Next week we'll begin treatment.

LISA: You mean there's treatment for this?

DR.: Oh, yes. We do have to have a little more history — but not much.

---

[47]This answer was the 'open sesame' of the case. It was now plain that all efforts directed at giving Lisa coital orgasms must fail as long as she could not bear to be seen having even masturbatory orgasms.

CHAPTER 5

Assertive Training

This is the first of several chapters dealing with methods for deconditioning anxiety-response habits. In point of logical sequence, we should be starting with an exposition of systematic desensitization, since that method so clearly parallels the method described in Chapter 1 for overcoming the conditioned unadaptive anxiety reactions of experimental cats; and since it is the most widely used of all anxiety-countering methods. But assertive training will be considered first, because it is frequently introduced early in therapy, right after the conceptual aspects of the patient's complaints have been put in perspective. It can frequently be initiated on the basis of relatively simple instructions, so that therapeutic change is effected by the patient carrying out prescribed behavior between sessions.

Assertive training is pre-eminently applicable to the deconditioning of unadaptive anxiety habits of response to people with whom the patient interacts. It makes use of the anxiety-inhibiting emotions that life situations evoke in him. A great many emotions, mostly 'pleasant' in character, seem to involve bodily events competitive with anxiety (Wolpe, 1958, p.99). All categories of stimuli — sights, smells, sounds, words — may be sources of such emotions because of their immediate perceptual harmoniousness (esthetic effect) or because of previous conditioning. A perfume, for example, may be conditioned to strong romantic feelings. In like fashion, another person may arouse approval, affection, admiration, annoyance, or anger or other feelings, each of which produce bodily responses different from anxiety and possibly competitive with it. It seems that when such emotions are exteriorized in motor behavior their intensity is enhanced; and any anxiety that is evoked by the situation is more likely to be inhibited. *Assertive behavior is defined as the proper expression of any emotion other than anxiety towards another person.*

There has been relatively little psychophysiological research on the interrelations between the various emotional states since the early survey by Leschke (1914). Arnold (1945) marshalled the evidence of physiological antagonism between anger and anxiety. Ax (1953) expressed doubts about this, although his own data to some extent supported it. Arnold (1960) later collected further supporting data. Recent Soviet research (Simonov, 1967) has yielded unequivocal evidence of the existence of separate and reciprocally inhibitory centers for anger and anxiety in the midbrain. Both by drugs and by ablations, it is possible to do away with one of these patterns of emotional response with the effect of facilitating the other.

The contexts in which assertive behavior is an appropriate therapeutic instrument are numerous. In almost all of them we find the patient inhibited from the performance of 'normal' behavior because of neurotic fear. He is inhibited from saying or doing things that seem reasonable and right to an observer. He may be unable to complain about poor services in a restaurant because he is afraid of hurting the feelings of the waiter; unable to express differences of opinion with his friends because he fears that they will not like him; unable to get up and leave a social situation that has become boring because he fears to seem ungrateful; unable to ask for the repayment of a loan or to administer a legitimate reproof to a subordinate because he fears that his 'nice guy' image will be impaired; and unable to express affection, admiration, or praise because he finds such expression embarrassing. Besides the things he cannot do because of fear, there may be others that he cannot *stop* doing. For example, he may compulsively reach for the lunch check again and again to ward off a fear of incurring an obligation.

It should be noted that interpersonal anxiety responses of the kind exemplified above sometimes lead to the channeling of innate drives into unadaptive paths. Fear evoked by heterosexual peers may deflect the patient from normal sexual partnerships, to engage in deviations like homosexuality, pedophilia, or exhibitionism. In other cases, the suppression of action that would give outward expression to feelings results in continuing inner turmoil, which may produce psychosomatic symptoms and even pathological change in predisposed organs. In all such cases, the correct strategy of treatment aims not at the overt target (such as the sexual deviation *per se*), but at the neurotic interpersonal anxieties that are generally amenable to assertive training (see Cases 32 and 33).

A very common history in patients for whom assertive training is needed is of early teaching that has over-emphasized social obligations, engendering the feeling in the patient that the rights of others are more important than his own. An extreme, but not very unusual example, is a 36-year-old man whose parents had strongly insisted on polite sub-missiveness. During World War II, at the age of 8, he had gone to live for 2 years with an uncle who encouraged self-expression. That behavior was severely punished when he returned to his parental house, establishing a firm and enduring habit of timidity towards others, and especially towards authority figures.

The therapist's interventions are aimed at augmenting every impulse towards the elicitation of the inhibited responses, with the expectation that with each elicitation, there will, reciprocally, be an inhibiting of the anxiety, resulting in some degree of weakening of the anxiety-response habit (Wolpe, 1958, p. 72). Meanwhile, the motor behavior is reinforced by its favorable social consequences, such as the attainment of control of a social situation, reduction of anxiety, and the later approbation of the therapist. Thus, the counterconditioning of anxiety and the operant conditioning of the motor act take place simultaneously, facilitating each other. (For a fuller discussion, see Wolpe, 1958.) Operant conditioning of assertive behavior is employed alone in certain people who lack it, not because of anxiety, but because they have simply not acquired the appropriate motor habits for certain social situations.

Like all other methods of behavior therapy, assertive training is applied in specific contexts in which there is evidence of a need for it. Some patients are unassertive in a very wide range of interactions, and to these, Salter's (1949) appellation, 'the inhibitory personality,' is descriptively appropriate. In such cases, almost any social interaction might be suitable for assertive training. But in others, the indications relate to particular contexts. We find patients who are able competently to handle tradesmen and strangers, but are timorous and submissive with anybody important like a mother, a wife, or a lover—or to only one of these. By contrast, there are those who dominate (and occasionally tyrannize) over close associates, but are fearful, awkward, and in various degrees ineffective in their dealings with the 'outgroup.'

PRELIMINARY MEASURES

Before assertive training can begin, the patient must accept its reasonableness. Sometimes submission to the needs of others is bound up with the general philosophy that it is morally good to place the interests of others ahead of one's own. This is most often encountered in some devout Christians whose foremost emulation of Christ consists of turning the other cheek. I tell them that this kind of behavior is a practical proposition only for rare saintly individuals; and that from everybody else biology exacts its toll for behavior contrary to the interests of the organism (see discussion of the moral aspects of behavior therapy). I add that as long as they are socially anxious, they have no alternative but to behave as they do; but that, later, when this anxiety has been deconditioned, they will have the option of being magnanimous at times.

Most patients can be brought to recognize the need for appropriate assertiveness. Some have always been aware of it. The insight, as such,[1] however clear, produces no change (see Wolpe, 1958, p. 120; Rathus, 1972). The therapist must help the patient to translate the insight into action. Simple direct coaxing and goading is often all that is necessary. This consists in part of emphasizing the disadvantages of non-assertion — its inevitable winlessness, its frequently unpleasant emotional consequences, the unfavorable image it gives to others — and in part of promising increasing ease of execution of assertive acts as anxiety diminishes. I tell patients that the power to assert grows with action like a snowball rolling down a slope. Sometimes, I find it helpful to quote the example of a previous case or two.[2]

A suitable context for starting assertive training often emerges in a very natural way from the patient's narration of some recent incident. An alternative starting point may be found in the patient's responses to the Willoughby Personality Schedule (Appendix 1) — particularly if there are high numerical responses to the following questions: Are your feelings

[1]Pegging away at the patient's 'illogical self-verbalizations,' which Ellis (1958) conceives as the cause of neurotic behavior, is the essence of his 'rational-emotive psychotherapy.' This kind of thing can be sufficient only in neuroses based on misconceptions. Ellis provides no data to the contrary. Satisfactory data would take into account the nonspecific processes that work for all psychotherapies. It is interesting that Ellis (1970) has lately added assertive instructions to his treatment.

[2]If assertion results from these interventions it can be seen behavioristically as due to a summation between an already-present action-tendency (to protest, for example) and that which is added by the attitude and words of the therapist.

easily hurt? Are you shy? Does criticism hurt you badly? Are you self-conscious before superiors?

To take the first of these as an example, the therapist would ask for an example of a situation that hurts the patient's feelings, and follow this up by inquiring how he would handle the situation. If the handling was unassertive, he would propose an assertive substitute.

A useful route to the initiation of assertion in 'outgroup' contexts takes off from asking the patient how he behaves in a number of set situations. For some years I have been presenting these five questions:

1. What do you do if after having bought an article in a shop you walk out and find that your change is a dollar short?
2. Suppose that, arriving home after buying an article on the way, you find it slightly damaged. What will you do?
3. What do you do if somebody pushes in front of you in line (e.g. at the theater)?
4. At a shop, while you wait for the clerk to finish with the customer ahead of you, another customer arrives and also waits. What do you do if the clerk subsequently directs his attention to that customer ahead of you?
5. You order a steak rare and it arrives well done. How do you handle the situation?

In all these situations, a person ought to be able to stand up for himself. Insofar as he does not, assertive training is indicated.

INSTIGATING ASSERTIVE BEHAVIOR

Let us trace how assertive instigation may develop out of the third of the above questions:

THERAPIST: What do you do if you are standing in line for theater tickets and somebody gets in front of you?

PATIENT: I don't do anything.

THERAPIST: Well, how do you feel?

PATIENT: I feel mad. I boil up inside.

THERAPIST: So, why don't you do anything?

PATIENT: I'm afraid of making a scene.

Thus, it is the fear of making a scene which prevents him from taking action. But at the same time he is angry. The therapist must try to get him to inflate this anger by giving vent to it. Then the anger may be great enough to inhibit the anxiety.

THERAPIST: People are taking advantage of you. Here, this person is taking advantage of you. You cannot allow it. You must say to him, "Will you kindly go to the back of the line?" In doing this, you will be expressing your anger in a way that is appropriate to the situation and socially acceptable.

Each time the patient, by expressing his anger, inhibits his anxiety, he weakens in some measure the anxiety habit. But emotion is not the only component of the instigated behavior. There is also new verbal behavior. The patient now for the first time tells another person to go to the back of the line. He will have the approval of those in the line behind him; and the intruder will usually move back. These things will reinforce the patient's tendency to speak up, not only in this specific situation, but in similar ones. Since progress in assertion depends on success, the therapist must apprise himself of details of the situations in which action is likely to occur. One would, for example, caution the patient against insisting on his priority in line in a tough neighborhood.

In patients who have a great deal of anxiety about assertion, it may be necessary to grade the tasks in a way that parallels desensitization. On the whole, it is good practice to make this a general rule. In the words of Salter (1949), the pioneer of assertive techniques, "Therapy should begin where the patient's level of inhibition is lowest."

Salter proposed six modes of behavior of general use to patients who require assertive training (in his terms, 'excitation'). These are:

1. Feeling Talk By this Salter means the deliberate utterance of spontaneously felt emotions. An example he gives is, "Thank heavens, today is Friday and the weekend is here"; in contrast to saying drily, "Today is Friday."

2. Facial Talk This is the display of emotion in face (and movement) as far as is appropriate.

3. Contradict and Attack When the patient disagrees with someone, he is not to pretend agreement, but to contradict with as much feeling as is reasonable.

4. The Use of 'I' The word 'I' is used as much as possible so as to involve the patient in the statements he makes.

5. Express Agreement When You Are Praised   Praise should not be warded off, but accepted honestly. Self-praise should also be volunteered when reasonable.

6. Improvise   Try to make spontaneous responses to immediate stimuli.

Some activities related to the foregoing are going out of the way to greet people, asking 'Why?' instead of accepting statements *ex cathedra*, looking people in the eye, and avoiding justifying one's opinions.

The following is a sampling of assertive statements, expressing either hostility or commendation. The former are more numerous because they are easily most frequently relevant to the needs of therapy.

Assertive Statements
HOSTILE
1. Would you please call me back. I can't speak to you now.
2. Please don't stand in front of me.
3. Will you kindly stop talking during the play/movie/music.
4. This is a line. Please go to the back of it.
5. Do you have special privileges in this line?
6. You have kept me waiting for 20 minutes.
7. Do you mind turning down the heat?
8. It's too cold for me to go outside.
9. Please put those heavy packages in a *double* bag (at a supermarket).
10. Your behavior disgusts me.
11. I hate your duplicity.
12. I despise your intolerance/unreasonableness.
13. I can't stand your nagging.
14. If it is not inconvenient, will you pick up my parcel?
15. I'm sorry, but it won't be possible.
16. (To the stewardess on a flight that is late for a connection.) Would you ask the pilot to radio ahead to my connecting flight?
17. I would rather not say.
18. Why are you late?
19. If you persist in coming late, I am going to stop making appointments with you.
20. I insist that you come to work on time.
21. How dare you speak to me like that.
22. Pardon me – I was here first.
23. I enjoy talking to you, but please be quiet while I am reading/writing/thinking/listening.

COMMENDATORY
1. That's a beautiful dress/brooch, etc.
2. You look lovely, terrific, ravishing, glamorous, etc.
3. That was a clever remark.
4. What a radiant smile.
5. I like you.
6. I love you.
7. I admire your tenacity.
8. That was brilliantly worked out.

With a reasonable amount of pressure and encouragement, most patients begin to be able to assert themselves in a matter of days, or a week or two. At each interview, they report what they have done in the intervening time, and the therapist commends their successes and corrects their errors. They must be warned not to rest on their laurels, but to be alert for every opportunity for appropriate assertion. One rule must always be observed: *Never instigate an assertive act that is likely to have punishing consequences.* As the patient's interpersonal anxiety decreases in consequence of his efforts, acts of assertion become easier to perform.

The following is a typical assertion-instigating conversation:

THERAPIST: Let us talk about your mother-in-law.

MRS. A.: She is a bully, says a lot of things and does a lot of things to me that I sit back and take. I really should open my mouth and not be big about it. Personally, I don't care if the woman does not like me. I feel more for the guy in the line than I do for her, because she has done a lot of things that I feel are not right. She steps all over me and I let it boil up inside.

THERAPIST: Now what would happen if you let it out on your mother-in-law—which is what you really want to do, isn't it? Let us take an actual example.

MRS. A.: Well, she is always telling me for instance that my mother did not raise me properly.

THERAPIST: That is an insulting remark.

MRS. A.: Yes, it is, and I never say anything.

THERAPIST: Well, do you mind the remark?

MRS. A.: It cuts me, like you would stab me.

THERAPIST: And you let her get away with it. What should you do?

MRS. A.: I should say, "It is my mother. Please don't talk about her."

THERAPIST: Right. And the effect will be to increase her respect for you.

MRS. A.: My in-laws don't like the way I behave, by the way; they really don't.

THERAPIST: That's not surprising. Let me give you a contrast. Suppose you are visiting at somebody's house and you notice two men there. They are your hosts' two sons-in-law. One of them is meek and ingratiating all the time, while the other one speaks up to his in-laws. Which one gives you a better impression?

MRS. A.: The one that speaks up. You don't have to make up an example. This new fiancee of my sister-in-law is living at my in-law's house right now with them and he speaks up. They love him.

A little later in the interview, Mrs. A. expressed concern that her husband might object to her new behavior to his mother.

MRS. A.: Suppose my husband starts up with me, "You shouldn't talk like that to my mother. You are not cementing relationships; you are putting them farther apart." How do I handle that situation?

THERAPIST: You have to say, "If your mother makes unjust remarks I have to tell her and I will tell her. If your mother makes reasonable criticisms, I will be very interested in what she has to say. But she is always at me, and she has gotten into the habit of it because I have been allowing her to say whatever she likes. I am not going to have it any more."

Some patients have great difficulty in performing any assertive acts at all. The therapist must ascertain why. He may discover a 'phobic' reaction to some aspect or implication of assertion. For example, the patient may have a strong conditioned anxiety-response to perceiving himself behaving aggressively or to the idea of *having* behaved aggressively (i.e. guilt about aggression). A preliminary program of systematic desensitization to the relevant stimulus configurations is then needed (Chapter 6). Marked fear of aggression from others (which is always a possible response to assertiveness) similarly requires desensitization.

When the patient finds assertive behavior difficult even though no such fears are evident, more vigorous direct efforts are made towards eliciting assertion. It may suffice simply to increase the patient's motivation by strongly contrasting the negative and unprepossessing effects of timidity with the benefits that assertion is expected to yield; or the therapist may refuse to see the patient until he can report some action. Another possibility is behavior rehearsal (see below).

The quintessence of assertive behavior is to do towards others what is reasonable and right. It is well brought out in the following excerpts from a statement written by a patient (Wolpe, 1958, p. 118):

> "I have been given the assignment of winning emotional victories in daily life . . . . . This is the important discovery I have made — and it is a satisfying one emotionally. Other people's opinions and feelings count — *but so do mine*. This does not mean that I have become aggressive, unpleasant, or inconsiderate to other people . . . . This new method of coping with interpersonal situations simply boils down to doing the things which, if you were an onlooker watching the situation, would seem fair and fitting."

The interrelations between assertive and other categories of behavior are illustrated in Fig. 3. Assertive behavior, defined as expressing emotions other than anxiety in a socially acceptable way, involves many categories of emotional behavior. The most common of these categories is oppositional behavior (e.g. standing up for reasonable rights). Types of oppositional behavior outside the assertive category are the provocative, the aggressive, the violent and, often, the sarcastic.

Many of the issues regarding assertive behavior are explicated at length and with clarity in a small book by Alberti and Emmons (1970) which also contains numerous illustrations and instructions for assertive training. It is a book that can be used with profit by practitioners and also by some of their patients.

Fig. 3. Interrelations between assertive, oppositional, and affectionate categories of behavior. (Courtesy of Graphic Communications, Eastern Pennsylvania Psychiatric Institute, Philadelphia.)

LIFEMANSHIP

There are circumstances in which direct assertion is inappropriate, but in which it is, nevertheless, desirable for the patient to achieve some kind of control. For example, it is not often advisable for an employee to give his employer 'a piece of his mind.' If assertion is necessary, it calls for subtle tactics. These are sometimes suggested by special knowledge of the other person's weaknesses; but there are gambits that may be applied to almost anybody — statements that automatically put the recipient at a disadvantage, without revealing an aggressive intent on the part of the speaker. A widely usable example is, "Is anything wrong? You don't seem to be quite your usual self today."

A large variety of clever instances of behavior of this kind are described in a series of little books by the late Stephen Potter, who referred to them as 'oneupmanship.' Although Potter's aim was humor and not psychotherapy, there is much that the psychotherapist can use. For example, Potter (1971, p. 13) describes how one day he and Professor Joad were playing tennis against two Oxford University students — fine, upstanding young men, Smith and Brown. Smith's first service, delivered to Joad, was an ace which Joad did not get near. He then served to Potter with the same result. At the next service, Joad managed to get his racket to the ball, which went flying over the net and hit the bottom of the back netting on the students' side. Then, as Smith was crossing over to serve the *coup de grace*, Joad called across the net, in an even tone: "Kindly say clearly, please, whether the ball was in or out."

SMITH: I'm so sorry — I thought it was out. (*The ball had hit the back netting twelve feet behind him before touching the ground.*) But what did you think, Brown?

BROWN: I thought it was out — but do let's have it again.

JOAD: No, I don't want to have it again. I only want you to say clearly, if you will, whether the ball is in or out.

This slight suggestion of unsportsmanlike behavior was sufficiently upsetting to undermine the students' performance and make them lose the game.

BEHAVIOR REHEARSAL

This technique was originally called 'behavioristic psychodrama' (Wolpe, 1958). It consists of the acting out of short exchanges between the therapist and the patient in settings from the patient's life. The patient represents himself, and the therapist someone towards whom the patient is unadaptively anxious and inhibited. The therapist starts with a remark, usually oppositional, that the other person might make, and the patient responds as if the situation were 'real.' His initial response will usually be variously hesitant, defensive, and timid. The therapist then suggests a more appropriate response; and the exchange is run again, revised. The sequence may be repeated again and again until the therapist is satisfied that the patient's utterances have been suitably reshaped. It is necessary to take into account not only the words the patient uses, but also the loudness, firmness, and emotional expressiveness of his voice, and the appropriateness of accompanying bodily movements. (For the last-mentioned purpose, the Behavior Therapy Unit has recently made good use of the modelling of behavior by a well-trained actress.) The aim of such modelling, shaping, and rehearsing is frequently an effective preparation for the patient to deal with his real 'adversary' so that the anxiety the latter evokes may be reciprocally inhibited, and the motor assertive habit established.

Case 4 is a typical example of the shaping that is done during behavior rehearsal, excerpted from a case study (Wolpe, 1970). The patient had been brooding over having been unfairly criticized by her father and wanted to rectify the matter.

THERAPIST: Well, let's do an experiment. Let's sort of act it out. Suppose you just go ahead and pretend I am your father and say to me what you think you would like to say to him.

PATIENT: About the other night, I would like to say that I think you were exceptionally unfair in assuming that I did not want to come up and that I was the one who was being unjust or the villain because I wasn't coming up to make the family happy. The family hasn't been much of a family actually for a number of years and that when it comes down to it, the family doesn't mean that much to me. I would be much happier spending Christmas by myself. And then he would probably say, "Well, you just go ahead and do that."

THERAPIST: Wait a minute. Never mind. Don't you worry about him. I am he, so don't put words in my mouth. Besides this, in general I would like to correct your approach. You are doing it in a way that leaves you too vulnerable. First of all, it is very unsatisfactory for you to complain to somebody that he is *unfair*, because if you do that you are really in some sense putting yourself at his mercy. A better line of approach would be: "I want to tell you that you had no right to assume the other night that I had no intention of coming for Christmas. You know very well that I have always come. You accused me of lacking feeling. I have a great deal of feeling, and perhaps too much. Your attack was absolutely unwarranted." In saying this, you are not asking for justice or fairness, you are simply stating what you feel was wrong in his behavior. Now, do you think you could redo it in some fashion?

PATIENT: Okay. I would like to set some matters straight—about your call the other night. When you called me I just couldn't think of this right away. I was so taken by surprise, but I have been thinking about it and I would just like to say a couple of things.

THERAPIST: I must interrupt you again. You started fine—the first sentence was fine, but when you begin to explain why you didn't say it the other night, that weakens your position. For example, it might invite him to say "Yes, that is like you, isn't it? You never answer at the right time. You always have to brood for 3 days before you can say anything." He *could* say something of that sort. But in any case, it is a kind of under-dog statement, and we don't want that.

PATIENT: All right. About the call the other night, I had not entirely given up on the idea of coming up to have Christmas with you and Mom. I was doing what I thought was best according to what I gathered from the conversation I had with Mom. I felt that Mom wanted me to have Christmas with grandma and grandpop—have Christmas dinner, and I wanted to be both places, but I just felt that the drive might be too much.

THERAPIST: I am sorry, but I must interrupt you again. You see, you are explaining yourself. You are giving a kind of excuse. Actually, the important part of this conversation is to bring out the point that it was not right for him to plunge into a criticism that assumed that you had made up your mind not to come.

PATIENT: How about—I don't think it was right for you to call me last night, and say what you did, because I don't think you had the facts straight from Mom. I think you should have checked with her first and be sure you understood the situation. I had talked with Mom earlier and felt that this was what we had worked out and I think you should have checked with her and made sure that—

THERAPIST: That's enough. The fact that you keep on suggests that you are not very confident; so stop. Now, let him say something.

Actually, a *good deal of deconditioning of anxiety frequently takes place during the behavior rehearsal itself.* For example, an intelligent woman of age 42 had so much anxiety at the idea of inconveniencing people that she could not be persuaded to make even the most miniscule demands of anybody except her closest friends. In behavior rehearsal with her, I took the role of one of her office colleagues who lives near her, and told her to ask me for a ride home (that would only take me out of my way one block). She had difficulty even in formulating this request. I therefore gave her this sentence to use: "If you are going home after work, would you mind giving me a ride home?" Her first enunciation of this was very awkward, and she stated that it had evoked a good deal of anxiety (70 *suds*). My reply was, "I will take you with pleasure." With repetition, she articulated the sentence with greater ease and expression, while the level of her anxiety progressively fell. After a total of 8 repetitions in two sessions, she could request that ride with practically no anxiety. During subsequent sessions, the distance she was taking me out of my way was progressively increased. These 'rehearsals' enabled the patient comfortably to make reasonable requests in reality.

The ability of 'put on' behavior to bring about real therapeutic change is in accord with some observations on actors reported by Simonov (1967). Especially (but not only) when the actor has been trained by the Stanislavsky method (which requires him to try to *live* each part), he evinces autonomic responses in the direction of the emotions that he is simulating. Simonov states, "The actors were asked to pronounce certain words under various mentally reproducible conditions .... The changes in the heart rate, recorded in the actor when he was fulfilling the task, confirm that he was actually reproducing an emotionally colored situation and was not copying intonations formerly noticed in other people. This conclusion was confirmed by comparison with the results of analyzing speech in natural situations." However, there are differences, too, because if the actor is doing his part well he gets a pleasurable feeling intermixed with the anxiety or anger that he is enacting. A detailed account of this work is, unfortunately, available only in manuscript form (Simonov, 1962).

More than any other methods under the rubric of behavior therapy, the teaching of assertive training profits from practical demonstrations. Technical nuances are more readily conveyed by them than by written accounts. Films and tape recordings have a very useful role. A tape of my own that *inter alia* demonstrates assertive training is *The Case of Mrs. Schmidt* (1964).*

---

*Published by Counsellor Recordings, Nashville, Tenn.

Two behavior therapy films that have sections showing assertive training are *Behavior Therapy Demonstration*,* and *Behavior Therapy In A Case Of Overdependency.*†

*Available from Psychological Cinema Register, Penn State University, University Park, Penna.

†Available from Behavior Therapy Presentations, Eastern Pennsylvania Psychiatric Institute, Philadelphia, Penna.

CHAPTER 6

Systematic Desensitization

INTRODUCTION

Systematic desensitization is one of a variety of methods for breaking down neurotic anxiety-response habits in piecemeal fashion, modelled on the therapy of experimental neurosis. A physiological state inhibitory of anxiety is induced in the patient by means of muscle relaxation, and he is then exposed to a weak anxiety-arousing stimulus for a few seconds. If the exposure is repeated several times, the stimulus progressively loses its ability to evoke anxiety. Then successively 'stronger' stimuli are introduced and similarly treated. This method has given us the power to overcome a great many neurotic habits, often in a short time. It has enabled us to treat these habits in almost any order that we choose, and as far as we choose.

Employing a counteracting emotion to overcome an undesirable emotional habit *step by step*, has a precedent in an age-old method: a child is gradually accustomed to a situation he fears by exposing him to small doses of it in circumstances in which other emotions are also present. For example, if the child fears a visitor's long black beard, he is quite likely to become reconciled to it by deconditioning events that may occur if he sits on his father's lap while the latter speaks to the visitor. The child may at first intermittently glance at the beard so that the anxiety arousals are small each time. Since they occur against a background of warm and pleasant responses to the father, these small fear arousals are presumably inhibited; and, gradually, as the fear subsides, the child tolerates lengthening looks at the beard.

Besides being inadvertent agents to such spontaneous therapy, parents quite often 'instinctively' treat established fears of their children in an essentially similar way (deliberately and fairly systematically). When a child is afraid of bathing in the sea, the parent will, at first, take him by the hand to the very fringe of the approaching waves and lift him up when a wave approaches; then, when the child has become comfortable about this, the parent encourages him to dip his foot into a wave, and later his ankle, and so on. Conquering his fear by degrees, the child eventually becomes able to play in the sea with pleasure. This is very much like the routine followed in primitive societies to prepare individuals to undergo ceremonial ordeals, and in our own world in the training of mountaineers and trapeze artists. The first known example of the deliberate use of counteracting responses to overcome neurotic anxieties by gradually approaching the peak stimulus was in the use of feeding to overcome children's phobias in the cases of Mary Cover Jones (1924) described in Chapter 1.

THE FORMAL BASIS OF SYSTEMATIC DESENSITIZATION

The systematic desensitization technique has its roots in the experimental laboratory (Wolpe, 1948, 1952, 1958). Having produced experimental neurosis in cats confined in a small cage by administering to them high-voltage, low-amperage shocks (as described in Chapter 1), I found that the neurotic anxiety responses to the cage and related stimuli and to an auditory stimulus that had preceded the shocks were extremely resistant to the normal process of extinction. Neither prolonged nor repeated exposure of the animals to the environment of the cage led to decrement in the intensity of the anxiety responses even though the animals were never again shocked. This failure to extinguish is, of course, also regularly found in the neuroses of man. Furthermore, animals, however hungry, could not be tempted to eat pellets of fresh meat scattered on the floor of the experimental cage. In other words, the anxiety produced total inhibition of so basic an adaptive response as eating in a very hungry animal. It seemed likely that this depended on the greater relative strength of the anxiety. Now, the animals showed less anxiety in the experimental laboratory and still less in other rooms, according to their degree of resemblance to the laboratory. It seemed reasonable to offer them food in these various places in descending order. Sooner or later I found a room where the evocation of anxiety was not great enough to inhibit feeding. Then, successive offerings of food would be accepted with increasing readiness while the signs of anxiety receded and finally disappeared. The room next in resemblance to the experimental laboratory could then be used. After several similar steps, eating behavior was eventually restored in the experimental cage itself, and this made possible the total elimination of all signs of anxiety there. In parallel piecemeal fashion, anxiety was deconditioned from the auditory stimulus that had preceded the shocks.

While these observations led to a search for methods by which the neurotic habits of humans might also be broken down bit by bit, they did not immediately suggest the systematic desensitization technique. This emerged only after a succession of further experiences. Since 1947, I had been trying to bring about changes in patients through getting them to behave differently in their life situations. The most common enterprise was the instigation of assertive behavior. I was greatly encouraged in these activities by their buoyant advocacy in Salter's *Conditioned Reflex Therapy* (1949); and, in fact, was moved by its optimism to applying instruction in self-expressive behavior to all patients. I was influenced in this way by the positiveness of Salter's report, although it was not clear to me how this treatment could affect those neuroses in which the stimuli controlling the neurotic reactions were in no way brought into the interpersonal situations in which the assertive behavior was induced.

However, I soon realized that non-interpersonal neuroses were *not* responding to assertive behavior training precisely as theoretical considerations had indicated. Conditioning theory requires that to eliminate or change a habit of reaction to a stimulus, that stimulus must be present in the deconditioning situation. Such deconditioning as occurs through acts of assertion can affect only the anxiety-response habits to stimuli that are present. If a patient has a fear of being alone, this will not be diminished by assertive behavior (if only because assertion implies the presence of another person). Certainly, now and then, benefit is noted in special cases in which a chain of other habits may be secondarily altered when interpersonal fear has been diminished (for example, in certain cases of agoraphobia; see below). In general, however, assertion towards persons is irrelevant where anxiety responses are to such non-personal stimulus constellations as enclosed spaces, animals, heights, the sight of blood — in short, in most classical phobic reactions. It is also irrelevant in the case of anxiety responses that other people elicit in contexts where action on the part of the patient would be inappropriate — for example, where the fear is evoked by the mere presence of particular persons, by being the center of attention, or by a feeling of 'rejection,' such as in a social situation where it seems to the patient that too little attention is being directed to him.

A case which at that time starkly displayed the irrelevancy of interpersonal expressiveness was that of a woman who was severely anxious at manifestations of illness in other people. Successful schooling in expressive behavior failed to diminish her anxiety and the case was sorrowfully abandoned as a failure. At that time I knew no way to inhibit anxieties aroused by stimuli to which no relevant *action response* could be proposed for the patient — stimuli that oppress the patient 'without *animus.*'

Soon afterwards, I had the good luck to come across Edmund Jacobson's *Progressive Relaxation* (1938). Here was described an anxiety-inhibiting response that did not call from the patient *any kind of motor activity towards the source of his anxiety.* I began to give relaxation training to patients for whose neuroses assertion was not applicable. However, an enormous relaxation potential was necessary to inhibit the anxiety evoked by a major real-life phobic stimulus. I conjectured that Jacobson's patients were enabled to inhibit *high* levels of anxiety because of their assiduous training and long and diligent practice.

I began to organize programs of exposure to graduated phobic stimuli *in vivo* for patients who had acquired some facility in relaxing, usually after 6–10 sessions. But since it is often very awkward to arrange for graded real-life situations, I began to explore the possibility of making use of imaginary situations in the place of real ones — being encouraged in this by the writings of practitioners of hypnosis. I was gratified to find that magnitudes of experienced anxiety diminished progressively at repeated presentations of imaginary situations that were weakly anxiety-arousing. Increasingly strong imaginary stimuli could one by one be divested of their anxiety-evoking potential. Furthermore, there was transfer of the deconditioning of anxiety to the corresponding real situations. At first, influenced by certain of Pavlov's experiments, I presented only one stimulus of any class at a session, but cautious trials of multiple presentations revealed no adverse effects. This opened up the prospect of greatly accelerating therapy.

GENERAL STATEMENT OF DESENSITIZATION PARADIGM

The autonomic effects that accompany deep relaxation are diametrically opposed to those characteristic of anxiety. Jacobson (1939, 1940) long ago showed that pulse rate and blood pressure were diminished by deep muscle relaxation. It was subsequently demonstrated (Drvota, 1962; Clark, 1963; Wolpe, 1964a) that skin resistance increases and respiration becomes slower and more regular during relaxation. More thoroughgoing studies have recently appeared. Paul (1969) has shown that muscle relaxation produces effects opposite to those of anxiety on heart rate, respiratory rate, and skin conductance. Obvious effects can be obtained even by simple instructions to relax; but they are significantly enhanced if the instructions are given in an hypnotic setting and even more significantly if they follow relaxation training. Van Egeren, Feather, and Hein (1971), in an elaborate psychophysiological study involving skin conductance, heart rate, digital pulse amplitude, and rate of respiration, found that relaxed subjects showed less decrease in skin resistance to phobic stimuli than those who were not relaxed. These autonomic effects of relaxation (and the related subjective calmness) cannot be secondary to the relaxed state of the muscles. The complete or almost complete relaxation induced by curare-like drugs may be accompanied by very severe anxiety. The calming effects of Jacobsonian relaxation appear to be concomitants or consequences of the voluntary efforts the subject makes to diminish the tonus of his muscles.

A pilot psychophysiological study by Wolpe and Fried (1968) provided evidence that the galvanic skin response (on Lathrop's (1964) variability measure) shows decrements during desensitization that are parallel to the decrements of anxiety that patients report. Figure 4 shows the averaged changes of four patients, to whom hierarchical phobic scenes were presented three times on each of two sessions. The decrease of response from one presentation to the next should be noted, as well as the 'savings' between Session 1 and Session 2.

Thus, not only are the effects of relaxation opposite in kind to those of anxiety, but, if counterposed to anxiety-evoking stimuli, they diminish the anxiety responses that these stimuli are able to evoke. Van Egeren (1970) reported that with repetitions of the phobic stimuli, the magnitude of their effects decreased progressively in relaxed subjects, but remained much the same in the unrelaxed. In a non-therapeutic experiment comparing the effects of presenting hierarchical stimuli in a standardized repetitive way to relaxed and non-relaxed subjects (Wolpe and Flood, 1970), a consistent downward trend of autonomic arousal as measured by galvanic skin response was noted across sessions with respect to each stimulus in the case of relaxed subjects but not in non-relaxed ones. In a clinical context, Paul (1969) demonstrated that autonomic arousal by a stressful stimulus decreases with repetition as a function of the extent

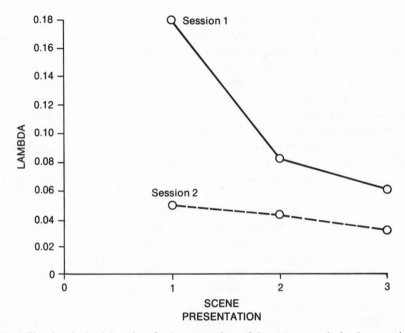

Fig. 4. Showing the lambda values for 3 presentations of the same scene during 2 successive desensitization sessions. The figure averages the readings for four different patients. Note that reactivity not only declines during each session but the decrement obtained at the end of Session 1 is maintained at the beginning of Session 2.

to which previously induced relaxation has contrary-to-anxiety effects.

In the neuroses of cats it was found that feeding can be used to counteract an anxiety response only if the latter is weak. Similarly, in human beings the autonomic effects of relaxation will be able to counteract only relatively weak anxiety responses. I have found again and again that a stimulus evoking a *strong* anxiety response may be presented many times to the relaxed patient without the strength of anxiety diminishing in the least. By contrast, if the anxiety response is weak, it is found that from one presentation of the stimulus to the next the amount of anxiety is diminished until at last there is none whatsoever. These clinical observations have been impressively supported by an admirably controlled animal experiment by Poppen (1970).

In contrast to the foregoing, it must be noted that some recent observations, including those of Wolpe and Flood noted above, indicate that response decrement does occur if stronger stimuli are administered insistently enough. The possible interrelations with flooding have yet to be explored.

The potency of relaxation in systematic desensitization has been experimentally demonstrated. Working independently, on spider and snake phobias respectively, Rachman (1965) and Davison (1965) have found that subjects to whom the whole desensitization sequence of procedures is applied show significantly more improvement than either those receiving relaxation training without scene presentations or others to whom scenes are presented without relaxation. A recent study pointing in the same direction has been reported by Farmer and Wright (1971).

Traditionalists have seized on the suggestion by Valins and Ray (1967) that the basis for desensitization may be, not emotional reconditioning, but changing the subject's cognitions about his internal reactions to the feared object. Obviously, this will not be possible if we are correct in regarding neurotic fears as conditioned habits involving the emotional centers of the midbrain, since these would not be altered merely by changing cortical associations. Valins and Ray provided some snake phobic subjects with false heart-rate feedback while viewing slides of snakes. Because these subjects subsequently approached closer to a snake than a control group did, Valins and Ray concluded that cognitions about internal reactions might be responsible for successful desensitization. Their study, however, has a variety of internal weaknesses (Wolpe, 1969, 1970). Recent and better controlled replications of the study by Sushinsky and Bootzin (1970) and by Kent, Wilson, and Nelson (1972) have failed to demonstrate any significant effect of cognitive manipulation on avoidance or emotional behavior. Furthermore, a psychophysiological experiment by Gaupp, Stern, and Galbraith (1972) indicates that whenever the cognition, "That stimulus has not affected me internally," is induced in relation to the Valins and Ray snake slides, it is veridical in nature and based on actual reduced physiological responding.

Another idea that has recently been put forward is that much of the effect of systematic desensitization depends on 'therapeutic instructions' (Leitenberg, et al., 1969 and Oliveau, et al., 1969). In experiments conducted by these workers, snake phobic subjects who thought they were being desensitized as a therapeutic measure improved significantly more than those who underwent the procedure in the belief that it was a physiological experiment, though the latter group did better than a control group. This contrast in outcomes was not replicated by McGlynn, Reynolds, and Linder (1971). Reports of the relevance of other 'peripheral' factors such as suggestion (e.g. Efram and Marcia, 1967; McGlynn and Williams, 1970) and real-life exposure (Sherman, 1972) have of late appeared with increasing frequency. They should be viewed with considerable reserve since they deal with relatively weak fears. Bernstein and Paul (1971) have pointed out that unless the fears that are the subject matter of an experiment have the severity that characterizes clinical phobias they do not constitute a true analogue of the latter.

Once a stimulus to weak anxiety has ceased to arouse any anxiety, it is possible to present a somewhat 'stronger' one to the fully relaxed patient, and this 'stronger' stimulus will now evoke less anxiety than it would have done before. Successive presentations will bring the amount of anxiety aroused down to zero. More and more potent stimuli are thus brought within the anxiety-inhibiting capacity of the subject's relaxation. To illustrate this, if there are ten stimuli which in their variations along a single dimension evoke in a subject quantities of anxiety which vary from one to ten, and if through the inhibiting effects of relaxation the anxiety aroused by the stimulus evoking one unit is reduced to zero, the stimulus originally evoking two units of anxiety will be found to be evoking only one unit. This is illustrated in Fig. 5. Thus, in an acrophobic subject who

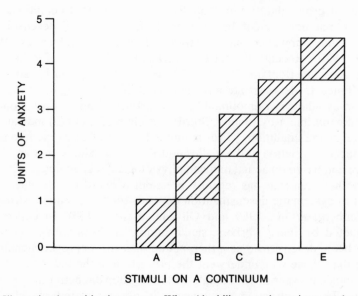

Fig. 5. Illustrating desensitization process. When A's ability to evoke anxiety goes down from 1 unit to 0, B evokes 1 unit in place of an original potential of 2 units; and when B's evocation is 0, C evokes 1 unit; and so forth.

has one unit of anxiety produced by looking out of a second-floor window, and two units by looking out of a third-floor window, reduction of the amount of anxiety from the second-floor window to zero would have the effect that the amount of anxiety evoked at a third-floor window would be diminished to one unit. Then, when anxiety at the third floor is zero, there is only one unit at the fourth floor — and so forth. (This linear relationship is used for clarity of exposition. The actual relationship is a simple power function.)

It is appropriate at this point to note that although it has been usual to refer to the weaker anxiety-evoking stimuli as 'generalized stimuli,' this does not accurately apply to all instances. A generalized stimulus incorporates some measure of a feature of the conditioned stimulus; and the magnitude of the shared feature is the basis of a generalization gradient (Hull, 1943). But sometimes weaker anxiety evocation is a function of stimuli that have been conditioned to anxiety through being *on the pathway* to the central conditioned stimulus. These pathway stimuli, obviously, do not depend on their resemblance to the central conditioned stimulus for their anxiety-evoking potential. The difference is illustrated in Fig. 6.

THE TECHNIQUE OF SYSTEMATIC DESENSITIZATION

The problems posed by the patient are always carefully considered by the therapist before deciding on any particular technique. His first task is often the correcting of misconceptions; and in respect of some fears

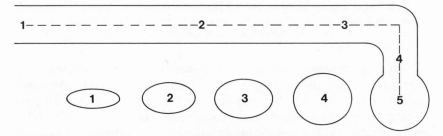

Fig. 6. Two stimulus continua — shape generalization and pathway stimuli. The strength of an anxiety response can be diminished either by exposing the subject to a shape progressively dissimilar to the circle (Shape 5) or by placing him at points on the pathway increasingly remote from Shape 5. Note that in the latter case the influence of distance is greater with increasing proximity in accordance with the observation that a simple power function is in operation in this dimension. (Courtesy of Graphic Communications, Eastern Pennsylvania Psychiatric Institute, Philadelphia.)

nothing more may be needed (see Fig. 2). Then, if changed behavior is required in social, sexual or other life situations, this will usually be worked on next, most often through the medium of assertive training (Chapter 5). If systematic desensitization is indicated, it is started as soon as possible and may be conducted in parallel with any measures that may have been prescribed for the life situation. The technique involves four separate sets of operations:

1. Training in deep muscle relaxation.
2. The establishment of the use of a scale of subjective anxiety.
3. The construction of anxiety hierarchies.
4. Counterposing relaxation and anxiety-evoking stimuli from the hierarchies.

1. Training in Relaxation

The method of relaxation taught is essentially that of Jacobson (1938), but instruction is completed in the course of about six interviews, in marked contrast to Jacobson's very prolonged training schedule. The patient is asked to practice at home for two 15-minute periods a day.

In introducing the subject of relaxation, I tell the patient (who has by now usually gained a general idea of the nature of conditioning therapy) that relaxation is just one of the methods in our armamentarium for combating anxiety. I continue as follows:

> Even the ordinary relaxing that takes place when one lies down often produces quite a noticeable calming effect. It has been found that there is a definite relationship between the extent of muscle relaxation and the production of emotional changes opposite to anxiety. I am going to teach you how to relax far beyond the usual point, and with practice you will be able to 'switch on' at will very considerable emotional effects of an 'anti-anxiety' kind.

There is no necessary sequence for training the various muscle groups in relaxation, but the sequence adopted should be orderly. My own practice is to start with the arms because they are convenient for purposes of demonstration and their relaxation is easy to check. The head region is done next because the most marked anxiety-inhibiting effects are usually obtained by relaxations there.

The patient is asked to grip the arm of his chair with one hand to see whether he can distinguish any qualitative difference between the sensations produced in his forearm and those in his hand. He is told to take special note of the quality of the forearm sensation because it is caused by muscle tension in contrast to the touch and pressure sensations in the hand. He is also enjoined to note the exact location of the forearm tensions in the flexor and extensor areas. Next, the therapist grips the patient's wrist and asks him to bend his arm against this resistance, thus making him aware of the tension in his biceps. Then, by instructing him to straighten his bent elbow against resistance, he calls his attention to the extensor muscles of the arm. The therapist goes on to say:

> I am now going to show you the essential activity that is involved in obtaining deep relaxation. I shall again ask you to resist my pull at your wrist so as to tighten your biceps. I want you to notice very carefully the sensations in that muscle. Then I shall ask you to let go gradually as I diminish the amount of force exerted against you. Notice, as your forearm descends, that there is decreasing sensation in the biceps muscle. Notice also that the letting go is an activity, but of a negative kind — it is an 'uncontracting' of the muscle. In due course, your forearm will come to rest on the arm of the chair, and you may then think that you have gone as far as possible — that relaxation is complete. But although the biceps will indeed be partly and perhaps largely relaxed, a certain number of its fibers will still, in fact, be contracted. I shall, therefore, say to you, "Go on letting go. Try to extend the activity that went on in the biceps while your forearm was coming down." It is the act of relaxing these additional fibers that will bring about the emotional effects we want. Let's try it and see what happens.

The therapist then grips the patient's wrist a second time, and asks him to tense and then gradually to relax the biceps. When the forearm is close to the arm of the chair, the therapist releases the wrist, allowing the patient to complete the movement on his own. He then exhorts him to "go on letting go," to "keep trying to go further and further in the negative direction," to "try to go beyond what seems to you to be the furthest point."

When the patient has shown by relaxing his biceps that he fully understands what is required, he is asked to put both hands comfortably on his lap and try to relax all the muscles of both arms for a few minutes. He is to report any new sensations that he may feel. The usual ones are tingling, numbness, or warmth, mainly in the hands. After a few minutes the therapist palpates the relaxing muscles. With practice he learns to judge between various grosser degrees of muscle tension.

Most patients have rather limited success when they first attempt to relax, but they are assured that good relaxation is a matter of practice, and whereas initially twenty minutes of relaxation may achieve no more than partial relaxation of an arm, it will eventually be possible to relax the whole body in a matter of a minute of two. However, there are some fortunate individuals who from the first attempt experience a deepening and extending relaxation, radiating, as it were, from the arms, and accompanied by general effects, like calmness, sleepiness or warmth.

I customarily begin the *second lesson* in relaxation by telling the patient that, from the emotional point of view, the most important muscles in the body are situated in and around the head, and that we shall, therefore, deal with this area next. We begin with the muscles of the face, demonstrating the tensions produced by contracting the muscles of the forehead. These muscles lend themselves to a demonstration by the therapist of the 'step-like' character of deepening relaxation. The therapist simultaneously contracts the eyebrow raising and frowning muscles in his own forehead very intensely, pointing out that an anxious expression has thus been produced. He then says: "I am going to relax these muscles in a controlled way to give you an impression of the step-like way in which decrements of tension occur during attempts at deep relaxation, although, when you are learning to relax, the steps take much longer than in my demonstration." The muscles are then relaxed, making an obvious step-down about every five seconds until, after about half-a-dozen steps, no further change is evident. At this point, it is clearly stated that relaxation is continuing and that this relaxation 'beneath the surface' is the part that matters for producing the desired emotional effects. The patient is then told to contract his own forehead muscles, and given about ten minutes to relax them as far as possible. Many report spontaneously the occurrence of 'relaxation feedback' in their foreheads, which they may feel as tingling, warmth, or "a feeling of thickness, as though my skin were made of leather." These sensations are, as a rule, indicative of a degree of relaxation beyond the normal level of muscle tone.

This lesson usually concludes by drawing attention to the muscles in the region of the nose by getting the patient to wrinkle his nose, and to the muscles around the mouth by making him purse his lips and then smile. All these muscles are now relaxed.

At the *third lesson* the patient is asked to bite on his teeth, thus tensing his masseters and temporales. The position of the lips is an important indicator of relaxation of the muscles of mastication. When these are relaxed, the lips are parted by a few millimeters. The masseters cannot be relaxed if the mouth is resolutely closed. On the other hand, an open mouth is no proof of their relaxation.

At the same lesson, I usually also introduce the muscles of the tongue. These may be felt contracting in the floor of the mouth when the patient presses the tip of his tongue firmly against the back of his lower incisor teeth. Relaxing the tongue muscles may produce such local sensations as tingling or a feeling of enlargement of that organ.

Patients who have special tensions in the neck region are now shown how to relax the pharyngeal muscles—which can be located by preparing to clear the throat. Other muscle groups that receive attention only for special purposes are those of the eyeball (which are first identified by having the eyes turned in succession left, right, up, and down), and the infrahyoid group (which the patient can be made to feel by trying to open his jaws against resistance).

The *fourth lesson* deals with the neck and shoulders. The main target in the neck is the posterior muscles that normally maintain the head's erect posture. Most people become aware of them merely by concentrating on sensations at the back of the neck. Relaxing these muscles makes the head fall forward, but because in the unpracticed individual the relaxation is incomplete, the head's whole weight is imposed on the few muscle fibers that are still contracted, producing discomfort and even pain in the neck. As Jacobson pointed out, persistent practice, in despite of the discomfort, leads to a progressive yielding of these muscles; and usually in a week or so the patient finds his neck comfortable with his chin pressing against his sternum. Those who find the discomfort of the forward leaning head too great are instructed to practice relaxing the neck muscles with the back of the head resting against a high-backed chair.

Shoulder muscle tensions are demonstrated by the following routine. The deltoid is contracted by abducting the arm to the horizontal, the lateral neck muscles by continuing this movement up to the ear, the post-humeral and scapulo-spinal groups by moving the horizontal arm backward, and the pectorals by swinging it forward across the chest. In relaxing these muscles the patient is directed to observe their functional unity with those of the arm.

The *fifth lesson* deals with the muscles of the back, abdomen, and thorax. The procedure with respect to the first two areas follows the usual pattern. The back muscles are contracted by backward arching of the spine. The abdominal muscles are tensed as if in anticipation of a punch in the belly. After contracting these muscles, the patient lets them go as far as he can. The thoracic muscles, or, more accurately, the muscles of respiration, are necessarily in a different category—for total inhibition of breathing is not an achievement to try to promote! But the respiratory rhythm can often be used to augment relaxation. Attention to the musculature during a few fairly deep breaths soon reveals that while some effort is involved during inhalation, expiration is essentially a 'letting-go.' Some patients find it very helpful to coordinate relaxation of various other muscles with the automatic relaxation of the respiratory muscles that takes place with the exhalation during *normal* breathing.

In making patients aware of the muscles to be relaxed in the lower limbs, during the *sixth lesson*, it has been my custom to start with the feet, and work upwards. The flexor digitorium brevis is felt in the sole by bending the toes within the shoe, the calf muscles by placing some weight on the toe, the peroneal and anterior tibial muscles by dorsiflexing the foot, the quadriceps femoris by straightening the knee, the hamstrings by trying to bend the knee against resistance, the adductors of the thigh by adduction against hand pressure on the inner aspect of the knee, and the abductors (which include some of the gluteal muscles) by abduction against pressure. All these muscles are the subject of the sixth lesson, and the patient should be allowed enough time for relaxing them.

The assessment of a patient's ability to relax depends partly upon his reports of the degree of calmness that relaxing brings about in him, and partly upon impressions gained from observing him. By the second or third lesson, most patients report ease, tranquility, or sleepiness. A few experience little or no change of feeling. It is an advantage to have objective indicators of relaxation. Jacobson (1939, 1964) has used the electromyogram, but mainly as a corroborative measure. Recently, more convenient equipment has become available that translates muscle potentials into auditory signals whose pitch drops as tension decreases (Budzinski, Stoyva, and Adler, 1970). This also facilitates relaxation by providing feedback to the patient. Fortunately, the reports of patients usually serve as a sufficiently reliable guide to their emotional state, especially with the help of the subjective anxiety scale. Quite a number of them, especially those who start with little or no ongoing anxiety, report a positive feeling of calm after only one or two sessions of relaxation training. Some fortunate individuals appear to possess a kind of relaxation-radiation zone (usually in the arms or face), from which relaxation spreads to other regions when the radiation zone is relaxed.

2. The Construction of Hierarchies

An anxiety hierarchy is a list of stimuli on a theme, ranked according to the amount of anxiety they evoke. My own practice has always been to place the stimulus evoking greatest anxiety at the top of the list. Sometimes hierarchy construction is an easy matter: the themes are clear and the rank order of the stimuli obvious. In other cases it can be very difficult. Case 31 in Chapter 14 illustrates how complicated a matter hierarchy construction can be.

The theme, or common core, of a family of anxiety-evoking stimuli most often consists of something extrinsic to the patient—like spiders or criticism; but the core may be internal—such as a feeling of losing control. Sometimes a number of physically disparate extrinsic stimulus situations all induce a common internal response. For example, a case of claustrophobia (Wolpe, 1961) had the same kind of trapped feeling when she had irremovable nail polish on her fingers or was wearing a tight ring as when she was physically confined. Such commonality of response is the basis of secondary generalization (Hull, 1943, p. 191).

Hierarchy construction usually begins at about the same time as relaxation training, and is subject to alterations or additions at any time. It is important to note that both the gathering of data and its subsequent organizing are done in an ordinary conversational way and *not under relaxation*, since the patient's *ordinary* responses to stimuli are what the therapist needs to know.

The raw data from which hierarchies are constructed come from four main sources: (a) the patient's history (see Chapter 3); (b) responses to the Willoughby questionnaire (Appendix 1 or 2) which reveals anxieties mainly in certain interpersonal contexts; (c) a Fear Survey Schedule[1] (Wolpe and Lang, 1964) (see Appendix 3); and (d) special probings into situations in which the patient feels unadaptive anxiety. If needed, further information may be sought by assigning to the patient the homework task of listing all situations, thoughts, or feelings that he finds disturbing, fearful, embarrassing, or in any other way distressing.

When all the identified sources of neurotic disturbance have been listed, the therapist classifies them into themes. Usually, there is more than one theme. In a good many cases, these are fairly obvious, but there are frequent exceptions. For example, a fear of going to movies, parties, and football games may suggest a fear of public situations and yet turn out to be really a claustrophobia or a fear of scrutiny. Frequently, fear and avoidance of social occasions turn out to be based on fear of criticism or rejection; or the fear may be a function of the mere physical presence of people, varying with the number to whom the patient is exposed. One patient's ostensible fear of social situations was really a conditioned anxiety response to the smell of food in public places. A good example of the importance of correct identification of relevant sources of anxiety is to be found in a previously reported case (Wolpe, 1958, p. 152) where the anxiety underlying a man's impotence turned out to be due, not to any aspect of the sexual situation as such, but to the idea

[1]A more extensive inventory (Wolpe and Lang, 1969) is commercially available. (Educational & Industrial Testing Service, San Diego, California)

of inflicting physical trauma. (An attempt at defloration had aroused high anxiety in this patient, and this anxiety had been conditioned to the sexual act.) The strategy of treatment was shifted by this revelation from *in vivo* use of the sexual response to systematic desensitization to tissue damage.

It is not necessary for the patient actually to have experienced each situation that is included in a hierarchy. The question posed is, "If you were today confronted by such and such a situation, *would you expect* to be anxious?" To answer this question he has to *imagine* the situation concerned, and it is generally almost as easy to imagine a supposed event as one that has at some time occurred. The temporal setting of an imagined stimulus configuration scarcely affects the responses to it. A man with a phobia for dogs will usually have about as much anxiety at the idea of meeting a bulldog on the way home tomorrow as at recalling an actual encounter with this breed of dog.

The following list of fears supplied by a patient will be used to illustrate some of the intricacies of hierarchy construction. This list is reproduced exactly as the patient presented it.

Raw List of Fears

1. High Altitudes
2. Elevators
3. Crowded Places
4. Church
5. Darkness — Movies, etc.
6. Being Alone
7. Marital Relations (pregnancy)
8. Walking any Distance
9. Death
10. Accidents
11. Fire
12. Fainting
13. Falling Back
14. Injections
15. Medications
16. Fear of the Unknown
17. Losing My Mind
18. Locked Doors
19. Amusement Park Rides
20. Steep Stairways

With the help of a little clarification from the patient the items were sorted into categories, thus:

A. ACROPHOBIA

1. High Altitudes
19. Amusement Park Rides
20. Steep Stairways

B. CLAUSTROPHOBIA

2. Elevators
3. Crowded Places
4. Church
5. Movies (darkness factor)
18. Locked Doors

C. AGORAPHOBIA
6. Being Alone   8. Walking any Distance (alone)

D. ILLNESS AND ITS ASSOCIATIONS
12. Fainting   14. Injections
13. Falling Back   15. Medication

E. BASICALLY OBJECTIVE FEARS
7. Marital Relations (pregnancy)   11. Fire
9. Death   16. Fear of the Unknown
10. Accidents   17. Losing My Mind

Before considering the truly neurotic hierarchical groups A–D to which desensitization is relevant, some remarks must be made about group E. The patient's fears of pregnancy, accidents, death, and fire were all in contexts in which fear can be reasonable, but in her case, apprehension about these matters was somewhat more than normal. I considered that this might be a function of a generally elevated level of anxiety — which is quite often found in neuroses — and would probably disappear when the major neurotic anxiety sources had been removed by therapy. Her fear of the unknown was bound up with the idea of death. Her fear of losing her mind, an inference from the bizarre and uncontrollable feelings that characterized her neurosis, was overcome by strong assurance that her condition was not related to insanity and could *never* lead to it, assurance that was reinforced by demonstrating that hyperventilation could precipitate many of her symptoms. There are some cases in whom *all* fears would belong to group E, in which instance, of course, desensitization would not be relevant; and supplying corrective information, with the addition, sometimes, of thought-stopping would be indicated.

On scrutinizing the stimulus groups A–D, the reader should observe that the items are very general and not sufficiently well-defined for hierarchical ranking. In fact, the items of each group are merely exemplifications that can generate stimulus situations specific enough to be ranked only after further communication between patient and therapist. But this may not be immediately obvious to newcomers to behavior therapy. They often attempt to form such exemplifications into hierarchies. One day, I asked a group of 25 members of a behavior therapy class (none of whom had previously treated more than two or three patients) how they would proceed to build a hierarchy out of the five claustrophobia items of group B. The majority of them were disposed to ask the patient to rank elevators, churches, movies, etc., hierarchically, and to assume that the influence of modifying factors, like *size* of elevator, would automatically be bounded by the hierarchical ranking. But, actually, these five items were merely various settings that in a general way embodied space-constriction. Further questioning of the patient showed quite clearly that the claustrophobic anxiety was an inverse function of the size of the enclosing space and a direct function of duration of confinement. Desensitization, consequently, involved two hierarchical series: First, the patient was 'confined' for a constant length of time in progressively smaller rooms; and, secondly, she was 'confined' in a very small room (4 ft square) for increasing periods.

Similarly, in group A, acrophobia, each of the three items refers to a whole range of concrete situations. They do not have the specificity that would permit them to be used in desensitization; but particularizing within the areas they encompass provided a range of concrete situations evoking responses of different intensities. Questioning disclosed that increasing heights were increasingly fearful, starting from about 20 feet (or a second floor window), and that at all heights motion aggravated the fear. Similarly, group D yielded a fairly extensive hierarchy, some of whose items, ranked in descending order, were:

1. Feeling of being about to lose consciousness.
2. Feeling of falling backwards.
3. Marked dizziness.
4. Feeling of lightness in head.
5. Moderate dizziness.
6. Smell of ether.
7. Receiving an injection.
8. Racing heart (anxiety increasing with rapidity of heart beat).
9. Weak knees.
10. Seeing syringe poised for an injection.
11. Sight of bandages.

It may be observed that the stronger stimuli (1–5) are all endogenous, and most of the weaker ones exogenous. What is common to all is the feeling of personal threat.

In other cases, besides multiplicity of hierarchies, one encounters multiple 'dimensions' within a single hierarchy. For example, in a patient having claustrophobic reactions in social situations five variables controlled the intensity of the reaction. The reactions were the *stronger*:

1. The greater the number of people present.
2. The more strange the people.

3. The greater the difficulties in the way of leaving the room (both physical factors and social propriety being relevant).
4. The shorter the time since her last meal (this factor determining the measure of a fear of vomiting).

They were *weaker* if she was accompanied by

5. Protective persons—husband, mother, and close friend (in descending order of effectiveness).

Sometimes, the inadequacies of a hierarchy become evident only after attempts at desensitization have begun, when it may be seen that the anxiety level does not diminish after repeated presentations of the weakest scene contained in the hierarchy, even though relaxation is manifestly good. The problem is then to seek still less disturbing stimuli whose evoked anxiety is weak enough to be inhibited by the patient's relaxation. In many cases, it is obvious where to look for weaker stimuli. For example, in a patient who had an anxiety hierarchy on the theme of loneliness, the weakest item in the original hierarchy—being at home accompanied only by her daughter—was found to evoke more anxiety than was manageable. To obtain a weaker starting point all that was needed was to add to the situation two or more companions. But it is not always so easy, and the therapist may have to use a good deal of ingenuity to procure weak stimuli.

For example, following an accident three years previously, a woman patient had developed severe anxiety reactions to the sight of approaching automobiles. I had been led to believe that the patient noticed the first glimmerings of anxiety when a car was two blocks away, and that the anxiety increased gradually up to a distance of half a block, and then much more steeply with further approximation. This seemed to promise straightforward progress; but at the first desensitization session even an imagined distance of two blocks from the car aroused anxiety too great to be inhibited by the counteraction of relaxation. Further questioning revealed that the patient really had considerable anxiety at the very prospect of even the shortest journey by car, since the whole range of threatening possibilities was already present for her the moment a journey became imminent; but she had not thought this amount of anxiety worthy of report. As in all other cases, desensitization could not begin unless the amount of 'danger' contained in scenes from the hierarchy was under control. What was required was a sharp delimitation of the implications of each situation. Accordingly, an imaginary enclosed field, two blocks square, was drawn on paper. The patient imagined that she sat in her car 'placed' in one corner of the field while a trusted person drove his car up to an agreed distance from her car, and then to ever-closer agreed points as the patient progressed. The 'danger' was thus always circumscribed. This, and later steps in the treatment of the case are described in some detail in Chapter 14.

Another case in whom it was difficult to obtain sufficiently weak anxiety-evoking stimuli was a patient with a death phobia, whose items ranged in descending order from human corpses to funeral processions to dead dogs. Presentation of scenes of dead dogs produced marked and un-diminishing anxiety, even when they were imagined at distances of two or three hundred yards (where they were hardly discernible). A solution was found in the use of a temporal dimension, beginning with the histor-ically inaccurate sentence, "William the Conqueror was killed at the Battle of Hastings in 1066."

A third example concerns a woman who had very severe reactions to the idea of anybody fainting or 'losing power.' Imagining even the most trivial sign of weakness in a person or an animal produced more anxiety than her relaxation could counteract. The first scene to be successfully used in her desensitization was in the context of her being conducted around a campus. Her escort points to a platform and says, "That is where, 5 years ago, an animal was given an injection that paralyzed it for 5 minutes." Desensitization subsequently involved first reducing the time gap and then increasing the duration of the paralysis.

An ever-present question in constructing hierarchies is whether the items constitute a reasonably evenly-spaced progression. If items are too similar, time will be wasted; if adjacent items differ too widely in anxiety-evoking potential, progress will be halted upon moving from the lesser to the greater. The patient may even occasionally be further sensitized, i.e. conditioned to higher levels of anxiety as the result of severe anxiety being evoked. (It is not clear why, but this hardly ever happens with social stimuli to anxiety.) When a hierarchy is based on a directly measurable dimension such as distance, a well-spaced progression is relatively easy to obtain. However, this is not a linear function: a simple power function is involved, whose index exceeds unity in some cases and is fractional in others (Wolpe, 1963). In phobias in which anxiety increases with proximity to the feared object small changes in the physical dimension affect anxiety more with increasing closeness of the object. The opposite applies to acrophobia and agoraphobia. Where fear is a function of number of feared objects, small increments are more potent at low numerical levels. Further reference to this topic will be made later (pp. 127–132).

It is always an advantage for a hierarchy to be in clearly quantifiable form; and the therapist should exercise every effort to achieve this. Often, it requires the utilization of a setting that is far removed from the patient's problem. For example, in a 42-year-old woman with a fear of traveling alone of 21 years' duration, it became evident that the center point of her disability was a fear of *being alone* away from home. It would certainly have been possible to deal with this in the context of traveling, but her sensitivity was extreme and aloneness would have been difficult to quantify in terms of distance. It was possible to obtain much better control of her reactions by using an elevator as the vehicle of her separation from the outside world. The weaker items of the hierarchy were set in a completely open elevator in which she ascended an increasing number of floors up to 100. Then she was 'placed' in an elevator that had a single one-foot-square window, and in this a similar sequence was followed. The same was then done in an elevator with a window whose dimensions were 9 in. × 3 in., an elevator with a 2 in. peephole, and finally a completely opaque one. Desensitization to these items was attended by a progressive increase in her capacity to travel afield, even though distance had not figured at all in the desensitization up to this point. But now a new series was started embracing special anxiety-conditioned stimuli belonging to journeys of various kinds.

The problem of determining reasonably evenly spaced differences is much more difficult when the hierarchy does not depend upon an externally measurable independent dimension — when it depends upon secondary generalization — for example, a hierarchy based on the strength of feelings of rejection. This and many other difficulties of quantification that arise not only in doing desensitization, but in psychotherapy in general, are greatly aided by the use of the *subjective anxiety scale*.

3. Some Examples of Hierarchies

1. A Cluster of Hierarchies Involving People

Case 5

Miss C. was a 24-year-old art student who came for treatment because marked anxiety at examinations had resulted in repeated failures. Investigation revealed additional phobic areas. The hierarchies are given below. All of them involve people, and none belong to the classical phobias. Note, in the examination series, that the hierarchical order of the top 5 items does not correspond with the temporal order. (Freedom from anxiety to the highest items of each of these hierarchies was achieved in 17 desensitization sessions, with complete transfer to the corresponding situations in actuality. Four months later, she passed her examinations without anxiety.)

Hierarchies in Descending Order of Reaction Intensity

A. EXAMINATION SERIES
1. On the way to the university on the day of an examination.
2. In the process of answering an examination paper.
3. Standing before the unopened doors of the examination room.
4. Awaiting the distribution of examination papers.
5. The examination paper lies face down before her.
6. The night before an examination.
7. One day before an examination.
8. Two days before an examination.
9. Three days before an examination.
10. Four days before an examination.
11. Five days before an examination.
12. A week before an examination.
13. Two weeks before an examination.
14. A month before an examination.

B. SCRUTINY SERIES
1. Being watched working (especially drawing) by ten people.
2. Being watched working by six people.
3. Being watched working by three people.
4. Being watched working by one expert in the field. (Anxiety begins when the observer is ten feet away and increases as he draws closer.)
5. Being watched working by a non-expert. (Anxiety begins at a distance of four feet.)

C. DEVALUATION SERIES
1. An argument she raises in a discussion is ignored by the group.
2. She is not recognized by a person she has briefly met three times.
3. Her mother says she is selfish because she is not helping in the house. (Studying instead.)
4. She is not recognized by a person she has briefly met twice.
5. Her mother calls her lazy.
6. She is not recognized by a person she has briefly met once.

D. DISCORD BETWEEN OTHER PEOPLE
1. Her mother shouts at a servant.
2. Her young sister whines to her mother.
3. Her sister engages in a dispute with her father.
4. Her mother shouts at her sister.
5. She sees two strangers quarrel.

2. A Variety of Hierarchies on the Theme of Sickness and Injury   The examples that follow illustrate individual differences in the content, order, and number of items making up hierarchies of the same theme in different patients. In each of the cases there was fear of both external and internal stimuli. All three required and received training in assertive behavior in addition to desensitization.

Case 6
Mrs. D., aged 35, was also agoraphobic. She had never actually experienced any of the possible events in the endogenous series.

EXTERNAL SERIES
1. Sight of a fit.
2. Jerky movement of another's arm.
3. Sight of someone fainting.
4. An acquaintance says "That man across the street has some form of insanity."
5. The word 'insanity.'
6. The word 'madness.'
7. Insane-sounding laughter.
8. An acquaintance says, "That man across the street has an anxiety state."
9. The sound of screaming (the closer the more disturbing).
10. A man with a fracture lying in bed with ropes and pulleys attached to his leg.
11. A man propped up in bed short of breath because of heart disease.
12. An acquaintance says, "That man across the road is an epileptic."
13. Seeing a man propped up in bed short of breath because of pneumonia.
14. A man walks by with a plaster cast on his leg.
15. A man with Parkinson's disease.
16. A man with blood running down his face from a cut.
17. A person with a facial tic.

ENDOGENOUS SERIES

1. Having a fit.
2. Fainting.
3. Tremor of her hand.

Case 7

Mrs. E., aged 32.

EXTERNAL SERIES

1. The sight of physical deformity.
2. Someone in pain (the greater the evidence of pain the more disturbing).
3. The sight of bleeding.
4. The sight of somebody seriously ill (e.g. heart attack).
5. Automobile accidents.
6. Nurses in uniform.
7. Wheelchairs.
8. Hospitals.
9. Ambulances.

ENDOGENOUS SERIES

1. Tense (explosive) sensation in head.
2. Clammy feet.
3. Perspiring hands.
4. Dry mouth and inability to swallow.
5. Dizziness.
6. Rapid breathing.
7. Racing heart.
8. Tense feeling in back of neck.
9. Weakness at knees.
10. Butterflies in stomach.

Case 8

Mrs. F., aged 52, also had a severe phobic system on the theme of death.

EXTERNAL SERIES

1. Child with two wasted legs.
2. Man walking slowly – short of breath due to weak heart.
3. Blind man working lift.
4. Child with one wasted leg.
5. A hunchback.

6. A person groaning with pain.
7. A man with a club foot.
8. A one-armed man.
9. A one-legged man.
10. A person with a high temperature due to a relatively non-dangerous disease like influenza.

ENDOGENOUS SERIES
1. Extrasystoles.
2. Shooting pains in chest and abdomen.
3. Pains in the left shoulder and back.
4. Pain on top of head.
5. Buzzing in ear.
6. Tremor of hands.
7. Numbness or pain in fingertips.
8. Shortness of breath after exertion.
9. Pain in left hand (old injury).

It will be noted that the heterogeneous material in all of the foregoing hierarchies is unavoidable. It is impossible to abstract from any of them a common feature that can be varied quantitatively. It is quite different in the following example in which the heterogeneity is superfluous.

1. At large university cocktail party talking with strangers.
2. At departmental luncheon with friends.
3. Entering common room of residents where people glance up at you.
4. People look at you walking down street.
5. Reading in library, glanced at by two men at opposite table.
6. At library, conscious of girl looking at you.

The essence of this hierarchy could have been more profitably rendered as a function of social exposure on a numerical dimension in a single arbitrarily chosen setting, e.g. at a library being looked at by increasing numbers of people. If it eventually turned out that different settings added their own anxiety, these could have been dealt with in a new hierarchy in which the persons present could be kept at a constant large number.

Although most hierarchies vary in a single dimension, there are many which incorporate two or more factors. It is then helpful to set them out in the tabular form illustrated by Table 2 in which a woman's fears of the negative opinions of others varied according to the adjective applied to

Table 2. Bidimensional hierarchy set out according to the *sud* score resulting from the interplay of pairs of factors.

	Uncle Charlie	Florence	Sharon	Geraldine	Shopkeeper She Barely Knows
Uses People	95	65	70	50	20
Irresponsible	90	75	50	40	20
Selfish	90	75	40	50	20
Unreliable	80	60	30	40	10
Lazy	60	50	10	20	0
Untidy	50	40	20	10	0
Awkward	40	30	10	10	0

her and with the person applying it. It should be noted that the true hierarchical order of the impact of the words varies somewhat from speaker to speaker. The usual way of treating hierarchies of this kind is to have the patient imagine herself overhearing the named person attributing a particular quality to her while unaware of being overheard.

3. The Subjective Anxiety Scale Knowledge of the magnitude of the patient's anxiety responses to specific stimuli being indispensable to desensitization, it is desirable to have reliable ways of gauging it.

The scale is introduced to the patient by addressing him as follows: "Think of the worst anxiety you have ever experienced, or can imagine experiencing, and assign to this the number 100. Now think of the state of being absolutely calm and call this zero. Now you have a scale of anxiety. On this scale how do you rate yourself at this moment?" Most subjects give a figure without much hesitation, and with practice come to be able to indicate their feelings with increasing confidence in a way that is much more informative than the usual adjectival statements. The unit is the *sud* (subjective unit of disturbance). It is possible to use the scale to ask the patient to rate the items of the hierarchy according to the amount of anxiety he would have upon exposure to them. If the differences between items are similar, and, generally speaking, not more than 5 to 10 *suds*, the spacing can be regarded as satisfactory. On the other hand, if there were, for example, 40 *suds* for item number 8, and 10 *suds* for item number 9, there would be an obvious need for intervening items.

4. Desensitization Procedure: Counteracting Anxiety by Relaxation

The stage is set for the desensitization procedure when the patient has attained a capacity to calm himself by relaxation, and the therapist has established appropriate hierarchies. Many of them are adequately calm when relaxation training has gone halfway or less. While a desensitization program makes it highly desirable for the patient to achieve a positive feeling of calm, i.e. a negative of anxiety, it is not mandatory, and one can be well satisfied with zero subjective units of disturbance. In a fair number who have considerable levels of current anxiety (whether or not this is pervasive — 'free-floating' — anxiety), it has been found that a substantial lowering of the level — say, from 50 to 15 *suds* — may afford a sufficiently low anxiety baseline for successful desensitization. Apparently, an anxiety-inhibiting 'dynamism' can inhibit small quanta of intercurrent anxiety even when it does not fully overcome current anxiety. Desensitizing effects are only rarely obtainable with levels in excess of 25 *suds*; and in some individuals a zero level is indispensable.

It is natural to hope for a smooth therapeutic passage, and such is often the case, but there are many difficulties that may encumber the path. I shall first describe the technique and the characteristic course of uncomplicated desensitization.

The first desensitization session is introduced by saying, "I am now going to get you to relax; and when you are relaxed I will ask you to imagine certain scenes. Each time a scene is clear in your mind indicate this by raising your index finger about one inch."

While the patient sits or lies comfortably with his eyes closed, the therapist proceeds to bring about as deep as possible a state of relaxation by the use of such words as the following: "Now, your whole body becomes progressively heavier, and all your muscles relax. Let go more and more completely. We shall give your muscles individual attention. Relax the muscles of your forehead. (Pause 5–10 seconds.) Relax the muscles of your jaws and those of your tongue. (Pause) Relax the muscles of your eyeballs. The more you relax, the calmer you become. (Pause) Relax the muscles of your neck. (Pause) Let all the muscles of your shoulders relax. Just let yourself go. (Pause) Now relax your arms. (Pause) Relax all the muscles of your trunk. (Pause) Relax the muscles of your lower limbs. Let your muscles go more and more. You feel so much at ease and so very comfortable."

At the first desensitization session, which is always partly exploratory, the therapist seeks some feedback about the state of the patient, asking him to state on the subjective scale how much anxiety he feels. If it is zero or close thereto, scene presentations can begin. If the patient continues to have some anxiety despite his best efforts at direct relaxation, various imaginal devices may be invoked. Those most commonly used are:

1. "Imagine that on a calm summer's day you lie back on a soft lawn and watch the clouds move slowly overhead. Notice especially the brilliant edges of the clouds."
2. "Imagine an intense, bright spot of light about eighteen inches in front of you." (This image is due to Milton Erickson.)
3. "Imagine that near a river's bank you see a leaf moving erratically on little waves."

There is a routine manner of proceeding with the introduction of the scenes at the first desensitization session. The observations that the therapist makes at this session frequently lead to modifications of technique to fit in with particular requirements of the patient.

The first scene presented is a 'control.' It is neutral in the sense that the patient is not expected to have any anxious reaction to it. I most commonly use a street scene. Sometimes it is 'safer' to have the patient imagine himself sitting in his living room, or reading a newspaper; but there is no guarantee of safety unless the subject matter has actually been explored beforehand. At one time I used to employ a white flower against a black background as a standard control scene. One day, a patient evinced considerable anxiety to it, because he associated it with funerals, and, as it subsequently turned out, he had a neurosis about death.

There are two reasons for using a control scene. First, it provides information about the patient's general ability to visualize anxiety-free material. Second, it provides indications of certain contaminating factors: the patient may have anxiety about relinquishing control of himself, or about 'the unknown.' In either case, anxiety is present that has nothing to do with the target of desensitization, and that must be dealt with if therapy is to succeed.

For many years, the preferred method of introducing scenes was the one that I first described in detail in 1954. In brief, the patient was asked to imagine the scene, and then instructed to desist after 'sufficient' time had passed (usually 15–20 seconds). He was then requested to raise his finger if the scene had caused even the slightest rise of anxiety.

This procedure has the disadvantage that the therapist cannot tell when visualization has actually begun. Consequently, there may be wide variations in duration of a scene from one presentation to the next. The method to be described here is free from this disadvantage. It has been consistently used and taught in the Behavior Therapy Unit since 1968.

The patient is asked to imagine a number of scenes that will be described to him. He is to raise his left index finger about one inch the moment the image is clearly formed. The therapist then presents a scene and lets it remain for exactly as long as he wants to—usually 5–7 seconds. He terminates it by saying, "Stop the scene"; and then asks the patient to state how much it disturbed him in terms of *suds*. After a few sessions, the patient gets into the habit of stating the number of *suds* automatically upon the termination of the scene. While the use of a verbal report possibly disrupts relaxation more than the raising of a finger, the adverse effects have to date in no case seemed to be important. Any disadvantages are certainly outweighed by dispensing with the need to allow 'long enough time' to be sure that the patient has visualized the scene, and by the immediate and precise feedback of amount of disturbance.

In order to illustrate what is typically said and done, let us make use of the cluster of four hierarchies of Miss C. (p. 115).

THERAPIST: I am now going to ask you to imagine a number of scenes. You will imagine them clearly and they will generally interfere little, if at all, with your state of relaxation. If, however, at any time you feel disturbed or worried and want to draw my attention, you can tell me so. As soon as a scene is clear in your mind, indicate it by raising your left index finger about one inch. First, I want you to imagine that you are standing at a familiar street corner on a pleasant morning watching the traffic go by. You see cars, motorcycles, trucks, bicycles, people, and traffic lights; and you hear the sounds associated with all these things.

After a few seconds the patient raises her left index finger. The therapist pauses for five seconds.

THERAPIST: Stop imagining that scene. By how much did it raise your anxiety level while you imagined it?

MISS C.: Not at all.

THERAPIST: Now give your attention once again to relaxing.

There is again a pause of 20–30 seconds.

THERAPIST: Now imagine that you are home studying in the evening. It is the 20th May, exactly a month before your examination.

After about 15 seconds Miss C. raises her finger. Again she is left with the scene for 5 seconds.

THERAPIST: Stop that scene. By how much did it raise your anxiety?
MISS C.: About 15 units.

THERAPIST: Now imagine the same scene again — a month before your examination.

At this second presentation the rise in anxiety was five *suds* and at the third it was zero. The successive figures vary both with the individual and the scene. When the initial figure is over 30, repetition is unlikely to lower it. But there are exceptions. There are also occasional patients in whom an initial rise of 10 is too great to be diminished by repetition.

Having disposed of the first scene of the examination hierarchy, I could move on to the second. Alternatively, I could test Miss C.'s responses in another area, such as the discord hierarchy — thus:

THERAPIST: Imagine you are sitting on a bench at a bus stop and across the road are two strange men whose voices are raised in argument.

This scene was given twice. After the patient reported on her response to the last presentation I terminated the desensitization session.

THERAPIST: Relax again. Now I am going to count up to 5 and you will open your eyes, feeling calm and refreshed.

The responses of this patient were unexceptional. Since visualization was clear, and there was evidence of decrease of anxiety with each repetition of a scene, it seemed likely that we would make our way through all four hierarchies without much trouble, an expectation that the course of events bore out.

Procedure at later sessions takes much the same course as at the first, but there is a tendency for the preliminaries to take less and less time. Whenever the patient is judged sufficiently relaxed, he is informed that scenes will be presented to his imagination and at early sessions reminded that if anything should disturb him unduly he should at once communicate this fact to the therapist. Exposure, and prolonged exposure in particular, to a very disturbing scene can seriously increase phobic sensitivity. If at the previous session there was a scene at whose repeated presentations anxiety diminished, but not to zero, that scene is usually the first to be presented. But if at the previous session that scene ceased to arouse any anxiety, the scene next higher in the hierarchy will now be presented. There are, however, some patients who, though having had no anxiety at all to the final scene at a session, again show a small measure of anxiety to that same scene at the next session—a kind of 'spontaneous recovery' of anxiety. The scene must then be repeated until the anxiety is entirely eliminated, before proceeding to ascend the hierarchy. In some of these patients, the need for back-tracking can sometimes be eliminated by overlearning at the earlier session, i.e. presenting a scene 2 or 3 times more after it has ceased to arouse anxiety.

All relevant occurrences during the desensitization session are noted on a card by a concise notation. The following is the record summarizing Miss C.'s desensitization session as described above:

S. D. by rel. Scene 1—corner ([xl] 0). 2—studying at home one month before exam ([x3] 15, 5, 0). 3—two strange men argue across road ([× 2] 15, 10).

"S. D. by rel." stands for "systematic desensitization by relaxation." The numbers in square parenthesis show how many presentations were given. Those to their right are the *sud* scores for the successive presentations.

The usual plan followed in assigning numerical indices to scenes is to use an integer to indicate the class of subject matter, and letters for variations of detail. For example, in Miss C.'s case, the imaginary situation of being at home working 2 weeks before the examination was given the index 1 a, one week before the examination was 1 b, and so forth. The advantages of employing these indices are: (1) they obviate repeatedly writing out the features of scenes; (2) they make it easy to find particular scenes when one consults the record; and (3) they facilitate later research work.

QUANTITATIVE CONSIDERATIONS

There is great variation in *how many themes, how many scenes from each*, and *how many presentations are given* at a desensitization session. Generally, up to four hierarchies are drawn upon in an individual session, and not many patients have more than four. Three or four presentations of a scene are usual to bring the response to zero, but ten or more may be needed. The total number of scenes presented is limited mainly by availability of time, but sometimes by the endurance of the patient. On the whole, available time increases as therapy goes on, and eventually almost the whole interview period may be devoted to desensitization; so that whereas at an early stage eight or ten presentations may be the total at a session, at an advanced stage the number may be 30 or even 50. The usual duration of a desensitization session is 15–30 minutes. However, Wolpin and Pearsall (1965) reported totally overcoming a phobia in a single session conducted continuously for 90 minutes.

While the foregoing generalizations apply to the great majority of patients, there are rare individuals who manifest marked perseveration of even the mild anxiety aroused by a single scene presentation. Yet, anxiety decreases from session to session. In such individuals only one scene should be given at a session. Marked perseveration of anxiety can also occur in the usual run of patients after the presentation of an unduly disturbing scene. When this happens, the session should be terminated.

It has hitherto been the accepted principle in systematic desensitization to use only weakly anxiety-evoking stimuli. While this is obviously prudent when one depends on reciprocal inhibition for change, it is not necessarily always the most economical thing to do. There are clinical reports suggesting that more rapid progress sometimes follows larger steps (Rachman, personal communication.) It is conceivable that there is some personality factor that determines responsiveness to change, ranging from 'desensitizability' at one extreme to 'floodability' at the other.

The *duration* of a scene is usually of the order of 5–7 seconds, but it may be varied according to several circumstances. It is quickly terminated if the patient indicates strong anxiety. Whenever the therapist has special reason to suspect that a scene may evoke a strong reaction he presents it with cautious brevity—for one or two seconds. By and large, early presentations of scenes are briefer, later ones longer. A certain number of patients require fifteen or more seconds to construct a clear image of a verbally triggered scene. The character of the scene also necessarily plays a part in determining the time allowed for it. A clap of thunder takes less time than making a speech.

The *interval* between scenes also varies. It is usually between ten and thirty seconds, but if the patient has been more than slightly disturbed by the preceding scene, the interval may be extended to a minute or more, during which time he may be given repeated suggestions to be relaxed and tranquil. Until the therapist is well acquainted with the patient's reactions, he should frequently check the basal relaxation level between scenes. For this purpose, the *sud* scale is invaluable.

The *number* of desensitizing sessions required depends on the number of scene presentations necessary to overcome the phobic constellations of the patient. Relevant factors are the number of such constellations, the severity of each, and the degree of generalization or involvement of related stimuli in the case of each. One patient may recover in half a dozen sessions, another may require a hundred or more. The patient with a death phobia (p.114), on whom a temporal dimension had to be used, also had two other phobias and required a total of about a hundred sessions. To remove the death phobia alone, a total of about 2,000 scene presentations were given.

The *spacing* of sessions does not seem to matter greatly. As a rule, sessions are once or twice a week, but may be separated by many weeks, or take place daily. Some patients, visiting from afar, receive 2 sessions a day, and occasionally as many as four. Whether sessions are massed or widely dispersed, there is practically always a close correlation between the extent to which desensitization has been accomplished and the degree of diminution of anxiety responses to real stimuli in the phobic areas. Except when therapy is almost terminated and nothing remains of a phobia but a few weak reactions that may be overcome by the competition of emotions arising spontaneously in the ordinary course of living (Wolpe, 1958, p. 99), very little change occurs, as a rule, between sessions. In one case of severe claustrophobia, a marked but incomplete degree of improvement achieved by a first series of sessions remained almost stationary during a $3\frac{1}{2}$-year interval, after which further sessions led to complete elimination of the phobia. The patient mentioned earlier with a disabling fear of cars, who had daily sessions for a week or two every 5 weeks or so, greatly improved during the treatment phases, but not at all during the intervening weeks (see Case 31).

Rate of change is neither haphazard nor purely an individual matter. At least in the case of desensitization of the classical phobias it follows consistent quantitative laws. A study of 20 phobias of 13 patients (Wolpe, 1963) was prompted by the casual observation that during desensitization the number of presentations of a scene required to bring the anxiety level down to zero is not uniform, but tends to increase or decrease on the way up the hierarchy. An attempt was made to establish quantitative relations by a study of those phobias that vary along a physical dimension. It was found that in claustrophobia and those phobias in which the patient becomes more anxious with increasing proximity to the feared object, the cumulative curve relating number of scene presentations to therapeutic progress is a positively accelerating function. In agoraphobias, acrophobias, and those in which anxiety depends on the number of objects, the cumulative curve is a negatively accelerating function. No exceptions were found, as may be observed by studying Figs. 7–10, each of which contains the curves of a particular group. In order to make them comparable, the curves have been subjected to percentile transformations.

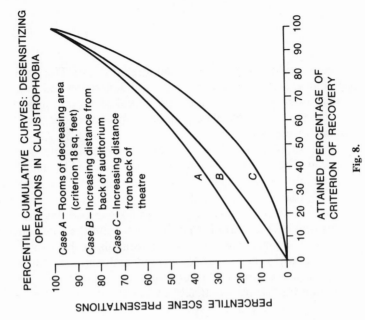

PERCENTILE CUMULATIVE CURVES: DESENSITIZING
OPERATIONS IN CLAUSTROPHOBIA

Case A – Rooms of decreasing area
(criterion 18 sq. feet)

Case B – Increasing distance from
back of auditorium

Case C – Increasing distance
from back of
theatre

Fig. 8.

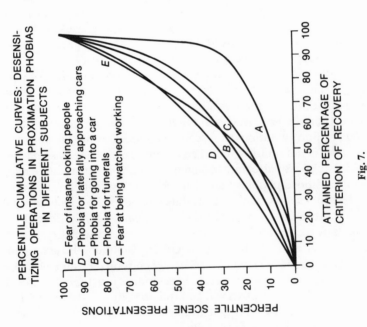

PERCENTILE CUMULATIVE CURVES: DESENSITIZING OPERATIONS IN PROXIMATION PHOBIAS
IN DIFFERENT SUBJECTS

E – Fear of insane looking people
D – Phobia for laterally approaching cars
B – Phobia for going into a car
C – Phobia for funerals
A – Fear at being watched working

Fig. 7.

128

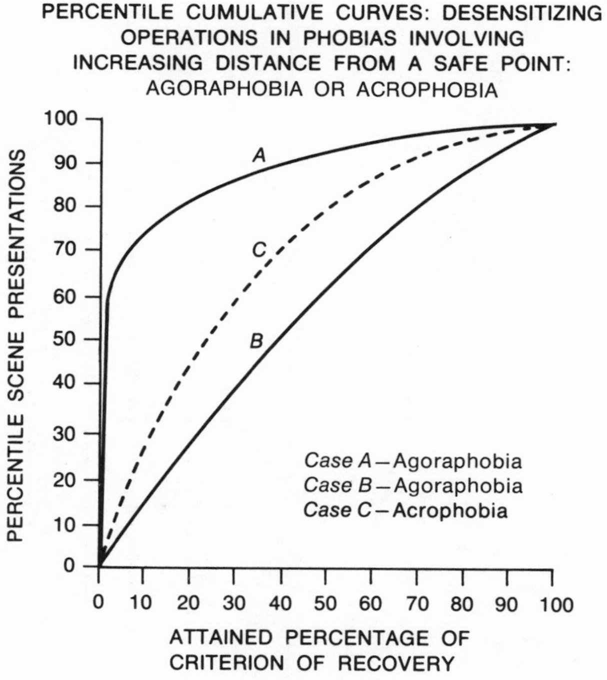

PERCENTILE CUMULATIVE CURVES: DESENSITIZING
OPERATIONS IN PHOBIAS INVOLVING
INCREASING DISTANCE FROM A SAFE POINT:
AGORAPHOBIA OR ACROPHOBIA

Case A – Agoraphobia
Case B – Agoraphobia
Case C – Acrophobia

Fig. 9.

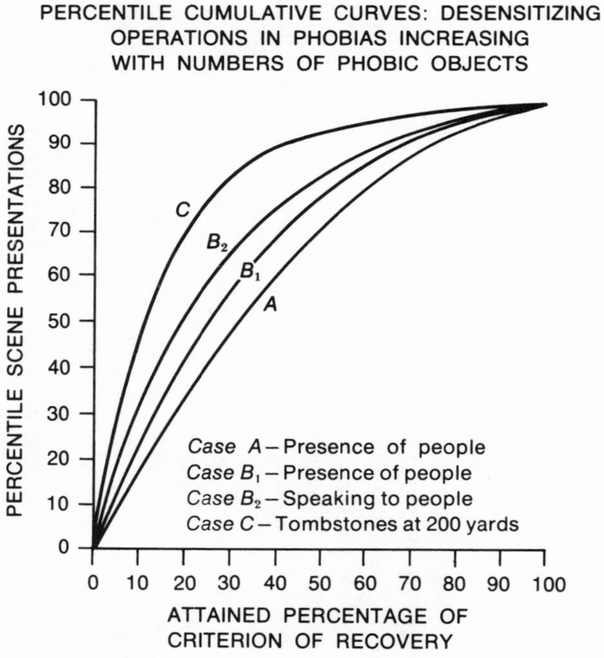

PERCENTILE CUMULATIVE CURVES: DESENSITIZING
OPERATIONS IN PHOBIAS INCREASING
WITH NUMBERS OF PHOBIC OBJECTS

Case A – Presence of people
Case B₁ – Presence of people
Case B₂ – Speaking to people
Case C – Tombstones at 200 yards

Fig. 10.

129

The horizontal axis shows attained percentage of criterion of recovery, and the vertical axis scene presentations as a percentage of the total number employed to overcome the whole hierarchy.

Figure 11 illustrates that it is not the personality of the patient but the type of phobia that determines the shape of the curve. The three curves in this figure were obtained from a single patient. That displaying negative acceleration (B) delineates the desensitization of the anxiety response to an increasing number of tombstones at 200 yards. The positively accelerating curves belong respectively to proximation phobias to a dead dog (A) and to a stationary automobile (C), and are strikingly concordant.

Mathematical analysis of the curves reveals that, with the exception of that for agoraphobia Case A, and Curve C in Fig. 10 (which will be commented upon subsequently), they express the same kind of functional relation as has been found by Stevens (1957, 1962) in relating the physical magnitude of a stimulus to its perceived intensity – the 'psycho-physical

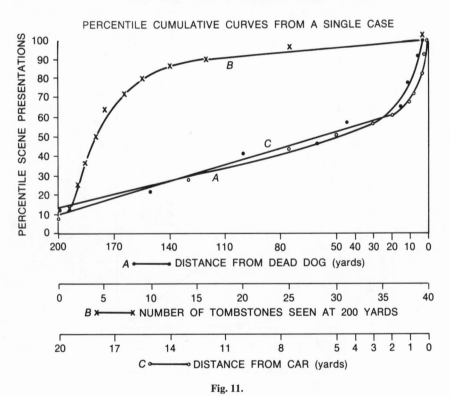

Fig. 11.

law.' This is a general empirical law that the psychological (subjective) magnitude is a power function of the stimulus magnitude. This means that to make one stimulus seem twice as strong as another, the physical energy must be increased at a fixed ratio, no matter what the initial intensity level. The relationship is expressed by the formula:

$$P = kS^n$$

where P stands for perceived intensity (psychological magnitude), S for stimulus magnitude, k is a constant, and n the exponent of the relationship. The exponent is determined empirically by the formula:

$$n = \frac{\log 0.5}{\log r}$$

where r is the ratio between the physical magnitude of a given stimulus and the physical magnitude of the stimulus that appears twice as strong as the given stimulus.

Insofar as the desensitization curves portray this kind of functional relation, it may be deduced that the amount of work required for each measured unit of progress in overcoming these phobias is a function of the correlated magnitudes of the subject's pre-treatment response. The relevant indicator of response here is *autonomic response magnitude* rather than perceived magnitude. To test this presumption, it is necessary to compare the curve of directly measured autonomic magnitudes of response at different points in hierarchies *before treatment*, with the desensitization curves subsequently obtained. No direct comparison has as yet been attempted, but Lang, *et al.* (1970) have found that the curve correlating pulse rate change with hierarchical position of the stimulus in snake phobias is very similar to the proximation phobia curves in Fig. 7.

For several of the curves, the value of the exponent n was determined by Stevens' formula (v.s.), the value of r being derived from the point on the x axis at which $y = 50\%$ (0.5). Among the proximation phobias (Fig. 7) the exponent of the middle curve, C, is about 3.0. Among the phobias varying with numbers of phobic objects (Fig. 8) the value for Curve B_2 is 0.43. The middle curve, C, in the remoteness phobia group (Fig. 9) is almost identical with this.

As mentioned above, curve A of the remoteness group does not conform to a power function but the case was unusual in that the desensitization distances reflected in the curve ranged from 20 yards to 100 miles. It is obvious that a person's perception of differences of yards may vary in quite a dissimilar way from differences of miles. It was found upon plotting separate curves for 0–1 and for 1–100 miles that two power function curves were obtained, the first (0–1) being similar to the theoretical curve $n = 0.44$, and the second (1–100) conforming almost exactly to the theoretical curve $n = 0.26$ (Wolpe, 1963). Curve C in Fig. 8 fits an exponential function [$(P = 76.11\ (1-0.85^n))$] a good deal better than a power function, but remains close enough to the power curve $n = 0.3$ not to constitute a damaging exception to the rule.

Awareness of these quantitative relations makes it possible both to predict in general at what stages, in cases of this class, progress will be slowest, and, more specifically, to calculate, after treatment has proceeded long enough to provide the essential data, how much more treatment will be needed to overcome a particular phobia. Furthermore, the curves characterizing different dimensions help the therapist to decide which dimension to work with first in a multidimensional hierarchy. For example, in a woman with a dread of being seen vomiting, the fear increased with numbers of witnesses and with proximity. The knowledge that the numbers curve accelerates negatively and the proximation curve positively led me first to present increasing numbers at a hundred yards. This allowed the number dimension to be mastered with very little effort. Then the numerous witnesses could be gradually brought closer. If the reverse order had been adopted I would ultimately have had to work at the steep ends of both curves simultaneously.

6. Some Snags and Pitfalls

Sometimes, despite having carried out the preliminaries conscientiously and apparently successfully, the therapist is chagrined to find that desensitization is not proceeding according to his expectations. Either the patient experiences no decrement of anxiety to successive presentations of scenes, or reports no improvement in his reactions to real situations to correspond with progress during sessions. Human variations are so complex and subtle that even the most extensive experience can provide no absolute insurance against disappointments. What the therapist must be able to do is to retrieve the situation. To do this he must first find out what accounts for his failure. The usual reasons are of three kinds, which will be discussed in turn.

1. Difficulties of relaxation.
2. Misleading or irrelevant hierarchies.
3. Inadequacies of imagery.

1. Difficulties of Relaxation   When relaxation is inadequate, efforts may be made to enhance it by doses of meprobamate, chlorpromazine, or codeine, or other tranquilizer given an hour before the interview. Which drug to use is a matter of trial and error. When pervasive ('free-floating') anxiety impedes relaxation, the use of carbon dioxide-oxygen mixtures by La Verne's single inhalation technique is of the greatest value, and with some patients comes to be used before every desensitization session. Inhalations are given until anxiety reaches an irreducible level—usually by the fourth inhalation. In a few patients who cannot relax but who are not pervasively anxious, attempts at desensitization may nonetheless succeed, presumably because interview-induced emotional responses inhibit the anxiety aroused by the imagined stimuli. This is a supposition that requires experimental testing.

Relaxation is sometimes enhanced by hypnosis. I employ, most often, the levitation technique described by Wolberg (1948). The patient may have been hypnotized in an exploratory way during one or more earlier interviews, but more often the first attempt at hypnosis is made during a desensitization session. In those who are difficult to hypnotize, the procedure is soon abandoned. But some patients certainly relax better in a formal hypnotic context.

The therapist may be under the impression that the patient is well relaxed when, in fact, he is not. A patient will often say that he feels relaxed when he is, in fact, moderately tense. This may be for various reasons. He may not yet be sufficiently aware of the internal indications of tension, or he may not think they are worth reporting, or it is so long since he has experienced a true state of calm that any substantial drop in tension *seems* like relaxation to him. The use of the quantitative subjective anxiety scale decreases the likelihood of miscommunications of this type occurring (though it does not eliminate them). The diagnosis can often be made by psychophysiological monitoring, for which the simplest indicator is auditory feedback from muscle potentials (Budzinski, Stoyva, and Adler, 1970; Leaf and Gaarder, 1971). It takes very careful questioning of the patient to reveal the true state of affairs; and then, of course, the therapist should intensify his efforts to improve relaxation either by further direct training or by the introduction of carbon dioxide or drugs (Chapter 9).

There are also patients who find it difficult to relax as part of a general fear of 'letting go.' Some of these make an effort to relax their muscles and perhaps succeed to an extent, but remain afraid. The autonomic excitations that comprise the anxiety response are unchanged, and may even increase. The solution to this problem varies. Sometimes it is possible to achieve a physiological state adequate for desensitization simply by telling the patient to get calm and comfortable in his own way, without attempting to 'let himself go.' In other cases, one may attempt prior desensitization of the fear of letting go by an *in vivo* method (Chapter 8) and then perhaps go on to attack all the other neurotic anxiety constellations in the same way. In yet others, one may have recourse to one or other of the electrical methods of counteracting anxiety, such as 'anxiety-relief' or the recently introduced non-aversive sensory interference technique (Chapter 7).

2. Misleading or Irrelevant Hierarchies   Even when the hierarchies he has obtained have none of the faults of conception or construction that may be imputed to elementary errors, there are occasions when the therapist finds himself making no headway. He should suspect that his hierarchies are off the track. Sometimes he is misled by the fact that the patient's fears are frequently experienced in certain contexts that are, in fact, only the occasion for fear, not its source. For example, after a man had been treated for 20 sessions with minimal benefit for claustrophobia and agoraphobia it was found that both were superimposed upon a fear of dying. He was anxious when his freedom of movement was restricted or when he was far from home because each of these conditions implied difficulty in getting help if he should collapse. While I was struggling with this patient, another man with very similar presenting phobias was responding to desensitization in classical fashion—for in him the space stimuli were the true antecedents of anxiety.

A common kind of case in which hierarchies are obtained which are not amenable to desensitization occurs in unhappily married women low in self-sufficiency (see p. 230). Apparently simple phobias, that have originated in the course of the marriage, turn out in reality to be fear reactions to stimulus situations related to some aspect of the marriage that evokes tension and aversion. This has also been independently noted by Fry (1962). These cases most frequently take the form of agoraphobia, and comprise the majority of cases of that syndrome. Such phobias may be regarded as true symbolic reactions, provided that the word 'symbolic' is understood in the conventional terms of semantics and learning theory, and not psychoanalytically. It is quite possible that encounters with cases having this feature are what led Freud to the presumption that all phobias have a hidden source.

An unusually instructive case of this kind, Case 9, was one that I treated as a demonstration in front of a group at Haverford State Hospital about 5 years ago. She was an attractive 26-year-old woman with four children who had been married at the age of 14 to a man who showed her no affection or even consideration. It was quite characteristic of him that, a few weeks after the marriage, he offered her as a sexual partner for the night to a friend of his who visited them. The patient wished desperately to get out of the marriage, but, being very low in self-sufficiency, was unable to do so, and in a matter of months became very fearful of going out alone, even for a distance of a few blocks. It was with this complaint, together with several others of phobic nature, that she presented herself for treatment. The history itself provided unusually clear evidence of the relevance of the marriage to the agoraphobia. About three years previously, the patient had met a man who had fallen in love with her and to whom she had felt attracted. She had gone to live with him for a month in another city, and during this time had been able to go about on her own any distance without the least discomfort. When she returned to her husband, the agoraphobia reappeared in full force. Her treatment followed three parallel lines — training in assertiveness, measures to enable her to move out of the common domicile with her husband, and desensitizing her to her other fears. Moving out became possible on the basis of an increase in self-sufficiency, achieved mainly by assertive training combined with arrangements for her to live elsewhere that took account of her rights in terms of the state laws of Pennsylvania. After about 9 months, she moved away to the house of a friend, and in the course of the first week the agoraphobia gradually disappeared. She stayed for one more week and then, for legal reasons, returned to live with her husband. There was then no recurrence of the agoraphobia because she now felt detached and free from her husband, and the thought of being alone was no longer threatening. She continued to put up with him for several more months, until arrangements for permanent separation were made, and ultimately, divorce.

A non-agoraphobic example, Case 10, is of a 34-year-old woman whose primary complaint was of a feeling of being closed in and a powerful urge to escape when engaged in conversations with adults — except interchanges on the most casual plane, such as asking the time. This reaction had begun eight years previously during the patient's first pregnancy. At the time when conditioning therapy began, no satisfactory precipitating cause of the neurosis could be elicited. She was trained in relaxation and the phobic stimuli taken at their face value. The first hierarchy to be used was based on the theme of being stared at, the patient's reactions increasing with the proximity of the starer. The scenes presented to her imagination aroused very little anxiety until a distance of 15 feet was reached—and then there was a *severe* reaction. Various other dimensions were then severally tried, including number of people at a distance, age of starer, duration of stare, and intensity of illumination—in each instance with the same consequence. It was obvious that something was being missed, but I could not tell what. I was about to abandon the case in despair when the patient, whom tranquilizers had helped but little, asked, "Is there nothing that could diminish my distress?" I replied, "At times of special stress you might try a little alcohol." After a long pause she said, "My husband doesn't let me drink." This was the first time I had heard her make an adverse remark about him; but it was the thin end of a wedge that prised open long-suppressed anger and frustration at his absolute domination over each and every one of her activities. The first pregnancy had precipitated the neurosis because it had seemed to block forever a way out of the marriage—which to the outer world and partly to herself she had represented as a great success.

The phobia now appeared to be primarily a fear of peering or prying. The impulse to get away from these situations summated with the claustrophobic feeling chronically engendered by the marriage. Thus, an unacknowledged life situation was the real basis of the phobia. Instigation to assertion with her husband now became the foremost therapeutic tactic. In case the reader is calculating that in *this* case psychoanalysis would have been the treatment of choice, it must be added that the patient had recently undergone psychoanalysis for two years without any success. The crucial aspects of the marital situation had not emerged during its course, in which, it appears, major attention was focused on oedipal attitudes and the like. The more specific rules of psychoanalytic practice often prove to be a straitjacket that prohibits the full exploration of a patient's reactive possibilities. In any event, the insight gained about the marriage did not of itself produce therapeutic effects.

3. Inadequacies of Imagery   Most patients are able to project themselves into imagined anxiety-evoking situations in a way that evokes something of the reality of the situations and a corresponding amount of anxiety. I have found this to be the case in about 90 percent of both South African and American patients. In England, however, the percentage may be considerably lower, according to my personal impression and recent comments by Meyer (1963). It may be that traditional English training that encourages underplaying manifestations of feeling also impairs the ability to associate emotion with imagery.

There are some patients who are unable to conjure up either visual or auditory images—at any rate, in response to the requirements of the therapist. Far more commonly, the trouble is that while images can be formed they have no sense of reality for the patient. Occasionally, action taken by the therapist leads to the difficulty being overcome. The action is of various kinds: providing much verbal detail of the situation to be imagined, inducing a 'deep' trance in good hypnotic subjects, or getting the patient to describe what he imagines. Darwin and McBrearty (1969) have found that in speech-anxious subjects significantly more rapid progress is made during desensitization if the patient describes the scenes instead of merely imagining them. An apparently effective program for the deliberate training of the capacity to imagine realistically has been put forward by Phillips (1971). All these efforts may be without avail; and therapeutic change is then dependent upon the use of the real stimuli, or their physical representations.

Occasional patients visualize satisfactorily until an advanced point in the hierarchy, and then seem to detach themselves from the imagined situations, viewing them as if from the standpoint of a disinterested spectator. An example is Case 34 in Chapter 14. He had a cleanliness compulsion of an extreme form, based upon a fear of contamination with his own urine. When transfer from the imaginary to the real situations ceased to occur, his relaxation was counterposed to real stimuli instead. On this basis the onslaught on his neurosis was brought to final victory.

RESULTS OF SYSTEMATIC DESENSITIZATION

It is useful to know how successful one may expect to be in applying desensitization to appropriate cases. In making a separate evaluation one should bear in mind that it is not a method *sui generis*, but merely a partic- ular application of a principle. In a statistical study (Wolpe, 1962), I used as subject matter 39 patients whose case records were extracted in random fashion from my therapeutic files. Many of these patients also had other neurotic habits that were treated by different methods deemed more appropriate.

The details of the study are tabulated in Table 3, in which outcome of treatment is indicated on a 5-point scale ranging from 4-plus to zero. A 4-plus rating means complete or almost complete freedom from phobic reactions to all situations in the area of the phobia *encountered in ac- tuality*. A 3-plus rating means an improvement of response such that the phobia is judged by the patient to have lost at least 80 percent of its

Table 3. Basic case data.

Patient Sex, Age	No. of Sessions	Hierarchy Theme	Outcome	Comments
1 F, 50	62	a Claustrophobia	++++	
		b Illness and hospitals	++++	
		c Death and its trappings	++++	
		d Storms	+++	
		e Quarrels	++++	
2 M, 40	6	a Guilt	++++	
		b Devaluation	++++	
3 F, 24	17	a Examinations	++++	See Case 4
		b Being scrutinized	++++	
		c Devaluation	++++	
		d Discord between others	++++	
4 M, 24	5	a Snakelike shapes	++++	
5 M, 21	24	a Being watched	++++	
		b Suffering of others	++++	
		c 'Jealousy' reaction	++++	
		d Disapproval	++++	
6 M, 28	5	Crowds	+++	
7 F, 21	5	Criticism	++++	
8 F, 52	21	a Being center of attention	0	No disturbance during scenes
		b Superstitions	0	Was in fact not imagining self in situation
9 F, 25	9	Suffering and death of others	+++	
10 M, 22	17	Tissue damage in others	++++	
11 M, 37	13	Actual or implied criticism	++++	
12 F, 31	15	Being watched working	+++	
13 F, 40	16	a 'Suffering' and eeriness	++++	This case has been
		b Being devalued	++++	reported in detail
		c Failing to come up to expectations	++++	(Wolpe, 1959)
14 M, 36	10	a Bright light	++++	
		b Palpitations	++++	
15 M, 43	9	Wounds and corpses	+++	
16 M,	51	a Being watched, especially at work	+++	No anxiety while being watched at
		b Being criticized	++++	work, Anxious at times while playing cards
17 M, 33	8	Being watched at golf	+++	

Table 3. (Contd.)

Patient Sex, Age	No. of Sessions	Hierarchy Theme	Outcome	Comments
18 M, 33	8	Talking before audience (stutterer)	0	No imagined scene was ever disturbing
19 M, 40	7	Authority figures	++++	
20 M, 23	4	Claustrophobia	++++	
21 F, 23	6	a Agoraphobia	0	Later successfully
		b Fear of falling	0	treated by conditioned motor response method
22 M, 46	19	a Being in limelight	+++	
		b Blood and death	++++	
23 F, 40	20	Social embarrassment	++++	
24 F, 28	9	Agoraphobia	0	
25 F, 48	7	Rejection	+++	
26 M, 28	13	a Disapproval	+++	
		b Rejection	++++	
27 M, 11	6	Authority figures	++++	
28 M, 26	217	a Claustrophobia	++++	
		b Criticism (numerous aspects)	+++	Finally overcome completely by use
		c Trappings of death	+++	of 'flooding'
29 F, 20	5	Agoraphobia	++++	
30 M, 68	23	a Agoraphobia	++++	
		b Masturbation	++++	
31 F, 36	5	Being in limelight	++++	
32 M, 26	17	a Illness and death	+++	
		b Own symptoms	+++	
33 F, 44	9	a Being watched	++++	
		b Elevators	++++	
34 F, 47	17	Intromission into vagina	+++	
35 M, 37	5	a Disapproval	++++	
		b Rejection	++++	
36 F, 32	25	Sexual stimuli	++++	
37 M, 36	21	a Agoraphobia	++++	
		b Disapproval	++++	
		c Being watched	++++	
38 M, 18	6	a Disapproval	+++	
		b Sexual stimuli	++++	Instrumental in overcoming impotence
39 F, 48	20	a Rejection	++++	Stutter markedly
		b Crudeness of others	++++	improved

Table 4. Summary of data of Table 3.

Patients	39
Number of patients responding to desensitization treatment	35
Number of hierarchies	68
Hierarchies overcome	45 ⎫
Hierarchies markedly improved	17 ⎬ 91%
Hierarchies unimproved	6 ⎫ 9%
Total number of desensitization sessions	762
Mean session expenditure per hierarchy	11.2
Mean session expenditure per successfully treated hierarchy	12.3
Median number of sessions per patient	10.0

original strength. A zero rating indicates that there is no definite change. It will be noted that only 4-plus, 3-plus and zero ratings were applicable to the patients in this series.

Table 4 summarizes the data given in Table 3. There were 68 anxiety-response habits among the 39 patients, of whom 19 had multiple hierarchies. The treatment was judged effective in 35 patients. Forty-five of the anxiety-response habits were apparently eliminated (4-plus rating) and 17 more markedly ameliorated (3-plus rating), making 90 percent in all. It is probable that many of the latter group would have reached a 4-plus level had there been additional sessions. In Cases 16 and 29, progress had diminished when sessions were discontinued, but not in any of the others.

Among the failures, Cases 8 and 18 were unable to imagine themselves within situations; Case 22 could not confine her imagining to the stated scene and repeatedly exposed herself to excessively disturbing images. She was later treated with complete success by the conditioned motor response method outlined on page 147. Case 25 had interpersonal reactions that led to erratic responses and, having experienced no benefit, sought therapy elsewhere.

The mean number of sessions per phobia was 11.2; the median number of sessions per patient 10.0. It should be noted that a desensitization session usually takes up only part of a ¾-hour interview period, and in cases that also have non-phobic neurotic problems there may be other interviews in which a desensitization session does not occur, and these are not included in this tally.

CHAPTER 7

Variants of Systematic Desensitization

The advantage of having a principle to utilize is that it provides the potentiality of generating logically parallel variations of tested procedures. If conventional systematic desensitization proves to be unsuitable in a particular case or class of cases, attempts can hopefully be made to implement, in other ways, the principle of reciprocally inhibiting small 'doses' of anxiety at a time. And even where conventional desensitization is quite successful, it is worth experimenting with other elaborations of the principle because of the possibility of their being more efficient or economical.

Several variations of technique are described in this chapter. Some of them have been held in reserve to be tried when conventional desensitization cannot be successfully carried out. Others have been the subject of controlled experiments that suggest them to be superior to conventional desensitization at least for the kinds of neurotic fears figuring in the experiments.

The desensitization variants can be divided into three categories: 1. Technical variations of the standard consulting-room procedure, 2. Alternative counter-anxiety responses for use with imaginal stimuli, and 3. Methods involving the use of exteroceptive sources of anxiety.

TECHNICAL VARIATIONS OF THE STANDARD DESENSITIZATION PROCEDURE

The essence of systematic desensitization is the presentation of graded imaginal stimuli to a relaxed patient. There are ways of carrying it out that reduce the amount of time the therapist has to spend with his patients, and increase the number he can see. One way is to automate some of the procedures so that they do not need the physical presence of the therapist. The second consists of desensitizing patients with similar neurotic fears in groups.

1. Mechanical Aids to Systematic Desensitization

Lang (1966) was the first to demonstrate that desensitization could be successfully accomplished by a machine. Phobias for snakes were overcome by the use of two tape recorders, one carrying hierarchy items and the other relaxation instructions. The patient controlled buttons to obtain relaxation, repetition, change, or cessation of scene. Taking a cue from Lang's observations, Migler and Wolpe (1967) used a single specially modified tape recorder to treat a patient who was severely disturbed by inferred disapproval and derision, especially when he was speaking to a group. The patient himself recorded both the hierarchy items and the relaxation instructions under supervision. He then took the tape recorder home and completely desensitized himself in seven sessions. He was free from his original fears when followed up two years later.

The following technical details are reproduced with minor modifications from Migler and Wolpe (1967). One may use either a Wollensak T-1600 tape recorder or a Uher Universal 5000, each of which has two necessary features. First, it has a pause switch by which the tape motions can be instantly stopped. This switch is connected to a microswitch which the patient can hold in his hand and, as desired, stop the tape motion at any time, for any duration. Second, the recorder has two metal sensing strips on each side of the recording heads. When a metal foil which has been placed on the tape makes contact with the two sensing strips on the right side an internal circuit is closed and the tape recorder automatically switches from playback to rewind. These two strips are, for the present purpose, bypassed by the tape and a pushbutton wired in parallel with them, so that now momentary depression of the pushbutton switches the recorder from playback to rewind. The second pair of sensing guides, to the left of the recording heads, functions to stop the rewinding and return to playback when another specially placed metal foil reaches these guides. This is not altered. The pushbutton and the microswitch are held together by adhesive tape, to make a combined remote control unit that the patient can hold in his hand. Depression of the microswitch (hereafter called the 'pause switch') stops the playback for as long as it is depressed. Momentary depression of the pushbutton (hereafter called the 'repeat button') produces the following sequential effects: the tape recorder stops playback and switches to rewind; rewinding continues until a metal foil is detected by the sensing guides to the left of the recording head; and when rewinding has stopped, playback begins again.

In preparing the tape for desensitization Migler and Wolpe took the following steps. (They used the patient's voice throughout.)

1. Relaxation instructions were taped—"Relax your calves, thighs, forearms, upper arms, shoulders, neck, jaws, forehead, etc." (In using this section of the tape, the patient was instructed to press the pause switch after each anatomical part was named and concentrate on that part until it felt free of muscular tension, then to release the pause switch and let the tape continue.)

2. A metal foil was attached to the tape at the end of the relaxation instructions. A similar metal foil came after each scene recorded on the tape. Their function is given in steps below.

3. Just beyond the metal foil (and before the first scene) were a few brief relaxation instructions: "Relax your arms, legs, stomach, chest, neck, and all your facial muscles. Now pause until you feel relaxed." (The patient was instructed to press the pause switch at this point until he felt relaxed.)

4. Following these relaxation instructions, the tape contained instructions to visualize the first scene in the hierarchy:—"Now imagine, etc." Pause. (The patient was instructed to press the pause switch at this point until the visualization was clear, and then to let the tape continue.)

5. Ten seconds of recorded silence followed the instruction to pause, permitting ten seconds of clear visualization. The silence was terminated by the words, "Stop visualizing it. Press the repeat button if that scene disturbed you at all." (If the patient felt any negative emotional response to the scene he was to press the repeat button, which would rewind the tape back to the metal foil (Step 2 above) so that the brief relaxation instructions, the scene, and the remainder of the sequence would recur. If the repeat button was not pressed, the tape recorder continued to the next metal foil, which, like the first, was followed by relaxation instructions, after which came Scene 2 of the hierarchy—and so forth.)

These elaborate arrangements make it easy for the patient to carry out desensitization. Much simpler equipment that can take its place, at much lower cost, calls for more effort from the patient. The first essay of this kind was by Kahn and Baker (1968) who devised a phonograph recording that patients could use at home for any hierarchy. It contains instructions for scene presentations followed by silence into which the patient inserts his imaginery hierarchical scenes as directed beforehand by the therapist. Relaxation instructions precede each scene, and the recording is worded in such a way that the patient can repeat a particular scene as many times as necessary.

Tape recorders are now widely used for desensitization at home. Very inexpensive ones are quite suitable. They offer far more flexibility than a phonograph recording. Denholtz (1971) has described the home use of tape recorders for both relaxation training and the presentation of anxiety-evoking scenes. Each relaxation lesson is recorded during the treatment session on the patient's own tape, which he then takes home ".... having been instructed to play it twice daily until his next visit. At subsequent visits, instructions are taped again, becoming progressively shorter because the patient is becoming conditioned to relaxation. Eventually the instructions are usually only 2–5 min long." The procedure is ".... particularly valuable for the not uncommon patient who is simply too anxious in the presence of the therapist to be able to let go. .... Some of these patients... learn relaxation in this way at home, and can later do it in the office."

For the purpose of homework desensitization, Denholtz usually tapes one scene from each hierarchy at each session. ".... If, however, there are a variety of settings that belong to a particular hierarchical step, (he) may tape as many as three scenes for that step. It is always important to ensure that the taped scenes evoke only a small amount of anxiety — generally no more than 10–15 units on the *sud* scale. Relaxation instructions are renewed between scenes. .... The patient is told to use this tape recording daily until his next session when he will usually report no longer having anxiety to any of the taped scenes. He is then ready to move upward in the hierarchy." It is not surprising that the use of such homework material reduces the amount of time the therapist has to spend with the patient.

2. Group Desensitization

If several patients suffer from the same phobia, it is reasonable to expect that, after having been trained to relax, they might be desensitized simultaneously, even if the slopes of their hierarchies (p. 130) are not identical, provided that the therapist ensures that each scene has ceased to evoke anxiety in every patient before proceeding to the next scene. Obviously, this arrangement can be very time-saving for the therapist. For example, an average of less than 2 hours of therapist's time per client was expended by Paul and Shannon (1966) in the treatment of severe 'social evaluative' anxiety in college students, manifested by fear and disablement in public-speaking situations. At a two-year follow-up, Paul (1968) found that the improvement achieved by this treatment had been maintained or increased.

It is possible that part of the reason why Paul and Shannon's patients were more rapidly desensitized is that exteroceptive stimuli from the other members of the group were involved in the deconditioning maneuvers. This possibility seemed in a small way to be supported by an experience I had in 1966 during a series of behavior therapy seminars, in which I invited all participants with fears of public speaking to submit to group desensitization in front of the class of 30. Eight volunteered. The treatment sessions—each lasting 15 minutes—took place at the end of a two-hour seminar. The group sat before me in the front row of the lecture room. The first session was devoted to relaxation training, with which they were already familiar, and which some of them had already been practicing. At subsequent sessions, imaginary scenes of speaking in public were presented to the group. The first scene was speaking to an audience of three. By the fifth desensitization sessions, the five of these subjects who went through with the therapy were able to imagine themselves speaking to a group of 50 without anxiety. Evidence of transfer to the real situation was subsequently obtained from two of the participants. One of them reported giving a lecture to a group of 75 without any anxiety at all. Since the total time spent on the group therapy was 90 minutes, then for the five subjects who completed the course we have a mean therapist time expenditure per patient per phobia of 18 minutes. While it is not wise to infer too much from this somewhat casual experiment, it does suggest that therapeutic change may have been accelerated by the subjects' awareness of sitting in a group while desensitization to imaginary groups was being carried out. There is a preponderance of evidence suggesting that desensitization with real stimuli is more potent than that with imaginary ones. These subjects had both.

Successful treatment in group settings has been reported for a variety of phobias, e.g. test situations (Donner and Guerney, 1969; Cohen and Dean, 1968; and Ihli and Garlington, 1969). Donner and Guerney (1969) used an automated technique with the groups and, at a follow-up, Donner

(1970) found that the gains had been maintained. Robinson and Suinn (1969) reported on the group treatment of spider phobias using massed desensitization sessions.

Group desensitization has also been part of a general group behavior therapy program (Goldstein and Wolpe, 1971). Each patient is first seen individually so that the therapist may take a history, perform a behavioral analysis, and decide on the goals of therapy. Group therapy is recommended when the patient has special problems in personal interactions. Five to seven patients and one or two therapists take part in a group. One advantage of the group setting is that the therapist is able to observe the patient's behavior in response to various other people; it may elicit behavior patterns of which the patient may not have been clearly aware. The first session lasts about two hours during which structure is minimal; the therapist stating that, since all the patients have similar problems, the initial sessions will largely be devoted to getting acquainted. The therapist then assumes the role of a facilitator to initiate the development of a suitable interactive atmosphere. By the fifth meeting, the sessions last between three and five hours. Since each session has to involve each patient in some concentrated way, it is necessary to allow approximately 45 minutes per patient, although the time is not allotted in any set way. The procedures mainly used are modeling, behavior rehearsal, and *in vivo* desensitization.

ALTERNATIVE COUNTER-ANXIETY RESPONSES FOR USE WITH IMAGINAL STIMULI

1. Therapist-evoked Responses

There is no doubt that the psychotherapeutic interview itself evokes emotional responses in many patients. Sometimes the emotion is anxiety, but more often, it would seem, it is a mixture of hopeful expectation, confidence in the expert, and other positive emotions conditioned to doctors and their consulting rooms. Altogether, it probably corresponds to the psychoanalyst's 'positive transference' in the loose sense. When it occurs, it is capable of inhibiting relatively weak anxiety responses that are verbally evoked during the interview (Wolpe, 1958, p. 193). It is probably the chief basis for the very similar psychotherapeutic effects that therapies other than behavior therapy obtain (Eysenck, 1952, 1965). Of course, behavior therapists profit from it as well, but only to a relatively minor extent indicated, perhaps, by the amount of change found in the 'attention-placebo' group of Paul's (1966) controlled study (see p. 270).

The foregoing effects of therapist-evoked emotion are inadvertent and unsystematic. It is, however, possible to make systematic use of it. In subjects who are unable to learn to relax or who resist 'letting-go' it is still worth presenting hierarchical scenes in the hope that therapist-evoked emotion will inhibit the anxiety. It is, apparently, the usual basis of successful desensitization without relaxation. In addition, it probably plays a leading part in desensitization *in vivo* (see below). Under the present heading, however, we shall be concerned with those modes of anxiety-inhibition that the therapist can deliberately induce.

2. Responses Triggered by Electrical Stimulation

1. Desensitization Based on Inhibition of Anxiety by a Conditioned Motor Response   This technique, first reported a good many years ago (Wolpe, 1954), has been used very little, although it has a very credible experimental basis. It was suggested by an observation by Mowrer and Viek (1948) that if the noxious stimulus applied to an animal is constantly discontinued when the animal performs a definite motor response, upon repetition of the stimulation the animal develops conditioned inhibition of the autonomic responses that are evoked at the same time. By contrast, an experimental twin that receives exactly the same duration of noxious stimulation terminated at each due time without reference to the animal's motor behavior fails to develop any inhibition of the emotional response which, instead, is likely to increase.

In the clinical application of this finding, the patient with an anxiety hierarchy is asked to imagine a scene in the usual way and to signal when the image is clear. The therapist then passes a fairly mild shock into the forearm, in response to which the patient flexes his arm, having been instructed in advance to do so. In an extreme case of agoraphobia that was successfully treated by this method and is elsewhere described in detail (Wolpe, 1958, p. 174), it was found that 15 to 25 flexions were generally needed to bring down to zero the anxiety response to a disturbing scene.

In the case referred to, flexion of the arm seemed indispensable for decreasing the anxiety response. But since we now know that weak electrical stimulation without a motor response can also weaken anxiety habits (see below), we may wonder how much the motor response really contributed to the change that was noted. However, there is some clinical data that suggests that muscle activity can be an anxiety-inhibiting agent (Wolpin and Raines, 1966; Farmer and Wright, 1971).

2. *External Inhibition* The possibility of utilizing this phenomenon (Pavlov, 1927, p.46) became apparent to me a few years ago while observing Dr. William M. Philpott perform a rather elaborate procedure to eliminate conditioned anxiety with the aid of mild electric shocks. The patient was lying on a couch with electrodes strapped to his forearm and with his eyes closed. He was given a scene to imagine, and, when he indicated that it was clearly formed, the therapist called out words on the following pattern: "Muscles of the arms, respond to the will; relax". Some controlled experiments that I shortly afterwards organized at the University of Virginia showed that the verbal patter was unnecessary and in itself ineffective, and that the weak electrical stimuli could produce all the effects demonstrated by Philpott. It seemed that the kind of interference typical of external inhibition was at work.

Shorn of redundancies, the technique is as follows. Encircling the patient's forearm are two saline-soaked gauze strips, 1½ in. wide, one just above the wrist and the other about 3 in. higher. Each strip is held in place by a stainless steel alligator clip connected to the source of current—a 90-volt dry cell whose output is controlled by a 50,000 ohm variable resistor. (Silver electrodes may be used instead of the gauze strips.) Pulses are delivered by the therapist pressing on a soft pushbutton switch for about half-a-second. The level of current correct for the patient is that which is strongly felt *without being aversive*. In some cases a very weak pulse suffices; in others no therapeutic effects occur until the electrical stimulus is strong enough to produce vigorous contraction of the forearm muscles. (It has frequently been noted that if the patient has pervasive anxiety 8 to 10 pulses per minute will gradually reduce it, so that in 20 or 30 minutes it may be brought down from 60 *suds* or more to zero.)

Once the appropriate level of shock has been established, the desensitizing procedure is begun. First, the weakest item in the hierarchy is presented alone once or twice to the patient's imagination in order to determine how many *suds* it evokes. He is then asked to imagine the scene again and to signal by raising his index finger when it is well-defined. At this point, the therapist administers two brief stimuli of the predetermined strength separated by about a second. After about five seconds, the patient is instructed again to imagine the scene, signaling as before.

After a series of 5 to 20 repetitions, a check is made on the status of his reaction to the scene by presenting it without any shock.

An early case to be treated by this method was a woman whose many-faceted neurosis had been largely overcome by the usual behavior therapy methods. An important remaining neurotic problem was a phobia for driving alone. Originally, she had been unable to drive up her own drive-way without feeling anxious. With conventional desensitization, she had progressed steadily, though slowly, until she was able to drive three-quarters of a mile without any discomfort. But a disturbing incident half-a-mile from home had set her back to that distance. Rather than resume the desensitization that had been so tedious, I decided to try external inhibition. Mild stimulation proved to be completely ineffective; but shocks strong enough to cause muscle contraction while she visu-alized herself at that critical place half-a-mile from home led to decreasing anxiety. With 20 repetitions of the scene the anxiety decreased to zero. The procedure was then repeated for the ¾-mile point. When she later tested herself at that point, she found herself completely free from anxiety. Continuing this method, the patient made much more rapid progress than she had previously done with conventional desensitization.

3. Responses Evoked by Verbally-induced Imagery

Falling under this heading are three methods — emotive imagery, induced anger, and direct suggestion. In the first of these, the emotional state counter active to anxiety is evoked by the setting into which the anxiety-evoking stimuli are introduced; in the latter two, it depends on repeated and insistent verbal inputs, and the setting is mainly background.

1. Emotive Imagery   This is the name of a procedure, first described by Lazarus and Abramovitz (1962), in which hierarchical stimuli are presented to the patient in an imaginary situation in which other elements evoke responses antagonistic to anxiety. These responses thus take the place of relaxation as the source of inhibition of anxiety.

One of their cases was a 12-year-old boy who greatly feared darkness. In the room he shared with his brother, a light constantly shone at night next to his bed. He was especially afraid in the bathroom, which he only used if accompanied by another member of the household. Attempts at relaxation training had failed. The child had a passion for two radio serials, 'Superman' and 'Captain Silver.' He was asked to imagine that Superman and Captain Silver had appointed him their agent. Subsequent procedure was as follows:

The therapist said, "Now I want you to close your eyes and imagine that you are sitting in the dining-room with your mother and father. It is night time. Suddenly, you receive a signal on the wrist radio that Superman has given you. You quickly run into the lounge because your mission must be kept a secret. There is only a little light coming into the lounge from the passage. Now pretend that you are all alone in the lounge waiting for Superman and Captain Silver to visit you. Think about this very clearly. If the idea makes you feel afraid, lift up your right hand."

An on-going scene was terminated as soon as there was any indication of anxiety. When an image had aroused anxiety, it would either be repeated in a more challengingly assertive manner, or altered slightly so as to appear less threatening. At the end of the third session, the child was able to picture himself alone in the bathroom with all the lights turned off, awaiting a communication from Superman. There was complete transfer to the real situation. A follow-up 11 months later revealed that the gains had been maintained.

The technique has also been used with adults. For example, a man with a claustrophobia that was especially related to theatres and restaurants was instructed to imagine himself seated in a theatre (at the aisle in the back row, initially) watching a striptease. The sexual arousal inhibited the weak anxiety response and was thus the basis for part of the deconditioning of the latter.

2. Induced Anger This procedure, which Goldstein, Serber, and Piaget (1970) found effective in six out of ten cases, consists of getting the patient to pair anger-arousing imagery (augmented by appropriate vocal and motor behavior) with fear-arousing imagined scenes (or real stimuli in the consulting room). Later, the patient uses the images to arouse anger in spontaneously occurring fear-producing real-life situations. The concern that such treatment might leave patients angry instead of fearful has not been borne out by experience. They ultimately become indifferent to the previously disturbing stimuli, supporting the viewpoint that the essential therapeutic process is the conditioning of inhibition of fear responses to the particular stimuli.

One of their cases was Mr. F., aged 23, who complained of fears of riding public conveyances, walking in certain neighborhoods, and being in the presence of seemingly aggressive people. These fears more or less confined him to his home. He ventured out only to attend therapy sessions, walking an excessive distance to avoid public transport and certain streets.

Although some progress was made in systematic desensitization to the fear of buses, none occurred in the area of interpersonal situations. When asked to imagine even very weak interpersonal scenes, Mr. F. would reach near-panic states which completely destroyed the previously achieved tenuous relaxed state. He was then asked to imagine being accosted on the street by an aggressive man (a reconstruction of an actual past event). When he felt afraid he was to imagine punching the man. Mr. F. found that he was unable to imagine effectively punching the man because each imagined episode of attack led to a sequence in which the attempted blow missed. But by starting with imagining simply talking back to the man and gradually increasing the amount of aggressiveness, Mr. F. was eventually able to imagine effectively punching, kicking, and finally chopping the man up with an axe. With each increase of aggression less fear and more anger was felt. At one point, he said, "I feel like screaming and actually hitting something." He was given a large pillow and encouraged to do so and vocalize according to his feelings. Thereafter, his images of being accosted on the street were accompanied by actual screaming of obscenities, pounding on the pillow, and imaginary counter-aggression. After 3 sessions of 10 repetitions per session of scenes appropriate to his fears, Mr. F. reported complete freedom of fear in most of the situations which had previously been frightening and said that he was traveling freely wherever he desired. He still felt somewhat fearful at plays and some movies if there were a number of people in the audience who seemed to him to epitomize aggressiveness. He was instructed to continue to attend these places and upon becoming anxious to imagine getting up on the stage and mowing down the audience with a machine gun. He did so and developed other variations of imagined aggression which led to his being able to attend theatres with complete absence of fear. *No hostile feeling took the place of the fear*; the result was complete indifference to the audience. At a 6-month follow-up Mr. F. reported that he was free of fears, was planning marriage, and was going to attend graduate school in a distant city.

In another of their cases the anxiety-evoking stimuli were countered by the anger *in vivo*. This was a 34-year-old woman with a history of severe and constant anxiety coupled with feelings of dizziness and unsteadiness in the legs. She felt relatively calm only when sitting down at home in the presence of her husband or close friends. She was fearful of losing her balance, or, if away from home, of being unable to return.

Behavior analysis showed that her anxiety was most severe at the anticipation of an anxiety-evoking situation. Standard desensitization had failed because the patient did not become anxious at imaginary scenes; and *in vivo* desensitization had failed because the fear aroused by the real situations was too great to be inhibited by her muscle relaxation.

It was then that the patient was taught the expression of anger, to be used later contiguously with anxiety-producing stimuli. She was shown how to express righteous indignation at the top of her lungs: "I'm not afraid! I don't want to be afraid! It is stupid and unfair—I will not be afraid!" She accentuated this verbal behavior by punching a pillow in front of her. Three training sessions were given and the patient was requested to practice at home for half-an-hour a day. She was instructed to expose herself to various situations that disturbed her, such as standing alone in a locked room for 10 mins and using the anger responses she had practiced whenever she had any awareness of disturbance. Therapy was terminated after a total of 19 sessions. Six months later she was free of all symptoms.

3. Direct Suggestion   Rubin (1972) has described a variant of systematic desensitization that depends on inducing various responses, often including relaxation, by strong verbal suggestion. It seems likely that suggested counter-anxiety responses are the key feature of this technique, although Rubin presents them as part of a package. One feature of this is a detailed explanation of how the patient acquired his undesirable habit through learning and how the stimuli concerned, when juxtaposed with a different response, will come to evoke the latter instead. Another feature is to tell the patient not actually to imagine a particular scene until the therapist gives a prearranged signal. Scenes are generally presented to the patient's imagination without regard to their hierarchical position, but a weaker scene is used if the chosen one is found to be too distressful.

Rubin's technique may be illustrated by reference to one of his cases — a 37-year-old woman who had conditioned anxiety reactions to numerous situations, including sitting at the dining table, applying cosmetics, sitting down to work, and going to the beauty shop. All of these reactions had ramified from an occasion two years previously when she had been seized with trembling of her hands while drinking coffee in a restaurant at the same time as she became aware of a feeling of posterior cervical spasm. An important background fact was that, five years previously, her mother had suffered a stroke which had rendered her aphasic. The thought had crossed the patient's mind that the cervical spasm had implications of an impending stroke. The following is the edited continuation of a transcript of Rubin's treatment after he had explained to her how serial conditioning had eventuated from the original anxiety experience:

> Now I am going to describe a series of scenes to you. Please listen carefully while I describe them, but do not attempt to visualize until I have given you the proper signal of counting to three. You will indicate that visualization is taking place by raising your index finger and dropping it only when visualization is complete.
>
> The very first scene that I would like you to visualize is one in which you are sitting down to eat in your own kitchen. You have prepared a delicious-looking filet mignon and you are quite hungry. As you sit there eating the filet, you feel quite comfortable and relaxed, and it is such a wonderful feeling to enjoy the food and feel relaxed. You are really not worried or concerned. You do have a feeling of some pain and discomfort in the back of your head and neck, but in spite of this you feel good. It is such a wonderful feeling to sit there feeling relaxed and enjoying the food. When I count to three, you may begin to visualize and indicate this to me by raising the index finger of your left hand and keep it elevated until visualization is completed.

As long as the patient indicated satisfactory visualization, the description was augmented by comments similar to those given initially. Additional scenes were now offered—applying cosmetics, being seated while at work, visiting and eating at other people's homes, eating in restaurants, and other situations which would ordinarily provoke anxiety. The following excerpts from the transcript dealing with visiting the beauty shop show how the therapist used his own experiences to augment the intended effects.

> You go to the hairdresser's. You are familiar with the place and you enter feeling very comfortable and relaxed. I know that when I go to the barber, it is an opportunity for me to relax and, frequently, I almost doze off. Sometimes, because of the position I am in, I develop some pain and discomfort in my head and neck. However, it doesn't disturb or frighten me, and that is exactly the way I want you to feel. So, when I give you the proper signal, I want you to picture yourself in the beauty shop feeling very comfortable and relaxed. You have some discomfort in the back of your head and neck, but it doesn't worry you or disturb you. You realize that it has no significance. It certainly does not indicate that you are going to have a stroke, and so, when I count to three, please start feeling calm and relaxed.

The patient was seen a total of four times, improving markedly, so that she was able to return to work. A follow-up nine months later revealed that all the improvement was maintained.

This technique makes the hypnotist's repertoire of response evocation available to the practice of behavior therapy. The common form of hypnotic therapy, which has consisted of 'suggest away' symptoms or reactions, leaning largely on post-hypnotic suggestion, has been notoriously unimpressive. Rubin's technique brings directly suggested responses into direct opposition with anxiety responses. It is worth noting that something like this seems to have been done at times by Bernheim (1895).

Initial attempts in the Behavior Therapy Unit to utilize this procedure, albeit in a modified way, have been encouraging. The first case I treated, 15 months ago, was markedly changed after a single session. The patient was a 45-year-old executive who had just begun a $50,000 a year job which entailed a great deal of flying. Following a fearful experience 10 years previously, he had developed a severe aerophobia. Because he had come from Boston to consult me and was due to fly half-way across America a few days later, I decided to try counterconditioning by direct suggestion. I elicited from him aspects of being in a plane to which he reacted pleasantly – the feeling of freedom, the decor, and the reassuring tones of the Captain's voice. I then had him close his eyes and imagine that he was sitting in a stationary chamber with the decor of a plane and strongly responding to the foregoing pleasant stimulations. When he indicated that he was having the required feelings at considerable strength, I had him imagine that the chamber was in motion as in flight. He was able to sustain this image without any anxiety for several minutes. I then instructed him to practice the image several times a day, and told him that on boarding the plane he was to focus his attention on the pleasant aspects and respond to them exclusively. After the scheduled flight, he telephoned to say that he had had slight anxiety initially and then none. Four months later, he informed a behavior therapist in Boston to whom I had referred him for other kinds of problems about the 'miraculous cure' of his fear of flying in a single session, enabling him to fly all over the country freely.

4. Responses Due to Special Physical Maneuvers

This heading covers practices mainly associated with the Far East – Oriental defense exercises, transcendental meditation, and Yoga. An Occidental paradigm is also now available for tapping: Cabanac (1971) has shown that physical stimuli can be made pleasurable by applying them against a suitable background state – e.g. localized cold against general hotness. Methods involving the more commonplace activity of reading (Everaerd, 1970 and Stoffelmayr, 1970) may well be considered in the same category.

1. Oriental Defense Exercises   In two cases who could not be satisfactorily treated by standard desensitization, Gershman and Stedman

(1971) used Oriental defense exercises as the source of reciprocal inhibition of anxiety, on the reasonable supposition that "if a therapist identifies a counterconditioner which is idiosyncratic to a patient it is likely to have special therapeutic efficacy."

One of their cases was a man who routinely practiced karate to keep himself in physical condition. His fear of flying was treated by having him imagine flying situations in hierarchical order, and, at each presentation, engage in vigorous karate exercises. In two sessions, anxiety to all items was reduced to zero on the *sud* scale.

In their other case, Kung Fu exercises were rapidly effective in overcoming a severe claustrophobia by having the patient initiate them immediately upon locking him in a room. The periods of his confinement were progressively increased from 10 seconds to 1 hour, and the duration of 'Kung Fu-ing' progressively diminished though, if the patient at any time felt a twinge of anxiety, he could again resort to the exercises to dissipate it.

Six-month follow-ups found both of these patients free from the anxiety habits that had been treated. It seems likely that motor competition is the basis of these changes; but the role of concomitant emotional effects cannot be ruled out.

2. Yoga   Insofar as the practices of yoga lead to control of autonomic responses, their potential as a means to breaking unadaptive emotional habits is obvious. Boudreau (1972) has described the case of a 40-year-old schoolteacher whose severe suffering from excessive perspiration was only partially alleviated by assiduous practice of muscle relaxation. She then took a summer course of training in yoga exercises. Her practice consisted of a half-hour daily of yoga exercises, with additional practice during tense moments. After three months of practice of this technique, her mild perspiration decreased to below one hour every day while her excessive perspiration disappeared.

Barber's (1970) studies indicate the considerable therapeutic potentialities residing in yoga.

3. Transcendental Meditation   Wallace (1970) has reported physiological changes during transcendental meditation, including decreased metabolic rate, increased skin resistance, and diminished heart rate. Boudreau (1972) made use of this observation in the treatment of a college student with several disabling phobias. At first, systematic desensitization was tried without noticeable improvement. At this point, the patient indicated that he was adept at transcendental meditation. He was instructed to practice meditation following imaginal phobic scenes for a half-hour every day and also at the actual appearance of fear-evoking situations. Marked improvement followed. Within one month, the avoidance behavior to enclosed places, being alone, and elevators had all disappeared. Once his tension level had decreased, he did not experience abnormal physiological sensations, and this reassured him as to his physical and mental state.

5. Responses Produced by Relief from Distress

These substitutes for relaxation in the context of standard desensitization have developed out of the anxiety-relief paradigm (Wolpe, 1958) which had its original use for overcoming anxiety in real-life settings.

1. Aversion Relief The essence of this method, which was first employed by Thorpe, *et al.* (1964), is to present a phobic stimulus to the subject at the moment that he presses a button to terminate a continuous unpleasant electrical stimulation. Solyom and Miller (1965) and Solyom (1969) have made extensive use of the following modified procedure.

The patient, who has prepared a tape recording consisting of both past and possible anxiety-provoking events, is seated in an armchair, separated from the experimenter by a one-way screen. Items from this tape recording are presented to him, one at a time, through earphones. After a period of silence about 30 seconds long, an unpleasant electrical stimulation is administered to the patient's finger. By pressing a button, he terminates the electric shock and at the same time sets off an anxiety item from his tape. For example, a cat phobic patient might, upon pressing the button, hear her own voice saying, "I see a gray cat" simultaneously with the cessation of the shock. The intensity of shock is determined for each individual by selecting the main point between his shock reception and shock tolerance thresholds. Solyom and Miller have summarized the treatment of 8 patients, among whom 6 were free from fears after a mean of 19.5 treatment sessions—without symptom substitution at follow-up.

2. Respiratory Relief A similar method that appears to have emerged independently of the foregoing is respiratory relief (Orwin, 1971). The patient is asked to hold his breath voluntarily as long as he can and to signal when he can no longer maintain it. At that moment the phobic stimulus is presented to his imagination so that the relief that comes on with the resumption of breathing can compete with the anxiety. Orwin states that 6 patients rapidly lost life-long phobias. Four spider-phobic patients were able to touch a spider in one or two 30-minute sessions. One of them subsequently allowed a large house spider to run over her hands and arms without concern. The phobic constituents of chronic obsessional conditions were also "surprisingly easily controlled by respiratory relief" and all patients showed marked improvement.

I have recently tried this method on two patients with some indication of its effectiveness in one of them. The technical simplicity of the method makes it worth investigating.

6. Pharmacological Inhibition of Anxiety by Carbon Dioxide-Oxygen Inhalation

The powerful effect that carbon dioxide-oxygen has in reducing pervasive anxiety (page 182) has made it appear a potentially valuable agent for overcoming specific anxiety habits as well. Philpott (1967) reported that he had been able to use the gas in this way by presenting hierarchical stimuli while the patient inhaled the gas so as to maintain a moderate degree of hyperventilation for several seconds.

During the past years, I have several times had occasion to attempt desensitization with carbon dioxide by this method. In each case, marked effects were obtained, and it was possible to present scenes much higher up the hierarchy than would be possible using relaxation. In a case of classroom phobia, apparent recovery was obtained in two sessions. In an unusual phobia for certain configurations of the opposite sex that had resisted all other available methods, it took eight sessions to obtain marked reduction in anxiety responses to the stimuli concerned presented *in vivo* during inhalations two to three minutes long. The indications are that this gas is a particularly powerful anxiety-inhibitor and deserves extensive clinical trials.

DESENSITIZATION USING EXTEROCEPTIVE STIMULI TO ANXIETY

An exteroceptive stimulus is one that comes from outside the body of the responding organism, by contrast with an endogenous stimulus that originates within the organism—e.g. a visceral sensation or a mental image. The exteroceptive stimuli that are employed in desensitization are either actual feared objects or pictorial representations of them. The former, have until now, been by far the more widely used. A variety of counter-anxiety responses have been involved, as will be indicated. The procedures fall into two main classes—(a) *in vivo* desensitization; in which exteroceptive stimuli are presented to the patient in graded amounts on the general lines of conventional desensitization, and (b) *modelling*; in which the patient observes a fearless subject make increasingly intimate contact with a feared object.

1. *In vivo* Desensitization

It has often been a practical policy to ask patients to try exposing themselves in reality to situations to which they have just been desensitized in imagination. For example, a person with a fear of driving is asked to go out driving up to the last desensitized point. I used to regard this as a consolidating maneuver and a means of getting 'feedback.' A controlled study by Garfield, Darwin, Singer, and McBrearty (1967) indicates that it positively accelerates desensitization. Sherman (1972) has reported a similar finding, but because he worked with weak fears the applicability of his findings to clinical conditions is uncertain (Bernstein and Paul, 1971).

Desensitization *in vivo* has its chief indication as the prime method in the 10 or 15 percent of patients in whom imaginal stimuli are useless for desensitization because they do not arouse emotional responses similar to those produced by the corresponding real situations. Cooke (1966) found that in snake phobias desensitization proceeded with the same speed, whether imagined or real stimuli were used.

The successful use of real-life graduated exposures in an institutional setting was first reported by Terhune (1948) working empirically and without awareness of the learning principles involved. The first account of *in vivo* therapy directly based on the desensitization paradigm was in connection with two agoraphobic cases treated by Meyer (1957). It was followed in 1960 by Freeman and Kendrick's report of the overcoming of a cat phobia by getting the patient to handle pieces of material progressively similar to cat fur, exposing her to pictures of cats, then a toy kitten, followed by a real kitten, and eventually grown cats. A phobia for earthworms was treated in a similar way by Murphy (1964). More recently, Goldberg and D'Zurilla (1968) have overcome fears of receiving injections by the use of slide projections of the stages of activity involved in an injection; and Dengrove (1968) has used moving film to overcome phobias for bridges.

Desensitization *in vivo* is usually quite a straightforward affair, though obviously less convenient than conventional desensitization. The above mentioned therapists relied on interpersonal and other 'natural' stimuli to evoke anxiety-inhibiting emotional responses and this often suffices; but relaxation (e.g. Case 34, Chapter 14) or other deliberate measures (e.g. anxiety-relief conditioning) may be needed. There is graded exposure of the patient to real fear-evoking stimuli while the therapist is present in the double role of guide and anxiety-inhibitor. For example, a woman whose anxiety level was related to distance from a 'reliable' person was brought by her husband to meet me in a public park in the quiet of the early morning. In the course of about 10 meetings, I effected increasingly distant separations, the anxiety presumably having been inhibited by her emotional responses to me.

The stimulus requirements are not always so obvious. Special 'dramatic' or technical arrangements sometimes have to be contrived. For example, in treating a patient whose fear of public speaking was based on a fear of humiliation, I first had him intentionally give wrong answers to simple arithmetical problems. The anxiety this at first produced faded away with repetition. I then gave him more difficult problems, some of which he really could not answer correctly; and then had him stumble in his own field – at each stage deriding his errors. Additional witnesses were later introduced, one by one, to watch the sequence of failures. As he became able to endure this progression of 'humiliations' without anxiety his public-speaking fear declined.

Case 11

A case that called for technical inventiveness was a young woman who was practically confined to her home by the fear that she would die if her heart beat too fast. She was admitted to a hospital; and when conventional desensitization had proved to be inapplicable, I arranged the following series of procedures in collaboration with Dr. John S. Jameson: (1) The induction of tachycardia by stepping on and off a stool an increasing number of times, (2) Intravenous injections of increasing doses – up to 1 c.c. – of epinephrine hydrochloride 1 : 1000, (3) Epinephrine with 'feedback' from an oscilloscope that grossly exaggerated the tachycardia, (4) Inhalations of amyl nitrite (3 c.c. capsules crushed in a handkerchief), and (5) Locking her up for increasing periods up to 2 hours in an isolated room in the basement of the hospital. Following these measures the patient was greatly improved, though not 'cured.' She has been working regularly for the past 54 months, making an occasional telephone call to boost her confidence. Lately she has been phoning no more than twice a year.

Case 12

This is a case in which desensitization *in vivo* occurred in the first place inadvertently and was later deliberately continued. The patient, who had an 11-year-long fear of confinement in social situations, was being treated as a demonstration case in front of 20 members of a Behavior Therapy Institute I was conducting in Holland in August, 1966. After training in relaxation and with his hierarchies prepared, he was asked at his fourth interview to visualize being in a movie house in circumstances of varying difficulty of egress; but none of them evoked the slightest anxiety. I then told him that it would be necessary for us to work with real stimuli. He replied, "Something interesting has already happened, Doctor. During my first session here I was very nervous in the group, but every day my nervousness has decreased; and today I don't feel nervous at all." He had been unwittingly desensitized to the audience of 20. As it happened, 160 psychologists were expected at the Institute the next day, and I decided to make use of them for continuing the treatment. Accordingly, the next morning, in the large lecture hall, I had the patient at first sit with me on the platform while the original 20 Institute members sat in the forward rows of seats. The patient reporting no anxiety, I gave a prearranged signal for 20 more people to enter the hall. When they did so, he reported anxiety and was instructed to relax. After a minute he stated that he felt comfortable, and then another 20 people were permitted to enter. Again anxiety appeared and was relaxed away. The same procedure was repeated until all 160 members were seated. The patient spent the remainder of the afternoon seated comfortably in the front row of the audience. Subsequently, further *in vivo* operations were arranged — such as jamming him in the front row of spectators at a tennis tournament. These measures resulted in marked improvement of his neurosis.

Anxiety-relief Conditioning   This counter-anxiety measure (Wolpe, 1958, p. 180) is unique in having to date been used exclusively *in vivo*. Essentially, it depends on the direct conditioning of an anxiety-inhibiting response to a neutral stimulus word ('calm') by administering an uncomfortable continuous faradic shock to the patient who has previously been instructed to say the word aloud when he strongly desires the shock to stop. The termination of the shock produces a feeling of relief which, upon repetition, often becomes conditioned to the word 'calm.' This happens only in individuals who experience some degree of emotional disturbance (and not only sensory discomfort) in response to shock. In these people, the feeling of relief when the shock stops may be quite strong. It may be made stronger and the conditioning may be facilitated by the administration of drugs that augment sympathetic responses, e.g. amphetamines (Eysenck, 1963). If, subsequently, the patient utters the word 'calm' subvocally in disturbing life situations, his anxiety level may be sharply reduced and conditioned inhibition of the anxiety habit may result.

2. Modelling

This recent innovation (Bandura, 1968) shows signs of being a significant practical advance. In the first study reported (Bandura, Grusec, and Menlove, 1967), young children who were very fearful of dogs were assigned to one of four groups, each receiving eight brief treatment sessions. One group observed a fearless peer-model exhibit progressively more fear-arousing interactions with a dog. The modelled approach-behavior was presented within a highly positive party context, designed to counteract anxiety reactions. After the jovial party was well under way, the fearless model, a 4-year-old boy entered the room leading a dog, and performed a prearranged sequence of interactions with the dog for approximately three minutes. Further sequences were provided at each subsequent session, the fear-provoking properties of the modelled displays being gradually increased from session to session by simultaneously varying the physical restraints on the dog, the directness and intimacy of the approach responses, and the duration of interaction between the model and the dog. A second group of children observed the same graduated performances, but outside the party context. A third group observed the dog in the party context, but with the model absent. The fourth group participated in the party activities, but was never exposed to either the dog or the modelled displays. Children's phobic behavior was measured separately toward two different dogs following completion of the treatment program and again a month later. The two groups of children who had observed the peer-model interact nonanxiously with the dog displayed significantly greater approach behavior toward both the experimental and an unfamiliar animal than children in the dog exposure or the control conditions, who did not differ from each other. The party context added only slightly to the favorable outcomes of modelling. While 67 percent of children receiving the modelling treatment were eventually able to remain alone in the room confined with the dog, this was attained by relatively few children in the two control conditions.

Bandura, Blanchard, and Ritter (1968) studied the effects of modelling on snake-fearful adults. Their groups were exposed to four conditions. The first group observed a graduated film depicting young children, adolescents, and adults engaging in progressively more fear-provoking interactions with a large king snake. They were taught to induce and to maintain anxiety-inhibiting relaxation throughout the period of exposure. The rate of presentation of modelling stimuli was regulated by the client through a projector equipped with remote control starting and reversing devices. Clients were instructed, whenever a particular modelled performance proved anxiety-provoking, to reverse the film to the beginning of the aversive sequence, and to reinduce deep relaxation. They then reviewed the threatening scene repeatedly until it was completely neutralized before proceeding to the next item in the hierarchy. The second group of clients received a form of treatment in which, after observing intimate snake-interaction behavior repeatedly modelled by the therapist, they were aided through demonstration to perform progressively closer approaches to a snake. The third group received conventional desensitization. As in the other conditions, the treatment was continued until the clients' anxiety reactions were totally extinguished, or the maximum time allotment of six hours of treatment (not counting relaxation training) was completed. A control group received before-and-after assessments without any intervening treatment. The final assessments showed that live modelling combined with guided participation was the most effective treatment, eliminating the snake phobia in 92 percent of subjects. The desensitization and symbolic modelling groups also showed substantial change, but the control group was unchanged. A one-month follow-up assessment revealed that the beneficial changes were maintained and had transferred to real-life situations. Ritter (1968) found a similar superiority for modelling combined with guided participation in the treatment of snake-phobic children.

The mechanism by which the guided participation group achieves more rapid changes is not entirely clear. Bandura (1968) suggests that what is added is "positive reinforcement of a sense of capability through success." This proportion is not easy to test. It seems at least as plausible that the guided participation amounts to an *in vivo* desensitization that augments the effects of symbolic desensitization, in conformity with the findings of Garfield, *et al.* (1967).

CHAPTER 8

The Treatment of Inhibited Sexual Responses

Uninhibited sexual responding is correlated with intense pleasurable arousal during sexual intercourse. While some cases of chronic sexual inhibition are due to failure of physical development or to physical pathology, the great majority are the result of conditioning. Usually anxiety responses have become conditioned to the stimuli associated with sexual responding, and, being incompatible with the latter, inhibit it. The same inhibitory effect may be due to other conditioned emotions, like shame or disgust. Temporary inhibitions may, of course, result from intercurrent stresses or interfering stimuli of all kinds.

Anxiety inhibits sexual responding in a particularly direct way, because it involves some of the very autonomic functions concerned in the sexual response. Pre-orgasmic sexual arousal is predominantly parasympathetic in character (Langley and Anderson, 1895; Masters and Johnson, 1966), while anxiety is essentially a sympathetic function. Therefore, the more intensely anxiety is aroused, the more inhibition there will be of the sexual response (Wolpe, 1958). Reciprocally, sexual responses may be used for overcoming the anxiety habits that inhibit them. As always such utilization depends upon arranging for the sexual response to be strong enough to dominate the anxiety response so that it may inhibit it; for thus it will diminish the anxiety habit. Napalkov and Karas (1957) have shown that experimental neuroses in dogs can be overcome by counterposing sexual excitation to neurotic anxiety. Clinical neuroses have been successfully treated on the same basis – as will be described below. Of course, other inhibitors of anxiety can also be used to treat the anxiety that affects sexual responding.

163

As might be expected, it is usually in connection with anxieties related to sexual stimuli that sexual arousal has therapeutic application. But its potential is not confined to these stimuli. The neurotic reactions of the dogs treated by Napalkov and Karas were conditioned to nonsexual stimuli. Similarly, sexual emotions can be instrumental in overcoming human nonsexual neuroses. Quite frequently, such therapeutic effects occur fortuitously in life. A fortunate twist in a person's life may provide him with an exciting new sexual relationship that has therapeutic consequences. The emotion then involved is often not purely sexual excitation—but a broad-based arousal that can be called love. A case in point was an exceptionally intelligent young woman who felt herself disparaged by all intelligent people whom she encountered, especially at social gatherings, where she became exceedingly anxious. Then she married a man with whom she had fallen deeply in love. Now, suffused with amorous feelings, constantly reinforced by reciprocation, she found that she no longer had anxiety in social contexts. Years later, when the phase of high romance was long past, she was still free from her original anxiety. The anxiety had presumably undergone conditioned inhibition due to its reciprocal inhibition in social situations when love was on the wing.

As a matter of fact, many other nonanxious emotions can also produce therapeutic changes without the intervention of a therapist. It is probable that the majority of neuroses that people acquire are mild, and that most of them are in time overcome by the competition of the intercurrent emotions aroused by life events (Wolpe, 1958, p. 198).

THE TREATMENT OF IMPOTENCE

The most common deliberate use of the anxiety-inhibiting effects of erotic arousal is in the treatment of inhibited sexual responding in the male, called impotence, which is generally manifested as inadequacy of penile erection or premature ejaculation or both. Penile erection is a parasympathetic function. The sympathetic discharges that characterize anxiety tend both to inhibit erection and to facilitate ejaculation, which is subserved by the sympathetic (Langley and Anderson, 1895). Thus, the key to the problem of impaired sexual performance is the subtraction of anxiety from the sexual encounter. Sometimes the anxiety has nonsexual antecedents, e.g. a fear of traumatization of human flesh (Wolpe, 1958, p. 152), but in the great majority of cases its stimuli are to be found within the sexual situation.

In using the sexual response as an anxiety-inhibitor, the first requirement is to ascertain at what point in the approach anxiety begins and what factors control it. Perhaps the man begins to feel anxiety the moment he enters the bedroom, or perhaps it is when he is lying in bed in the nude with his wife. The basic idea of the treatment is explained to him – that the sexual response, being antagonistic to anxiety, can weaken his habitual anxiety if it can be consistently counterposed to anxiety that is relatively weak. He can arrange for this by limiting his sexual approaches always to the point where anxiety begins. He obviously has to obtain the cooperation of his wife since she would certainly regard his behavior as odd if he were to institute it without explanation. She has to know that a treatment program is under way. The essence of her role is to avoid making her husband tense and anxious. She must not mock him or goad or press him to achieve any particular level of performance. Though this may mean her enduring a good deal of frustration, she may expect to reap the reward of her helpfulness eventually. Actually, many women obtain a reasonable degree of relief from digitally induced orgasms during this treatment. In the case of the man who begins to feel anxiety when just lying next to his wife in bed, he must do nothing more active until he no longer has anxiety in that situation. Usually after 2 or 3 occasions he will be able to say, "I feel perfectly comfortable, now – only sexually excited." Then, he can go on to the next stage – perhaps to turn towards her and lie facing her on his side and fondle her breasts while she remains on her back. When this can be done without anxiety, he again advances – this time perhaps to lying on top of her, but not attempting intromission. At the next step, the penis may be approximated to the clitoris or other parts of the vulva, but still without intromission. After this he is permitted a small degree of entry, and later greater degrees, followed by small amounts of movement and then greater movement. The precondition for advancing beyond a stage is the disappearance from it of all anxiety.

The details of the treatment, naturally, must be decided from case to case. A procedure that is frequently of great value was suggested by Semans (1956). The wife manipulates her husband's penis to a point just short of ejaculation and then stops. After an interval, she does the same again. The procedure may be repeated several times during a session, and over several sessions. Its effect is to increase the latency to ejaculation – sometimes from a few seconds to half an hour or more. It is easy to see how helpful this may be for prolonging intercourse when the time comes. Semans describes his technique, which Case 13 in part illustrates, as follows.

If fatigue is present in either partner, he or she should sleep for a brief period of time. After this love play is begun and progresses to mutual stimulation of the penis and clitoris. Each is instructed to inform the other of the stage of sexual excitement being experienced. When the husband feels a sensation which is, for him, premonitory to ejaculation, he informs his wife and removes her hand until the sensation disappears. Stimulation is begun again and interrupted by the husband when the premonitory sensation returns.... By continuing the technique described above ejaculation can eventually be postponed indefinitely. Both husband and wife are advised that if erection subsides more than temporarily, a brief sleep or postponement of further stimulation is to be preferred to continuing their efforts at that time. Next, each is told separately, and later together, that ejaculation occurs more rapidly with the penis wet than dry. It is necessary, therefore, to use a bland cream or other means to lubricate the penis while the procedure is repeated.*

Masters and Johnson (1970) describe a maneuver that can facilitate this technique. They state that when ejaculation seems inevitable it can be inhibited by the woman applying gentle pressure on the penis at the coronal sulcus, one finger pressing on the urethra and another on the dorsum.

Case 13

Mr. I., a 36-year-old realtor had suffered from premature ejaculation ever since the beginning of his coital life at the age of 16. Ejaculation generally occurred within 15 seconds of intromission. He had married at 24. His wife, though deriving some satisfaction from digital orgasms, had become increasingly conscious of her incomplete fulfillment, and had in the past two years been showing interest in other men. About 18 months previously, Mr. I. had had about 25 consultations with a 'dynamic' psychiatrist. Though he had found the probing type of approach irritating, his general confidence had been improved by the treatment, but his sexual performance had remained unchanged. In three short-lived extramarital affairs, his sexual performance had been no better than with his wife. He usually felt that he was doing the 'chasing,' and was being accepted to some extent on sufferance.

Mr. I.'s Willoughby score was 30, with highest loadings for humiliation, stage fright, and being hurt. He lacked assertiveness in relation to people close to him, but not at all in business affairs. A program of assertive

*From Semans, J. H. (1956). Premature ejaculation: A new approach. *Southern Medical Journal*, V. 49, p. 354. By special permission obtained from author for this publication only. Not for other publication or reprint without author's permission.

training was seen as a secondary, but very relevant therapeutic requirement.

Mrs. I., briefly interviewed, expressed great willingness to take part in a behavior therapy program. She stated that digital orgasms satisfied her physically, but not emotionally. She felt that even a relatively small degree of prolongation of intromission would enable her to have coital orgasms. She regarded her marriage as very satisfactory in all other respects.

Therapy of the sexual inadequacy based upon use of sexual responses made combined use of two lines of approach: (1) Graded penile stimulation by the technique of Semans (see above), and (2) Gradual advances towards coitus. Mr. I. kept a detailed record of his performances, which he timed as accurately as possible with a bedside clock. The data of the early and middle stages of his record are reproduced below. Each figure refers to the *number of minutes of manual stimulation of the penis by his wife that brought him just short of ejaculation* for each successive sequence of stimulations.

First occasion (Saturday) 8, 6, 6, 6, and 3 minutes.

Second occasion (Saturday) 11, 7, 3, 4, and 4 minutes.

Third occasion (Sunday) 8, 6, 5, and 18 minutes.

Fourth occasion (Sunday) 17 minutes.

Fifth occasion (Monday) 33 minutes. At this juncture he felt confident enough to have Mrs. I. stimulate him as he sat astride her. The time to 'pre-ejaculation' on two successive sequences was 2 minutes and 3 minutes.

Sixth occasion (Monday) lying face to face sideways the pre-ejaculatory point was reached in 10 minutes and was maintained for 20 more minutes, when Mrs. I. desisted because of fatigue.

After this occasion, Mr. I. declared that he had never before been able to reach and maintain so high a level of excitement, but this became the norm subsequently.

Seventh occasion (Monday) Same as sixth occasion, but 'pre-ejaculation' was reached in 14 minutes and again maintained to a total of thirty minutes.

Eight occasion (Tuesday) Same as sixth occasion, but 'pre-ejaculation' was reached in 12 minutes and maintained to 30 minutes.

Ninth occasion (Wednesday) Penile stimulation while astride: 5, 12+, and 9+ minutes.

Tenth occasion (Wednesday) Penile stimulation while astride: 12 and 11 minutes.

Eleventh occasion (Thursday) Penile stimulation while astride: $12\frac{1}{2}$, 12, and 23 minutes. After the last, Mr. I. inserted just the glans of his penis into the vagina, maintaining it there for 5 minutes. In the course of this time Mrs. I. became excited. Thereupon he withdrew, and they both had orgasms digitally.

Twelfth occasion (Friday) Partial insertion (glans penis) for 20 minutes during which Mrs. I. alone moved and in this way gradually manipulated the penis deeper. At the end of the period Mr. I. withdrew as he felt ejaculation imminent.

Mr. I. now reported with satisfaction that he was feeling very much less anxious than before at partial insertion of his penis. He was finding that his stimulation of his wife was the greatest factor increasing his own excitation. The next objective was to increase both depth and duration of insertion, and thereafter to add small amounts of movement. In the meantime at each meeting with the therapist the patient was receiving training in progressive relaxation.

Thirteenth occasion (Friday evening after meeting with therapist) Partial intercourse lasted 30 minutes — partial insertion 80 percent of the time and full insertion about 20 percent, for about a minute at a time. During this minute Mr. I. would move constantly, without feeling any danger of ejaculation, but when Mrs. I. moved 5–10 times ejaculation would become imminent.

Fourteenth occasion (Saturday) Partial intercourse as above, 23 minutes and then Mr. I. ejaculated during an attempt to reverse positions.

Fifteenth occasion (Saturday) Fifteen minutes, much the same as the thirteenth occasion.

Sixteenth occasion (Sunday) Ejaculation after four minutes.

Seventeenth occasion (Monday) Forty minutes, varying between one-quarter to half insertion of penis. Ejaculation was several times imminent, but Mr. I. averted it by relaxing each time.

Now the therapist directed Mr. I. to concentrate first on prolonging full intromission, and then gradually to introduce movement, but preventing excessive excitation by avoiding stimulation of Mrs. I. He was told always to keep well within his capacity to control. After a few minutes of this it would be permissible to go on to orgasm, concentrating then on clitoral pressure by the penis.

Eighteenth occasion (Monday) Orgasm after 15 minutes of complete insertion with small movements.

Nineteenth occasion Orgasm after 29 minutes of small movements. Mrs. I. said that she too had been on the point of orgasm.

Further sexual occasions enabled gradually increasing excursions of movement, and finally a major breakthrough occurred after the thirteenth therapeutic interview. While Mr. I. retained his erection, Mrs. I. had four orgasms, and he ejaculated during the last of them. From this time onward there was mutually satisfactory sexual performance that gradually improved. There were 14 therapeutic interviews in all, over 5 weeks. Mr. I.'s Willoughby score at the last interview was 13.

The course that events took in the treatment of Case 13 is typical. Some patients do not make this kind of progress because they cannot maintain the low levels of anxiety essential to success in the real sexual situations, even though these are delimited. Usually, the imagination of these patients takes them beyond the reality to the eventual 'threat' of actual coitus. Systematic desensitization to the stages of the sexual approach is then indicated; or the use of tranquilizing drugs may be considered.

In occasional cases of premature ejaculation, recovery may be obtained in a much more simple way. The couple are told to have coitus as frequently as possible. The husband is instructed to try to enjoy himself as much as possible, just letting himself go and not caring how soon he ejaculates. The wife is asked to endure the situation if she can, and, of course, some cannot. It is quite helpful in cases like this to encourage the procural of orgasm in the wife by noncoital means – by manual and oral manipulations. A method that Semans (1962) has found effective is for the woman to move her clitoris rhythmically against the husband's thigh.

In general, patients who complain of erectile failure or insufficiency are more difficult to treat than those with premature ejaculation, for theirs is a more profound inhibition of response. In some of them, there is clearly a biological factor involved. The onset of biologically based impotence is insidious, with erectile power diminishing over a period of months or years. The history usually reveals a lifelong low level of sexual function. If there is no evidence of anxiety or other reactive source of sexual inhibition, a biological causation is highly probable. The diagnosis may be settled by laboratory estimation of urinary testosterone (Cooper, *et al.*, 1970). Less directly relevant, but more easily available, is the estimation of urinary 17-ketosteroid excretion. A distinctly low testosterone assay is a strong indication for hormone therapy; but even with a moderately high reading the patient need not be denied the possible benefits of testosterone treatment although most of those so treated fail to respond (Cooper, *et al.*, 1970).

For some of those who do not respond to the relatively simple methods described above, a two-week spell with spouse in St. Louis. Mo. at The Reproductive Biology Research Foundation (Masters and Johnson, 1971) should be considered. This is, in essence, a highly-structured opportunity for reconditioning sexual responses, although the principals are not very explicitly cognizant of the conditioning principles involved.

It was mentioned in the opening paragraph of this chapter that various intercurrent stresses may cause temporary inhibition of sexual responding. Chronic stress that has nothing to do with the sexual relationship as such may in parallel fashion cause chronic sexual inhibition. Prolonged stress may come from an enduring real misery, such as an incurable illness in the wife. Most often it is bound up with disharmonies in the relationship of a nonsexual kind. A program for mutual readjustment should then be undertaken. Sometimes two or three joint sessions with the couple on a 'commonsense' basis are all that is needed. Other cases require more formal arrangements involving 'contracts,' score cards, and a token economy, as described by Stuart (1969). Case 33 affords a striking example of the disruptive effects of general anxiety on sexual behavior.

A less common form of male sexual inadequacy is ejaculatory incompetence. One case was successfully treated by desensitization to the idea of the penis in the vagina (Razani, 1972).

Problems of Female Collaboration

A cooperative sexual partner is indispensable to the success of most of the techniques described above. Many patients have a partner readily available. Others are less fortunate. Sometimes one has to wait months before the patient finds somebody sufficiently interested in him to be willing to make the effort and bear the discomforts required for his treatment. Sometimes, although the patient has a wife or paramour, she is unable to participate as needed, either because she is contemptuous of her mate's impotence, or, more often, because a long history of disappointment and frustration has quenched her amorous responses. If the woman is unmoved by her husband's prefiguration of the behavior therapy program, the therapist should arrange to speak to her himself. If she can be persuaded to take the first steps, and if she is encouraged by early advances, the rest can be plain sailing.

When all feasible efforts have failed to extract from the wife the affectional behavior needed for the therapeutic program, it seems entirely reasonable to encourage the husband to seek out another woman who may be more responsive to him. If moral justification is required, it may be said that if the man's sexual potency should be established through his relationship with the other woman, it may lead to reconstruction of the marriage; and even if it does not, the man is better off biologically and psychologically to be able to have outside satisfactions than to be doomed to lifelong chastity.

Provided that reasonable safeguards are observed, it is best for a therapeutic extramarital relationship to be conducted with somebody in whom there is some wider personal interest, but, when this is not possible, paid help has to be sought. The casual 'pick up' will not do, as she is likely to be interested only in her own immediate pleasure. Perhaps there will some day be a 'pool' of accredited women who will sell their services to men with sexual problems. At present there seems to be no other recourse than to seek out a regular prostitute – and it is usually no easy matter to find one who is both personally appealing and able to muster enough sympathetic interest to participate in the therapeutic program. One patient, with a 16-year history of impotence, tried about 10 prostitutes before he found a warm-hearted and considerate one with whose help his sexual anxiety was overcome and his potency restored. Others have found help more easily.

The Results of Behavior Therapy of Inhibited Male Sexual Responses

Among 18 cases I surveyed retrospectively in 1966, 14 (78%) recovered to the extent of achieving entirely satisfactory sexual performance. Another 3 cases (17%) attained a level that was acceptable to their partners. The mean span of time required was 11.3 weeks and the median 8.0 weeks. Table 5 gives some details of these cases.

(See overleaf for table of results)

Table 5. Results of behavior therapy in eighteen cases of impotence.

Patient Number	Age	Therapeutic Time Span	Outcome and Remarks
1	31	1 week	Recovered
2	40	8 weeks	Recovered
3	46	10 weeks	Recovered
4	46	20 weeks	Recovered
5	40	4 weeks	Recovered
6	41	12 weeks (intermittent and furtive)	Much Improved
7	50	6 weeks	Recovered but no transfer to wife.
8	49	2 weeks	Recovered (major factor was removal of anxiety through wife taking contraceptive pills).
9	20	6 weeks	Recovered (major factor was resolution of fears about masculinity from psychoanalytic reading).
10	49	10 weeks	Improved from almost complete erectile failure to functionally sufficient erections to make marriage possible and to satisfy and impregnate wife.
11	35	6 weeks	Markedly improved when therapist left country. Appropriate assertion towards wife major factor.
12	36	5 weeks	Recovered (Case 2)
13	44	16 weeks (infrequent opportunities)	Unimproved. No apparent sexual anxiety. Hypersensitivity of glans penis.
14	40	9 weeks	Recovered (See Case 10, Wolpe 1960)
15	35	8 weeks (preceded by 12 weeks of overcoming interpersonal fears)	Improved from no erection to strong ones. Coitus improving when therapist left country.
16	18	66 weeks (very irregular opportunities at first)	Recovered
17	53	3 weeks	Recovered with new consort. Previously no benefit in 12 weeks with uncooperative consort.
18	39	12 weeks	Recovered. At first erections occurred only after testosterone injections.

THE TREATMENT OF FRIGIDITY

Frigidity is an unfortunate term inasmuch as it seems to suggest emotional coldness—a total lack of sexual response, but it is too late to do away with it now. The best we can do is to recognize that there are all grades of inhibition of sexual response in women, from absolute frigidity (no response whatever of a sexual kind) to the inability to achieve coital orgasm in spite of very high sexual arousal.

Two kinds of cases must be distinguished. In 'essential frigidity,' the lack of response is in relation to males in general, while in 'situational frigidity' it is relative to a particular male who in many cases is, unfortunately, the patient's husband. The solutions required are of very different kinds.

Essential Frigidity

Essential frigidity may be either absolute or relative. Some cases of absolute essential frigidity have an organic basis. Occasionally, one encounters a woman whose sexual response system seems somehow to have failed to develop. She does not recall ever having known sexual arousal and gives no history of distressing sexual experiences that might have led to conditioned inhibition. It must be supposed that her deficiency is constitutional; and there seems to be no available solution to the problem. In organically-based relative frigidity, the woman is erotically arousable to at least some degree, but coitus is precluded, usually by some painful pathological condition of the vagina—usually either a zone of scar tissue or an inflammatory lesion. I once saw a woman who had been psychoanalyzed for the whole 4 years of her marriage for vaginal spasm that was really due to a painful ulcer. A gynecological examination should be advised in every case of frigidity in which there is the slightest possibility of physical pathology.

In the great bulk of cases, essential frigidity is a matter of conditioned inhibition. Some women are absolutely or relatively frigid due to early experiences that have attached negative, and usually anxious, feelings to sexual stimuli. Sometimes, the relevant experiences have consisted of anti-sexual indoctrination that may have had a religious basis, or may have come from a mother who herself had unhappy or fearful sexual experiences. The patient may have been told that sex is filthy and disgusting and permissible only for the purpose of having children. The emotions customarily attached to these adjectives would have been evoked in the little girl and thus conditioned to the sexual stimuli, so that later, when she grows up, they inhibit any sexual response that tends to be evoked. In other cases that originate in early life, the frigidity is the direct result of traumatic experiences related to sex. Sometimes, the inhibition originates from having been punished or frightened in the context of masturbation.

Frigidity that develops after puberty may follow attempted rape or other sexual trauma, or may be a consequence of sexual arousal having repeatedly been frustrated in one way or another. Often the patient relates that she has rarely or never achieved a satisfactory coital orgasm; and repeated frustration has created a growing revulsion towards sexual activity. Frigidity sometimes develops out of the very goodness of a relationship — a satire of circumstance — as in Case 14.

The treatment of essential frigidity depends upon what the stimulus-response analysis of the case reveals. Where there has been faulty indoctrination, it is necessary to remove misconceptions about sex and sexual activity and to re-educate the patient. Having done this, one is almost always still left with a negative emotional attitude to sex, bound up with anxiety towards various aspects of the sexual situation. The treatment is generally then systematic desensitization whose details are determined by the identified stimulus antecedents of the anxiety. In yet other cases, frigidity is a byproduct of an endless stream of simmering resentments at the spouse's 'failings' which would be corrected if she were able to make her wishes known; and here the cure may lie in assertive training.

Case 14

A woman who had for years had a very good relationship with her husband in all respects developed a vaginitis which made intercourse painful. However, because of her great affection for her husband she had gone on permitting intercourse; but it was very aversive so that she had become completely frigid, developing marked vaginismus. Even after the vaginitis had been treated and intercourse was no longer painful, the vaginismus had persisted, so that it was impossible for her husband to gain entry. When I first saw her this state of affairs had been going on for 3 years.

In the case of vaginismus that afflicted Case 14, the spasm was found to be part of an anxiety reaction to the entry of any object into the vagina. Treatment consisted of a combination of standard desensitization and *in vivo* desensitization. I instructed the patient to relax and to imagine, at first, a very thin rod (about $\frac{1}{8}$ in. in diameter) being inserted a depth of $\frac{1}{2}$ in. into her vagina. This produced anxiety. I continued repeating the scene until the anxiety disappeared. I then gradually increased the length of the rod's insertion, and subsequently repeated the sequence with progressively wider rods. When the width of the imaginary rod had reached ½ in., I arranged for the construction of a set of wax rods (bougies) that varied in diameter from ⅛ in. to 1½ in., that the patient was to use at home, starting with the insertion of the ⅛ in. bougie into her vagina, slowly, inch by inch. Thereafter, *in vivo* 'shadowing' a few widths behind the imaginary diameter was continued. When we reached about ¾ in. diameter in imagination, movement such as would occur during coitus was introduced. This was a new source of anxiety which required repeated scene presentations for its desensitization. Then, movement with the bougie was started. Increasingly rapid movement came to be comfortably tolerated. At this point, I began to encourage careful experimentation with actual coitus, which became possible very soon, without producing vaginismus or any other manifestation of anxiety.

Case 15

The following is a case of a much more common kind. Because of a fearful experience at puberty, a woman of 32 had a revulsion against sex. She had, nevertheless, married. She had borne 4 children in 6 years, because being pregnant was a defense against sex. She had been treated by various methods, drugs, and electro-convulsive therapy, all without benefit. Her psychiatrist, not a behavior therapist, had then decided to try systematic desensitization. This had been a fiasco. The weakest item on his hierarchy was the sight of naked female breasts. When the psychiatrist presented this image to the patient it had produced such a severe anxiety reaction that is was impossible to go on. Then he referred her to me. I added to the weak end of the hierarchy several items that were quite remote from the bedroom. The first scene was at a swimming pool where there was only one male present, 50 yards away, with his bare chest exposed. This man was later brought progressively closer. Next, we utilized, first at a distance of 50 yards and then closer, a completely nude male statue in a park. A later item in the hierarchy was seeing a little nude boy of four gambolling in a paddling pool. Eventually, after many steps, she was successfully desensitized to such images as dogs fornicating, French pictures of nude males, four-letter words, and, finally, personal coital contingencies. It became possible for her to indulge in and enjoy sexual intercourse with her husband.

Case 16

A somewhat similar case was the subject of a week-to-week demonstration to a group of psychiatric residents here some years ago. The patient was a 27-year-old woman with several interpersonal neurotic problems in addition to frigidity. Her interpersonal anxieties called for teaching her to assert herself. She caught on to the idea very quickly and soon began to implement it. After the fifth session, the main thrust of therapy was turned to the frigidity. Though she had worked as an actress, and actresses are by repute rather free and easy sexually, this lady had been extremely reticent. She had often been darkly warned by her mother about the evils of sex. Those warnings had been vindicated by an attempted sexual assault by a much older man about the time of puberty. After her marriage, she had found sex unpleasant and tried as much as possible to avoid it. The essence of her problem was a tense abhorrence of the male sex organ. In treating this by desensitization, I started by having her imagine looking at a nude male statue in a park, from a distance of 30 feet. After coming progressively closer to the statue, she eventually imagined herself handling the stone penis with equanimity. The next series of scenes began with her imagining herself at one end of her bedroom and seeing her nude husband's penis 15 feet away. As desensitization proceeded, he was brought closer and closer. Then she imagined that she quickly touched the penis. With repetition this gradually stopped arousing anxiety. I then gradually increased the duration of contact. By about the 20th therapeutic session, she was enjoying sexual relations and having coital orgasms on about 50 percent of occasions.

It is quite often helpful to employ tranquilizing drugs in deconditioning the neurotic anxieties on which frigidity is based. Brady (1966), who treated frigidity by desensitization, but used intravenous Brevital as an adjuvant to relaxation, gained the impression that his cases improved more quickly than if he had used relaxation alone. If this impression is confirmed, its relevance is not likely to be confined to the special field of frigidity (see p. 188).

A technique has recently been described that seems to be especially applicable to subjects who are sexually arousable to a considerable and often marked extent, but who have never experienced full coital orgasm. Many of these women are easily able to have frictional clitoral orgasms — some of them even during coitus when special efforts are made to continue clitoral stimulation then. Even so, the experience is unsatisfactory because this kind of orgasm has a restricted sensory locus in contrast with the widespread excitation that characterizes a full orgasm.

An effective solution to this kind of problem seems to lie in the induction of a 'clinical orgasm' by suggestion (MacVaugh, 1972). A similar procedure has been described by Rubin (1972). Rubin's schedule is considerably the simpler. The following is a summary of MacVaugh's procedure, which has the advantage of the availability of a detailed written account.

First, the patient is shown that it is possible, in general, to induce emotions – to turn on, modify and erase hate, jealousy, and love by the presentation of appropriate cues. It is pointed out that an orgasm involves a kind of control of emotions. Then, some general facts about sex are discussed to combat any idea that it is unclean or sinful, and to convey that it is a mature and desirable activity which a woman should not feel ashamed to initiate. The next step consists of drawing attention to the anatomical features of the female sex organs – the sensory zones and the controlling muscles. She is made to practice contracting and relaxing these muscles. The typical sensations in the build-up of the orgasm are then described, and the comparative male and female excitation curves shown. After this, the patient is shown a list of the common colloquial words for the male and female organs, and for coitus, and is asked to read out the words until it becomes comfortable to do so, and then to put as much feeling as possible into their enunciation.

MacVaugh then goes on to show a series of slides portraying the stages in lovemaking of a Japanese couple, from their getting out of a car, through their entrance into a pagoda and bathing together, up to lying together on a Japanese floor mattress. What is emphasized throughout is that the woman initiates and controls every stage: she takes off his shoes; she does the washing in the bath. This may be of importance because of its marked differences from the female passivity which is the mode in European lovemaking, and especially notable in frigid women. MacVaugh states (1972) that his success rate has risen from 25 to 90 percent since he introduced this Japanese sequence.

After obtaining evidence of responsiveness to suggestion, MacVaugh goes on to suggest the successive steps of an imaginal lovemaking with a stimulating partner previously chosen, giving a good deal of attention to pelvic sensations, and later, when appropriate, suggesting pelvic movements. He builds upon these finally to elicit a full orgasm. The tape recordings I have heard are utterly convincing. The whole procedure takes up to about 3 hours. Once the clinical orgasm has been induced, orgasmic behavior is in the women's repertoire, available for elicitation in her real sex life. The whole of this schedule is unlikely to be always necessary, and a behavioral analysis beforehand should indicate what parts might be omitted.

Situational Frigidity

Behavior analysis often reveals that a woman who complains of frigidity is not negatively conditioned to sexual stimuli in general, but unresponsive to the particular man with whom she consorts. The question then is why she does not respond to him. In many cases, one finds that she simply does not care for him as a person. Perhaps she did once, but no longer does. One patient had fallen in love with her husband for his wisdom and erudition, only to discover after marriage that she had been misled. When his image slumped, so did her ability to respond to him erotically. But sometimes the deficiencies are not easy to define. There may be a general lack of communion. I know of nothing that can be done about this. Perhaps one day we shall have ways of making people like things that they do not like, but we do not have them now.

However, one should make every effort to identify sources of inhibition and to see whether change is possible. As a rule one discovers something potentially changeable in the husband's behavior. It may be that he does not show his wife reasonable consideration. Perhaps he comes home from work at irregular hours without ever telling her in advance or phoning her. Such behavior can be extremely disturbing, and, if persistent, may transform a woman's attitude from affection to revulsion, and her sexual pattern from passion to frigidity. One patient in whom this has happened has a husband who is an 'empire builder,' busy establishing branches of his business all over the United States. He is usually out of town. When he gets home, he gives his wife scant attention, rushes out to play golf, and watches baseball or football on television. Though he protests that he loves his wife (who is, in fact, very attractive), all efforts to change his behavior have failed. He has a paternalistic attitude towards her and regards her demands as childish. It is Ibsen's *A Doll's House* in the flesh. But since, for practical reasons, she cannot leave him, nobody can blame her if she takes a lover.

Fortunately, a few husbands are as immovable as this one. Quite often, if the wife learns to behave with well-tempered assertiveness, the husband's behavior will also change favorably. In one case of situational frigidity, the husband, deeply involved in international affairs, treated his spouse essentially as a servant and caterer. He would bring home many visitors, often without notice, requiring her to prepare countless dinners and entertainments. Her behavior was extremely passive and compliant. In the context of assertive training I had her start structuring activities in such a way as to follow the principle: "If you will do things for me I will do things for you." This almost at once made his attitude towards her more pleasant. The next step was for her to make a stand regarding their way of life: "This kind of living does not suit me. I cannot have people here every night. I need some personal life, and I would like you to do something about it." He acceded to this, a much closer relationship progressively developed, and a sex life gratifying to both of them.

This unilateral approach to readjustment of marriages is not always appropriate. Discord is often a matter of spiralling resentments on both sides. One partner's feelings are hurt, and he withdraws affection or retaliates against his spouse in some other way, provoking further nega- tive behavior from the latter. It is necessary to break a vicious circle which, sometimes, has gone on for a very long while. This can only be done by some kind of contractual arrangement involving both partners. Stuart (1969) has devised a detailed program that includes a 'marital contract,' a written undertaking by each person to do things that the other desires, and score cards. In effect, each partner is given the opportunity to learn that if he positively reinforces the other he will be compensated commensurately.

CHAPTER 9

The Use of Drugs in Behavior Therapy

SYMPTOMATIC USES

When a person suffers more or less continuously from considerable anxiety or other emotional disturbance it is usually desirable and often possible to obtain amelioration by the use of a drug or combination of drugs. Many people resort to sedatives on their own, the most common substance being, of course, alcohol. Contrary to what is generally believed, anxiety is not often entirely allayed by drugs in the usual doses. It does not, however, seem that their use is ever inimical to the achievement of the fundamental changes at which behavior therapy aims; and there is little doubt that in some cases they actively promote such changes. The hazard of addiction is small when the duration of drug treatment is limited. As the neurotic reactions are deconditioned the dosages required for symptomatic relief become less, so that it is often possible to dispense with medication altogether a good while before the conclusion of therapy.

As every experienced clinician knows, it is trial and error that ultimately decides what drug will be effective in an individual case. Meprobamate, 400–800 mg., three or four times a day, Dexamyl (100 mg. of amobarbital combined with 5 mg. of dextroamphetamine sulphate) one or two tablets morning and midday, and Librium (chlordiazepoxide) 10–30 mg. three times a day are all useful, and it has been my practice to give these preference, though not necessarily in the order given. If there is depression, Dexamyl will usually be tried first. When none of the foregoing drugs succeeds, any of a considerable number of others may be tried—phenothiazine derivatives [e.g. chlorpromazine (Thorazine), trifluoperazine (Stelazine), thioridazine (Mellaril)], ethchlorvynol (Placidyl), or the diphenyl methane derivative Atarax. To these may be added various antidepressants such as Parnate and Nardil, on the strength of Sargant and Dally's report (1962) of their efficacy in relieving the symptoms of many cases of neurosis. A recent addition to the armamentarium is the beta-adrenergic blocking agent propanolol (Granville-Grossman and Turner, 1966).

Symptom control by drugs does not always require routine diurnal dosage. If anxieties are only evoked by specific predictable situations, the drug should be administered an hour or so in advance of each expected situation—and only then. For example, a patient who has a fear of 'public scrutiny' may take a tranquilizing preparation an hour before making a speech, and one who has a fear of flying may do the same before a journey by air. Many patients discover that they can protect themselves against foreseeable anxiety sources in this way.

Symptomatic control by drugs of syndromes other than anxiety has also been reported. Imipramine (Tofranil), an antidepressant, has controlled enuresis (Destounis, 1963) and encopresis (Abraham, 1963). Systematic use of the drug can achieve what Drooby (1964) has called a 'reliable truce' with certain disabilities when attempts at reconditioning are impracticable or unsuccessful. Drooby found that enuresis ceased completely or almost completely in a matter of days in every one of 45 children to whom he administered imipramine (25 mg.) two or three times a day according to age. The treatment was not curative, for when the drug was withheld enuresis recurred. When the drug was withdrawn after a year of use, 30 percent of the subjects remained free from enuresis —the same proportion as in an untreated control group. This means that the drug relieves the child and his parents from the misery of enuresis without impeding the development of whatever processes lead to recovery with the passage of time. It is thus an especially worthwhile measure when circumstances preclude the use of deconditioning procedures. It is similarly possible to achieve a 'truce' with stuttering, as shown, for example, in the 'good' or 'very good' effects of meprobamate in 13 out of 18 patients treated by Maxwell and Paterson (1958).

Drooby (1964a) has also successfully used imipramine and other drugs such as Mellaril, Valium, and Nardil (v.s.) (each sometimes in combination with ergotamine) to curb anxiety and delay ejaculation in cases of premature ejaculation. Similar experiences have been reported by others (e.g. Singh, 1963). Sometimes the repeated successful performance of sexual intercourse under the influence of these drugs enables the patient later to perform satisfactorily without them (see below).

In many female patients, especially those at the menopause or approaching it, emotional reactions may be accentuated (if not caused) by hormonal factors. In most of these cases, exacerbation of symptoms occurs in the week before menstruation and may continue throughout the menstrual period. Marked amelioration may be obtained by the administration of female sex hormone preparations. In most cases, it suffices to employ the same preparations and dosages as are used for contraceptive purposes, e.g. Ovulen, Anovlar, Enovid, or Ortho-novum (Guttmacher, 1961). One is sometimes surprised to find that the improvement in symptoms is not confined to the late phases of the cycle, but extends through the whole of it. Some cases in whom 'contraceptive pill' medication is not particularly successful reportedly respond well to large doses of progesterone by intramuscular injection or rectal suppository (Dalton, 1964). It seems that oral synthetic progestogens are not a satisfactory substitute.

An interesting new possibility for symptomatic treatment has emerged from the observation of Pitts and McClure (1967) that in patients with anxiety neuroses anxiety attacks can be produced by intravenous infusions of lactate ion, and that the anxiety symptoms can be largely prevented by the addition of small amounts of calcium ion in the form of calcium chloride. This suggests that the oral administration of calcium chloride might be tried for controlling anxiety symptoms.

ADJUVANT USES OF DRUGS

Various drugs can be used to reduce anxiety when the effects of active relaxation are insufficient for the purposes of systematic desensitization. Here, too, the effectiveness of a particular drug can only be determined by experiment. The drugs are most often needed when there is a very high ongoing anxiety level, but sometimes also when the patient is a poor relaxer. The ongoing anxiety may be due to specific external stimuli or thought-contents, or else 'free-floating' (see below). The drug, one of the tranquilizers named above, is taken an hour or so before the interview.

Carbon Dioxide-Oxygen

When the anxiety is pervasive (free-floating) i.e. anxiety that is apparently conditioned to pervasive aspects of stimulation, such as space, time, and bodily sensations (Wolpe, 1958), by far the most satisfactory measure is to administer to the patient one to four single, full-capacity inhalations of a mixture of carbon dioxide and oxygen. The technique we use is not the original one of Meduna (1947), in which the patient inhales a mixture of 30 percent carbon dioxide and 70 percent oxygen until he loses consciousness, but that of LaVerne (1953), in which a stronger mixture is inhaled, one breath at a time. The mixture that has become our standard consists of 65 percent carbon dioxide and 35 percent oxygen; but a cylinder of 40 percent carbon dioxide and 60 percent oxygen should be available for those patients for whom the higher concentration is found to be irritating or excessively drastic in its effects, and also a cylinder of 100 percent carbon dioxide for refractory cases. As a matter of fact, in the behavior therapy unit we have found it most satisfactory to use separate cylinders of oxygen and carbon dioxide and to mix the gases as needed (see Fig. 12).

The therapist first ascertains the patient's anxiety level in terms of the subjective (*sud*) scale. He then tells the patient what he proposes to do and what the probable effects will be. The exact manner of presentation varies, but a fairly typical speech is the following:

Your constant high level of anxiety makes it difficult for relaxing to decrease your anxiety very much. We sometimes find that we can get relaxation from inhalations of

Fig. 12. Patient receiving carbon dioxide-oxygen mixture. The patient, at the end of inhalation, has just emptied the pre-filled bag containing the mixture of gases.

a mixture of carbon dioxide and oxygen. Carbon dioxide stimulates the breathing – and is frequently used to revive patients under anesthesia. Now, in these cylinders, there is a concentration of carbon dioxide exceeding what you normally have in your lungs. When I have filled the bag, I am going to ask you to inhale the gas mixture through this mask – just one breath. After a delay of a few seconds, you will begin to notice certain symptoms which are unusual, but not really unpleasant. You will notice that you become short of breath, that your heart quickens, your face flushes, and your extremities tingle. You may become rather dizzy, and possibly also have some other sensations. These reactions will reach a peak in about five seconds or so.

Now, this is what I want you to do. Take the mask in your hand. Watch as I fill the bag with the mixture of gases. (*Pause while the bag is filled.*) In a few seconds I am going to ask you to do the following things. First, empty your lungs; exhale as far as you can. Then apply the mask over your nose and chin quite firmly. After this, press the button on top of the mask. This releases the gas; and, mainly through your mouth, breathe in until you have about half-filled your lungs with the gas. Then remove the mask from your face.

In some cases, even half-filling the lungs with the gas mixture elicits a substantial respiratory reaction. In others, little or no effect is produced, so that increasingly full inhalations are subsequently given, and, if necessary, higher concentrations of carbon dioxide. It is usually advisable not to try to fill the lungs completely the first time – the more so when there is any reason to believe that the patient may be disturbed by the unusual sensations brought on by the gas. It is always very important to inquire beforehand whether the patient has any fear of suffocation or of anesthetics. In the case of those who do, a very slow and careful approach should be made to this method of treatment, devoting to an 'habituation program' a few minutes of each of several successive sessions. At first, the patient is asked to do nothing more than handle the mask; then he may sniff it cautiously while the gas mixture flows through the open valve; then he may take a short sniff out of the full bag, and thereafter increasingly deep breaths until he eventually inhales fully. A few individuals are so distressed by the sensations produced that it never becomes possible for carbon dioxide to be profitably employed on them.

Unless the mixture produces a marked respiratory reaction it is unusual to find any significant lowering of the level of anxiety. When even a full capacity inhalation fails to obtain hyperventilation, it can often be elicited by asking the patient to hold his breath for as long as he can after inhaling, by two or more inhalations in succession, or by raising the concentration of carbon dioxide, if necessary, to as much as 100 percent.

After each inhalation the therapist asks the patient to state the *sud* level of anxiety, which he records by the convenient notation illustrated in the following example:

"Carbon dioxide-oxygen ($\times$ 5) 60 $\rightarrow$ 45 $\rightarrow$ 35 $\rightarrow$ 25 $\rightarrow$ 20 $\rightarrow$ 20."

This means that four inhalations brought subjective anxiety down from 60 to 20 and that a fifth inhalation had no effect. The failure of the score to go lower is an indication for terminating administration of the gas mixture. While a level of 20 is not ideal, it is self-evident that the patient's efforts at relaxation are far more likely to reduce anxiety to zero from that level than from the original 60 *suds*.

In about four-fifths of neurotic subjects, pervasive anxiety responds to carbon dioxide inhalations. On the other hand, schizophrenic anxiety seems never to decrease and sometimes gets worse, which gives the inhalations some value as a simple diagnostic test, though far less decisive than pupillography (Rubin, 1970).

The mechanism of the anxiety-reducing effects of carbon dioxide-oxygen mixtures is not known. It has been suggested (Wolpe, 1958) that they might result from reciprocal inhibition of anxiety by the immediate responses to the gas, by the post-inhalation reactive relaxation, or both. One thing that seems reasonably certain is that the effect is not a direct pharmacological one dependent upon the presence of carbon dioxide in the body, for any surfeit of the gas is dissipated in a matter of minutes (Gellhorn, 1967); yet one or two inhalations sometimes removes pervasive anxiety for weeks or months, and usually for at least a good many hours (Wolpe, 1958). Exposure to a specific anxiety-evoking stimulus situation seems always to be prerequisite to re-establishing the pervasive anxiety that has been removed by the inhalations; and it is only if for a particular patient such exposure is rare that he is free from pervasive anxiety for long periods. Only a conditioning hypothesis appears to be consonant with these facts. Leukel and Quinton (1964) have shown that the acquisition of avoidance conditioning in rats is impaired by the administration of carbon dioxide. The sooner the gas is given after the conditioning, the greater the negative effect.

Granted that carbon dioxide has its effects due to a learning process, it would be both interesting and of practical importance to know precisely how. The first step is to determine what components of the procedure produce these effects. A controlled study by Slater and Leavy (1966) indicates that neither the act of inhaling air from anaesthetic equipment nor mimicking the deep respiratory movements that carbon dioxide induces decreases pervasive anxiety. In an experiment by Weinreb

(1966), strong stimulation by sniffing aromatic spirits of ammonia failed to reduce pervasive anxiety significantly, making it seem unlikely that the effects of carbon dioxide are due to suggestion augmented by a very strong sensory experience. On the other hand, Mack (1970) found amyl nitrite inhalations to be almost as effective as carbon dioxide.

Much more experimental work needs to be done. At the moment, it seems likely that carbon dioxide diminishes anxiety by eliciting a powerful anxiety-inhibiting excitation because of the fact that the excitatory effects of the gas can be used to decondition specific anxiety habits. Psychophysiologically, the indications of an ongoing investigation are that after an inhalation the pulse slows and skin conductance falls (Shmavonian and Wolpe, 1972).

Intravenous Anxiety Inhibitors

Methahexitone sodium, which goes under the trade names of Brietal and Brevital, is used as a means of tranquilization for the purposes of desensitization. It is regarded by some of its users (Friedman, 1966; Friedman and Silverstone, 1967) as a primary anxiety-inhibiting agent. Others, like Reed (1966) and Brady (1966), regard it as essentially an adjuvant to relaxation, and always give relaxation instructions when using it. A controlled study by Mawson (1970) has shown methohexital to be not only a self-sufficient anxiety-inhibiting agent, but significantly more effective than relaxation.

Brady (1966) has made particular use of methohexital in cases of frigidity and describes with great clarity his use of it. After an introductory explanation, he has the patient relax comfortably in a reclining chair and starts the injection of a 1 percent solution.

> During the 2–4 minutes required for the drug to have its maximum effect, suggestions of calm and relaxation are given such as might be used to induce hypnosis. When a deeply relaxed state is attained, the patient is instructed to imagine the first or weakest scene in the hierarchy. For example, "Now I want you to imagine as vividly as possible that you and your husband are seated in the living room, fully clothed, and he is kissing you affectionately on the lips. Visualize this scene—imagine yourself there—what you might hear and what you might see. You remain calm and relaxed." The patient is permitted to visualize this scene for about 2 minutes and is then instructed to stop thinking of this scene and simply relax. After a minute of rest, the same scene is again suggested for about 3 minutes. After another rest period, and assuming that no anxiety is evident, the next scene in the hierarchy is suggested, and so forth.... Brevital is cleared from the body at such a rapid rate that usually the relaxant and sedative effect of the drug is appreciably diminished after 4–5 minutes. Hence, an additional amount is usually required after this time. During a typical session, a total of 50 to 70 mg. are

administered. After the last suggested scene is terminated, the patient is allowed to remain recumbent in the chair for about 10 minutes.

Four of Brady's five cases were greatly improved in a mean of 11.5 sessions. Follow-ups did not reveal relapse or new symptoms.

A drug of a much earlier vintage, thiopental sodium (Pentothal), may regain its lost prominence in psychiatry if the findings of Hussain (1971) are confirmed. Everybody who was on the psychotherapeutic scene during World War II can recall the vogue of narcoanalysis and the great hopes that were pinned on it as a short cut to fundamental psychotherapy. The narcosis induced by intravenous Pentothal made it easy for soldiers with war neuroses to recount in vivid detail the incidents during which their neuroses had begun. It seemed to provide an immediate conduit to material trapped in the recesses of the 'unconscious mind,' enabling rapid de-repression. In short, it promised the presumed benefits of instant psychoanalysis, The promise was not borne out by results, and the method fell out of favor. Hussain (1971) reports the treatment of 40 patients with agoraphobia and other severe phobias, 20 by desensitization and 20 by flooding. Half of each group had their first 5 treatment sessions under Pentothal and the second 5 without the drug, and in the other half the order was reversed. It was found that the Pentothal made little difference to desensitization, but very greatly increased the effectiveness of flooding. Flooding under Pentothal produced much more change than any of the other three therapeutic arrangements. It is, however, worth noting that Hussain's subjects showed virtually no change when flooded without Pentothal, a finding that contrasts strongly with those of others who have worked with this method.

Yeung (1968) has reported the successful treatment of a subway phobia and of snake phobias on the basis of a single large intravenous injection of diazepam. Pecknold, Raeburn, and Poser (1972) gave intravenous injections of this drug to two patients who were too anxious to be able to calm themselves by muscle relaxation. The drug-induced calmness in each patient was used for desensitization, but after a few sessions it was found that the desensitization could be continued with the calmness of muscle relaxation alone.

Male Sex Hormone

From time to time reports appear in the literature on the beneficial use of male sex hormone in the treatment of cases of impotence (e.g. Miller, Hubert, and Hamilton, 1938). In the course of 20 years of psychotherapeutic practice, I have twice succeeded in augmenting a very low sexual drive in males by daily injections of testosterone to an extent that sexual performance became possible and subsequently continued satisfactorily without further use of hormones. Presumably, the sexual response was conditioned to contiguous stimuli. (See also Cooper *et al.*, 1970.)

THE USE OF DRUGS FOR SPECIFIC DECONDITIONING

From various reports published during the last half century both in Russia (e.g. Pavlov, 1941) and in the United States (Dworkin, Raginsky, and Bourne, 1937; Masserman and Yum, 1946), it is evident that lasting recovery or improvement may be procured in neurotic animals by keeping them under the influence of such sedative drugs as bromides, barbiturates, or alcohol for long periods. It would appear, although it is not always specifically stated in the reports, that at various times while under the influence of the drugs the animals were exposed to the stimuli conditioned to the neurotic reaction. But none of these experimenters deliberately and systematically brought the stimuli into play as part of the therapeutic design.

This was done for the first time in an experimental study by Miller, Murphy, and Mirsky (1957). Using electric shock as the unconditioned stimulus, they conditioned 4 groups of rats to perform an avoidance response at the presentation of a buzzer. For the purpose of studying extinction of the avoidance response under different conditions, the animals in two of the groups received injections of saline, and those of the other two groups injections of chlorpromazine on each of four consecutive days. One of the two saline-injected groups (Group I) and one of the two chlorpromazine injected groups (Group II) received 15 unreinforced presentations of the buzzer on each of the four days, while the animals of the other two groups were simply returned to the living cage after receiving their injections. During these four days, Group II animals made far fewer avoidance responses (less than 5 percent of trials) than Group I (more than 70 percent of trials). On the fifth and subsequent days, when all groups were given unreinforced trials without receiving any further injections, Group II manifested a much lower percentage of avoidance responses than any of the other groups. Whereas the other groups showed an average of about 60 percent avoidance responses, Group II showed only about 20 percent; and in eleven of the fifteen animals that comprised the group the level did not go above that observed during the four days under the influence of the drug. That this lasting therapeutic effect was related to the autonomic action of the chlor-promazine and not to the supression of motor responses was indicated by repeating the experiment with phenobarbital in a dosage that had pre-viously been equated with chlorpromazine in terms of motor retardation effects. In the animals given phenobarbital the level of avoidance re-sponses after stopping the drug was not diminished. It is crucial to note that chlorpromazine has lasting effects only if, in the authors' words, "the opportunity for relearning is afforded during the administration of the agent."

It is reasonable to propose that reciprocal inhibition was the mechanism of this relearning. The animals were, through earlier conditioning, capable of responding also to other stimuli in the environment where the buzzer was heard; but without the 'protection' of the chlorpromazine the avoid-ance response to the buzzer was overwhelmingly strong. In animals who had been given chlorpromazine any remnant of the avoidance response (and concomitant anxiety) could presumably have been reciprocally inhibited by whatever responses were being evoked by other stimuli in the environment. Obviously this explanation calls for systematic study; but some support for it is given by Berkun's observation (1957) that animals in whom weak anxiety-cum-avoidance responses have been conditioned, can overcome these responses by mere exposure, first to situations similar to those associated with the original conditioning, and then to the original situation.

Clearly, if the paradigm of the Miller, Murphy, and Mirsky experiment can be extended to human clinical neuroses great therapeutic economies are possible. The crucial therapeutic events take place in life. The therapist's main role is to establish which drug is effectively tranquilizing and in what dosage. Thereafter, he need only check occasionally, and relatively briefly. But astonishing as it must seem, no systematic inves-tigation has been undertaken in the course of so many years. Promising indications have emerged from experimental treatment of individual cases, as well as from some incidental observations in a study by Winkel-man (1955). Winkelman gave his patients chlorpromazine for 6 months or more in doses sufficient to obtain marked diminution of neurotic symptoms, and then gradually withdrew the drug. He found that improve-ment persisted for at least 6 months after the withdrawal in 35 percent of the patients. Unfortunately, there was no control study to show what would happen to patients given a placebo instead of chlorpromazine. There is also other information that would be of great interest—for example, would more lasting effects result from maintaining the original dosage for the full period of treatment?

Since 1956, I have from time to time treated patients with drug protection, using at first chlorpromazine, meprobamate, or codeine. After consistently taking the drug before exposure to disturbing situations, some of them found themselves later not having the expected disturbance when exposed without the drug. To achieve this result, the drug had to be taken absolutely consistently for weeks or months so that no significant anxiety was ever produced by exposure to the relevant situations. For example, finding that the severe classroom anxiety experienced by a student was markedly ameliorated by meprobamate, I kept him on an adequate dosage of the drug on every school day for 6 weeks. Then I gave him a drug-free test-day on which he found his anxiety to have diminished by 40 percent from its original level. A second test after 6 more weeks showed a further 30 percent decrement of the anxiety – an overall improvement of about 70 percent. Among cases in which I have achieved complete recovery, I may mention a fear of physical deformities for which codeine was the drug used, a barber's chair phobia (see also Erwin, 1963) using meprobamate and alcohol, and a fairly mild airplane phobia that was overcome by the use of alcohol on three flights of about an hour's duration each.

There have been many scattered reports by others of successful treatment by this method. Reference was made (p. 181) to the lasting effects that sometimes follow when premature ejaculation is controlled by anxiety-inhibiting drugs (e.g. Drooby, 1964a). Similarly, among the cases of stuttering treated by meprobamate in the Maxwell and Paterson (1958) study was that of a 25-year-old butcher who was eventually able to dispense with the drug and still maintain marked speech improvement.

It has recently become apparent that chlordiazepoxide (Librium) and its relatives, Valium and Serax, may have a special value in treatment of this kind, because unlike meprobamate their tranquilizing effects increase with increasing dosage, and without much in the way of adverse accompaniments as a rule. Librium and Valium sometimes produce drowsiness in high dosage, but Serax reportedly does not (Berger, 1968). My own interest in the potentialities of this group of drugs was first aroused by Miller (1967) who had achieved striking effects in four phobic cases. In his first two cases – a woman with a fear of eating in public and a man with agoraphobia – doses of 50 and 75 mg. respectively were needed. Miller states, "The medication was taken only for the purpose of desensitization and never on a routine basis. The patients 'planned' a phobic exposure, took the medication, waited until it began to exert its effect and then exposed themselves to the phobic situation (in real life, not in fantasy). The course of the therapy was four weeks in one case and six weeks in the other." Both patients were completely free of their phobias without the use of any medication when followed up six months after the treatment.

The first case with whom I systematically employed Librium in this way was a physician in whom a year previously a severe emotional reaction to noise had been conditioned, when he had been exposed to insistent hammering while trying to sleep in a hotel. The sensitivity had generalized to other noises, of which the most distressful had become the sound of automobile horns, perhaps because of its frequency. He had improved moderately on relaxation and a masking procedure involving white noise. He was then instructed to determine the dose of Librium that could entirely block his emotional response to noise, and to take this dose (which was 30 mg.) in every circumstance in which he could anticipate being exposed to any considerable amount of honking. This schedule led to very marked diminution of the response without the drug in the course of four months.

Two points must be underlined. First, that the effectiveness of such programs almost certainly depends upon insuring that high anxiety evocation never occurs; for, whenever it does, it may be expected to recondition a substantial degree of anxiety and lose hard-won ground. Second, not every drug that inhibits anxiety will do. The site of action is critical. No lasting effects can be expected of peripherally acting drugs like propanolol (Suzman, 1968).

CHAPTER 10

Procedures Involving Strong Anxiety Evocation

Contrasting with the desensitization strategies and their weak responses are those treatments that involve very strong responses. The oldest of these is abreaction, in which memories of distressful events are stirred up to evoke the strong responses. More recent treatments evoke the strong responses by exposure to either real situations or contrived imaginal situations, and are known as flooding techniques.

The flooding techniques belong very properly to behavior therapy and will, therefore, be considered first, even though the paradigm of experimental extinction that generated them is almost certainly not their true explanation. But they can be instituted at will, and their components can be quantitatively varied. The therapist, therefore, can control the therapeutic event by controlling the stimulus input. Abreaction, on the other hand, is not strictly a behavior therapy technique, because all that the therapist can do is to try to create conditions for triggering its occurrence. When it occurs, both its content and its outcome are unpredictable. More often than not, it is not therapeutic. Even when the therapist can influence the stimulus input, he shoots in the dark because he does not know how to influence the process beneficially. But the fact that abreaction can be dramatically beneficial entitles it to our consideration and to our efforts to elucidate the factors that control it. Nevertheless, it might well turn out that abreaction and flooding work through the same processes. There is a published example of my own which seems to partake of both (Wolpe, 1958, p. 197).

FLOODING

The first account of a case successfully 'flooded' is, I believe, E. R. Guthrie's. The patient concerned was an adolescent girl with a phobia for automobiles. She was kept compulsorily at the back of a car in which she was continuously driven for 4 hours. Her fear soon reached panic proportions, and then gradually subsided. At the end of the ride she was quite comfortable, and henceforth was free from her phobia. The recent development of interest in flooding therapy started from the work of Malleson (1959), Frankl (1960), and Stampfl (1964).

Malleson described treating several cases by the evocation of intense anxiety on the supposition that experimental extinction of the anxiety habits would occur. One was an Indian student who was very afraid of examinations. He was asked to tell of the awful consequences that he felt would follow his failure — derision from his colleagues in India, disappointment from his family, financial loss. Then he was to try to imagine these things happening — the fingers of scorn pointed at him, his wife and mother in tears. At first, as he followed the instructions, his sobbings increased. But soon his trembling ceased. The effort needed to maintain a vivid imagining increased, and, inversely, the emotion he could summon began to ebb. Within half an hour he was calm. Malleson instructed him to repeat the exercise of experiencing his fears. When he felt a little wave of spontaneous alarm he was not to push it aside, but to try to experience it more profoundly and more vividly. If he did not spontaneously feel fear, every 20 or 30 minutes he was to make a special effort to try and do so, however difficult and ludicrous it might seem. He was seen twice a day over the next 2 days until his examination. Malleson states that, being an intelligent man and an assiduous patient, he practiced the exercises methodically and by the time of the examination reported himself almost totally unable to feel frightened. He had, as it were, exhausted the affect in the situation. He passed his examination without apparent difficulty.

When intense anxiety evocation is employed therapeutically by existential psychiatrists (Frankl, 1960; Gerz, 1966) they call it paradoxical intention. Of course, they are not guided to it by the idea of experimental extinction or other learning paradigm, but by the expectation that "if the patient were to try intentionally to bring on these symptoms he would not only find difficulty in doing so, but also change his attitude towards his neurosis." But there is no essential difference between their practical procedures and Malleson's. In a good many of their cases, treatments are given repeatedly over several months. One of Gerz's cases was a 29-year-old woman who had fears of heights, of being alone, of eating in a restaurant in case she vomited, and of going into super-markets, subways, and cars. She was instructed to try to expose herself to the conditions that she feared. She was to try to vomit while dining out with her husband and friends, so as to create the greatest possible mess. She was to drive to markets, hairdressers, and banks "trying to get as panicky as possible." In six weeks she had lost her fears in her home situation, and shortly thereafter drove all by herself to Gerz's office, about five miles from her home. Four months later, she drove with her husband to New York City, a hundred miles away, across the George Washington Bridge, back through the Lincoln Tunnel, and attended a goodbye party on the lower deck of an ocean liner. Gerz states that 2 years later she was free of symptoms.

Stampfl's strategy is basically the same, but relies on the patient's imagination, and is called implosive therapy. In his early writings, quoted by London (1964), Stampfl expressed the view that if the patient were insistently exposed to the conditioned anxiety-producing stimulus situa-tions, and the anxiety not reinforced (by an unconditioned stimulus) the anxiety response habit would extinguish. He would, accordingly, arrange for the frightening stimulus to be presented in circumstances from which the subject could not escape. The resulting continuous exposure to the stimulus was expected to cause it to lose all power to elicit anxiety. Stampfl advocated using every resource to frighten the patient as much as possible and for as long as possible at each sitting. The patient was made to imagine himself realistically in the relevant fear situation, while the therapist described in great detail the most vivid horrors possible.

Although later accounts (e.g. Stampfl and Levis, 1967) have continued to stress maximal stimulation as a matter of principle, in practice they invoke weaker stimuli in the initial phases. They prescribe an 'avoidance serial cue hierarchy,' and the 'hypothesized cues' which are low on this hierarchy (that is, cues that have low anxiety loadings) are presented first. This incorporation of a gradual approach would seem to be incon-sistent with Stampfl's central thesis. This is Stampfl and Levis' (1967) description of how they ascend the ladder of increasing stimulation:

> Once the implosive procedure is begun, every effort is made to encourage the patient
> to 'lose himself' in the part that he is playing and 'live' the scenes with genuine emotion
> and affect. . . . The scenes which contained the hypothesized cues are described at first
> by the therapist. The more involved and dramatic the therapist becomes in describing
> the scenes, the more realistic the presentation, and the easier it is for the patient to

participate. At each stage of the crisis an attempt is made by the therapist to obtain a maximal level of anxiety evocation from the patient. When a high-level anxiety is achieved, the patient is held on this level until some sign of spontaneous reduction in the anxiety-inducing value of the cues appears (extinction). The process is repeated, and again, at the first sign of spontaneous reduction of fear, new variations are introduced to elicit an intense anxiety response. This procedure is continued until a significant diminution of anxiety has resulted. . . . Between sessions the patient is instructed to reenact in his imagination the scenes which were presented during the treatment session.*

The prescription of practice between sessions is noteworthy. However, its efficacy in accelerating progress has not been demonstrated.

One distinguishing feature of the work of these authors is that while basing their methods on Mowrerian learning theory, they also assume the validity of psychoanalytic theorizing, and derive some of their scene material from it. Stampfl and Levis (1968) state that "castration dangers and Oedipal time conflicts are not foreign to the implosive therapy approach in that they are hypothesized to be a product of primary or secondary aversive conditioning events." Some of the scenes based upon psychoanalytic assumptions do evoke anxiety that in due course diminishes. The authors take this as evidence that such material has special therapeutic relevance. Actually, a variety of stimulus material with the same essential elements would be more or less interchangeable.

In the first edition of this book, I expressed reservations about the optimism and wide-ranging success with flooding claimed by both existentialists (e.g. Gerz, 1966) and implosive therapists (e.g. Levis and Carrera, 1967). I felt also that the method was not without risk. While I am now convinced of the wide efficacy of the method, and satisfied that the risks are small, I still advocate a cautious attitude, for little is really known of the ingredients for success, and prolonged *in vivo* exposure does exacerbate some neuroses (see Case 20).

There are also good experimental grounds for caution. So far, nobody has cured an experimental neurosis simply by exposing the animal for long periods (hours or days) to the stimuli to which anxiety has been maximally conditioned (see, for example, Masserman, 1943; Wolpe, 1958; Appel, 1963). Goldstein (1972), in an exploration of this matter, confirmed that the anxiety response of neurotic cats to a conditioned auditory stimulus did not decline (and sometimes increased) if that stimulus was presented continuously or frequently; but it did decline if

*From Stampfl, T. G. and Levis, D. J. (1967) Essentials of implosive therapy: A learning-theory-based psychodynamic behavioral therapy. *J. Abn. Psychol.* 72: 496.

presented following the presentation of a graded sequence of generalized stimuli. This makes it exceedingly unlikely that experimental extinction can be the mechanism of the favorable effects of flooding. Two contrasting clinical reports strengthen this conclusion. In snake phobias, Wolpin and Raines (1966) obtained good results by 5–10-minute periods of flooding, whereas Rachman (1966) failed entirely with 100 two-minute floodings (over 10 sessions) with spider phobias. If extinction had been at work, Rachman should have done much better.

The deductions which these observations seem to generate are that flooding should employ only moderately strong anxiety-evoking stimuli, but these should act on the patient for a relatively long time. They should continue until there is clear evidence of anxiety decrement in their presence, for this is the indication that the flooding has produced anxiety-response inhibition. If the stimulation is removed early, there is not enough time for the inhibitory process to develop, and the anxiety-drive reduction which follows removal reinforces the anxiety habit. This process, incidentally, appears to be the major reason for the resistance to extinction of neurotic habits, both animal and human (Wolpe, 1958, pp. 24–29).

The question, however, needs to be faced why in at least some clinical cases improvement has seemed to follow the use of extremely strong stimulation. Some possible clues to an answer have come from observations made in the Behavior Therapy Unit on an experimental *in vivo* flooding.

Case 17:   Multifaced experimental flooding
The subject of the experiment was a woman in her late twenties with long-standing severe phobias for dead birds and for bats. She had heard of flooding and believed that it might be a rapid way of overcoming her phobias. At first, an attempt was made to induce it by images based on verbal descriptions, but very little emotion was aroused in this way. The decision was then made, with her full agreement, to subject her to real dead birds. (She agreed to the taking of repeated blood samples during the experiment so that the changes in cortisol levels provoked by the treatment could be measured.)

On the appointed day, the patient sat in a comfortable armchair, and an indwelling cannula was inserted into a vein in her left arm which was immobilized on a board to insure immobility. Baseline blood samples were taken by Dr. George Curtis for two hours. In the meantime, two birds, a small blackbird and a pheasant, had been prepared in accordance with the patient's description of what for her provided maximal stress – exposure of the neck by the removal of most of the feathers. The patient was then told that the blackbird would be brought in, and a vivid verbal description was given. This produced a certain amount of manifest uneasiness, and the patient reported some anxiety, but not much. She was then asked to close her eyes, and the bird was brought in by Dr. Edna Foa, held by the feet, with head dangling down, and in this position kept about 7 feet away from her. She was asked to look at it, but refused. After two minutes, she shot a glance at the bird, and gave vent to a loud shriek and a great deal of generalized movement. She said that she would not look again. After firm but gentle coaxing, however, she did glance at it again with loud screams of terror and much movement. The patient's great reluctance to look at the bird so close led to our deciding to move it a little farther away – to about 10 feet. She seemed pleased at this, and after half a minute or so, opened her eyes and looked at the bird for about 3 seconds, again screaming and contorting her body. She subsequently opened her eyes for progressively longer periods, and the fifth time she was able to observe the bird continuously. Even then, though she was relatively undisturbed most of the time, she would occasionally relapse into screaming. When questioned about this, she said that at those times the bird assumed an aspect which made it seem as though it was getting 'under her skin,' suggesting a perceptual organization process that permits the turning on and off of the impact of a stimulus.

Eventually, these 'spontaneous' outbursts ceased, and then an interesting thing was noticed. Every time the bird was jerked or the angle of presentation changed, there was a further flurry of anxiety. After about five minutes, the patient could no longer be stirred up, no matter what was done with the bird at ten feet, though rating her basal level at 20 *suds*. It seemed as though all the angles and varieties of movement had been deconditioned at ten feet. The bird was now brought closer through three stages until it was only about three feet from the patient. Again, at each point of approach, there was a need to present the bird at different angles and with different movements, but the reactions were smaller and quite quickly overcome. At this point, the suggestion was made that the patient stroke the bird's feathers. She resisted this, but allowed herself to be persuaded to move her finger closer and closer, and eventually touched it. Thereafter, she was able to continue stroking it with decreasing anxiety. The next step was to get her to hold the bird herself, which she finally did, without any increase in the anxiety level beyond the 20 *suds* baseline level. At a second session, anxiety fell to zero in 20 minutes.

The following cases illustrate how various are the ways in which flooding may be done and how diverse the stimulus antecedents of the anxiety. As in the case of desensitization, the applicability of flooding extends far beyond the limits of the classical phobia. Observe that, although persevering exposure to anxiety-evoking stimulation is a cardinal feature of flooding, its effective duration was quite brief in Case 10. By contrast, we have seen equally successful cases in which, at the initial flooding session, anxiety showed its first decrease after about 45 minutes (e.g. from 90 to 80 *suds* in a case who feared to be seen urinating and who was treated *in vivo*).

Case 18:   Successful imaginal flooding

Imaginal stimuli were employed with Dr. E., a dentist who had had an extraordinarily severe and widespread neurosis, that had in most respects responded very well to varied and sometimes prolonged applications of the commoner behavior therapy techniques, such as assertive training and systematic desensitization. But two disabling neurotic constellations remained—an inability to give dental injections because of a fear of the patient dying in the chair, and an extravagant fear of ridicule. Since attempts to desensitize Dr. E. to these were making insufferably slow progress, I decided to try flooding. Under light hypnosis he was asked to imagine giving a patient a mandibular block, then, withdrawing the syringe, standing back and seeing the patient slump forward, dead. Dr. E. became profoundly disturbed, sweating, weeping, and wringing his hands. After a minute or so, noticing that the reaction was growing weaker, I terminated the scene and told him to relax. Two or three minutes later, the same scene evoked a similar, but weaker reaction. The sequence was given three more times, at the last of which no further reaction was observed. Dr. E. said that he felt he had been through a wringer—exhausted, but at ease. At the next session, the fear of ridicule was introduced. Dr. E. imagined that he was walking down the middle of a brilliantly lighted ballroom with people on both sides pointing their fingers at him and laughing derisively. At the fifth flooding session, it was clear that nothing remained to be treated. Four years later, at an interview with Dr. E., it was evident that his recovery had been fully maintained.

Case 19:   Successful in vivo flooding

In vivo flooding is exemplified by the case of Mrs. C., a woman with agoraphobia so severe that she was unable to go on her own more than two blocks by car without anxiety. Attempts at systematic desensitization had failed—apparently because she was unable to imagine scenes realistically. After other measures had also proved ineffective, I decided to persuade her to expose herself to flooding, which had to be *in vivo* because of the demonstrated inadequacy of her imagination. After resisting strenuously for some weeks, she agreed to take the plunge. Plans were made for her husband to place her, unaccompanied, on a commercial aircraft one hour's flight away from the airport where I would await her. When Mrs. C. in due course alighted from the plane, she walked towards me smiling. She had felt increasing anxiety for the first fifteen minutes of the flight, and then gradual subsidence of it. During the second half of the journey she had been perfectly comfortable. She flew home alone the next day without trouble. This single experience resulted in a great increase in her range of comfortable situations away from home. She was now able, without anxiety, to drive her car alone three or four miles from home and to make unaccompanied trips by plane without any anxiety. Plans to build up this improvement by further treatment were foiled by distance plus other practical obstacles.

Case 20:   Unsuccessful in vivo *flooding*

The following is an example of a patient made worse by attempts to 'flood' him. Dr. K. was a physician with a severe phobia for insane people and insane behavior. He was in military service, and soon after he began to consult me was offered a transfer to a psychiatric hospital. I encouraged this, thinking that the phobia might be overcome by flooding. On my advice, he exposed himself continuously to the presence of schizophrenic patients, sometimes for hours at a stretch. Far from decreasing, his reactions to these patients grew progressively worse, and, in addition, he developed a rising level of pervasive anxiety. By the end of the second day he was so extremely anxious that he had to be relocated. He had become much more sensitive than ever before to 'insane stimuli.' He was now a far more difficult problem than when I had first seen him, and far more effort was now needed to overcome his neurosis by desensitization.

Evaluation of Flooding Therapy

To make the most of flooding, we would have to understand how it works. Even though it was originally modelled on the paradigm of experimental extinction, it seems most unlikely that it leads to change on the basis of extinction. Extinction is defined as the progressive weakening displayed by a habit when the response concerned is evoked repeatedly without reinforcement. In the case of motor habits, the more strongly the response is evoked the more rapidly it extinguishes (Hull, 1943, p. 279).

Goldstein's experiments, cited above, show that in the case of strongly conditioned anxiety what happens is exactly the opposite: only when response evocation is always maximal or nearly so is there no response decrement. There is uniform non-extinguishability of experimental neuroses by prolonged exposure to maximal stimulation. The clinical failures of flooding, as in Case 20, and similar cases – such as the many aerophobias that do not improve in repeated fear-filled flights – are of a piece with this.

Goldstein's experiments, Case 19, and Stampfl's clinically-derived gradualness all point to the conclusion that for flooding to succeed the fear must be masterable. If so, by what process does anxiety habit decrement take place? One straw in the wind is the observation that, generally, the therapist has been directly involved in the immediate therapeutic situation when habit decrement has occurred. It is possible that the anxiety is inhibited by the response to the therapist (which seems also to be crucial in other circumstances). Another possibility is this: if the stimulation is not so strong as to cause the subject to withdraw or 'switch off' entirely, the continuing strong stimulation leads, after a time (which varies from case to case), to transmarginal inhibition (Pavlov, 1927; Gray, 1964) of the response. (In this connection, it must be stated that the suggestion made in the first edition of this book that an epinephrine rebound might be behind this, is now clearly untenable. Change of stimulus would not renew anxiety as it did in Case 17 if this were the mechanism.)

Recently, there have been several reports of controlled comparisons of flooding and desensitization. The conclusions from laboratory studies (Willis and Edwards, 1969; DeMoor, 1970; Mealiea and Nawas, 1971) dealing with the uniform subject matter of small animal phobias are that flooding is less effective than desensitization and, in contrast to the latter, somewhat liable to relapse. On the other hand, in comparisons involving severe clinical phobias, flooding has been reported to achieve better results than desensitization (Boulougouris, Marks, and Marset, 1971; Gath and Gelder, 1971). The use of untrained therapists by the former creates a bias against desensitization, but the same objection does not apply to Gath and Gelder's study, in which flooding was found more effective than desensitization in agoraphobia, but less effective in some other phobias. (For a review of research on flooding see Morganstern (1973).)

Time will no doubt reveal that there are individual differences, too, that determine responsiveness to flooding methods, and to desensitization. We also need to have some way of identifying the occasional individual whose anxiety flooding may exacerbate.

ABREACTION

Abreaction is operationally defined as the re-evocation with strong emotional accompaniment of a fearful past experience. Some abreactions are followed by therapeutic changes, while others are not, and may even leave the patient worse off than before. If we could predict which individuals would respond favorably to it, and could induce it at will, we would expedite therapy in many cases. As matters stand, the induction of abreaction is unreliable, and its effects unpredictable. It would seem, however, that in some neurotic patients the unadaptive emotional responses have been conditioned to intricate stimulus compounds that neither current nor contrived stimulus situations can adequately cover; and then abreaction may be well-nigh indispensable (Wolpe, 1958, p. 198)—or at least it may be necessary to use the recalled images of the causal situation introduced in some therapeutic context.

The therapeutic efficacy of abreaction, judging from Grinker and Spiegel's experiences (1945) with war neuroses, bears no relation to the previous *accessibility* to recall of the abreacted experience. The one apparent essential is for it to take place in a protected setting such as the psychotherapeutic relationship affords (Grinker and Spiegel, 1945). This observation was the basis for the suggestion (Wolpe, 1958, p. 196) that the therapeutic effects obtained during abreaction might be a special case of the nonspecific effects that occur in a proportion of cases receiving any form of psychotherapy. In other words, abreaction succeeds when anxiety is inhibited by other emotional responses that the therapeutic situation induces in the patient. Thus, though the source of the stimulus material differs, abreaction and flooding may operate through the same process.

Abreactions take place in a variety of circumstances. Sometimes they arise unbidden, during history-taking or systematic desensitization.

Case 21:   Abreaction during history-taking

A truck driver had, following an accident, a marked phobia for driving (in addition to considerable pervasive anxiety). After training in relaxation and the construction of a hierarchy on the theme of driving, he was asked, during his first desensitization session, to imagine himself sitting at the wheel of a car that was stationary and whose engine was not running. He suddenly began to verbalize the details of the accident, broke into a sweat and became very agitated. After about a minute, when the reaction subsided, he was asked to open his eyes. When he did so he appeared tired but relieved, and said that he was no longer afraid to drive a truck. The test of reality proved him right.

Case 22 :   Abreaction during desensitization

Another example of unscheduled abreaction occurred in a 50-year-old lawyer who had been vaguely tense for decades, and who had come for treatment mainly because of increasing insomnia. During instruction in assertive behavior, he began to talk of his childhood, and mentioned that though his family had been very poor he would never take anything from other people. He recounted an incident at school when, being a good athlete, he had taken part in a race and had been the only contestant without spiked shoes. He had proudly refused to accept a pair as a hand-out from the school. He became very tearful during this narration. At the next interview, a week later, he said that he was feeling better and that the average duration of his sleep had gone up from four to six hours per night. At this interview he abreacted at telling the story of a friend in the Army towards whom he had been aggressive and who had been killed within a month. Further abreactions were subsequently deliberately induced in relation to this story under hypnosis. Each of these abreactions, though weaker than the first one, was followed by improvement. With the addition of assertive training and desensitization to receiving praise and favors, an apparently complete recovery was obtained in a total of 15 sessions.

If the therapist wishes to try to bring about an abreaction, there are several courses open to him. He may endeavor, either with or without hypnosis, to plunge the patient into re-experiencing some past situation *known* to be highly disturbing. He may also try to gain access to unknown material by asking the hypnotized patient to fantasize an unpleasant or fearful event out of the past. An impressive case of successful hypnotic abreaction of a war neurosis after 20 years was recently described by Leahy and Martin (1967). It is sometimes worth trying the 'age-regression' technique in which the patient imagines himself back in past phases of his life, starting relatively recently and then going back year by year. I have used this technique very occasionally, but have not seen the dramatic effects reported by others. As Barber (1969) has shown, this produces a restimulating, not a reliving.

The most practical way of pursuing an abreaction is by means of drugs. The first drug to gain widespread interest for this purpose was pentobarbital (Pentothal) whose use in this manner was introduced by Horsley (1936), and used widely during World War II. At that time, and for a few years following, I occasionally used it in the hope of obtaining beneficial abreactions; but though abreactions did occur fairly often – sometimes very vivid and exciting ones – in not a single case did I find marked and lasting benefit. Perhaps drugs that *elevate* arousal are more likely to lead to therapeutic abreactions. The most effective and hopeful of these are probably di-ethyl ether (in its excitatory phase) and lysergic acid diethylamide. The amphetamines (notably Methedrine) can also produce abreactions, but it has not been evident from the literature that these yield any lastingly beneficial after-effects, and sometimes (as has been my own experience) sensitization may afterwards be found to have been increased. Possibly, because these drugs favor responses of the sympathetic division of the autonomic nervous system, they actually militate against the therapeutic counterconditioning that we have presumed to be the basis of beneficial abreaction.

For a full description of the technique of obtaining excitatory abreaction with ether, the reader should consult the original accounts by Palmer (1944) and by Shorvon and Sargant (1947). While the patient lies on his back on a couch the therapist talks to him informally about events that preceded the incident on which it is hoped he will abreact. The ether-soaked mask is held a few inches from the face, and then rather rapidly approximated. In a matter of minutes the patient becomes excited and, in a successful case, begins to recite the events that led to the precipitation of his neurosis. He is encouraged to 'cry, shout, and struggle'; and it is very desirable to have an assistant at hand to restrain excessive movement. Shorvon and Slater express the consensus when they state that one is much more likely to produce emotional release in an individual suffering from a recent traumatic neurosis than in one with a long-standing illness. But even with recent cases, as they also point out, there are many failures. An interesting case was recently described by Little and James (1964), in which a neurosis originating in battle 18 years previously was progressively overcome in 5 sessions of ether abreactions. During the course of these, the patient pieced together the tremendously disturbing sequence of events that had precipitated the neurosis, beginning with his shooting of two young German soldiers while the three of them were in a ditch taking shelter from artillery shells.

Lysergic acid diethylamide (LSD 25) is a drug that may have great abreactive potentialities if its effects can be brought under control. It was introduced into psychiatry because of its ability to promote vivid imagery and strong emotional responses. Beneficial abreactions have frequently been reported (e.g. Sandison, 1954), but cannot be relied on. Costello (1964) reported attempting to turn the effects of the drug to use in accordance with conditioning principles. He reported rapid recoveries in three cases. My own limited experience with Costello's technique has been disappointing. None of three cases on whom I tried it made the hoped-for improvement, although two of them showed emotional responses during treatment not unlike those of Costello's cases.

CHAPTER 11

Operant Conditioning Methods

The physiological basis of learning (conditioning) is the establishment of functional connections between neurons (Wolpe, 1958). There is no reason to believe that there is more than one *kind* of learning. Variation depends on the identity of interconnected neuronal sequences. Thus, the distinction between respondent and operant conditioning is not in the nature of the conditioning, but in the fact that in the former 'nonvoluntary,' especially autonomic, behavior is predominantly involved, whereas in the latter the behavior is either motor or cognitive.

The conditioning of operants is certainly more obviously relatable to reinforcing events, and more clearly 'under the control of its consequences' (e.g. reward or non-reward) than the conditioning of autonomic responses. The difference, however, is probably a matter of details rather than of essence. There is impressive evidence that autonomic responses can be brought under the control of reward contingencies (Kimmel, 1967; Miller and DiCara, 1968; Lang, 1968). And the resistance of neurotic anxiety responses to extinction is evidently due to negative reinforcement — the anxiety reduction that follows the removal of the organism from the conditioned stimuli (Wolpe, 1952).

The operant procedures that are used in clinical practice generally follow experimental paradigms that have emerged from the work of B. F. Skinner and his associates. Explicit applications of these paradigms do not figure largely in the treatment of neuroses which are primarily autonomic habits. Nevertheless, we have noted the operant conditioning of motor responses that is part and parcel of assertive training. There are also numerous other unadaptive habits in whose treatment operant procedures are central, among them the learned habits of schizophrenics and a wide range of other unadaptive habits that have usually no particular relation to conditioned anxiety—such habits as nail-biting, trichotillomania, enuresis, encopresis, and thumb-sucking.

A concise account of operant conditioning methods follows. For more extensive expositions the reader is referred to Ayllon and Azrin (1968), Schaefer and Martin (1969), Bandura (1969), and Kanfer and Phillips (1970); for briefer accounts that introduce collections of cases, to Ullmann and Krasner (1965); Franks (1965); and Ulrich, Stachnik, and Mabry (1966).

Six operant techniques are distinguishable: positive reinforcement, extinction, differential reinforcement, response-shaping, punishment, and negative reinforcement. Punishment, as far as behavior therapy is concerned, is referred to in Chapter 12. Differential reinforcement is a selective combination of positive reinforcement and extinction. Shaping is, in essence, a special case of positive reinforcement. We shall here consider positive reinforcement, negative reinforcement, and extinction.

POSITIVE REINFORCEMENT

Any state of affairs that, following a response, serves to increase the rate of responding may be called a reinforcer. When 'reward' is that state of affairs it is called a positive reinforcer. Food, water, sex, money, domination, approval, or affection are all operational reinforcers when they increase the rate (or strength) of a response in a given stimulus situation—as they will under the appropriate conditions of hunger, etc. Homme (1965) has extended the range of clinical reinforcers to include high probability (preferred) behaviors, on the strength of Premack's (1965) observation that these reinforce low probability behaviors that they follow. When the rate of responding is increased by relief from anything aversive—pain, discomfort, or tension—we speak of this as 'negative reinforcement' (see p. 213).

Examples of the habit-building power of positive reinforcement are legion, ranging from pecking habits in pigeons to the most complex rituals of mankind. In the field of therapeutic behavior change, it has already been noted that the motor behavior of assertion is reinforced by such consequences as the achievement of interpersonal domination, and the approval of the therapist, but the context is a relatively complex one. Simple examples are easy to find in relation to commonplace behavior problems of children. A child habitually screams to get what he wants, and getting what he wants (sooner or later) maintains the habit of screaming. Now the child is told, "You will never get it (e.g. a toy) if you scream. You will get it if you say quietly, 'Please, may I have it?'" If he asks as directed, he is at once rewarded, which immediately increases the likelihood of his asking in this new way again. Consistently rewarding the new behavior results in its displacing the old.

The therapeutic potentialities of positive reinforcement have been strikingly demonstrated in recent years. Most of the earlier work was done on chronic schizophrenics; though it must at once be stated that 'cure' of the psychosis is neither obtained nor claimed, but only change in particular habits. This is not surprising since a variety of evidence, genetic (Kallman, 1953), physiological (Rubin, 1970), biochemical (Gottlieb and Frohman, 1972), and others suggests that schizophrenia is basically an organic illness (Wolpe, 1970). The organic abnormality seems to be directly responsible for some of the psychotic behavior while at the same time predisposing the individual to the acquisition by learning of unadaptive habits that are often bizarre.

Lindsley (1956) was the first to explore the possibilities of operant conditioning schedules in psychotic subjects. This work was later vastly extended by Ayllon and Azrin (1964, 1965). One of the clever treatment schedules devised by Ayllon (1963)* is worth presenting at length. The patient was a 47-year-old schizophrenic woman who had been in a state hospital for nine years. Among other strange habits she always wore an excessive amount of clothing—about 25 pounds. In order to treat this, a scale was placed at the entrance to the dining room. The requirement for entering (to receive food reinforcement) was a predetermined weight.

Initially, she was given an allowance of 23 lbs. over her current body weight. This allowance represented a 2 lb. reduction from her usual clothing weight. When the patient exceeded the weight requirement, the nurse stated in a matter-of-fact manner, "Sorry, you weigh too much, you'll have to weigh less." Failure to meet the required weight resulted in the patient missing the meal at which she was being weighed. Sometimes, in an effort to meet the requirement, the patient discarded more clothing than she was required. When this occurred, the requirement was adjusted at the next weighing time to correspond to the limit set by the patient on the preceding occasion.

At the start of this experiment, the patient missed a few meals because she failed to meet the weight requirement, but soon thereafter she gradually discarded her superfluous clothing. First, she left behind odd items she had carried in her arms, such as bundles, cups and handbags. Next, she took off the elaborate headgear and assorted

*Ayllon, T. (1963) Intensive treatment of psychotic behavior by stimulus satiation and food reinforcement, *Behav. Res. Ther.*, 1: 53.

'capes' or shawls she had worn over her shoulders. Although she had worn 18 pairs of stockings at one time, she eventually shed these also.

At the end of the experiment, the patient's clothing weighed a normal 3 pounds and subsequently remained stable at this level. One result of dressing normally was participation in small social events at the hospital. Another was that her parents took her out for the first time in nine years.

Anorexia nervosa is one of the few conditions classified as neurotic in which positive reinforcement has been successfully used as the main method. Some years ago, I was involved to an extent in the treatment of the first two cases to be so treated, one of which has been reported in detail by Bachrach, Erwin, and Mohr (1965).* This was a 37-year-old woman whose weight had fallen to 47 pounds in the face of various medical treatments. For the purposes of the operant conditioning program, she was transferred from her attractive hospital room to a barren one, furnished only with a bed, nightstand, and chair. Each of the three authors had one meal a day with her. The reinforcement schedule involved verbal reinforcement of movements associated with eating.

When the patient lifted her fork to move toward spearing a piece of food, the experimenter would talk to her about something in which she might have an interest. The required response was then successively raised to lifting the food toward her mouth, chewing, and so forth. The same scheduled increase in required response was applied to the amount of food consumed. At first, any portion of the meal that was consumed would be a basis for a postprandial reinforcement (a radio, TV set, or phonograph would be brought in by the nurse at a signal from the experimenter); if she did not touch any of the food before her, nothing would be given until the next meal. More and more of the meal had to be consumed in order to be reinforced until she eventually was required to eat everything on the plate.

After two months, when she had gained 14 pounds, she was discharged to out-patient treatment, and positive reinforcement treatment was continued at home with the cooperation of her family. Eighteen months later her weight was 88 pounds. A number of other cases successfully treated by operant methods have been reported (e.g. Hallsten, 1965; Blinder, Freeman, and Stunkard, 1970; Scrignar, 1971).

While operant procedures have generally not had an important role in

*Bachrach, A. J., Erwin, W. J., and Mohr, J. P. "The control of eating behavior in an anorexic by operant conditioning techniques." In *Case Studies in Behavior Modification*, L. Ullmann and L. Krasner (Eds.). New York: Holt, Rinehart and Winston, 1965.

the treatment of phobias, they are probably very relevant in those in whose maintenance physical avoidance plays a major part. This is a feature of certain cases of agoraphobia, and, probably more often, of school phobias. Ayllon, Smith, and Rogers (1970) have reported the operant treatment of a school phobia in an 8-year-old. The problem was redefined as zero or low probability of school attendance. The implementation of techniques for increasing the probability involved getting the child's mother to withdraw the rewards of staying at home. Then a home-based motivational system was used to reinforce school attendance, and refusal to attend school resulted in punishment. School attendance was generated quickly and maintained even after the procedures were withdrawn a month later. No 'symptom substitution' was noticed either by the parents or the school officials within the 9 months of follow-up.

Operant programs have in recent years been increasingly applied to problem behavior in children. Much of the work has been directed at classroom behavior (e.g. Homme et al., 1971; Patterson and Gullion, 1968) but specific psychiatric syndromes have also received a great deal of attention.

Kimmel and Kimmel (1970) have described a method for treating nocturnal enuresis by which the child, drinking water and other liquids without restriction, is rewarded with cookies or other desired items for 'holding in' his urine for increasing periods. At the beginning, the child is given the reward for inhibiting urination for five minutes after his first report of a need to urinate, and later the period of inhibition is lengthened. Apparently, a habit of inhibition of urination is established by positive reinforcement. In three cases in which this method was used, complete cessation of bed-wetting was achieved in about a week.

Neale (1963) cured several cases of encopresis by rewarding defecation at the toilet with candy. Similar cases have been reported by Madsen (1965) and Tomlinson (1970). Edelman (1971) used a combination of negative and positive reinforcement to the same end.

The rewarding quality of the masturbatory orgasm appears to be a powerful agent for transferring male sexual interest from deviant objects to women (Marquis, 1970). The patient is instructed to masturbate to the point where he feels the inevitability of orgasm, using whatever fantasy is most arousing. Then he is to switch to the female fantasy that has previously been agreed on as appropriate. He is warned that he may experience some difficulty at first, but that he will not lose his sexual arousal at that point. After he has successfully shifted to the appropriate stimulus four or five times, he is instructed to start moving the introduction of the appropriate fantasy backward in time toward the beginning of masturbation. An attempt is made at the outset to get a commitment from the client never to continue picturing the inappropriate fantasy through the occurrence of an orgasm, whether in masturbation or overt sexual behavior. Any decrease in sexual arousal upon switching is seen as evidence that the client has exchanged fantasies too soon, and he is instructed to drop back to the original fantasy and switch at a higher level of sexual arousal. Of the fourteen cases Marquis reports, five were cured, and seven much improved.

Exploratory applications of operant conditioning techniques to delinquent behavior (Schwitzgebel and Kolb, 1964; Burchard and Tyler, 1965) have yielded encouraging results. The former authors treated 40 adolescent delinquents by reinforcement procedures. A three-year follow-up study of 20 of them revealed a significant reduction in the frequency and severity of crime in comparison with a matched-pair control group. Burchard and Tyler produced a marked decrease in the 'destructive and disruptive behavior' of a 13-year-old delinquent boy by systematically isolating him when he performed in an anti-social way and by rewarding socially acceptable behavior.

Thomas (1968)* has listed a number of conditions that relate to the effectiveness of positive reinforcement.

1. The response to be reinforced must first be emitted, otherwise reinforcement is impossible.
2. Reinforcement must not be delayed; in general, the more immediate the reinforcement, the better.
3. Reinforcement of every desired response emitted is most effective for establishing behavior.
4. Not reinforcing every desired response during response establishment, while less effective in achieving immediate high rates of responding, is generally more effective in producing responses that endure after reinforcement is terminated.
5. The stimuli suitable to reinforce one individual's behavior may not be the most appropriate for another. Recent research suggests that one important clue to what the reinforcing conditions are in the profile is simply the rank order of activities in which a person engages in his free time (see Premack, 1965; Homme, 1965).

*From Thomas. E. J. Selected sociobehavioral techniques and principles: An approach to interpersonal helping. Reprinted with permission of the National Association of Social Workers. From *Social Work*, Vol. 13, No. 1 (January 1968), p. 18.

Cautela (1970) has described a procedure that he calls covert rein-forcement. In this, the response to be reinforced and the reinforcer of that response are both presented in imagination. Cautela reports that he has successfully employed it to treat phobias, obsessions, homosexuality, and obesity The first necessity is to identify stimuli that will appro-priately function as reinforcers. This can conveniently be done on the basis of the patient's responses to a reinforcement survey schedule (Cautela and Kastenbaum, 1967). Any item to which the patient indicates a high degree of pleasure is tested for visual clarity and for the ease with which the patient can conjure up the image of it. The patient must be able to evoke the image within about five seconds if the item is to be usable as a reinforcer.

We may illustrate the method with reference to material from a case reported by Wisocki (1970). The patient had a neatness compulsion that included, among other things, the habit of folding articles of clothing again and again, smoothing them down more perfectly each time. In applying the covert reinforcement procedure, the therapist instructed the patient to imagine herself in various situations involving two types of behavior: (1) Refraining from repeating the obsessive-compulsive behavior, (2) Making responses antagonistic to that behavior. When the patient signalled imagining the appropriate response, the therapist immed-iately said "reinforcement," which was the cue for the patient to imagine a predetermined reinforcing item, such as walking in a forest, practicing ballet, or eating an Italian sandwich. Thus, the therapist would instigate a reinforcing image when the patient signalled that she was thinking "I don't care if it is wrinkled; it doesn't matter," or if she imagined folding a laundered item quickly and putting it on top of the finished pile though it was a little wrinkled. This patient's obsessive-compulsive behaviors were eliminated in eight two-hour sessions. At a twelve month follow-up, there was no recurrence of the compulsive behavior.

Thought-Stopping

The likely basis of this procedure is the establishment of an inhibitory habit by positive reinforcement. Perseverating trains of thought that are unrealistic, unproductive, and anxiety-arousing are a common clinical problem. If chronic, they are called obsessions. Many are only episodic. A businessman, for example, constantly brooded upon the possibility of a fire breaking out in one of his warehouses, after a friend of his suffered a severe financial loss. Thought-stopping is a particularly effective way of

treating episodic brooding. It also sometimes succeeds with true obsessions (see below). In either type of case, however, the treatment of
anxiety must not be neglected.

A thought-stopping program begins by asking the patient to close his
eyes and to verbalize a typical futile thought-sequence. During the
verbalization the therapist suddenly shouts, "Stop!" and then draws
attention to the fact that the thoughts actually do stop. This is repeated
several times, and then the patient is urged to test the efficacy of the procedure by interrupting his unadaptive thoughts by saying, "Stop!"
subvocally. He is warned that the thoughts will return; but every time
they do he must interrupt them again. The main effort later is directed at
learning to stifle each unwanted thought at birth. The moment it threatens
to appear the patient quickly inhibits it by concentrating on something
else. The thoughts in many cases return less and less readily and eventually cease to be a problem.

Modifications of the method are sometimes successful with patients
with whom the standard procedure fails. A fairly uncomfortable faradic
shock accompanying the "Stop" signal may successfully disrupt the negative thought sequence. Alternatively, the patient may be asked to keep
his mind on pleasant thoughts and to press a button which activates a
buzzer as soon as any disturbing thought intrudes. Upon the buzzer
sounding, the therapist instantly shouts, "Stop!" There is frequently a
progressive decline in buzzer-pressing, which may be steep, e.g. from 20
per minute to one every two minutes in the course of a 15-minute treatment period.

Some years ago, I took advantage of an opportunity to observe the
effects of this procedure on myself. I had been involved in a legal dispute
that was finally settled at a meeting of principals and lawyers. Later that
day, reflecting upon the proceedings, I became very disturbed at realizing
how ineptly I had handled an important interchange. Dwelling continuously on the matter, I became increasingly distressed. I decided to try
thought-stopping. I found it very difficult to do, for the thoughts were
seemingly borne along by the anxiety that they themselves had stirred
up; but I worked at it assiduously, and after an hour noticed that the
general anxiety level was distinctly lower. After two more hours, I was
no longer troubled by these thoughts. Even when my anxiety was high,
it seemed that the successful exclusion of a thought slightly diminished it;
but when the anxiety was low this effect was quite clear.

On the basis of this personal experience, supported to some extent by
the testimony of patients, it is reasonable to think that a habit of thought-

inhibition is reinforced by the anxiety-reducing consequence of each successful effort at thought-inhibition. This hypothesis could be tested by psychophysiological monitoring.

Thought-stopping was introduced by J. G. Taylor in 1955 (see Wolpe, 1958); but, unknown to him, it had already been advocated by a largely forgotten writer, Alexander Bain (1928). Taylor (1963) has also described the application of the idea to the treatment of a case of compulsive eyebrow-plucking of 31 years' duration. The habit was overcome in ten days.

While thought-stopping has its most frequent use for episodic preoccupation or brooding, it is also occasionally of great value in the treatment of true obsessions. In an obsessional neurosis of eight years' duration reported by Yamagami (1971), it was the sole agent of recovery. The patient was a 24-year-old male graduate student whose obsession consisted in verbalizing in thought the names of colors, counting numbers, and typing words in fantasy. The color obsession was predominant, occurring an average of 110 times per day. Colored sticks, which could trigger the color obsession, were placed in front of the subject. He was told to look at them and not to try to suppress whatever obsessional thinking came to mind. He was to signal the onset of the obsessive thoughts by raising a finger. At this point the therapist would shout, "Stop," which he was instructed to repeat. By the fourth session, the obsession had diminished by about 80 percent. Treatment was continued for a total of 17 sessions, in the course of which 3 variations of the technique were used. In one of them an electric shock was substituted for the shouting of the word "Stop." At the time of the seventeenth weekly session the obsession had decreased to about five occurrences per day; and the patient could control it easily by saying, "Stop," subvocally, on any occasion. A month after the end of treatment, the color obsession disappeared completely. At a seven-month follow-up, it had not recurred, and the other obsessions were reported to be progressively decreasing.

NEGATIVE REINFORCEMENT

Negative reinforcement means increasing the rate or strength of a response by the removal of some source of pain or tension after the response. Negative reinforcement is often complicated by the fact that the therapist has to introduce the source of pain in the first place, and the immediate consequences of this have to be taken into account.

A beautiful example of the operation of negative reinforcement is afforded by Ayllon's (1963) treatment of another habit of the patient referred to on p. 207—towel hoarding. This woman would collect and store large numbers of towels which the nursing staff would remove from her room about twice a week. Ayllon instructed the staff to stop the routine towel removal and, intermittently each day, to hand the patient a towel without comment. The patient was delighted at this new policy, and arranged her growing stock in neat piles, first on the dressing table and chair, and later on the floor and bed. When there were several hundred, the piles became unmanageable so that increasing numbers of them began to lie about the room in disorder. The patient now began to ask the staff to stop bringing the towels, but without avail. When the number reached 600, additional towels seemed to become aversive, as surfeits are wont to do. One day, when there were 625 towels in the room, the patient seized the next towel that arrived and threw it out of the room. It did not come back, so there was negative reinforcement of the act of discarding a towel. Thereafter, the patient started taking them out, and no more were given her. During the next 12 months the mean number of towels found in her room was 1.5.

Cautela has extended his covert reinforcement idea to include covert negative reinforcement. He states that it is especially applicable to subjects who find it easier to evoke disagreeable images than pleasant ones. If the patient finds it unpleasant to be spoken to in a harsh tone, he will be asked to visualize this and, when he signals that the image is clear, to replace it by an image of the response to be increased. Great care is taken to insure that the patient can immediately withdraw the aversive stimulus upon request and replace it with the response to be increased. If, after a number of trials, there is still an overlap, a new aversive stimulus is chosen. This technique has not as yet been widely used, but has been successful in 90 percent of the cases in which Cautela (1970a) has used it.

EXTINCTION

Extinction is the progressive weakening or diminishing frequency of a response when it is repeatedly evoked without being followed by a reinforcer.

A case of Ayllon and Michael (1959) is one of the earliest clinical examples of a type of extinction program that is finding increasing use. The patient was a woman who, for a period of two years, had been entering the nurses' office on an average of 16 times a day. The nurses had resigned themselves to this activity on the grounds that such efforts as pushing her back bodily onto the ward had failed in the past and because the patient had been classified as mentally defective and, therefore, 'too dumb' to understand. In order to extinguish the problem behavior in question, the nurses were instructed that during the program the patient not be given any reinforcement (attention) for entering the nurses' office. It was found that, following the inception of the extinction schedule, there was a gradual and continuing diminution of entries to the nurses' office. The average frequency was down to two entries per day by the seventh week of extinction, at which time the program was terminated.

Behavior that is being extinguished diminishes at varying rates. As Thomas (1968) points out, resistance to extinction is often high in clinical cases because the responses have been sustained for long periods by intermittent reinforcement. For this reason, it is important that the cessation of reinforcement be abrupt and complete.

A massed practice type of extinction program was introduced by Dunlap (1932), who called it "negative practice." He described overcoming such habits as the repeated typing of errors, tics, and stuttering by persuading the subject to repeat the undesired act a great many times. The method has come to be mainly used in the treatment of tics (e.g. Yates, 1958; Jones, 1960; Rafi, 1962; Walton, 1964). In using this method it is imperative that the undesirable response is evoked to the point of exhaustion—so that a high degree of reactive inhibition is produced. Otherwise the tic may actually be reinforced, especially if it is not asymptotic to begin with. In any event, this is a tedious, time-consuming method. Kondas (1965) has reported that much more rapid change can be obtained if negative practice is combined with 'anxiety-relief' conditioning. While the patient repeats the tic, an unpleasant electric current is continuously applied; and it is switched off simultaneously with cessation of the tic sequence, a negative reinforcement of not doing the tic.

CHAPTER 12

Aversion Therapy

Aversion therapy consists, operationally, of administering an aversive stimulus to inhibit an unwanted emotional response, thereby diminishing its habit strength. For example, a painful stimulus may be employed to inhibit sexual arousal by a fetishistic object. It is thus a special application of the reciprocal inhibition principle. Aversion must be clearly distinguished from punishment, in which the aversive stimulus follows the response of concern instead of coinciding with it. Failure to make the distinction is very common. I was guilty of it in the first edition of this book. But there are circumstances in which aversion and punishment are both present.

The uses of aversion are largely in the treatment of obsessions, compulsions, fetishes, and habits of attraction to inappropriate objects, e.g. sex objects of the same sex. It also has some value in the control of drug addictions, but not, as yet, in a satisfactory way because we know so little of what goes into the making of drug habits, despite the pioneering efforts of Wikler (1948, 1972).

Aversion is not often the behavioral treatment of first choice. Usually, the homosexual or other maladaptive behavior to which aversion therapy might be applied is found to have a basis in neurotic anxiety, and this should be deconditioned first. If this is done, secondary maladaptive behavior will usually stop, having required no special attention. On the other hand, even when aversion therapy succeeds in removing the secondary behavior, deconditioning of anxiety is still likely to be needed. The

216

continued presence of neurotic anxiety can provide a basis for 'symptom substitution.' For example, some years ago I was consulted about a woman whose compulsive eating had been overcome by aversion therapy and who had thereafter become severely depressed. It was soon apparent that her neurotic anxiety habits had not been removed, and that the depression was the result of her having been deprived of what was for her the anxiety-reducing activity of eating.

The essence of aversion therapy is to present, in the presence of the stimulus to the undesired response, a strong aversive stimulus, such as strong electrical stimulation of a limb. Besides eliciting an avoidance response, the shock will inhibit the undesired emotional response. Whenever it does so, a measure of conditioned inhibition of the undesired response will be established—a weakening of its habit—of the bond between that response and its stimulus. At the same time, the stimulus may be to some extent conditioned to the response constellation which the shock evoked. The amount of positive conditioning is generally small or else transient (e.g. Raymond, 1964; O'Keefe, 1965). Pearce (1963) found that transvestites who had been treated by apomorphine later reported loss of interest rather than nausea at transvestite fantasies. Similarly, Rachman and Teasdale (1969) have noted a lack of evidence of conditioned fear developing in studies employing shock as the aversive stimulus.

Figure 13 exemplifies the experimental paradigm on which all aversive

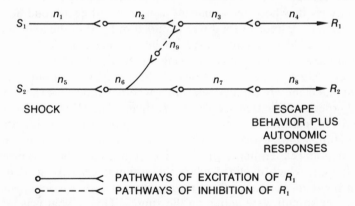

Fig. 13. When S_1 and S_2 are presented simultaneously and S_2 is relatively strong, R_2 is elicited, and R_1 inhibited by impulses from the inhibitory neurone, n_9. At the same time, S_1 is conditioned to R_2 (pathway not shown).

therapeutic procedures are based. An animal is placed in a cage that has an electrifiable grid on its floor. Food has been dropped audibly into a food box within easy reach, and the animal has eaten it. With repetition he has acquired the habit of approaching the food box at the sound of the food dropping into it. Appropriate autonomic responses accompany the approach — salivation, increased gastric motility, etc. Now, one day, as the animal is approaching the food box, we pass a strong shock into his feet through the grid on the floor of the cage. The shock inhibits the conditioned approach. It produces 'pain,' anxiety, and motor withdrawal. Since there are neural arrangements in the central nervous system that prevent the simultaneous activation of two incompatible responses (Gellhorn, 1967), the alimentary response is inhibited. Each time that response is inhibited, some weakening occurs of the habit tying it to its antecedent stimulus; and at the same time some conditioning takes place of that stimulus to the responses to the other stimulus, namely, the shock. After several repetitions of the maneuver, the sound of food dropping into the food box evokes exclusively an anxiety-and-avoidance response in place of the approach response and its autonomic concomitants. However, it should be noted that there may be an 'interphase' when eating is inhibited and anxiety-and-avoidance not yet quite established. This 'interphase' is probably the end point of most aversion therapy.

The electrical stimulus is an unconditioned stimulus. The same inhibition of an approach response can be achieved with a conditioned aversive stimulus. This was clearly demonstrated some years ago (Wolpe, 1952) in cats in whom the sound of a buzzer had been conditioned to evoke anxiety. Attractive food was dropped in front of the animal under a particular table in a laboratory. As he approached, the buzzer was sounded. He stopped abruptly, showing mydriasis and other sympathetic responses. After several repetitions of the procedure the animal at all times avoided the area under that table whether food was there or not. Second order conditioning of anxiety clearly mediated this avoidance.

Wherever learning occurs, we expect to find a reinforcing state of affairs (Hull, 1943), especially when strong reactions are learnt. In both of the foregoing experiments, the aversive stimulus (e.g. buzzer) produced an excitation, which declined when the stimulus ceased — so that there was a *drive reduction* to reinforce the attachment of the anxiety responses to whatever stimuli were acting on the animal. This is what was referred to as negative reinforcement in Chapter 11.

The first formal usage of aversive therapy seems to have been by Kantorovich (1929) who gave alcoholic patients painful electric shocks in relation to the sight, smell, and taste of alcohol. In 1935, L. W. Max reported overcoming a homosexual's fetish by administering very strong shocks to the patient in the presence of the fetishistic object. Unfortunately, his promised detailed account of this historic case never reached print. Nevertheless, Max's report served to encourage others to repeat his procedure, and instigated my own maiden attempt, in South Africa, to treat a patient with it (Wolpe, 1954).

Case 23:   Aversion therapy of food craving

The patient was a 32-year-old spinster who, among other neurotic reactions, was preoccupied with warding off impulses to indulge in 'eating sprees,' impulses which invariably in a day or two proved irresistible. Her cravings involved two kinds of 'forbidden' food – doughnuts and similar sweet foods, and salty foods. The former were disallowed because they made her fat (and she had a particular horror of obesity), and the latter because rheumatic heart disease had several times sent her into cardiac failure – so that a salt-limited diet had been prescribed. She would try to avoid these foods by various stratagems, such as not keeping them in her apartment, and getting her African servant to lock her in the apartment when he went off at night. But at times her impulse was overpowering, so that she would go out, buy food, and eat. As she went on gorging she would have a rising feeling of disgust and despair that would culminate in a helpless state of prostration.

I had her list all items of food that figured in her obsession, and selected an item from the list. I then attached electrodes to her forearm, told her to close her eyes and to signal by a hand movement each time she clearly formed the mental image of the selected food. At the signal, I passed a very severe faradic shock into her forearm. Ten shocks were used at a session. After two sessions, she found that thinking of these foods at any time conjured up an image of the shock equipment, which produced anxiety. With further treatment, thoughts of the foods progressively decreased. After five sessions, she felt free of their burden for the first time in sixteen years. She began to enjoy company and bought clothes, which she had not done for years.

Aversion therapy has been applied to a considerable number of neurotic conditions, e.g. fetishism (Raymond, 1956), homosexuality (Freund, 1960; James, 1962; Feldman and MacCulloch, 1965), transvestism (Glynn and Harper, 1961; Blakemore, 1965) – and to the addictions –

alcoholism, drug addiction, and smoking (McGuire and Vallance, 1964; Getze, 1968). A large number of clinical reports have been critically surveyed by Rachman and Teasdale (1968).

It is extremely important to note that apart from the addictions, the foregoing conditions are characterized by pleasurable excitation by inappropriate objects, and that the approach behavior is generally secondary to this. Simultaneous aversive stimulation inhibits the pleasurable emotion and leads to the elimination of its habit. It is this that provides the answer to what Rachman and Teasdale (1968, p. xii) term "a major puzzle" about aversion therapy – why patients refrain from their deviant behavior after they leave the hospital. If the object of deviation no longer arouses pleasure, there is no impulse to approach it.

DESCRIPTION OF TECHNIQUES

Electrical Stimulation

An important advantage of electrical stimulation is that it can be precisely timed in relation to the behavior to be modified. Depending upon the circumstances of the case, one may administer the shock either in the presence of the actual objects or situations that form the basis of the obsessional or other undesirable behavior, or in relation to imaginary or pictorial representations of them. The preferred source of aversive stimulation is either faradic current or alternating current because these can, if necessary, be kept at steady levels for prolonged periods. The electrodes are usually attached to the patient's forearm. The baseline shock setting is determined by gradually increasing the current to a point where the patient reports it to be distinctly unpleasant. The starting point for aversive trials is then usually a current 25–50 percent stronger. The most satisfactory electrode is the concentric electrode (Tursky *et al.*, 1965) which greatly minimizes the risk of burning the skin. Wet electrodes of saline-soaked gauze are also quite satisfactory. Ordinary electrocardiographic silver electrodes may be used if necessary.

The aversive use of electrical stimulation varies in its details, but always follows the general lines of the obsessional eating described above. The stimulus to which a change of response is desired may be presented either in imagination or in the concrete.

Real stimuli have figured in the treatment of transvestism (Blakemore *et al.*, 1963) and of compulsive gambling (Barker and Miller, 1968). One of the latters' patients had been gambling steadily on 'fruit machines' for

12 years. A machine borrowed from an inn was installed in the hospital. Shocks at about 70 volts were administered to the patient's forearm. While standing gambling continuously for 3 hours (his usual practice), he withstood a minimum of 150 shocks delivered by a third party at random to all stages of the gambling procedure from insertion of the discs to 'pay-out.' He received 672 shocks altogether, designed to produce a tolerable degree of discomfort during 12 hours' 'gambling treatment,' although he lost all desire to gamble after only 6 hours. He did not resume gambling for 18 months when he relapsed following a period of stress. Six hours' booster treatment, using the same technique, prevented further gambling for at least 6 months.

Feldman and MacCulloch (1965) have made extensive use of pictorial representations of the object to which aversion therapy is directed in their program for treating homosexuality (see p. 238).

Rachman (1961) utilized both photographs and imagination in the treatment of a man who was sexually aroused by women's buttocks and bloomers. His five aversive conditioning sessions incorporated photographs of women in bloomers and imagined scenes of bloomers and of women with attractive buttocks. Electric shocks were applied to the fingers 10 to 15 times for each stimulus at each session. After the final session, the patient said that he no longer felt attracted by buttocks and disposed of his collection of pornographic photographs.

Abel, Levis, and Clancy (1970) have reported an elaborate "goal-gradient in reverse" technique in which tape-recorded descriptions of behavior were used in the treatment of sexual deviations. In three cases of exhibitionism, two of transvestism, and one of masochism, tapes were made involving descriptions of each subject's individual deviant behavior divided into three sequential segments. Five of the six subjects were placed on a schedule on which, at first, the final segment of the tape was followed by shock, and at later sessions the second, and ultimately the first segment. At each session, the shocked tape runs were followed by runs in which the patient avoided shock by verbalizing normal sexual behavior in place of the deviant segment. The sixth subject was given shocks out of relation to taped material, as a control. Treatment was evaluated by measuring penile responses to sexually deviant and non-deviant tapes, clinical interviews, and behavior reports. In the experimental subjects there was reduction of erectile responses to deviant tapes, but sustained responses to non-deviant tapes. Deviant responses became weaker and less frequent, and the improvement was maintained at follow-up 18 weeks later.

A technique in which aversion apparently works through the juxtaposition of unconditioned and conditioned aversive responses with both exteroceptive and imaginally evoked cognitions was introduced by Feingold (1966). His first patient was a girl of eleven who persistently kept her mouth open and thus made it unfeasible for her dentist to perform certain necessary procedures. The girl and her parents were instructed to bring the therapist a record of each occasion on which her mouth was noticed to be open. Then when she came to see him she was given as many strong shocks to the leg as there were recorded occasions of open mouth. The number of shocks needed decreased from 48 to zero in the course of 12 sessions, after which the mouth remained closed in a normal way, and the delighted dentist was able to proceed with his work. My own solitary experience with this technique was equally favorable.

Case 24 was a high school junior who, despite high intelligence, was getting low grades because he could not sit down to study in the evening. He felt he ought to be working between 7 and 11 p.m. He was asked to keep a record of his work each evening and told that he would receive a severe shock for each half-hour between 7 and 11 p.m. during which, in the course of the week, he did not work. At the end of the first week, he received four shocks, at the end of the second, three, and after that no more were necessary. His report of improved work habits was supported by his mother's report of a rise in grades from C to A-minus. It is presumed that the technique owed its efficacy to the juxtaposing of anxiety to the idea of not working.

Small portable shock equipment (e.g. McGuire and Vallance, 1964) has made it possible to program aversive events in the life situation of the patient. There is no alternative to this when the target behavior cannot be evoked to order in the consulting room. For example, there are rituals that particular situations elicit and that cannot be conjured up satisfactorily in imagination. Again, if aversion is to have much chance of success in the treatment of alcoholism or other drug addictions, it is not sufficient to administer aversive stimulation only in connection with the responses evoked by the sight, smell, and taste of the drug. It is also necessary to combat the 'craving' that arises endogenously. Since there is no way of producing the craving to order in the consulting room, aversion therapy must rely on portable shock apparatus to deliver aversive stimuli in real-life contexts.

Case 25 (Wolpe, 1965), a physician, who had for 5 years been taking

Demerol to alleviate emotional distress, had for 3 years noticed the increasing occurrence of a craving for the drug even in the absence of stress. This endogenous impulse had gradually become the dominating reason for indulgence. Now, about once a week, it would be irresistible, requiring 1000 to 1500 milligrams of the drug for its allayal. On the day following he would feel revolted and ashamed, but soon the craving would recur. I showed him how to work a portable shocker to give himself a painful shock to the forearm, and gave him the machine to take home, with instructions to use it whenever he felt a desire for the drug. On 3 occasions, 4, 3, and 2 severe shocks respectively dispelled the craving. After this the apparatus broke down, but for 12 weeks the patient felt only minor cravings that he could easily control, before he relapsed.

The effects noted in this single case clearly justify further trials. It may be that permanent suppression of craving can be produced by more thorough treatment and maybe not. But even suppressions lasting several months would be a boon if they were reliably repeatable. Current therapeutic resources for drug addiction are so pitifully inadequate that no lead should be disdained, as this one has been for seven years.

By what mechanism does the intrusion of electrical stimulation on a craving diminish the likelihood and strength of recurrence of the craving? We do not know the physiological responses that underlie the feeling of craving for a drug; but if they are mediated by nerve impulses they must be connected to their antecedents (whatever these may be) by neuronal chains. It should be possible to produce conditioned inhibition of these responses—even without identifying them—if they can be inhibited by the simultaneous evocation of an incompatible response. Strong electrical stimulation is quite apparently capable of procuring response inhibition, but research is needed to reveal to what extent habit decrement can be expected to follow in the very special case of habits whose stimuli are brought into being by the physiological effects of addictive drugs.

Aversion Therapy by Drugs

The treatment of alcoholism by an aversion method based on the nauseating effects of drugs was introduced many years ago by Voegtlin and Lemere (1942), and has been the subject of many subsequent reports, e.g. Lemere and Voegtlin (1950). It consists of giving the patient a nausea-producing drug, such as tartar emetic, emetine, apomorphine, or gold chloride, and then having him drink a favored alcoholic beverage. The combination of alcohol and emetic is given daily for a week to ten days, after which the effectiveness of the procedure is tested by giving the patient alcohol alone. If there is sufficient conditioning, the very sight of alcohol will produce nausea. Booster treatments are given two or three times during the following year.

Typically, the patient is given two ten-ounce glasses of warm saline solution containing 0.1 gram of emetine and 1 gram of sodium chloride to 20 ounces of water. This is just sufficient salt to mask the bitter taste of emetine. Immediately after this, he is given a hypodermic injection of 30 milligrams of emetine hydrochloride to produce emesis, 15 milligrams of pilocarpine hydrochloride for diaphoresis, and 15 milligrams of ephedrine sulphate for 'support.' The alcoholic beverage, e.g. whiskey, is held in front of the patient's nose and he is asked to smell deeply. He is then requested to sip the beverage and taste it thoroughly, swishing it around in his mouth and then swallowing it so that the sensory impact is at a maximum. Another drink is poured and the same procedure repeated. Nausea should begin immediately after this second drink if the timing has been right—as it must be if the treatment is to have its maximum effect.

Lemere and Voegtlin (1950) found that 38 percent of 4096 patients remained abstinent for 5 years or longer and 23 percent for 10 years or longer after their first treatment. The method is, however, extremely time-consuming, tedious, and messy and requires long-term accessibility of the patients. Trying it out in private practice in about a dozen patients in 1949, I found it so difficult and unrewarding that I gave it up in a few months. An institutional setting with routine arrangements for booster treatments would undoubtedly offer greater hope of success.

Drug-induced aversion for a behavioral problem was first reported by Raymond (1956). The patient was a 33-year-old man who had been arrested for acting out destructive fetishes towards perambulators (baby carriages) and handbags (pocket books). The fetishistic acts gave him a pleasurable erotic sensation. For purposes of treatment, "a collection of handbags, perambulators and colored illustrations was obtained and these were shown to the patient after he had received an injection of apomorphine and just before nausea was produced." Treatment was given two-hourly, day and night. At the end of the first week, treatment was temporarily suspended and the patient allowed home to attend to his affairs. Returning eight days later to continue the treatment, he reported jubilantly that he had for the first time been able to have intercourse with his wife without the use of the old fantasies. His wife said that she had noticed a change in his attitude to her, but was unable to define it. Treatment was resumed, save that emetine hydrochloride was used whenever the emetic effect of apomorphine became less pronounced than its sedative effect. After several more days' treatment the patient said that the sight of the objects made him sick. Six months later, it was suggested that he have a booster course of treatment, to which he agreed, although he did not consider it necessary. Nineteen months after the beginning of therapy, he stated that he had not again required the old fantasies to enable him to have sexual intercourse, nor had he masturbated with these fantasies. His wife said that she no longer worried about him and that their sexual relations had greatly improved. He had been promoted to a more responsible job.

Raymond carried out the above treatment under deprivation of food and rest, a condition that is almost certainly unnecessary as Raymond himself later seemed to recognize (Raymond and O'Keefe, 1965). Its omission has not apparently marred the efforts of other therapists. Glynn and Harper (1961), Lavin, et al. (1961) and Morganstern, Pearce, and Rees (1965) have all successfully treated cases of transvestism with apomorphine, the last-named authors having entirely overcome the habit in seven out of thirteen cases.

Another physiologically-acting group of aversive agents are curare-like drugs, such as succinylcholine (Scoline) (Sanderson, Campbell, and Laverty, 1963). These drugs, given in sufficient dosage, produce a temporary respiratory paralysis which, added to the patient's inability to speak or move in any way, is "a most terrifying experience." If alcohol is presented to the patient just at the height of his terror, a conditioned response of fear and aversion to the drug may be established. The subject is placed on a stretcher. Attached to him are a respirator and a polygraph which measures muscle tension and respiration, among other responses. A 20-mg. dose of Scoline is gradually injected. As soon as there is evidence of respiratory failure, the physician holds the bottle of alcohol to the lips of the subject and deposits a few drops into his mouth. During the period of apnea, which lasts between 30 and 150 seconds, the patient is enabled to breathe by the respirator. As soon as there are signs of natural breathing being restored, the alcohol is removed.

The original report by Sanderson's group was encouraging. Of twelve subjects, six were known to be abstinent several weeks later. However, the beneficial effects do not appear to be lasting (Laverty, 1966). Twelve cases were treated in this way by Farrar, Powell, and Martin (1968) and only two were abstinent at a one-year follow-up.

There is a general comment to be made about all aversion treatments of alcoholism. At best, they result in the patient 'recovering' on the condition that he no longer partakes of any alcohol at all. This does not amount to a restoration to normality. A cured patient would be one who could take a drink like anybody else. Such a result will remain beyond our reach until we know more about the processes that are involved in the formation of the drug-induced habits that we call addictions.

Covert Sensitization

This is the label Cautela (1966, 1967) has applied to the technique of pairing a verbally suggested aversive response with an imagined stimulus. This has been successful in a variety of conditions, notably obesity, homosexuality, and alcoholism. In the last-named condition, Ashem and Donner (1968) have recently noted that six out of fifteen alcoholics were abstinent six months after this treatment in contrast to none in an untreated control group—supporting to some extent an enthusiastic report by Anant (1967) of complete success in all of 26 patients without any relapse at a fifteen-month follow-up.

Cautela (1967) gives the following* exposition of his instructions in relation to an obese patient in whom he wishes to inhibit the eating of apple pie. The patient is relaxed and his eyes are shut.

> I want you to imagine you've just had your main meal and you are about to eat your dessert, which is apple pie. As you are about to reach for the fork, you get a funny feeling in the pit of your stomach. You start to feel queasy, nauseous, and sick all over. As you touch the fork, you can feel food particles inching up your throat. You're just about to vomit. As you put the fork into the pie, the food comes up into your mouth. You try to keep your mouth closed because you are afraid that you'll spit the food out all over the place. You bring the piece of pie to your mouth. As you're about to open your mouth, you puke; you vomit all over your hands, the fork, over the pie. It goes all over the table, over the other peoples' food. Your eyes are watering. Snot and mucous are all over your mouth and nose. Your hands feel sticky. There is an awful smell. As you look at this mess you just can't help but vomit again and again until just watery stuff is coming out. Everybody is looking at you with shocked expressions. You turn away from the food and immediately start to feel better. You run out of the room and, as you run out, you feel better and better. You wash and clean yourself up, and it feels wonderful.

It seems that the first report of the systematic use of aversion-evoking imagery was by Gold and Neufeld (1965), who used repulsive male images to overcome a 16-year-old boy's habit of soliciting men in public toilets. Davison (1967) used covert sensitization as part of a program to

*Reprinted with permission of author and publisher. Cautela, J. R. Covert sensitization. PSYCHOLOGICAL REPORTS, 1967, 20, 459–468.

eliminate a sadistic fantasy. Kolvin (1967) used it to treat a fetish and an addiction to the sniffing of gasoline.

Other Aversive Agents

Anything that is unpleasant is a potential source of aversive conditioning. Philpott (1967) claimed to overcome obsessional thinking by getting the patient to hold her breath as long as possible each time an obsessional thought obtruded itself. Lublin (1968) has described two aversive inhalation techniques for the smoking habit. One consists of puffing stale warm cigarette smoke from a machine into the face of the subject while he is smoking his own cigarette. In the other, the subject has to puff regularly at a cigarette, in time to the ticking of a metronome, inhaling every 6 seconds on the first cigarette and then puffing without inhaling every 3 seconds on a second cigarette. (This strikes a familiar chord. Parents have for generations done something like this to make their children desist from smoking.) They state that both methods are very aversive, hardly any subject ever finishing a whole cigarette. Of 36 patients who had an average of six half-hour sessions, 16 stopped smoking completely; and all of these are reported to have stayed off cigarettes, some for as long as a year.

In 1956, I treated two cases of obesity by approximating a vile-smelling solution of asafetida to their nostrils while they were handling, smelling, and tasting attractive items of food. (Both of these patients also received reciprocal inhibition therapy for interpersonal anxieties to which they responded well.) Temporary control of over-eating was achieved in one, and lasting control in the other who to this day has a sylph-like figure. Kennedy and Foreyt (1968) have described a very similar procedure using more sophisticated equipment to deliver noxious butyric acid gas.

Other physical stimuli that have been used for purposes of aversive conditioning are intense illumination and white noise. White noise was successfully employed in an unusual and interesting fashion by William Philpott in a case that I referred to him in 1964. The patient was a 30-year-old woman who for 15 years had had an extreme sensitivity to a variety of sharp sounds, such as bells, the jangling of keys, and a hammer on metal. Apart from this set of reactions, no unadaptive responses whatever were revealed in the analysis of her behavior. What Philpott did was to feed white noise at high intensity to her ears through earphones at the same time as he jangled a bunch of keys before her eyes. Thus, while she saw the moving keys, their sound was completely masked by the white noise.

The subject's hyperacusis was entirely overcome by this treatment. A follow-up inquiry in 1967 revealed that she had remained well and experienced no recurrence of this affliction.

Serber (1970) has reported the use of shame as an effective aversive agent for cases of transvestism, voyeurism, pedophilia, and exhibitionism. The subject must necessarily be one who is embarrassed at his deviant act being performed in front of witnesses. He is made to perform the act for 15 to 35 minutes in the presence of increasing numbers of observers. Voyeurs, for example, were placed on the observer side of a one-way mirror to look at someone undressing behind the mirror. The observers stood in the observation room away from the mirror, openly observing the patient observing. A pedophile was placed in a room with a consenting young secretary, who had agreed to stand in for his usual sexual objects, a neighbor's child or his own niece. Of the seven patients with the above diagnoses whom Serber treated, five were free of the deviant behavior at a six-month follow-up. Treatment was unsuccessful in a case of frotteurism. Some of the successful cases later relapsed.

The reader who wishes to inquire more fully into the theoretical and experimental studies of stimuli to which there is an avoidance response should consult the work of Church (1963), Solomon (1964), Azrin and Holz (1966), Rachman and Teasdale (1968, 1969), and Campbell and Church (1969). However, the reader should note that all these authors' discussions relate to the punishment paradigm; whereas, as we have already noted, aversion therapy depends on reciprocal inhibition of a target response by the aversive agent.

The following practical guidelines for aversion therapy in emotionally-based habits are derived and adapted from those provided by Azrin and Holz (1966) for the different purpose of eliminating motor habits by punishment.

1. The stimulus should be as intense as necessary to block the pleasurable response totally.
2. The aversive stimulus should be delivered contemporaneously with the response.
3. The aversive stimulus should not be increased gradually, but introduced at a previously determined high intensity.
4. The frequency of administration should be as high as possible; ideally the stimulus should be given with every evocation of the response to be eliminated.
5. An alternative emotional target should be available which will not

be punished, but which will produce the same or greater reinforcement as that to which the response is being eliminated. For example, a fetishist or exhibitionist needs to achieve normal sex relations.

6. *Aversion therapy should not be administered before seeking out the possible anxiety bases of the unadaptive behavior and treating them if found.* This course of action will frequently make it unnecessary to inflict pain on the patient. For example, in both Case 27 and Case 32 aversion therapy was in the cards, but was not needed.

CHAPTER 13

Some Special Syndromes

There are some categories of neurotic reactions that call for sequences of maneuvers in a particular order, or major variations of strategy according to the behavior analysis of the case. Some of the commoner of these categories are considered in this chapter.

AGORAPHOBIA

Although agoraphobia is customarily regarded as a classical phobia because the patient responds with anxiety to a well-defined class of stimuli — usually physical distance from a place of safety or the relative inaccessibility of a 'safe' person — it is only in a minority of agoraphobics that the level of anxiety is really controlled by distance from 'safety.' Much more often, the distance or the inaccessibility is only the setting for the evocation of the anxiety and not its stimulus.

In some of these cases the behavior analysis shows that what the patient really fears is some personal catastrophe. For example, he infers a heart attack when he feels a certain kind of pain in the chest; and the farther away he is from possible help at the time, the more anxious he becomes. The agoraphobia is thus incidental to a 'hypochondriacal' neurosis (see Case 11). Overcoming the fear response to the symptom will usually cure the agoraphobia.

The commonest of all cases of agoraphobia are found in unhappily married women of low self-sufficiency, appearing after several years of marriage. If a woman with normal self-sufficiency is dissatisfied with her husband and all her endeavors to change him have failed, she is able to consider divorce or separation. The woman with low self-sufficiency cannot seriously contemplate divorce because the threat of being on her own is too frightening. She has a strong desire to leave her husband, but the projected consequences of leaving make it too fearful to translate the desire into action. It would seem that fear of the physical situation of being alone is a generalization from the fear of the aloneness implied in the wished-for separation. In this kind of agoraphobia one must first work on the marriage, to try to make it satisfactory if possible, and, if not possible, to end it. Whatever happens with regard to the marriage, the treatment of the case cannot be regarded as complete until the patient has also overcome her fear of being alone, which can usually be accomplished by a combination of assertive training and systematic desensitization.

Case 26

Mrs. R. was a 26-year-old housewife who had suffered from agoraphobia for the previous 8 years. She had at the age of 14 married a man who treated her with scorn and indifference and whom she hated. She would have loved to leave him, but could not. Not only was her self-sufficiency extremely low (Bernreuter Self-Sufficiency score of 13), but she was of the Catholic faith and had five children. The relevance of the marriage to the agoraphobia was particularly clear in her case because she had run away for a month with a man to whom she was attracted two years previously, and during that month had been free from agoraphobia. After it became obvious that there was no chance of improving the marriage, my efforts were directed at enabling her to make a break from her husband while desensitizing her in some other areas of unadaptive anxiety and training her is self-assertion. After about 8 months (during which I saw her in front of a professional group once every two weeks), she felt herself ready for a temporary separation, which was arranged. She went to stay with a friend for two weeks. During the first week, her agoraphobia gradually faded away; and she was completely free of it in the second week. It was then necessary for her to return home in order to satisfy legal requirements for a permanent separation. Her return did not produce any resurgence of the agoraphobia since, apparently, her temporary absence had effected an emotional freeing from the marital situation.

FEAR OF SYMPTOMS

A kind of neurosis that frequently gives rise to difficulty for the therapist is that in which fear reactions are triggered by certain of the patient's bodily sensations. Endogenous stimuli are as susceptible to fear conditioning as exogenous ones. Quite commonly, the stimuli concerned are consequents of fear itself—rapid heart beat, headache, sweaty palms, and the various effects of hyperventilation such as dizziness, faintness, and dyspnea—so that a vicious cycle is set in motion by any stimuli that arouses fear—even 'normal' fear in the subject. But other sensations, not due to fear, are conditioned to fear responses just as often.

Most often encountered is the person who has strong fear responses to palpitations, rapid heart beat, or pain in the chest. The first necessity is, of course, to have an internist rule out actual cardiac disease. In some cases, the internist's reassurance is all that is needed to dissipate the fear. Sometimes the cognitive reorientation thus obtained needs to be consolidated by the unequivocal identification of the actual cause of the pain. This is usually traceable to gaseous distension of the stomach or intestines, which may be demonstrated by giving the patient a glass of orange juice into which a teaspoonful of sodium bicarbonate has been freshly added. Occasionally the pain can be shown to be autosuggested. But it may continue to elicit anxiety even after the patient is thoroughly convinced that it has nothing to do with heart disease, because in many cases the pain is directly conditioned to the anxiety response. Systematic desensitization is then indicated. Usually the hierarchy will consist of the characteristic pain 'placed' at decreasing distances from the middle of the chest, starting in the lower abdomen. If palpitations are a stimulus to anxiety, a hierarchy of numbers of missed beats may be appropriate.

When the patient is unable effectively to conjure up in imagination the symptoms that disturb him they will need to be produced in actuality. Pain may be evoked by a sharp object or by heat, and tachycardia and palpitations by hyperventilation or inhalations of carbon dioxide. Occasionally, we have resorted to intravenous adrenaline. Since it is usually very difficult to achieve quantitative control of such induced stimulation, the mode of treatment often then becomes flooding rather than desensitization.

STUTTERING

The dependence of most stuttering on social anxiety is demonstrated by the fact that almost every stutterer speaks fluently when he is alone or in the presence of people with whom he is quite comfortable. The greater the anxiety the social situation evokes, the worse the stutter is likely to be. A behavior analysis will identify the stimulus elements in the social contexts that trigger the anxiety; and upon these will depend the therapeutic strategy. Most often, assertive training or some form of desensitization will be indicated, or both, (For a case of stuttering treated by assertive training see Wolpe (1958, p. 128) and for one treated by desensitization Wolpe (1969, p. 23).) The deconditioning of anxiety is often all that is needed to alleviate the stutter more or less completely, and lastingly. However, in some cases motor operants will keep the stutter going to some extent after the anxiety has been removed and their separate extinction will be needed. Since the modifiability of dysfluency by punishment was first convincingly demonstrated (Flanagan, Goldiamond, and Azrin, 1958; Goldiamond, 1965; Siegel and Martin, 1967), a variety of applications of operant principles have been described—for example, Leach (1969) used cash rewards for fluent speech and Shames (1969) verbal reinforcement. A very convenient method was suggested by Migler (1967), and yielded very promising results in the few cases in which it was tried. It consists of forbidding the subject to complete any word that begins with dysfluency, so that only fluent behavior is rewarded—by being completed and by the social results thereof.

Meyer and Mair (1963) and Andrews, et al. (1964) re-examined from a behavioral viewpoint the therapeutic potentialities of the previously disdained observation that dysfluencies are decreased when speech becomes rhythmic. Meyer and Mair used a metronome, and Andrews and Harris verse-like scanning. They obtained lasting improvement in many cases and complete fluency in some. Building on these observations and on experiments of his own, Brady (1971) has elaborated a very practical treatment of stuttering. His procedure involves the use of a miniature electronic metronome worn behind the ear like a hearing aid, which it resembles.* The first step is to find conditions under which the patient can be highly fluent with the aid of a desk metronome. For a severe, chronic stutterer this may require being alone with the therapist and pacing one syllable of his speech to each beat of a loud metronome set as slow as 40 beats per minute. Almost always, conditions can be found under which the patient speaks in an easy, relaxed, and fluent manner.

Once fluent verbalizations appear, albeit at a low rate, the task is gradually and systematically to use the micrometronome to 'shape' verbalizations to approximate the rate and cadence of normal speech and to help

*This metronome, called the Pacemaster is obtainable from Associated Auditory Instruments, Inc., 6796 Market St., Upper Darby, Pa. (19082). Both its frequency and its volume can be varied.

the patient extend this fluency to other situations to which anticipatory anxiety and tension have been conditioned. The series of small steps corresponds to a hierarchy of speaking situations arranged from those associated with minimal stuttering to those associated with severe stuttering. For example, the first situation on the list might be 'speaking with wife' and the last 'giving an impromptu after-dinner speech.'

During this phase of treatment it is not uncommon for the patient to experience unexpected difficulty in some situations from time to time. If this occurs, it is essential for the patient to regain fluency in the situation as soon as possible by the same means he has used before, viz., by reverting to a slower rate of speech and, if necessary, to more strict pacing (one syllable or one word per beat). When he becomes more fluent and regains the feeling of 'control' of his speech, he may gradually return to more rapid speech and less strict pacing on a trial basis. This in an important principle and sometimes requires much coaching by the therapist. Often it is helpful for the patient to rehearse this procedure in the therapist's office by simulating outside speaking situations.

Discontinuation of the metronome is done gradually and systematically, starting with the speaking situations in which the patient has the least amount of difficulty. During this phase many patients find it helpful to pace their speech to the beats of an 'imaginary' metronome. If in any situation the patient finds himself having appreciable speaking difficulty, he must again immediately return to stricter pacing of his speech even though the metronome is not present. Only a few sentences may be required before control is regained. If he continues to have difficulty in this and related situations, he may need to return to the use of the actual metronome again.

Of 23 patients who completed Brady's treatment program, 21 (or over 90 percent) showed a marked increase in fluency and an improvement in their general adjustment as well. These clinical results have persisted for follow-up periods that range from 6 months to over 3 years.

REACTIVE DEPRESSION[1]

Depression is a term applied to constellations of behavior among whose most characteristic elements are motor and verbal retardation, crying, sadness, loss of mirth response, loss of interest, self-devaluation, sleeplessness, and anorexia (Beck, 1967). Bleuler (1911) condensed them

[1]This section is based on a recent article (Wolpe, 1971).

into the 'melancholic triad' of depressive affect, inhibition of action, and inhibition of thinking. There are circumstances to which depression is a normal and fitting response—for example, when a person has suffered a serious loss or deprivation. Such normal depressions usually fade fairly soon, as new objects of need or desire supplant what was lost. It is possible that normal depression aids adaptive responding to loss—facilitating substitute-seeking, for example. A depression is judged 'pathological' when it is apparent that it is not serving to restore adaptive function— when it is excessively severe or too long-continued in relation to the deprivation that caused it, or if it has arisen out of context of a loss or deprivation.

Maier *et al.*, (1970) have found an experimental analogue for at least some reactive depressions. It will be recalled that experimental neuroses are producible by giving an animal about a dozen strong inescapable electrical stimuli. Maier studied the effects of much larger numbers. A dog, strapped in a hammock, was given 64 randomly spaced inescapable electrical shocks through electrodes attached to his foot. These elicited a variety of motor responses which after a time began progressively to fade out until, eventually, no more responding was discernible. Twenty-four hours later, the dog was put into another situation—a shuttle box, a cage divided by a barrier at shoulder height. A dim light was switched on and, after 10 seconds, was accompanied by a 4.5 milliampere floor shock, which was terminated either if the animal jumped the barrier or else after the lapse of 50 seconds. In the ten trials that were given, two-thirds of the animals pre-treated with inescapable shock failed to jump the barrier on at least nine. By contrast, 19 out of 20 animals not pre-treated *escaped* on 9 or more of the 10 trials. It would seem that during the period of inescapable shock in the hammock the animals' whole repertoire of escape behavior was extinguished.

To overcome this 'conditioned helplessness,' Maier tried removing the barrier from the shuttle box, calling to the animal, and dropping food on the non-electrified side—all without success. (Maier noted the similarity between this intractable negativity of behavior and that frequently observed in clinical depression.) The measure that eventually bore fruit was physically compelling the animal, by a rod attached to his collar, to walk across from the electrified side of the cage to the safe side. But change came slowly. Animals had to be pulled across in this fashion 20–50 times before there was, first of all, a decrease in the amount of force needed to effect passage, and eventually spontaneous passage. Once this occurred, recovery was complete and lasting.

There are three distinct sets of circumstances in which neurotic depression is seen: (1) As an exaggeration and prolongation of the normal reaction to loss, (2) As a consequence of severe and prolonged anxiety, and (3) As a consequence of failure to control interpersonal situations, such failure being due to the inhibiting effects of neurotic anxiety.

1.   Exaggeration and Prolongation of Normal Reaction to Loss

It is natural to be overcome with a sense of helplessness when death or some other irrevocable happening deprives one of something cherished, or if one has experienced a severe disappointment. The feeling then reflects a realistic helplessness. If the depression is extravagantly great or lasts unreasonably long, it must be presumed that there is a diminished capacity to make alternative responses that might break into the depression. It seems likely that a biological (endogenous) insufficiency is usually behind this (see Eysenck, 1970). But a conditioning process is sometimes evidently responsible—in individuals who have suffered repeated losses in the past. A conditioned helplessness triggered by a major deprivation might make up an inhibitory reaction of great strength.

When there is reason to suspect that there is an endogenous cause for an exaggerated reaction to loss, the case should be investigated so that appropriate biological measures can be taken. There may, for example, be a need for female sex hormones, or lithium in 'idiopathic' endogenous depression. If the over-reaction is due to conditioned helplessness established in association with repeated losses in the past, it will first be necessary to determine whether anxiety is involved. If so, it should be deconditioned. At the same time, whether there is an anxiety factor or not, a schedule should be devised by which the individual's efforts are systematically rewarded (Burgess, 1968), sometimes starting with such minor accomplishments as making a telephone call, mowing the lawn, or washing dishes. These behaviors are praised and in other ways rewarded by the therapist, and after a time come to give the patient a sense of satisfaction in themselves. They are then succeeded by more complicated activities which the patient himself often initiates.

2.   Reactive Depression Associated with Severe Anxiety

A patient with a history of attacks of severe and long-lasting anxiety will often report bouts of depression that are correlated with times of high anxiety. Generally, the depression follows the anxiety, and not infrequently comes to replace it. It seems likely, in the light of Maier *et al.* experiments, that the explanation lies in the development of conditioned helplessness. The patient has been severely anxious for days or weeks. He has performed many acts that have in the past been associated with anxiety reduction, and they have all now failed to reduce anxiety. He has consequently lapsed into the passivity and emotional depression indicative of conditioned helplessness. Under some conditions, the depression will dominate over and supersede the anxiety from whose bosom it arose.

It has been my experience, with regard to the great majority of cases of this form of reactive depression, that successful deconditioning of the anxiety, by systematic desensitization or assertive training or whatever other method is appropriate, progressively diminishes the occurrence of these depressions, their duration, and their intensity. And, when the neurotic anxiety has been overcome, the depression ceases to be in evidence.

3. Failure to Control Interpersonal Situations

Domination by one person over another is normally based on *force majeur* in terms of position, prestige, wealth, or physical strength. The underdog may be resentful, frustrated or resigned, but he is typically not depressed. Depression seems to arise only when the domination derives, not from real power, but from the conditioned submissiveness of the dominated one, who is unable to handle the other person effectively because of a conditioned anxiety-response habit to the thought of asserting himself or to certain projected implications of his assertiveness—such as hurting the other person's feelings (see Chapter 5). Unable to summon any motor response that would give him some mastery of the interaction, he is depressed. When this powerlessness extends to all or most of his relationships, he is likely to be chronically depressed. Here is the apparent basis for what has traditionally been called 'neurasthenia,' and for the aimless ineffectuality of those who are nowadays often categorized as having 'existential' neuroses.

Since depressions of this kind are bound up with lack of assertiveness due to fear of other people, treatment will include assertive training. It is likely that some of these cases would also benefit from programs of reinforcement of selected motor behavior as proposed by Burgess (1968) —as outlined above.

SEXUAL DEVIATIONS

Aversion methods figure prominently in published accounts of the behavioral treatment of sexual deviations. While there is no doubt that these methods have an important place, they should never be the first resort. Each case must first be investigated for unadaptive anxiety responses, which will usually be found; and, if found, should be treated first.

Homosexuality is the commonest sexual deviation. Our experience with a large number of cases in the Behavior Therapy Unit has led us to conclude that it is generally based on one or more of three kinds of learned habits:

1. Conditioned anxiety reactions evoked by women in contexts of emotional closeness or physical proximity.
2. Conditioned interpersonal anxiety of the kind that calls for assertive training, this conditioning having its greatest strength in these cases at the female end of the social spectrum.
3. Positive erotic conditioning to males.

Aversion therapy is appropriate only when the homosexuality rests on the last factor. If one or both types of anxiety conditioning are present, treatment should be directed to them first. If the treatment is successful it will often be found that there is no need for aversion therapy because sexual interest has 'spontaneously' transferred from males to females (see Cases 32 and 33 in Chapter 14). It is in those subjects in whom homosexual interest persists after the deconditioning of anxiety that aversion therapy is indicated.

The most commonly used method is that of Feldman and MacCulloch (1967, 1970) in which approach attitudes to females are conditioned in coordination with the deconditioning of positive feelings to males. The patient is asked to examine a number of slides of males both clothed and nude, and to rank them in a hierarchy of attractiveness. This hierarchy will later be worked through in ascending order of attractiveness. The patient also arranges in rank order a number of female slides to be worked through in descending order, i.e. the most attractive first. Next, a level of shock is determined that the patient finds very unpleasant.

The patient is then told that he will see a male picture and that several seconds later he may receive a shock. He can turn off the slide by pressing a switch, whenever he wishes to do so, knowing that the moment the slide leaves the screen the shock will also be turned off. He is told that he will never be shocked when the screen is blank, and urged to leave the slide on the screen for as long as he finds it sexually attractive. The first slide is then presented. Should he switch it off within eight seconds he is not shocked, this being termed an avoidance response. At 8 seconds, the shock begins and continues. If its strength is not sufficiently high to cause the patient to switch it off immediately, it is increased until he does so. The moment he presses the switch the slide is removed and the shock terminated. This is termed an escape response. The patient is also told to say, "No" as soon as he wishes the slide to be removed, in the hope that further strength will be given to the avoidance habit by this additional element. The usual course of events is: several trials in all of which escape responses are made; a sequence of trials in some of which the patient escapes, and some of which he avoids; a sequence of trials in which the patient avoids every time. When he reports that his previous attraction to the slide has been replaced by indifference or even actual dislike and when, in addition, he switches off within one to two seconds of the slide appearing, the next more attractive slide is introduced and the process repeated.

In combination with the aversive conditioning to male stimuli, Feldman and MacCulloch attempt to induce a positive attitude to females and approach behavior towards them by introducing a female slide at the moment of the removal of the male slide. Thus, anxiety-relief is associated with the introduction of the female image. The patient can request the return of the female slide after it has been removed. The rationale of this is that the absence of a female slide means that a male slide, by now associated with shock, may reappear. The patient gradually becomes more motivated to request the return of the female slide. However, since this request is sometimes granted and sometimes not, the patient cannot predict the consequences of his asking for the return of the female slide. This is thought to aid the program designed to lead to avoidance of males and approach to females.

The rule of giving therapeutic priority to anxiety habits applies also to other forms of sexual deviation, although there is an impression that anxiety is less often relevant. Years ago, a case of exhibitionism (Wolpe, 1958) was successfully treated by a combination of assertive training and systematic desensitization, and a shoe fetish by assertive training. The treatment by desensitization of another case of exhibitionism was reported in some detail by Bond and Hutchinson (1960). Stevenson and Wolpe (1960) overcame three cases of sexual deviation by assertive training. Marquis (1970) has effectively used orgasmic reconditioning in the treatment of a dozen cases.

CHARACTER NEUROSES

A character neurosis may be defined as a neurosis whose habit patterns include asocial or antisocial behavior, such as inability to hold a job, sexual promiscuity, repeated suicidal attempts (whether in earnest or for show), kleptomania, and tantrum behavior. This definition obviously also includes such sexual deviations as voyeurism, frotteurism, and exhibitionism. Almost invariably, anxiety is the antecedent of these habit patterns, and its deconditioning is the key to their elimination. This is illustrated by the following example.

Case 27: Desensitization in a case of kleptomania

Mrs. U., a 36-year-old housewife, married to a man of considerable substance, was referred to me by a probation officer because she had been caught shoplifting and was threatened with imprisonment. Since the age of 19, when she had gotten away with a suit stuffed into her shopping bag, she had stolen thousands of articles, mainly food and clothing. She said that getting something that she had not paid for gave her a feeling of satisfaction.

The crucial points that were yielded by the behavior analysis were that she felt an inner tension at either spending money or neglecting an opportunity to acquire something without spending money. Accordingly, two hierarchies were set up, the first in a Howard Johnson restaurant at which she would be having dinner with her three children. If the bill came to anything over $6, she would feel anxiety that increased with the amount of the excess. The theme of the second hierarchy was the awareness of not having taken something out of a shop when she easily could have; and here, the anxiety also increased with the value of the thing not taken. At the same session, she was given initial training in deep muscle relaxation at which she was found to be an exceedingly apt subject.

Desensitization to the first hierarchy commenced with having her imagine that the Howard Johnson bill came to $7. This produced 20 *suds* that came down to 0 at the third presentation. The amount was then progressively increased until she could imagine spending $13 without anxiety. At this point, she was asked to imagine having just sat down with her children in the restaurant and saying to them, "You can have anything on the menu." This produced no anxiety, in contrast to 30 *suds* when it was presented to her before desensitization began.

To deal with the second hierarchy, she was first asked to imagine that she was outside a supermarket remembering that she had been in a remote corner where she could easily have taken a 45¢ can of tuna and had not. This evoked 30 *suds*, coming down to 0 at the third presentation. In the course of 3 sessions, she came to be able to imagine without anxiety having left a $60 gown in a clothing store that she could easily have taken.

The effects of the treatment became increasingly apparent in her everyday life. She stated that she had a wonderful feeling of freedom walking through shops and not feeling driven to take things. During a two-month interval when she was seen only to discuss other matters such as the handling of her marital situation, there was no recurrence of impulses to steal. At this point, attention was turned to overcoming her inability to spend any substantial sum of money for clothing—an aim that was achieved in the course of three sessions. She is now able to purchase whatever she wants and, in the course of a 15-month follow-up, there has been no recurrence of her tendency to engage in shoplifting.

Case 28:   The treatment of a sociopath

Cases such as this are more complex. Six years ago I saw a man of 22 who was leading quite a sociopathic kind of existence. The prospective heir of a fortune, and the recipient of a considerable monthly income, he spent money like water, usually in such a way as to impress others. He had drunk heavily (though not so much recently) because it made him feel "like Superman". He was much given to daydreams on the Walter Mitty model. A few months earlier, he had walked into a motel, checked in, and then pulled a gun on the manager, saying, "This is a holdup." The manager had promptly knocked him down, taken the gun, and called the police, as a result of which he was currently on probation.

At the first interview, I noticed that he was very 'quick on the trigger' in his conversational responses—in fact, spoke almost continuously. He was also manifestly sensitive to the opinions of others, although his Willoughby score was only 24 (but his score for hurt feelings was 4 and for sensitivity to criticism 3). On the Maudsley Personality Inventory, his extroversion score was at the 89th percentile and his neurotic score at the 74th percentile.

Two lines of treatment were adopted. First, an attack was made on his primary reactiveness by showing him how to slow down his responses, first in the context of his answers to simple mathematical problems. Then he was shown how to delay or withhold his responses to my statements or questions. He enlisted the aid of his wife to control these behaviors at home. My second action was to obtain from him a list of situations in which his feelings were hurt and arrange them in a hierarchy according to how disturbed he felt, using this for desensitization. He responded rapidly to both of these modes of treatment. After seven sessions, he claimed that he was in very good control of himself, no longer so sensitive. He had taken a job as a used car salesman (at which he was very adept) and was managing well because he no longer felt a desire to "fly off the handle" if anybody irritated him, as he had been prone to do in the past. At a follow-up interview six months later, he stated that he was still doing well at selling used cars and getting on progressively harmoniously with his wife. He had no trouble with drinking, indulging in one or two drinks in the evening and a few more occasionally at parties. A year later, he made a telephone call from a city in the Midwest saying that he was still getting on well and staying out of trouble.

OBSESSIONAL NEUROSES

As pointed out in *Psychotherapy by Reciprocal Inhibition*, some obsessional behavior has the effect of reducing anxiety, and some the effect of elevating it; but anxiety is the usual trigger to both varieties. Certainly, there are cases in which obsessional behavior persists autonomously, after the deconditioning of antecedent anxiety, because it has become conditioned to other stimuli; but they are unusual.

The first target, in dealing with an obsessional neurosis—as with neuroses of other kinds—is the identification and deconditioning of antecedent anxiety. The mainstay of the deconditioning has been systematic desensitization although the frequent complexity of obsessional cases has very often required the use of other methods as well (see, for example, Walton and Mather (1963)). Even when the case responds to desensitization alone, the amount of effort required is usually very considerable, as exemplified by Case 34; though now and again the method overcomes an obsessional neurosis with remarkable ease. For example, for a mathematics professor with an obsession for tidiness that was destroying his marriage, I used a hierarchy of increasing degrees of disarray in his living room, starting with a one-inch-square piece of paper lying on the floor in a corner. In the course of five desensitization sessions he became able to imagine all reasonable degrees of disarray without disturbance. The change transferred to his life situation, to his wife's relief, and the gratification of both.

But the fact that much time is usually required to desensitize the hierarchies characteristic of obsessional neuroses has naturally stimulated research for more economical methods. Meyer (1966) was the first to attempt to treat these neuroses by prolonged exposure of the patient to the situation (e.g. 'contamination') from which the obsessional behavior provided an escape. He prolonged the exposure by precluding the customary washing and rituals. Both of his two cases improved markedly and lastingly. Recently, the idea has been taken up by others – Marks (1972), Rainey (1972), and Hodgson, et al. (1972). The last-named, in a pilot control study comparing desensitization, flooding, and flooding preceded by modelling, found indications of marked superiority of the last over the other two methods.

On the strength of these findings, we have recently been exploring the use of flooding for obsessions in the Behavior Therapy Unit, and have found some of the first results encouraging. An example involving the use of exteroceptive stimulation was in a girl of 20 who felt contaminated by tactile contact with any other person, so that she was engaged in washing rituals almost incessantly. She was successfully treated by copying Dr. Michael Ascher modelling the handling and wearing of garments that she had worn in the place where the revulsion had first come to be established (these garments having been mailed to us by her parents).

Case 29

Flooding by the use of imagery was applied to a history professor who was incapacitated by an obsessive fear of a negative response from a committee whom he was due to meet several months later to be con-sidered for a position he greatly coveted. He was treated by having him continuously imagine that he was actually meeting with this committee and receiving negative reactions all round. The scene raised his anxiety level to 100 *suds* in the first 15 minutes, and then the level gradually subsided to about 60 *suds* after an hour, when the flooding was ter-minated. At a second flooding with the same scene a week later, it was impossible to raise his anxiety above 40 *suds*, and in a few minutes it came down to zero and stayed there. He stated that his thoughts were now switching to alternatives – this possible defeat was no longer the end of the world. He remained markedly relieved and withstood his eventual actual rejection by the committee very well.

In those obsessions that have antecedents other than anxiety, and in those in relation to which anxiety is an appropriate response (for example, preoccupations about death), it is necessary to try to break the thinking habit directly. The usual method used is thought-stopping (Wolpe, 1958). Yamagami (1971) obtained complete recovery from an 8-year-old color-naming obsession by the exclusive use of thought-stopping (see p. 213).

Covert sensitization (Cautela, 1966) and covert reinforcement (Cautela,

1970) have been finding increasing use in the treatment of obsessions. The essential procedures in a case reported by Wisocki (1970) are given on page 211.

A measure of final resort, to be considered only when all else has failed in a patient who is severly disabled, is cingulotomy (Hunter-Brown and Lighthill, 1968). This improved form of lobotomy provides very good results in properly selected cases. Kelly (1972) has made the excellent recommendation that the operation be preceded by electrical stimulation of target areas to determine with accuracy where the section should take place.

OBESITY

Some cases of obesity have hormonal origins, but the great majority are attributable to overeating that is a matter of habit. Stuart (1967) was the first to exploit this realization and to devise a program to change habit rather than to manipulate food content. His original trial was successful in all of twelve cases, whose weight loss was maintained at one-year follow up. A slightly modified form of this program has been very effective in the Behavior Therapy Unit.

The patient is instructed to weigh herself at least once a day, either on rising or on retiring. She is given no particular diet, but told that she is under no circumstances to eat except when seated at a table. It is desirable, as far as possible, to eat in the company of other people; but if eating alone she is to do nothing else; i.e. she is to concentrate on eating and not engage in additional activities, such as watching television, listening to music, or reading. Then, once or twice during each meal she is to put down her knife and fork and concentrate on the food without eating, initially for a period of two minutes. This period is increased by one minute each week, up to a maximum of five minutes. The rationale of this is to build up a conditioned inhibition of the automatic response of eating at the sight of food. It seems to have the effect of making many patients feel generally much less hungry.

In some cases, as Stuart noted, it turns out to be necessary to inhibit eating between meals by covert sensitization, as described on p. 226. Stuart and Davis (1972) have recently proposed a more elaborate program that includes attention to diet, but this is probably not often necessary.

CHAPTER 14

Some Complex Cases

A neurosis may be complex in one or more of several ways (see p. 24) e.g.:

1. Multiple families of stimuli may be conditioned to neurotic reactions.
2. The reactions may include unadaptiveness in important areas of social behavior (e.g. sexual deviations, 'character neuroses').
3. The neurosis may have somatic consequences (e.g. asthma, neuro-dermatitis).
4. The neurosis may include obsessional behavior.
5. There may be pervasive anxiety in addition to that associated with specific stimuli.

The extended case summaries that make up this chapter are intended to illustrate how complex cases are handled by a behavior therapist. At all times, the stimulus-response relations perceived by the therapist determine his strategies. New information frequently leads to change of direction.

FEAR OF SYMPTOMS

Case 30: Anxiety with frequent urination, nausea, and diarrhea; obsession about wife's premarital loss of virginity

Mr. B. was a 31-year-old advertising salesman who four years previously had begun to notice himself increasingly anxious in social and business situations from which it was difficult to get away. Within a few

months, even five minutes in the office of a client would produce considerable anxiety accompanied by a strong desire to urinate. If he went
out and relieved himself, the urge would return after a further five minutes,
and so on. The only circumstances that could be associated with the onset
of Mr. B.'s neurosis were the unsettlement of having moved to a new
house in a new town, and his concern at the unexpected break-up of the
marriage of close friends whom he had regarded as ideally mated. His
only previous neurotic phase had been a brief one that had occurred upon
moving to a new school at the age of 16. This could conceivably have
conditioned anxiety to 'new places.' The Fear Survey Schedule revealed
very high anxiety to the following stimulus classes: strange places, failure,
strangers, bats, journeys especially by train, being criticized, surgical
operations, rejection, planes, being disapproved of, losing control, looking foolish, and fainting.

Mr. B.'s early history was quite conventional. A feature of interest was
a strong religious training with marked emphasis on 'the good and the
bad.' Churchgoing had played a prominent part in his childhood and
adolescence. In his middle teens he had come to resent it, but without
rebelling outwardly. He had done well in school and got on well with
both classmates and teachers. He had been trained in journal advertising,
but was now engaged in advertising salesmanship which he greatly
liked.

As regards his sexual history, Mr. B. had been stimulated by erotic
pictures at the age of ten. At thirteen, he had begun to masturbate, but
without fear or guilt. Dating and petting began at fourteen, and at eighteen
he had met his wife who attracted him by her intelligence, good looks, and
responsiveness to his jokes. The courtship was broken by Mr. B. after
she revealed that she had had an affair two years earlier. On reflection, he
condoned the episode, and at the age of twenty married her. The relationship turned out to be a very congenial one, and sexually very satisfying
to both; but Mr. B. was never really able to divest himself of the painful
idea that he had been 'dealt a dirty card.'

At the second session, Mr. B. described how embarrassing and incapacitating he found his neurotic anxiety and the associated urge to
urinate. Anxiety was greater in the presence of unfamiliar people and if
there was no easy access to a toilet. Other factors that increased it were
the importance of the occasion and the importance of the other person.
On the whole, there was more anxiety in anticipation of a meeting than at
the meeting itself.* Since it was evident that a desensitization program

---

*The therapeutic implication of this last observation will become apparent later.

would need to be undertaken, relaxation training was started at this interview.

At his next session, five days later, Mr. B. reported that he had practiced relaxing, and that by means of it had been able to desist from urinating while at home for a period of six-and-a-half hours despite quite a strong urge. Relaxation training was now extended, and the general desensitization strategy worked out. It was apparent that the duration of interviews with his clients was an important factor determining the strength of Mr. B.'s anxiety. It was therefore decided to treat an 'interview' hierarchy, using a time dimension for its easy quantifiability. I started the desensitization by having him imagine himself scheduled to a very brief meeting (of two minutes' duration) with the manager of an important firm. In spite of the fact that relaxation training had at this point involved only a limited part of his musculature, it was decided to begin desensitization at this session because he manifested considerable calmness. The first scene was presented to him as follows: "Imagine that you have just entered the office of a manager who has a rule that no representative is permitted to spend more than two minutes in his office." By the third presentation this scene produced no more anxiety; and scenes of meetings of four minutes and six minutes were then presented in succession.

In subsequent interviews, the duration of these meetings was progressively extended, until by the ninth he could imagine being with an executive for sixty minutes without anxiety. He now found himself much better at real meetings and social situations. While visiting relatives, he urinated only three times in five hours. However, anticipatory anxiety was almost as bad as it had ever been. There was some measure of it several hours before a prospective meeting, but it became much more noticeable half to one hour beforehand, and then increased rather steeply. At the ninth interview, then, desensitization of anticipatory anxiety was started. Anxiety decreased to zero in two to three presentations of each of the following scenes:

1. In his office, 60 minutes before visiting a client.
2. In his office, 30 minutes before visiting a client and preparing to leave.
3. Twenty minutes before visiting a client, entering his car to allow ample time.
4. In his car on the way to a client 10 minutes before the appointed time.
5. Emerging from his car at the premises of the client's office, with 8 minutes in hand.

6. Entering the waiting room of the client's office 6 minutes before the appointed time.
7. Announcing himself to the client's secretary 5 minutes before the appointed time.

At his tenth interview, a week later, Mr. B. reported considerably less anxiety in relation to anticipated business meetings. He had for the first time in many months taken his wife to a downtown restaurant. During the 25-minute ride to that restaurant he had not, as in the past, had to stop to relieve himself in a rest room. At first slightly anxious in the restaurant, he had become almost entirely calm after the first 10 minutes. Desensitization to the anticipation of interviews was continued to the point that he could calmly imagine himself in the client's waiting room 2 minutes before he was to be called in. This hierarchy was finally disposed of at the next session. Now Mr. B. spontaneously reported that he felt far greater confidence in all respects. He had been going out to get new business — at first feeling some strain, but later increasingly comfortably. He had spent one-and-a-half hours with a new and imposing manager of an important new client firm, with hardly any anxiety either beforehand or during the interview. He was no longer bothered at going into strange places because it no longer mattered whether or not he knew where the toilet was. For the same reason, he had ceased to fear using trains, airliners, buses, and other public transportation.

Attention was now turned to Mr. B.'s difficulty in asserting himself with strangers. Assertive behavior was instigated. To facilitate it he was desensitized to one relevant situation — telling a waiter "This food is bad." Anxiety disappeared at the second presentation of this. Two weeks later, at his fourteenth interview, Mr. B. stated that he was expressing himself where required with increasing ease. For example, he had immediately and effectively spoken up at a drugstore when another customer was taken ahead of him out of turn. He had become more and more comfortable making business calls, citing as an example a one-and-three-quarter hour interview with a particular executive. He commented that 3 months earlier he would in the course of so long a period have had to go out to urinate about 20 times. However, he still had to push himself to do some of the things he had become inured to avoiding.

From this point onward, the main focus of therapy was his distress about his wife's premarital affair. First, it was mutually agreed, after reference to Kinsey and others, that Mr. B.'s reactions were irrational. Then, an attempt was made to employ a kind of emotive imagery (p.

149) that was suggested by a discussion with Dr. Akhter Ahsen (1965) who bases some interesting operations that he calls "eidetic psychotherapy" upon an extremely fanciful conceptual system. The central practical idea is to ask the patient to imagine himself behaving in a new way in a past real situation that has been emotionally distressful. The idea was employed in the present case by having Mr. B. project himself back to the time of his wife's affair and imagine that while she was amorously engaged with her lover in a hotel he was in the next room. He was to force the connecting door open and beat up the paramour. In doing this, it was supposed that angry emotions would be counterposed to the anxiety that this image ordinarily evoked. Mr. B. was enjoined to practice this imaginary sequence 50 to 100 times a day. He felt himself making progressive improvement for about two weeks, when he stated that his obsession was about 20 percent less in incidence and 40 percent less in emotional intensity. But continuing the drill for a further four weeks yielded no further benefit. After the second week, he was also asked to practice imagining attacking Mrs. B. in the premarital amorous situation, but the only effect of this was to make him feel hostile towards her generally.

I decided, therefore, to tackle the problem by systematic desensitization. In order to desensitize Mr. B. to this long-past situation, I employed images from a fictitious film supposed to have been taken of his wife's premarital amorous activities by a hidden camera in her family's living room. Relaxed and with his eyes closed, Mr. B. was asked to imagine that his wife was sitting on a couch with her lover who kissed her and then put his hand on one of her breasts over her dress for exactly five seconds. He felt no anxiety at this. A fair amount of anxiety was evoked by the next scene in which the duration of contact was made 8 seconds, but at the third presentation of this scene anxiety disappeared. Two presentations were required to remove anxiety from imagining the hand over the breast for 10 seconds, and five presentations were required for 20 seconds.

At the following session, six weeks later, Mr. B. again felt anxiety to the 20-second hand contact, but it disappeared at the third presentation. Two weeks later, he reported that his feelings toward his wife were more detached and that he was thinking of her less. In general, his thoughts were turning away from the past and towards the present and future. Further scenes were presented, increasing the duration of the lover's hand upon his wife's clothed breast successively to 25 seconds, 30 seconds, 40 seconds, one minute, one-and-a-half minutes, two minutes, and three minutes, and her snuggling up to him. None of these scenes produced any disturbance. On opening his eyes, Mr. B. stated that "having got over the hump last time," he no longer cared what his wife had done in the past. Recovery from the obsession (as well as the other problems) had endured at last contact three years later.

The contrast between the marked effects of the desensitization and the limited impact of the 'eidetic' treatment appears to afford a valuable object lesson. In the desensitization, the relaxation systematically overcame the anxiety engendered by images of progressively greater liberties taken by Mrs. B.'s lover, desensitizing Mr. B. to the idea of her having permitted such liberties—which was precisely the therapeutic target. In the 'eidetic' treatment, the images mobilizing anger against the seducer produced some improvement, presumably by deconditioning anxiety for which the seducer was the stimulus. Practicing images of aggression towards the 'errant' Mrs. B. only led to hostility towards her. Since both eidetic images were off the main therapeutic target, neither could have been the vehicle for full recovery.

AUTOMOBILE PHOBIA

Case 31: Desensitization of a multidimensional automobile phobia

The following account of the case of Mrs. C. is excerpted and adapted from an experimental study (Wolpe, 1962). Mrs. C. was a 39-year-old woman who complained of fear reactions to traffic situations, and whom I first saw on April 6, 1960. Her story was that on February 3, 1958, while her husband was taking her to work by car, they entered an intersection on the green light. She suddenly became aware of a large truck that, disregarding the red signal, was bearing down upon the car from the left. She remembered the moment of impact, being flung out of the car, flying through the air, and then losing consciousness. Her next recollection was of waking in the ambulance on the way to the hospital. She was found to have injuries to her knee and neck, for the treatment of which she spent a week in the hospital.

On the way home, by car, she felt unaccountably frightened. She stayed at home for two weeks, quite happily, and then, resuming normal activities, noticed that, while in a car, though relatively comfortable on the open road, she was always disturbed by seeing any car approach from either side, but not at all by vehicles straight ahead. Along city streets she had continuous anxiety, which, at the sight of a laterally approaching car less than half a block away, would rise to panic. She could, however, avoid a reaction by closing her eyes before reaching an intersection. She was also distressed in other situations that in some sense involved lateral approaches of cars. Reactions were extraordinarily severe in making a left turn in the face of approaching traffic on the highway. Execution of the turn, of course, momentarily placed the approaching vehicle to the right of her car. There was a considerable rise in tension even when the vehicle was a mile or more ahead. Left turns in the city disturbed her less because of slower speeds. The entry of other cars from side streets even as far as two blocks ahead into the road in which she was traveling also constituted a 'lateral threat.' Besides her reactions while in a car, she was anxious while walking across streets, even at intersections with the traffic light in her favor, and even if the nearest approaching car were more than a block away.

Questioned about previous traumatic experiences, she recalled that ten years previously a tractor had crashed into the side of a car in which she was a passenger. Nobody had been hurt; the car had continued its journey, and she had been aware of no emotional sequel. No one close to her had ever been involved in a serious accident. Though she had worked in the Workmen's Compensation Claims office, dealing with cases of injury had not been disturbing to her. She found it incomprehensible that she should have developed this phobia; in London during World War II, she had accepted the dangers of the blitz calmly, without ever needing to use sedatives.

Her early history revealed nothing of significance. In England, during World War II, she had been engaged to a pilot, who was killed. After his death, she had lost interest for a time in forming other associations. Her next serious association was with her husband, whom she had met in 1955. They had married in May, 1957, about nine months before the accident. Until the accident, the marital relationship had been good. Sexual relations had been satisfactory, most often with both partners achieving orgasm. Since the accident, however, she had been negatively influenced by adverse comments that her husband had made about her disability, so that sexual behavior had diminished. Nevertheless, when coitus occurred, she still had orgasm more often than not.

In the second interview, training in relaxation and the construction of hierarchies were both initiated. Mrs. C. was schooled in relaxation of the arms and the muscles of the forehead. Two hierarchies were constructed. The first related to traffic situations in open country. There was allegedly a minimal reaction if she was in a car driven by her husband and they were 200 yards from a crossroad and if, 400 yards away, at right angles,

another car was approaching. Anxiety increased with increasing proximity. The second hierarchy related to lateral approaches of other cars
while that in which she was traveling had stopped at a city traffic light. The
first signs of anxiety supposedly appeared when the other car was two
blocks away. (This, as will be seen, was a gross understatement of the
patient's reactions.) The interview concluded with an introductory
desensitization session. Having hypnotized and relaxed Mrs. C., I presented to her imagination some presumably neutral stimuli. First, she was
asked to imagine herself walking across a baseball field and then that she
was riding in a car in the country with no other cars in sight. Following
this, she was presented with the allegedly weak phobic situation of being
in a car 200 yards from an intersection and seeing another car 400 yards
on the left. She afterwards reported no disturbances to any of the scenes.

At the third interview, instruction in relaxation of muscles of the
shoulder was succeeded by a desensitization session in which the following scenes were presented: (1) The patient's car, driven by her husband,
had stopped at an intersection, and another car was approaching at right
angles two blocks away; (2) The highway scene of the previous session
was suggested, except that now her car was 150 yards from the intersection and the other car 300 yards away. It was evident that these were
evoking considerable anxiety. Consequently, I subjected Mrs. C. to
further questioning, from which it emerged that she was continuously
tense in cars, but had not thought this worth reporting, so trifling was it
beside the terror experienced at the lateral approach of a car. She also
stated that all the car scenes imagined during the sessions had aroused
anxiety, but too little, she had felt, to deserve mention. Mrs. C. was now
asked to imagine that she was about to ride two blocks on a country
road. This evoked considerable anxiety!

At the fifth interview, it was learned that even the thought of a journey
raised Mrs. C.'s tension, so that if, for example, at 9 a.m. her husband
were to say, "We are going out driving at 2 p.m.," she would be continuously apprehensive, and more so when actually in the car. During the
desensitization session (fourth) at this interview, I asked her to imagine
that she was at home expecting to go for a short drive in the country in
four hours' time. This scene, presented five times, evoked anxiety that
did not decrease on repetition. It was now obvious that scenes with the
merest suspicion of exposure to traffic were producing more anxiety
than could be mastered by Mrs. C.'s relaxation potential.

A new strategy therefore had to be devised. On a sheet of paper I drew
an altogether imaginary completely enclosed square field, which was

represented as being two blocks (200 yards) long (see Fig. 14). At the southwest corner (lower left) I drew her car, facing north (upwards), in which she sat with her husband and at the lower right corner another car, supposed to be that of Dr. Richard W. Garnett, a senior staff psychiatrist, which faced them at right angles. Dr. Garnett (hereafter "Dr. G.") was 'used' because Mrs. C. regarded him as a trustworthy person.

This imaginary situation became the focus of the scenes presented in the sessions that followed. At the fifth desensitization session, Mrs. C. was asked to imagine Dr. G. announcing to her that he was going to drive his car a half-block towards her and then proceeding to do so while she sat in her parked car. As this elicited no reaction, she was next made to imagine him driving one block towards her, and then, as there was again no reaction, one-and-a-quarter blocks. On perceiving a reaction to this scene, I repeated it three times, but without effecting any decrement in the reaction. I then 'retreated,' asking her to imagine Dr. G. stopping after traveling one block and two paces towards her. This produced a slighter reaction, which decreased on repeating the scene, disappearing at the fourth presentation. This was the first evidence of change, affording grounds for a confident prediction of a successful outcome of therapy.

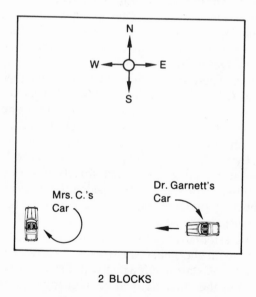

2 BLOCKS

Fig. 14. Imaginary enclosed square where Dr. Garnett makes progressively closer advances to Mrs. C.'s car.

At the sixth session, the imagined distance between Dr. G.'s stopping point and Mrs. C.'s car was decreased by two or three paces at a time, and at the end of the session he was able to stop seven-eighths of a block short of her (a total gain of about 10 paces). The following are the details of the progression. In parenthesis is the number of presentations of each scene required to reduce the anxiety response to zero:

1. Dr. G. approaches four paces beyond one block (3).
2. Six paces beyond one block (3)
3. Nine paces beyond one block (2).
4. Twelve paces beyond one block, i.e. one and one-eighth block (4).

At the seventh session, Mrs. C. was enabled to tolerate Dr. G.'s car reaching a point half-a-block short of her car without disturbance; at the eighth session, three-eighths of a block (about 37 yards); at the tenth, she was able to imagine him approaching within two yards of her without any reaction whatsoever.

The day after this, Mrs. C. reported that for the first time since her accident she had been able to walk across a street while an approaching car was in sight. The car was two blocks away but she was able to complete the crossing without quickening her pace. At this, the eleventh session, I began a new series of scenes in which Dr. G. drove in front of the car containing Mrs. C. instead of towards it, passing at first 30 yards ahead, and then gradually closer, cutting the distance eventually to about three yards. Desensitization to all this was rather rapidly achieved during this session. Thereupon, I drew two intersecting roads in the diagram of the field (Fig. 15). A traffic light was indicated in the middle, and the patient's car, as shown in the diagram, had 'stopped' at the red signal. At first, Mrs. C. was asked to imagine Dr. G.'s car passing on the green light. As anticipated, she could at once accept this without anxiety; it was followed by Dr. G.'s car passing one way and a resident physician's car in the opposite direction. The slight anxiety this aroused was soon eliminated. In subsequent scenes, the resident's car was followed by an increasing number of students' cars, each scene being repeated until its emotional effect declined to zero.

At the twelfth session, the roadway at right angles to Mrs. C.'s car was made continuous with the public highway system (as indicated by the dotted lines) and now, starting off again with Dr. G., we added the cars of the resident and the students, and subsequently those of strangers. Imagining two unknown cars passing the intersection produced a fair degree of anxiety, and she required five presentations at this session and

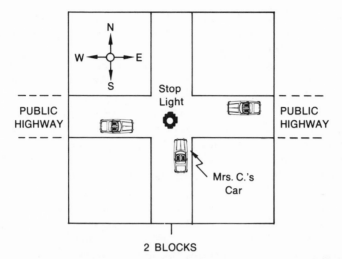

Fig. 15. Imaginary enclosed square with crossroads and traffic light added. Other cars pass while Mrs. C.'s car has stopped at the red light.

five more at the next before she could accept it entirely calmly. However, once this was accomplished, it was relatively easy gradually to introduce several cars passing from both sides.

We now began a new series of scenes in which, with the traffic light in her favor, she was stepping off the curb to cross a city street while a car was slowly approaching. At first, the car was imagined a block away, but during succeeding sessions the distance gradually decreased to ten yards.

At this point, to check upon transfer from the imaginary to real life, I took Mrs. C. to the Charlottesville business center and observed her crossing streets at an intersection controlled by a traffic light. She went across repeatedly with apparent ease and reported no anxiety. But in the car, on the way there and back, she showed marked anxiety whenever a car from a side street threatened to enter the street in which we drove.

I now made a detailed analysis of Mrs. C.'s reaction to left turns on the highway in the face of oncoming traffic. She reported anxiety at doing a left turn if an oncoming car was in sight. Even if it was two miles away she could not allow her husband to turn left in front of it.

To treat this most sensitive reaction, I again introduced Dr. G. into the picture. I started by making Mrs. C. imagine (while hypnotized and relaxed) that Dr. G.'s car was a mile ahead when her car began to turn. But this was too disturbing and several repetitions of the scene brought no diminution in the magnitude of anxiety evoked. It seemed possible that there would be less anxiety if the patient's husband were not the driver of the car since his presence at the time of the accident might have made him a conditioned stimulus to anxiety. Thus, I presented the scene with Mrs. C.'s brother as the driver of the car. With this altered feature, Dr. G.'s making a left turn a mile ahead evoked much less anxiety, and after four repetitions it declined to zero. We were then gradually able to decrease the distance so that she could eventually imagine making the turn with Dr. G.'s car only about 150 yards away. Meanwhile, when she was able to 'do' the turn with Dr. G. three-eighths of a mile away, I introduced two new left-turn series: a strange car approaching with her brother driving and Dr. G. approaching with her husband driving—both a mile away initially. Work on all three series went on concurrently. When Mrs. C. could comfortably imagine her brother doing a left turn with the strange car five-eighths of a mile ahead, I resumed the original series in which her husband was the driver, starting with a left turn while the strange car was a mile ahead. This now evoked relatively little anxiety, and progress ensued.

The interrelated decrements of reaction to this group of hierarchies are summarized in Fig. 16.

Other series of related scenes were also subjected to desensitization. One comprised left turns in the city in front of oncoming cars. Since cars in the city move relatively slowly, she felt less 'danger' at a given distance. The series where Mrs. C. was crossing streets as a pedestrian was extended, and she was enabled in imagination to cross under all normal conditions. She reported complete transfer to the reality. Altogether, 36 hierarchical series were used, as detailed in the original account of this case (Wolpe, 1962).

The total effect of desensitization to these interrelated series of stimulus situations was that Mrs. C. became completely at ease in all normal traffic situations—both in crossing streets as a pedestrian and riding in a car. Improvement in real situations took place in close relation with the improvement during sessions. Her tension headaches ceased. In all, 57 desensitization sessions were conducted, comprising a total of 1491 scene presentations. The last session took place on September 29, 1960.

Because Mrs. C. lived about 100 miles away, treatment was episodic. At intervals of from four to six weeks she would come to Charlottesville for about two weeks and be seen almost every day. Noteworthy reduction in the range of real situations that could disturb her occurred in the course of each period of active treatment, and practically none during the inter-

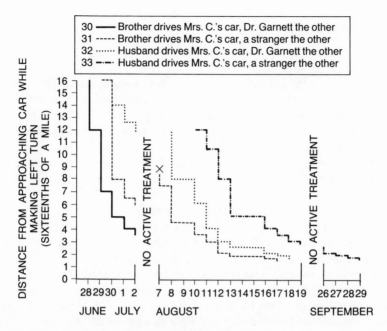

Fig. 16. Temporal relations of 'distances accomplished' in imagination in desensitization series 30, 31, 32 and 33. X: indicates some relapse in Hierarchy 31 following a taxi ride in which the driver insisted on exceeding the speed limit. The status of Hierarchy 32 was not tested before relapse in 31 was overcome.

vals. She was instructed not to avoid exposing herself during these intervals to situations that might be expected to be only slightly disturbing, but if she anticipated being very disturbed to close her eyes, if feasible, for she could thus 'ward off' the situation.

When Mrs. C. was seen late in December, 1960, she was as well as she had been at the end of treatment. Her sexual relations with her husband were progressively improving. At a follow-up telephone call in February, 1962, she stated that she had fully maintained her recovery and had developed no new symptoms. Her relationship with her husband was excellent and, sexually, at least as satisfying as before the accident. Two near-misses of accidents had had no lasting consequences. In 1969 she was still well.

HOMOSEXUALITY

*Case 32:   Reversal of homosexuality after overcoming general inter-personal anxiety**

Mr. R., a 32-year-old hairdresser, was first seen in April, 1954. Seven years previously he had become aware of a slowly progressive diminution in his general enjoyment of life. He had emigrated to South Africa early in 1952 and soon after began to suffer from a persistent feeling of tension, combined with a varying amount of depression. Over the next two years he was treated unsuccessfully by several psychiatrists who gave him electro-shock therapy, injections of vitamins, and some psychoanalytic psychotherapy.

Mr. R. was born in a small town in Sweden and had an only sister, seven years younger. His father was a very good-natured religious man, who never smoked, drank, or lost his temper. He was extremely submissive in all his personal relations and much dominated by his wife, a very ambitious woman who could never be satisfied. She had been very anxious for Mr. R. to do her credit by becoming someone important, and was very resentful when he did not turn out to be a particularly good scholar. She would repeatedly say how disappointed she was to have borne a son, and treated him like a girl—forbidding him to play football, for example. She used to force him to stay at home and amuse his sister when he would rather be playing with his friends. If anything went wrong, she would invariably blame him, screaming at him and often beating him. His predominant feeling towards her was fear. He also felt an impulse to please her and, particularly in later years, condoned her harshness towards him by the thought that she knew no better.

Mr. R. disliked school, was a poor scholar, and had few friends in childhood. On leaving school at 16, he was sent to work on a farm, but soon left to take up ladies' hairdressing. This greatly angered his mother, but he continued in this career notwithstanding her objections.

At the time of puberty, Mr. R. found himself attracted to men, although at first socially rather than sexually. As he became older, he experienced no sexual attraction towards women. When they occasionally made advances, he became extremely anxious and experienced no sexual arousal. By contrast, he found pleasure in the company of men and had formed a succession of attachments to men with whom he had sexual relations. He took the active role on about 90 percent of occasions. At the same time, he thought homosexuality sinful and shameful, and became

---

*A shorter account of this case appears in a paper by Stevenson and Wolpe (1960).

increasingly anxious about his activities. He struggled against his homosexual inclinations and tried to fortify himself with religious advice and acts of devotion. The failure of these efforts, combined with family stresses, was almost unbearable. He sought relief by emigrating to South Africa when he was 30, hoping that a drastic environmental change might effect a psychological change. Of course, this did not happen. His homosexual behavior continued in unstable relationships, and produced the severe anxiety that finally brought him to treatment.

The above history required nearly five interviews. These did not discover any causal sexual trauma, did not elicit any emotions of marked intensity, and were not accompanied by any change in the patient's condition. Toward the end of the fifth interview, because it seemed clear that his excessive devotion to religious matters was responsible for many of his stresses, an effort was made to provide a different perspective and he was given a copy of Winwood Reade's *Martyrdom of Man* to read. At his sixth interview a week later, he reported having read the book; and though upset by the criticisms of religion at first, he felt afterwards that his ideas about it had been clarified. He saw that he had taken sin, particularly in relation to sexuality, too seriously.

His reactions in most social situations were extremely fearful and submissive. Arguments of any kind were so unpleasant that he would avoid them at almost any cost. If a customer at the beauty shop where he worked made an unjust criticism of him he would feel hurt, helpless, and tearful, but make no rejoinder. He could not retrieve the considerable sums of money he had lent to some of his friends because he was quite unable to ask for repayment, even after a year or two had elapsed since the loan.

The learning of unadaptive fears was explained to him, and their susceptibility to unlearning. The five interviews of the next two months were devoted to guiding him in the use of assertive behavior for overcoming his social fears. He proved an apt pupil and soon became much more firm and positive in all his behavior. In two months, his symptoms had almost completely disappeared and he came to be practically completely at ease with his customers. In the meantime, he had formed a couple of new homosexual attachments, each of which, although satisfying while it lasted, had petered out in less than a month. He asked whether I could help him overcome his homosexuality; I gave a negative answer, because Kallman's (1952) twin studies had then convinced me that it had a genetic basis and was therefore impervious to conditioning methods.

Mr. R. did not come again until August 23, two months later. He had continued to advance in the handling of his personal relationships and had been free of symptoms. The quality of his work had greatly improved and, as a consequence, his clientele had practically doubled. He had been offered an administrative post which would begin a year later at a mission hospital in one of the African tribal reserves, and had been enthusiastically studying to equip himself for this.

When next seen on October 18, he said that he had again felt considerably depressed in the past two weeks because of uncertainties about the mission hospital job. The mission people were not particularly cooperative and if the project fell through all his study would have been in vain. At the same time, though better than ever at hairdressing, he was becoming dissatisfied with the job because he found his customers boring, and he felt that it was rather pointless and no real service to humanity. He was told that any work that ministers to human needs is a service, and was advised to give up the idea of going to the mission. A week later, he reported feeling much relieved after having told the mission people that he had decided to withdraw. On November 29, he said that he was feeling fine and getting on very well, especially at his work, which was giving him such great satisfaction that he had abandoned the idea of changing. All the same, he was interested in experiencing what it was like to work in some other country, like England or the United States.

He made another appointment in June, 1955 to tell the following story. Since his treatment he had given up worrying about the sexual problem and had been doing just what he pleased. He had formed a very pleasant homosexual association, but after two months had noticed that he was no longer responding to his friend sexually. A week or two later when he tried to have sex with another man to whom he felt attracted, there was similarly a failure of sexual response. "It felt funny." Two or three later attempts with other men also failed and Mr. R. now felt that, "If a man were to touch me I would hit him."

A few months earlier, Mr. R. had met a girl called Jean whom he had found very likable. She had an attractive personality and many tastes and interests in common with his own, so that he had grown fond of her. He had sometimes thought, "I would marry her if I were normal." When his associations with males became unsatisfactory, he began to take Jean out. It was very pleasant, and before long he wanted to see her every day. For about three months the relationship was purely platonic, but one night after a party when they were both slightly drunk and Jean became sentimental he kissed her and found to his surprise that it was pleasant.

From this time onward he began to respond to her in a sexual way. One evening he became so excited during petting that he was sure he could have had coitus. This kind of reaction had since then recurred many times with consistent erections. Even holding Jean's hand had become exciting. Intercourse had not been attempted because she was "not that kind of girl."

Mr. R. wanted to know whether he dared propose to marry her and was told that no objection could be seen. The next week he reported that Jean was considering his proposal favorably, but had not yet given a definite answer. He felt wonderful and expected at any moment to wake from a dream. He had decided to move to England, where, if they married, Jean was willing to accompany him. He reaffirmed at this interview that he had previously not felt the slightest physical attraction towards women, although he had always liked their company. But because of his inexperience with courtship, Mr. R. sadly mishandled this affair with Jean, damping her interest by his unbridled eagerness. When next seen, late in July, 1955 (at his 21st interview), he reported that she had rejected him, to his great disappointment, and he was leaving for England on his own. My parting advice to him was to make love only to women to whom he felt definitely attracted.

In January, 1956 he wrote from London. After a party he had taken a woman home who had suggested that he spend the night with her, but he had refused on the pretext of fatigue. A few nights later he had dinner at her apartment and, at the end of a pleasant evening, she suggested that he spend the night with her. Although strongly attracted, he felt very much afraid, excused himself, and got up to go home. But when he opened the front door it was raining heavily. He resigned himself to going to bed with her and risking the chagrin of failure. To his delight, however, his sexual performance was completely successful. At the time of writing, he had made love to this woman almost every night for a month, always with complete success, and with greater enjoyment than he had ever experienced with men. He was feeling jubilant. He regarded this affair as his final vindication, assuring him that he need never again feel inferior to other men.

I had follow-up interviews with Mr. R. in 1956 and again in 1957. He continued to be free from neurotic reactions, remained exclusively heterosexual and in 1957 began part-time courses in business administration. In January, 1959 I received a letter from him stating that he married a South American girl. His sex life was still in every way satisfactory, and his wife was expecting a baby.

The favorable sequence of events is explained as follows. Mr. R.'s anxieties evidently originated in his childhood association with his harsh, perpetually screaming mother. Although he was conditioned to be fearful and apologetic towards all people, men were further than women on a gradient of generalization from his mother. During adolescence he had a pleasant feeling of warmth and affection towards men, which naturally inclined him to seek greater closeness into which entered the expression of sexual impulses. Sexual satisfaction with men reinforced his tendencies to consort with them. Direct instigation of assertive behavior with a wide range of individuals led to an extinction of his fear of people. When this had been accomplished, and he was able to survey the world of men and women without anxiety, preference for females spontaneously emerged — a preference presumably established by social role conditionings very early in his life.

HOMOSEXUAL PEDOPHILIA

*Case 33: Assertive training in a case of homosexual pedophilia**

The patient, Dr. V., a 40-year-old physician, was seen late in June, 1971, for the treatment of three problems: sexual activity with his three sons (now aged 13, 9, and 5) for about 10 years; numerous longstanding interpersonal difficulties, mainly with his wife, but also with other adults; and mild, episodic impotence with his wife for two years. What precipitated him into behavior therapy was his wife's discovery that he had persuaded his eldest son to take an active role in one of their sexual encounters, i.e. to penetrate the patient anally. Even though she had known for almost two years about the sexual activity between the patient and the boys, this new development was the last straw. The marriage had been very shaky for the past two years, but the wife now saw no possibility of reconciliation even if he were cured. He was leaving in a couple of days for a month in Europe, which was to be the beginning of a legal separation.

Dr. V., slim, athletic, and youthful in appearance, seemed initially somewhat anxious in telling his story but, as the session progressed, became quite comfortable. His pedophilic behavior with his children had started soon after he discovered that his wife had an affair. Its frequency was variable, but averaged about once every two weeks. It involved all

*This case report has been provided by Dr. Neil B. Edwards, being condensed from a detailed account, Edwards, N. B. (1972) Case Conference: Assertive training in a case of homosexual pedophilia. *J. Behav. Ther. Exp. Pschiat.*, 3: 55.

three sons and consisted mainly of his rubbing his penis between a boy's buttocks to the point of orgasm. Since his wife's discovery of this behavior two years back, it had been a continual source of argument. Despite her pleas he had been unable to stop. It was during these two years that he had begun to have trouble maintaining erections during their infrequent attempts at intercourse.

Regarding Dr. V.'s background, he was the elder of two children, the younger being a married sister. He described his mother as "somewhat overbearing." His father was much more quiet than his mother, but "when he did say something, people listened." He was a stern disciplinarian, yet tended to be "overly fair." The patient described himself as having the latter characteristic also.

Dr. V.'s peer heterosexual adjustment had always been, at best, tenuous. Although he dated during high school his first sexual intercourse was at seventeen when he twice had intercourse with prostitutes, on both occasions contracting gonorrhea. This was quite frightening and succeeded in turning him off sexual intercourse for several years. About one year after his second gonorrheal infection he had his first pedophilic experience with the four-year-old son of a friend.

He first met his wife when he was in medical school. About six months after they met, they had intercourse. This enthused him so much that they were engaged two months later. At a brief vacation in Florida, during which "she was all for sex," they had sexual intercourse frequently. After the wedding she was less keen on sex, and almost immediately began "sitting around moping." This unexpected behavior began to turn him off. Even so, he continued "trying all sorts of ways to get sex" for a few months. Gradually, however, his efforts waned and after about a year of marriage, coitus was down to once every two or three months. Two years later, she started seeing another man. Though she claimed that sex was not involved, he was very broken up by this and told her to leave. After a nine-month legal separation, they were divorced. Two months later, they remarried. Sexually she was now the aggressor! He found this irritating; so that within a year they were back to coitus once every two or three months, a frequency which continued to be the mode. It was at this stage of their remarriage that he started turning to his children for sexual outlet.

Dr. V.'s relationship with his wife was strained on several other scores also. Since the early years of the marriage they were prone to arguments. She was "bored to death," but unwilling to take up sports, reading, or any other activity. She wanted to be given a good time, but did not want to invest much of herself.

At the end of the first interview, three things were done: (1) Since even when not engaging in pedophilic behavior he was troubled by pedophilic thoughts every day or two, he was shown thought-stopping, and told to use it whenever the pedophilic thoughts came to his mind; (2) He was told to avoid sex with anyone during the month he was away, and to concentrate on getting to know people instead; (3) Initial instructions were given on assertive behavior, and he was told to start practicing it. He agreed to come three times a week on his return from Europe.

On his return, he reported that the thought-stopping was working well, the frequency of the pedophilic thoughts having decreased to once or twice weekly. He was back with his wife and had had several good erections, but, following instructions, had not attempted intercourse. He seemed fairly well into assertive training. He was congratulated on this and instructed in the expression of positive feelings. The therapist smiled whenever he referred to his wife as "the wife" as was his wont. After about three sessions of this, he was routinely referring to her by her first name. Meanwhile, the smiling brought out some more feelings about her. What he disliked about her mainly was that she had been keeping him "one down." If she provoked him, he would be unable to assert himself, but stay angry for several days, feeling dissatisfied that he was not getting things straightened out. He was now beginning to feel that he was gaining some control.

Since Dr. V. now seemed ready to approach his wife sexually, he was instructed to do so, but to assume at least equality in control, not allowing her to domineer. At the fifth session, he reported intercourse, which he had initiated, culminating in simultaneous orgasms. He had one disturbing experience—an erection while watching cartoons with his children. He was worried that this would continue, but was assured that it was merely a habit that would extinguish.

He reported at the ninth session that he had misinterpreted a secret conversation between his wife and their eldest son as one of his wife's "subversive sessions." Although he was angry, he let it ride to see what would happen. He found later that this had been a wise course of action— the son had been in some minor trouble with the police (breaking lumber at a construction site) while Dr. V. was in Europe, and was afraid to tell him about it. His wife advised the son to tell his father about it and the next day, without prodding, he did. Dr. V. told his wife of his misgivings and apologized—then congratulated her on her course of action. She continued to move toward him.

At the twelfth session, Dr. V. reported that his wife was finally convinced that her "confidence" sessions with the eldest son were subversive in terms of family interaction and that she had agreed that they would stop.

The thirteenth session was the last. He reported that he had a minor lapse. He had allowed three issues to build up and became too angry to speak out. However, he recognized this in time and was able to express his anger to his wife, and in a couple of hours it was all over. He felt at this point that it would be a good idea for him to apologize to her for letting these things build up. He and his family were leaving for Oregon in a few days. He was advised to call periodically and, if necessary, return for consultation.

The total time span was four weeks — thirteen sessions. In December, 1971, the patient reported by telephone that he was still doing well in all areas.

WASHING COMPULSION

Case 34: A washing compulsion overcome by systematic desensitization to urinary 'contamination' using both imaginary and real stimuli*

Mr. T. was an eighteen-year-old youth with a very severe washing compulsion. The basis of this was a fear of contamination by urine, and most especially his own urine, mainly because he dreaded to contaminate others with it. When the treatment to be described began, the patient was almost completely impotentiated by his neurosis. After urinating, he would spend up to 45 minutes in an elaborate ritual of cleaning up his genitalia, followed by about two hours of hand-washing. When he woke in the morning, his first need was to shower, which took him about four hours to do. To these 'basic requirements,' were added many others occasioned by the incidental contaminations inevitable on any day. It is scarcely surprising that Mr. T. had come to conclude that getting up was not worth the effort, and for two months had spent most of his time in bed.

The neurosis evidently originated in an unusual domestic situation. Until he was 15, Mr. T.'s parents had compelled him to share a bed with his sister, two years older, because she had a fear of being alone. The very natural erotic responses aroused by this proximity to the girl had made him feel very guilty and ashamed. Anger towards his parents for imposing this on him led to hostile and, at times, destructive fantasies about them.

*This is an adaptation of an earlier report (Wolpe, 1964).

Horrified at these, he had come to regard himself as despicable. His urine had subsequently become the prime focus of his 'repulsiveness.'

Treatment in the first place consisted of conventional desensitization. Since he was disturbed even at the idea of anybody else becoming contaminated with urine, the first scene he was asked to imagine was of an unknown man dipping his hand into a forty cubic foot trough of water into which one drop of urine had been deposited. Even this scene produced some disturbance in Mr. T. at first, but it waned and disappeared in the course of a few presentations. The concentration of urine was then increased until the man was imagined to be inserting his hand into pure urine. Each scene was repeated until it no longer evoked any anxiety.

During the course of these procedures, which occupied about five months of sessions taking place about five times a week and each lasting, as a rule, about twenty minutes, there was considerable improvement in Mr. T.'s clinical condition. For example, his hand-washing time went down to about 30 minutes and his shower time to just over an hour; and he no longer found it necessary to interpose the *New York Times* between himself and his chair during interviews.

A new series of imaginary situations was now started in which Mr. T. himself was inserting his hand into increasingly concentrated solutions of urine. At first, he seemed to make some further progress, but then it became evident that there was diminishing transfer between what he could imagine himself doing and what he actually could do. Eventually, whereas he could unperturbedly imagine himself immersing his hand in pure urine, to do so in actuality was out of the question.

It was therefore decided to switch to desensitization *in vivo*. Relaxation was now opposed to increasingly strong real stimuli evoking anxiety. Mr. T. was, to begin with, exposed to the word 'urine' printed in big block letters. This evoked a little anxiety which he was asked to relax away. The next step was to seat him at one end of a long room and present a closed bottle of urine at the other end. Again, he had to relax away the anxiety. Then, step by step, the bottle of urine was moved closer until eventually he was handling it with only minimal anxiety which he could relax away. When the bottle of urine was no longer capable of evoking anxiety, a new series of maneuvers was started. First of all, a very dilute solution of anonymous urine (1 drop to a gallon) was applied to the back of his hand, and he was made to relax until all anxiety disappeared; and then, from session to session, the concentration was gradually increased. When he was able to endure pure urine, his own urine began to be used; and, finally, he was enabled unflinchingly to 'contaminate' all kinds of objects with his uriniferous hands—magazines, doorknobs, and people's hands.

The numerous acts of desensitization outlined were completed at the end of June, 1961. By then Mr. T. had achieved greatly increased freedom of movement; he was dressing daily, his hand-washing time had gone down to 7 minutes, his shower time to 40 minutes, and his cleaning-up ritual was almost eliminated. In September, 1961, he went back to school and was seen only occasionally until March 1962. During this time, without active treatment, he made virtually no further progress. In March, 1962, he began weekly sessions as an out-patient, and then improvement was resumed. When last seen in June, 1962, his hand-washing time was 3 minutes and his shower time 20 minutes. He said that he was coming to think of urine as "sticky and smelly and nothing else." In February, 1965, he reported that hand-washing took him about 10 seconds, and he "wasn't even using soap." He was leading a normal life. In September, 1967, a telephone call conveyed that his recovery had been maintained.

CHAPTER 15

Evaluation of Behavior Therapy

Since behavior therapy is the clinical application of experimentally established principles of learning, its use is almost exclusively in clinical states that learning has brought into being. The commonest of these states are the neuroses, so that it is particularly germane to evaluate the therapeutic effects of behavior therapy on them. As in *Psychotherapy by Reciprocal Inhibition*, therefore, our evaluative purview will concentrate on the neuroses. It will be seen that the tentative optimism expressed in that volume has become firmer and bolder.

Psychotherapists very easily acquire a belief in the efficacy of their own methods because, as has repeatedly been shown (e.g. Landis, 1937; Wilder, 1945; Eysenck, 1952), 40 percent or more of neurotic patients improve markedly with conventional therapies (not behavior therapy) despite widely differing theories and practices. Success with this degree of frequency provides more than enough intermittent reinforcement (Skinner, 1938) to maintain therapeutic habits very strongly. But the fact that the beneficial effects are rather uniform indicates that they are not attributable to specific features of the individual therapies, but to some process that is common to all of them — presumably the emotional impact on the patient of the therapist, a trusted and supposedly wise and competent person to whom he entrusts himself. Nobody who is aware of these nonspecific therapeutic effects is in any position to claim potency for his particular practices unless they yield either a percentage of recoveries substantially above the common average or greater rapidity of recovery.

Thus, if behavior therapy is to displace the present widely-accepted and well-organized psychoanalytically-oriented practices, there must be evidence that it is substantially more effective in overcoming neurotic disturbances. It is because there are factual grounds for believing that behavior therapy does exceed the common average in *both* percentage and speed of recoveries that its techniques are confidently offered in this volume. It is a confidence based partly on clinical experience, and partly on some well-controlled experimental studies.

CLINICAL STUDIES

An increasing number of reports of the successful treatment of individual cases or small groups treated by behavior therapy have been appearing during the past decade. Many of the earlier ones were conveniently brought together in two volumes edited by Eysenck (1960, 1964). A feature of these case reports that is unusual in the literature of psychotherapy is that they almost invariably display *clear temporal relationships between specific interventions and therapeutic change.** This, together with a highly predictable replicability of effects, is really more impressive than the statistical comparisons at present available.

There have been several uncontrolled statistical studies. In a survey (Wolpe, 1958) of my results with behavior therapy in private practice, 89 percent of 210 patients had either apparently recovered or were at least 80 percent improved in a mean of about 30 therapeutic sessions. The criteria were those suggested by Knight (1941). No case diagnosed as neurotic was refused treatment if time was available. Psychotics and psychopaths were not knowingly accepted, and, if treated through error of diagnosis, were transferred to other therapists when the mistake was discovered. When 45 of these patients were followed up two to seven years later all but one had at least maintained their gains.

Table 6, comparing the results of the foregoing two studies with those of a typical series from a general hospital, and two psychoanalytic series, shows a substantially higher percentage of recoveries for behavior therapy. More important than the relative percentages is the fact that the number of sessions spent in therapy is overwhelmingly less in behavior therapy. The mean number for psychoanalysis is in the region of 600 — 3 or 4 times a week for 3 or 4 years (Masserman, 1963); while the mean for behavior therapy is about 30. However, the series are not matched and therefore the validity of the comparison can be disputed.

*The cases in Chapter 14 are typical.

Table 6. Uncontrolled outcome studies of different types of therapy.

Series	No. of Cases	Apparently cured or much improved	Percentage recoveries
Behavior Therapy			
Wolpe (1958)	210	188	89.5
Psychoanalytic Therapy			
(Brody, 1962)			
Completely analyzed cases only	210	126	60
General Hospital Therapy			
(Hamilton and Wall, 1941)	100	53	53

Note: The *total* patient population in the psychoanalytic group was 595.

The following reports of results support the behavioristic approach in a general way, even though they relate to procedures that were off the beaten track in one way or another. Hussain (1964) claimed a 95 percent "complete or almost complete removal of symptoms" in 105 patients whose disturbed habits were treated by hypnotic suggestions based on the reciprocal inhibition principle; but the details of his method are not very clear, and the criteria of change are not reported in detail. However, Rubin's (1972) use of suggestion as a source of reciprocal inhibition may have much in common with Hussain's work. Burnett and Ryan (1964) treated 100 patients by giving them relaxation training, and then desensitization to both imaginary and real situations — in groups, and sometimes individually. Treatment continued for 5 weeks on the average. A one-year follow-up was possible on only 25 of the patients, of whom 15 (60 percent) were found to be either apparently cured or much improved. The brief exposure of the patients to behavior therapy and the predominance of group procedures tend to bias the outcome negatively because a full exploitation of available resources was precluded. Nevertheless, a 60 percent recovery rate after such brief therapy seems quite noteworthy.

Controlled Comparative Studies of Outcome

Several studies have compared behavioristic methods with various forms of nonbehavioristic psychotherapy. Most often the comparison has been made with systematic desensitization.

Paul (1966), in an ingeniously designed experiment, compared desensitization with two other methods in the treatment of students with severe fears of speaking in public. He enlisted the services of five experienced psychotherapists whose 'school' affiliation ranged from Freud to Sullivan. Nine subjects were allotted to each therapist so that he could use three different methods—each in three subjects. The methods were: (1) The therapist's own customary type of insight therapy, (2) A stylized procedure involving suggestion and support called 'attention-placebo' therapy, and (3) Systematic desensitization, which the therapist had to be trained to administer. Each patient had five therapeutic sessions. The results showed significantly superior effectiveness for systematic desensitization on a variety of measures—cognitive, physiological, and motor performance. On the conventional clinical criteria, 86 percent of the patients treated by desensitization were much improved and 14 percent improved (Table 7). This compares with 20 percent much improved and 27 percent improved for the insight group, and with none much improved and 47 percent improved for the attention-placebo group. In a follow-up two years later (Paul, 1968), the differences were found to have been maintained.

Lang has been the chief architect of an excellent series of controlled studies beginning with Lang and Lazovik (1963) and Lang, Lazovik, and Reynolds (1965). Their subjects were students who had severe phobic reactions to harmless snakes. They treated some groups of them by systematic desensitization, and compared the results with those obtained in control groups who either received no treatment or else 'pseudotherapy' (i.e. relaxation training followed by interviews focusing on problems of 'living,' with the subject in a state of relaxation). The desensitized students improved very much more than either of the control groups as shown by a snake avoidance test, and by the patient's self-rating of fear

Table 7. Percentage breakdown of cases in traditional 'improvement' categories from stress-condition data*

Treatment	N	Unimproved	Slightly Improved	Improved	Much Improved
Desensitization	15	—	—	14%	86%
Insight	15	7%	46%	27%	20%
Attention-Placebo	15	20%	33%	47%	—
Treatment-control	29	55%	28%	17%	—

*From Paul, Gordon L. (1966). *Insight versus desensitization in psychotherapy.* Stanford University Press. Reprinted with permission.

Table 8. T-tests of mean fear change scores from pre- to post-treatment in snake phobias

Groups	Avoidance test	Fear thermometer	FSS No. 38	Fear survey
Combined control *vs.* Desensitization	2.57*	2.12*	2.19*	1.25*
Combined control *vs.* 15 or more	3.26†	3.44†	3.99‡	2.52*
Combined control *vs.* Less than 15	0.14	0.41	1.85	0.41
Less than 15 *vs.* 15 or more	2.33*	3.28*	5.00‡	2.26*
Pseudotherapy *vs.* No treatment	1.67	0.48	0.58	0.12

*p < 0.05.   †p < 0.01.   ‡p < 0.001.
Lang, P. J., Lazovik, A. D., and Reynolds, D. (1965), Desensitization, Suggestibility and Pseudotherapy. *J. Abnorm. Psychol.* 10, 395–402.

reaction to snakes (Table 8). The difference is significant at the 0.001 level when 15 or more hierarchy items have been desensitized.

Moore (1965) was the author of the first well-planned and well-executed controlled investigation dealing with asthmatic patients applying for treatment at a clinic. She used a balanced incomplete block design (in which the subjects are their own controls) to compare the effects on these cases of three forms of treatment—(1) Reciprocal inhibition therapy, (2) Relaxation therapy, (3) Relaxation combined with suggestion. During the first four weeks of treatment, both subjectively, and objectively, as measured by maximum peak flow of respired air, all three groups improved, but the reciprocal inhibition group more than the others. After this time, progress continued in the reciprocal inhibition group, while the other two began to regress. Eight weeks from the beginning of treatment, in terms of maximum peak flow the superiority of improvement of the reciprocal inhibition group was significant at the 0.001 level (Fig. 17).

In contrast to the above are the 'controlled studies' of Cooper (1963), Gelder, Marks, Sakinovsky, and Wolff (1964), and Gelder and Marks (1965) which purport to compare the results in clinical practice, of behavior therapy with those of conventional 'dynamic' psychotherapy. Though their work is conscientious, it has serious flaws, some of which bias it negatively against behavior therapy. The comments that follow are partly based on personal correspondence with Dr. M. G. Gelder.

A behavior analysis such as described in this book is not generally performed, the 'deconditioning' being on the whole applied to the patient's complaints as presented. Desensitization *in vivo* is almost the exclusive technique in contrast to the considerable range that a well-schooled behavior therapist can offer. The therapists who carried out the behavior therapy were often unskilled, and sometimes novices. In later studies

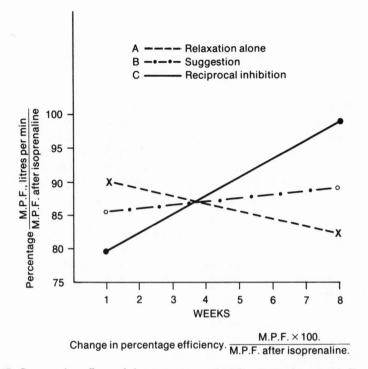

Fig. 17. Comparative effects of three treatment schedules on maximum peak flow of inspired air in asthmatic patients (Moore, 1965).

(Gelder, *et al.*, 1967; Gelder and Marks, 1968), using conventional desensitization, the inexperienced therapists obtained better results than before, but still less good than those of well-trained behavior therapists.

Paul (1969) has provided an extensive and penetrating review of studies of the outcome of behavior therapy with main attention to systematic desensitization, covering 75 papers. Twenty of the reports were controlled experiments, and 10 of these included designs which ruled out intraclass confounding of therapist characteristics and treatment techniques. The findings were overwhelmingly positive. Paul states that "for the first time in the history of psychological treatments, a specific therapeutic package reliably produced measureable benefits for clients across a broad range of distressing problems in which anxiety was of fundamental importance." Relapse and symptom-substitution were "notably lacking," though most of the authors were looking out for them.

THE CRITERIA OF THERAPEUTIC CHANGE

The central goal of psychotherapy is the same as that of any other branch of therapeutics—the lasting removal of the sources of suffering and disability. Since the behavior therapist views the therapeutic task as a matter of eliminating persistent unadaptive *habits*, an appropriate way of measuring his success would be to classify and enumerate the unadaptive habits before therapy, and then, after therapy, to assess to what extent each habit has been eliminated. In making such assessments the therapist can employ several kinds of information—the report of the patient, clinical observation, the observations of the patient's associates, and psychophysiological studies. The last-named are basic, and necessarily figure prominently in research.

The clinical criteria for therapeutic change that have been generally adopted by behavior therapists are those delineated by Knight (1941). They lend themselves well to comparative outcome research. Ironically, they were originally proposed for the purpose of improving psychoanalytic research but seem never to have been used by psychoanalysts. Knight's criteria are:

1. Symptomatic improvement.
2. Increased productiveness at work.
3. Improved adjustment and pleasure in sex.
4. Improved interpersonal relationships.
5. Enhanced ability to handle ordinary psychological conflicts and reasonable reality stresses.

'Symptomatic improvement' is a necessary criterion of change in every case of neurosis. One or more of the other criteria are relevant in most cases, but not in all. A man with neurotic anxieties in work situations may have a completely satisfying sex life and be at ease in social situations. 'Symptomatic improvement' in this context does not mean palliation by means such as drugs, but *fundamental* change in the sense that the stimuli that used to call forth inappropriate anxiety or other unadaptive responses can no longer do so *under the same conditions*. What the patient perceives as a symptom, the therapist perceives as a habit. By deconditioning the anxiety-response habit that is the basis of the symptom, he brings about a commensurate diminution of the symptom. If there have been other reactions that have depended on the presence of the anxiety, they, too, diminish or cease—whether they have appeared in the form of migraine, asthma, neurodermatitis, fibrositis, stammering, frigidity, impotence, or homosexuality. The decline of the secondary manifestations of neurosis can thus also be used as a measure of improvement. Moore's investigation of the treatment of asthma provides a good example of this. See also Table 1, Chapter 3.

There is one major reform that should be incorporated into future outcome studies. Marks and Gelder (1965) have drawn attention to the confusing consequences of the traditional practice of lumping together all kinds of neuroses. It is a practice that is due to the domination of psychoanalytic theory, which plays down the outward features of neuroses in the belief that the 'real' pathology is 'inside.' Although categorization is not always easy, particularly in complex neuroses, it would facilitate comparisons, and permit us to determine to what extent different syndromes may require different measures. Therapeutic comparisons confined to reasonably well-defined syndromes have recently been appearing (e.g. Bancroft, 1970; Gath and Gelder,. 1971; Hodgson, Rachman, and Marks, 1972).

ANSWERS TO SOME OBJECTIONS

It can scarcely be disputed that for unmaking unadaptive habits that have been acquired by learning, unlearning is the appropriate process to invoke; and when it succeeds nothing more remains to be done. Since to do behavior therapy is to apply principles of learning—such as reciprocal inhibition or positive reinforcement, as well as other experimentally established principles like generalization—it follows that for purely learned unadaptive habits behavior therapy uniquely fits the bill. To amend a dictum by Eysenck (1960, p. 9), "Get rid of the unadaptive habit and you have eliminated the neurosis." On the other hand, of course, when there are organic factors involved in unadaptive behavior—like the endogenous causes of depression, hyperthyroidism, or functional hyper-insulinism—behavior therapy is certainly not sufficient. If there is no ingredient of learning in a particular sample of unadaptive behavior, behavior therapy is not indicated.

However, there are those who urge that even when there is no organic factor, behavior therapy is insufficient. Adherents of the psychoanalytic systems hold that the effects of behavior therapy are 'superficial,' that it does not remove the basic neurosis, and that relapse and symptom-substitution are to be expected. This opinion follows logically from an acceptance of the psychoanalytic view of neurosis—a view which, however, there are many logical and factual reasons to doubt (Wohlgemuth, 1923;

Salter, 1952; Eysenck, 1953; Wolpe and Rachman, 1960; and Wolpe, 1961a). What is more persuasive than theoretical or methodological objections is the empirical fact that after behavior therapy has been successful, recurrence of symptoms is very unusual. Every instance of recurrence that has been investigated has been found to be due to reconditioning. Only one 'relapse' was found among 45 patients I followed up from 2 to 7 years (Wolpe, 1958). In none of 17 patients with whom I have been in touch for 20 years or more has there been any evidence of relapse or symptom substitution. These occur only when therapy has failed to deal with the autonomic core of the neurotic reactions. For example, when a case of obesity whose overeating relieved anxiety was treated by aversion therapy without deconditioning the anxiety, it was not surprising that she developed a reactive depression. (See also some of McConaghy's (1964) cases).

A related objection is that behavior therapy is narrowly focused on symptoms and unable to effect 'personality change.' If personality is defined as a person's totality of habits, it is obvious that even the elimination of a single neurotic habit is a personality change. Furthermore, when a patient is rid of his neurotic habits, he is more free to behave effectively in various directions. Motor habits, for example, are often changed – movements become more graceful and conversation becomes easier and more humorous when the patient is freed from neurotic tension. A great variety of other possible changes is implied in Table 1 (Chapter 3). Those who raise this issue of personality change do not define it. When they do, the way will be open for comparing behavior therapy with psychoanalysis and other methods as instruments of 'personality change.'

A popular fallacy is that behavior therapy is useful for simple cases, but not for complex ones. I made a re-examination (Wolpe, 1964) of some previously published results (Wolpe, 1958), dividing the cases into simple and complex. A neurosis was regarded as complex if it had one or more of the following features: (1) More than one family of stimuli conditioned to neurotic responses, (2) Reactions to which the conditioned stimuli were determined with difficulty, (3) Reactions that included social unadaptiveness (character neuroses), (4) Obsessional neuroses, and (5) Reactions that included pervasive anxiety. Of the 86 cases reviewed, 65 were complex in one or more of the senses defined. Fifty-eight of these (89 percent) were judged either apparently cured or much improved. This percentage was exactly the same as that obtained for the whole group. However, the median number of sessions for the complex group was 29 and the mean 54.8 in contrast to a median for the non-complex remainder of 11.5 and a mean of 14.9. Thus, while the complex cases responded to behavior therapy as often as the simple ones, therapy took longer.

The literature has recently brought forth a spate of 'critiques' of the red herring variety (e.g. Breger and McGaugh, 1965; Costello, 1970; Wilkins, 1972; Locke, 1971; Davison and Wilson, 1972), where spurious issues arise from the critic's lack of familiarity with basic data and arguments, especially those presented in *Psychotherapy by Reciprocal Inhibition*. For example, the theory of neurosis there presented is attacked as if it were conceived as a kind of avoidance behavior. As the reader of this book knows, the proposition of our theory is, on the contrary, that conditioned anxiety, an autonomic constellation of responses, is the core of most neuroses. Failure to extinguish the primarily autonomic behavior of experimental neuroses by simple evocation is the consistent finding of an extensive literature. Yet the fact itself is contested by quoting evidence that "conditioned avoidance responses can, indeed, be rapidly extinguished via exposure to the CS under appropriate conditions"!

The application of Sherrington's reciprocal inhibition principle to complex reactions is also attacked as "a massive extrapolation," which is easy enough to do by ignoring both the experimental evidence given in *Psychotherapy by Reciprocal Inhibition* and the findings of everyday observation. Reciprocal inhibition is an exceedingly widespread phenomenon (Gellhorn, 1967) which nature did not really reserve for the special purposes of psychotherapy. Innumerable pairs of possible reactions are mutually exclusive so that eliciting the currently 'stronger' member of a pair precludes (inhibits) performance of the 'weaker.' Intestinal cramps inhibit feelings of tenderness, anger inhibits smiling, and "accompanying the articulation of any work there is ordinarily an automatic inhibition of all simultaneous tendencies to pronounce other words" (Wolpe, 1954). Experimentally, anxiety has been shown to inhibit cats from eating even after being starved for a day or more (Masserman, 1943; Wolpe, 1958) and dogs from responding sexually (Napalkov and Karas, 1957). The reciprocal inhibition that Sherrington discovered in spinal reflexes is the prototype of a ubiquitous class of occurrences.

It has more recently been proposed (e.g. Bergin and Strupp, 1972) that the methods emanating from other approaches should be used in addition to those of behavior therapy. The argument is that different approaches may suit different problems and that patients benefit if the therapist has a wide range of methods on which to draw. The weakness of this position is that there is no evidence for the specific effectiveness of any of the non-behavioristic techniques these authors refer to (as distinct from the nonspecific effects mentioned earlier in this chapter). The likelihood is that spending therapeutic time on non-behavioristic measures will dilute behavior therapy effort and produce poorer results.

There is really no escape from the conclusion that knowledge of the factors influencing the making and breaking of habits is of central importance in modifying and eliminating unadaptive behavior that has been learned. This knowledge has generated a steady stream of clinical methods that are increasingly vindicated by their results. While it is not the only source of effective methods — some are occasionally found empirically — it is by its nature the most fruitful.

Willoughby Personality Schedule

Instructions: The questions in this schedule are intended to indicate various emotional personality traits. It is not a test in any sense because there are no right nor wrong answers to any of the questions.

After each question you will find a row of numbers whose meaning is given below. All you have to do is to draw a ring around the number that describes you best.

    0 means "No," "never," "not at all," etc.
    1 means "Somewhat," "sometimes," "a little," etc.
    2 means "About as often as not," "an average amount," etc.
    3 means "Usually," "a good deal," "rather often," etc.
    4 means "Practically always," "entirely," etc.

1. Do you get stage fright?—0 1 2 3 4
2. Do you worry over humiliating experiences?—0 1 2 3 4
3. Are you afraid of falling when you are on a high place?—0 1 2 3 4
4. Are your feelings easily hurt?—0 1 2 3 4
5. Do you keep in the background on social occasions?—0 1 2 3 4
6. Are you happy and sad by turns without knowing why?—0 1 2 3 4
7. Are you shy?—0 1 2 3 4
8. Do you daydream frequently?—0 1 2 3 4
9. Do you get discouraged easily?—0 1 2 3 4

10. Do you say things on the spur of the moment and then regret them? —
    0 1 2 3 4

11. Do you like to be alone? — 0 1 2 3 4

12. Do you cry easily? — 0 1 2 3 4

13. Does it bother you to have people watch you work even when you do
    it well? — 0 1 2 3 4

14. Does criticism hurt you badly? — 0 1 2 3 4

15. Do you cross the street to avoid meeting someone? — 0 1 2 3 4

16. At a reception or tea do you avoid meeting the important person
    present? — 0 1 2 3 4

17. Do you often feel just miserable? — 0 1 2 3 4

18. Do you hesitate to volunteer in a class discussion or debate? —
    0 1 2 3 4

19. Are you often lonely? — 0 1 2 3 4

20. Are you self-conscious before superiors? — 0 1 2 3 4

21. Do you lack self-confidence? — 0 1 2 3 4

22. Are you self-conscious about your appearance? — 0 1 2 3 4

23. If you see an accident does something keep you from giving help? —
    0 1 2 3 4

24. Do you feel inferior? — 0 1 2 3 4

25. Is it hard to make up your mind until the time for action is past? —
    0 1 2 3 4

Revised Willoughby Questionnaire for Self-Administration

Instructions: The questions in this schedule are intended to indicate various emotional personality traits. It is not a test in any sense because there are no right nor wrong answers to any of the questions.

After each question you will find a row of numbers whose meaning is given below. All you have to do is to draw a ring around the number that describes you best.

0 means "No," "never," "not at all," etc.
1 means "Somewhat," "sometimes," "a little," etc.
2 means "About as often as not," "an average amount," etc.
3 means "Usually," "a good deal," "rather often," etc.
4 means "Practically always," "entirely," etc.

1. Do you get anxious if you have to speak or perform in any way in front of a group of strangers? — 0 1 2 3 4
2. Do you worry if you make a fool of yourself, or feel you have been made to look foolish? — 0 1 2 3 4
3. Are you afraid of falling when you are on a high place from which there is no real danger of falling — for example, looking down from a balcony on the tenth floor? — 0 1 2 3 4
4. Are you easily hurt by what other people do or say to you? — 0 1 2 3 4
5. Do you keep in the background on social occasions? — 0 1 2 3 4
6. Do you have changes of mood that you cannot explain? — 0 1 2 3 4

7. Do you feel uncomfortable when you meet new people? – 0 1 2 3 4

8. Do you day-dream frequently, i.e. indulge in fantasies not involving concrete situations? – 0 1 2 3 4

9. Do you get discouraged easily, e.g. by failure or criticism? – 0 1 2 3 4

10. Do you say things in haste and then regret them? – 0 1 2 3 4

11. Are you ever disturbed by the mere presence of other people? – 0 1 2 3 4

12. Do you cry easily? – 0 1 2 3 4

13. Does it bother you to have people watch you work even when you do it well? – 0 1 2 3 4

14. Does criticism hurt you badly? – 0 1 2 3 4

15. Do you cross the street to avoid meeting someone? – 0 1 2 3 4

16. At a reception or tea do you go out of your way to avoid meeting the important person present? – 0 1 2 3 4

17. Do you often feel just miserable? – 0 1 2 3 4

18. Do you hesitate to volunteer in a discussion or debate with a group of people whom you know more or less? – 0 1 2 3 4

19. Do you have a sense of isolation, either when alone or among people? – 0 1 2 3 4

20. Are you self-conscious before 'superiors' (teachers, employers, authorities)? – 0 1 2 3 4

21. Do you lack confidence in your general ability to do things and to cope with situations? – 0 1 2 3 4

22. Are you self-conscious about your appearance even when you are well-dressed and groomed? – 0 1 2 3 4

23. Are you scared at the sight of blood, injuries, and destruction even though there is no danger to you? – 0 1 2 3 4

24. Do you feel that other people are better than you? – 0 1 2 3 4

25. Is it hard for you to make up your mind? – 0 1 2 3 4

APPENDIX 3

Fear Inventory

The items in this questionnaire refer to things and experiences that may cause fear or other unpleasant feelings. Write the number of each item in the column that describes how much you are disturbed by it nowadays.

	Not At All	A Little	A Fair Amount	Much	Very Much
1. Noise of vacuum cleaners					
2. Open wounds					
3. Being alone					
4. Being in a strange place					
5. Loud voices					
6. Dead people					
7. Speaking in public					
8. Crossing streets					
9. People who seem insane					
10. Falling					
11. Automobiles					
12. Being teased					
13. Dentists					
14. Thunder					
15. Sirens					
16. Failure					

	Not At All	A Little	A Fair Amount	Much	Very Much
17. Entering a room where other people are already seated					
18. High places on land					
19. Looking down from high buildings					
20. Worms					
21. Imaginary creatures					
22. Strangers					
23. Receiving injections					
24. Bats					
25. Journeys by train					
26. Journeys by bus					
27. Journeys by car					
28. Feeling angry					
29. People in authority					
30. Flying insects					
31. Seeing other people injected					
32. Sudden noises					
33. Dull weather					
34. Crowds					
35. Large open spaces					
36. Cats					
37. One person bullying another					
38. Tough looking people					
39. Birds					
40. Sight of deep water					
41. Being watched working					
42. Dead animals					
43. Weapons					
44. Dirt					
45. Crawling insects					
46. Sight of fighting					
47. Ugly people					
48. Fire					

	Not At All	A Little	A Fair Amount	Much	Very Much
49. Sick people					
50. Dogs					
51. Being criticized					
52. Strange shapes					
53. Being in an elevator					
54. Witnessing surgical oper- ations					
55. Angry people					
56. Mice					
57. Blood					
a — Human					
b — Animal					
58. Parting from friends					
59. Enclosed places					
60. Prospect of a surgical operation					
61. Feeling rejected by others					
62. Airplanes					
63. Medical odors					
64. Feeling disapproved of					
65. Harmless snakes					
66. Cemeteries					
67. Being ignored					
68. Darkness					
69. Premature heart beats (Missing a beat)					
70. Nude Men (a) Nude Women (b)					
71. Lightning					
72. Doctors					
73. People with deformities					
74. Making mistakes					
75. Looking foolish					
76. Losing control					
77. Fainting					
78. Becoming nauseous					

	Not At All	A Little	A Fair Amount	Much	Very Much
79. Spiders					
80. Being in charge or responsible for decisions					
81. Sight of knives or sharp objects					
82. Becoming mentally ill					
83. Being with a member of the opposite sex					
84. Taking written tests					
85. Being touched by others					
86. Feeling different from others					
87. A lull in conversation					

Bernreuter S-S Scale and Scoring Key

1. Yes No ? Would you rather work for yourself than carry out the program of a superior whom you respect?
2. Yes No ? Do you usually enjoy spending an evening alone?
3. Yes No ? Have books been more entertaining to you than companions?
4. Yes No ? Do you feel the need of wider social contacts than you have?
5. Yes No ? Are you easily discouraged when the opinions of others differ from your own?
6. Yes No ? Does admiration gratify you more than achievement?
7. Yes No ? Do you usually prefer to keep your opinions to yourself?
8. Yes No ? Do you dislike attending the movies alone?
9. Yes No ? Would you like to have a very congenial friend with whom you could plan daily activities?
10. Yes No ? Can you calm your own fears?
11. Yes No ? Do jeers humiliate you even when you know you are right?
12. Yes No ? Do you think you could become so absorbed in creative work that you would not notice the lack of intimate friends?
13. Yes No ? Are you willing to take a chance alone in a situation of doubtful outcome?
14. Yes No ? Do you find conversation more helpful in formulating your ideas than reading?

15. Yes No ? Do you like to shop alone?

16. Yes No ? Does your ambition need occasional stimulation through contacts with successful people?

17. Yes No ? Do you have difficulty in making up your mind for yourself?

18. Yes No ? Would you prefer making your own arrangements on a trip to a foreign country to going on a prearranged trip?

19. Yes No ? Are you much affected by praise, or blame, of many people?

20. Yes No ? Do you usually avoid taking advice?

21. Yes No ? Do you consider the observance of social customs and manners an essential aspect of life?

22. Yes No ? Do you want someone with you when you receive bad news?

23. Yes No ? Does it make you uncomfortable to be 'different' or unconventional?

24. Yes No ? Do you prefer to make hurried decisions alone?

25. Yes No ? If you were to start out in research work would you prefer to be an assistant in another's project rather than an independent worker on your own?

26. Yes No ? When you are low in spirits do you try to find someone to cheer you up?

27. Yes No ? Have you preferred being alone most of the time?

28. Yes No ? Do you prefer traveling with someone who will make all the necessary arrangements to the adventure of traveling alone?

29. Yes No ? Do you usually work things out rather than get someone to show you?

30. Yes No ? Do you like especially to have attention from acquaintances when you are ill?

31. Yes No ? Do you prefer to face dangerous situations alone?

32. Yes No ? Can you usually see wherein your mistakes lie without having them pointed out to you?

33. Yes No ? Do you like to make friends when you go to new places?

34. Yes No ? Can you stick to a tiresome task for long without someone prodding or encouraging you?

35. Yes No ? Do you experience periods of loneliness?

36. Yes No ? Do you like to get many views from others before making an important decision?

37. Yes No ? Would you dislike any work which might take you into isolation for a few years, such as forest ranging, etc.?

38. Yes No ? Do you prefer a play to a dance?

39. Yes No ? Do you usually try to take added responsibility upon yourself?

40. Yes No ? Do you make friends easily?

41. Yes No ? Can you be optimistic when others about you are greatly depressed?

42. Yes No ? Do you try to get your own way even if you have to fight for it?

43. Yes No ? Do you like to be with other people a great deal?

44. Yes No ? Do you get as many ideas at the time of reading as you do from a discussion of it afterwards?

45. Yes No ? In sports do you prefer to participate in individual competitions rather than in team games?

46. Yes No ? Do you usually face your troubles alone without seeking help?

47. Yes No ? Do you see more fun or humor in things when you are in a group than when you are alone?

48. Yes No ? Do you dislike finding your way about in strange places?

49. Yes No ? Can you work happily without praise or recognition?

50. Yes No ? Do you feel that marriage is essential to your happiness?

51. Yes No ? If all but a few of your friends threatened to break relations because of some habit they considered a vice in you, and in which you saw no harm, would you stop the habit to keep friends?

52. Yes No ? Do you like to have suggestions offered to you when you are working a puzzle?

53. Yes No ? Do you usually prefer to do your own planning alone rather than with others?

54. Yes No ?   Do you usually find that people are more stimulating to you than anything else?
55. Yes No ?   Do you prefer to be alone at times of emotional stress?
56. Yes No ?   Do you like to bear responsibilities alone?
57. Yes No ?   Can you usually understand a problem better by studying it out alone than by discussing it with others?
58. Yes No ?   Do you find that telling others of your own personal good news is the greatest part of the enjoyment of it?
59. Yes No ?   Do you generally rely on your own judgment?
60. Yes No ?   Do you like playing games in which you have no spectators?

*Bernreuter Key**

1. <u>Yes</u> No ?	21. Yes <u>No</u> <u>?</u>	41. <u>Yes</u> No ?
2. <u>Yes</u> No ?	22. Yes <u>No</u> ?	42. <u>Yes</u> No ?
3. <u>Yes</u> No <u>?</u>	23. Yes <u>No</u> ?	43. <u>Yes</u> No <u>?</u>
4. Yes <u>No</u> ?	24. <u>Yes</u> No ?	44. <u>Yes</u> No ?
5. Yes <u>No</u> ?	25. Yes <u>No</u> ?	45. <u>Yes</u> No <u>?</u>
6. Yes <u>No</u> ?	26. Yes <u>No</u> ?	46. <u>Yes</u> No ?
7. <u>Yes</u> No ?	27. <u>Yes</u> No <u>?</u>	47. Yes <u>No</u> ?
8. Yes <u>No</u> ?	28. Yes <u>No</u> ?	48. Yes <u>No</u> ?
9. Yes <u>No</u> ?	29. <u>Yes</u> No ?	49. Yes <u>No</u> <u>?</u>
10. <u>Yes</u> No ?	30. Yes <u>No</u> ?	50. <u>Yes</u> No ?
11. Yes <u>No</u> ?	31. <u>Yes</u> No <u>?</u>	51. Yes <u>No</u> ?
12. <u>Yes</u> No <u>?</u>	32. <u>Yes</u> No ?	52. <u>Yes</u> No ?
13. <u>Yes</u> No ?	33. Yes <u>No</u> ?	53. Yes <u>No</u> ?
14. Yes <u>No</u> ?	34. <u>Yes</u> No ?	54. <u>Yes</u> No ?
15. <u>Yes</u> No ?	35. Yes <u>No</u> ?	55. <u>Yes</u> No ?
16. Yes <u>No</u> <u>?</u>	36. Yes <u>No</u> <u>?</u>	56. <u>Yes</u> No ?
17. Yes <u>No</u> ?	37. Yes <u>No</u> ?	57. <u>Yes</u> No ?
18. <u>Yes</u> No <u>?</u>	38. <u>Yes</u> No <u>?</u>	58. Yes <u>No</u> ?
19. Yes <u>No</u> ?	39. <u>Yes</u> No ?	59. <u>Yes</u> No ?
20. <u>Yes</u> No ?	40. Yes <u>No</u> ?	60. <u>Yes</u> No ?

*Underlined answer scores one point.

Bibliography

Abel, G. G., Levis, D. J., and Clancy, J. (1970) Aversion therapy applied to taped sequences of deviant behavior in exhibitionism and other sexual deviations: A preliminary report, *J. Behav. Ther. Exp. Psychiat.*, 1: 59.

Abraham, D. (1963) Treatment of encopresis with imipramine, *Amer. J. Psychiat.*, 119: 891.

Ahsen, A. (1965) *Eidetic Psychotherapy*. Lahore, India, Nai Matboat Press.

Alberti, R. E. and Emmons, M. L. (1970) *Your Perfect Right*. San Luis Obispo, Calif.

Anant, S. (1967) A note on the treatment of alcoholics by a verbal aversion technique, *Canad. Psychol.*, 80: 19.

Andrews, G., Harris, M., Garside, R., and Kay, D. (1964) *Syndrome of Stuttering*. London, Heinemann Medical Books.

Appel, J. B. (1963) Punishment and shock intensity, *Science*, 141: 528.

Arnold, M. B. (1945) The physiological differentiation of emotional states, *Psychol. Rev.*, 52: 35.

Arnold, M. B. (1960) *Emotion and Personality*, Vol. 1. New York, Columbia University Press.

Ashem, B. and Donner, L. (1968) Covert sensitization with alcoholics: A controlled replication, *Behav. Res. Ther.*, 6: 7.

Ax, A. F. (1953) The physiological differentiation of anger and fear in humans, *Psychosom. Med.*, 15: 433.

Ayllon, T. (1963) Intensive treatment of psychotic behavior by stimulus satiation and food reinforcement, *Behav. Res. Ther.*, 1: 53.

Ayllon, T. and Azrin, N. H. (1964) Reinforcement and instructions with mental patients, *J. Exp. Anal. Behav.*, 7: 327.

Ayllon, T. and Azrin, N. H. (1965) The measurement and reinforcement of behavior of psychotics, *J. Exp. Anal. Behav.*, 8: 357.

Ayllon, T. and Azrin, N. H. (1968) *The Token Economy: A Motivational System for Therapy and Rehabilitation*. New York, Appleton-Century-Crofts.

Ayllon, T. and Michael, J. (1959) The psychiatric nurse as a behavioral engineer, *J. Exp. Anal. Behav.*, 2: 323.

Ayllon, T., Smith, D., and Rogers, M. (1970) Behavioral management of school phobia, *J. Behav. Ther. Exp. Psychiat.*, **1**: 125.

Azrin, N. H. and Holz, W. C. (1968) Punishment. In W. K. Honig (Ed.), *Operant Behavior*. New York, Appleton-Century-Crofts.

Bachrach, A. J., Erwin, W. J., and Mohr, J. P. (1965) The control of eating behavior in an anorexic by operant conditioning techniques. In L. Ullmann and L. Krasner (Eds.), *Case Studies in Behavior Modification*. New York, Holt, Rinehart & Winston.

Bain, J. A. (1928) *Thought Control in Everyday Life*. New York, Funk & Wagnalls.

Bancroft, J. H. J. (1970) A comparative study of aversion and desensitization in the treatment of homosexuality. In L. E. Burns and J. L. Worsley (Eds.), *Behavior Therapy in the 70's*. Bristol, England, Wright.

Bandura, A. (1968) Modelling approaches to the modification of phobic disorders, *Ciba Foundation Symposium: The Role of Learning in Psychotherapy*. London, Churchill.

Bandura, A. (1969) *Principles of Behavior Modification*. New York, Holt, Rinehart & Winston.

Bandura, A., Blanchard, E. D., and Ritter, B. (1968) The relative efficacy of desensitization and modelling therapeutic approaches for inducing behavioral, affective, and attitudinal changes. Stanford Univ. Unpublished manuscript.

Bandura, A., Grusec, J., and Menlove, F. (1967) Vicarious extinction of avoidance behavior, *J. Pers. Soc. Psychol.*, **5**: 16.

Barber, T. X. (1969) *Hypnosis: A Scientific Approach*. New York, Van Nostrand Reinhold Company.

Barber, T. X. (1970) *LSD, Marihuana, Yoga and Hypnosis*. Chicago, Aldine.

Barker, J. C. and Miller, M. B. (1968) Recent developments and some future trends in the application of aversion therapy. Unpublished manuscript.

Beck, A. T. (1967) *Depression*. New York, Harper & Row.

Berger, B. (1968) Personal communication.

Bergin, A. E. and Strupp, H. H. (1972) *Changing Frontiers in the Science of Psychotherapy*. New York, Aldine.

Berkun, M. M. (1957) Factors in the recovery from approach-avoidance conflict, *J. Exp. Psychol.*, **54**: 65.

Bernheim, H. (1889) *Suggestive Therapeutics*. New York, Putnam.

Bernstein, D. A. and Paul, G. L. (1971) Some comments on therapy analogue research with small animal 'phobias,' *J. Behav. Ther. Exp. Psychiat.*, **2**: 225.

Blakemore, C. B. (1965) The application of behavior therapy to a sexual disorder. In H. J. Eysenck (Ed.), *Experiments in Behavior Therapy*. Oxford, Pergamon Press.

Blakemore, C. B., Thorpe, J. G., Barker, J. C., Conway, C. G., and Lavin, N. I. (1963) The application of faradic aversion conditioning in a case of transvestism, *Behav. Res. Ther.*, **1**: 29.

Bleuler, E. (1911) *Dementia Praecox or the Group of Schizophrenias*. Trans. by J. Zinken. New York, International Universities Press.

Blinder, J., Freeman, D. M. A., and Stunkard, A. J. (1970) Behavior therapy of anorexia nervosa: Effectiveness of activity as a reinforcer of weight gain, *Amer. J. Psychiat.*, **126**: 1093.

Bond, I. K. and Hutchinson, H. C. (1960) Application of reciprocal inhibition therapy to exhibitionism, *Canad. Med. Ass. J.*, **83**: 23.

Boudreau, L. (1972) Transcendental meditation and yoga as reciprocal inhibitors, *J. Behav. Ther. Exp. Psychiat.*, **3**: 97.

Boulougouris, J. C., Marks, I. M., and Marset, P. (1971) Superiority of flooding (implosion) to desensitization for reducing pathological fear, *Behav. Res. Ther.*, **9**: 7.

Brady, J. P. (1966) Brevital-relaxation treatment of frigidity, *Behav. Res. Ther.*, 4: 71.

Brady, J. P. (1971) Metronome-conditioned speech retraining for stuttering, *Behav. Ther.*, 2: 129.

Breger, L. and McGaugh, J. L. (1965) Critique and reformulation of "Learning Theory" approaches to psychotherapy and neuroses, *Psychol. Bull.*, 63: 338.

Brody, M. W. (1962) Prognosis and results of psychoanalysis. In J. H. Nodine and J. H. Moyer (Eds.), *Psychosomatic Medicine*. Philadelphia, Lea and Febiger.

Budzinski, T., Stoyva, J., and Adler, C. (1970) Feedback-induced muscle relaxation: Application to tension headache, *J. Behav. Ther. Exp. Psychiat.*, 1: 205.

Burchard, J. and Tyler, V. (1965) The modification of delinquent behavior through operant conditioning, *Behav. Res. Ther.*, 2: 245.

Burgess, E. (1968) The modification of depressive behavior. In R. Rubin and C. Franks (Eds.), *Advances in Behavior Therapy*. New York, Academic Press.

Burnett, A. and Ryan, E. (1964) Conditioning techniques in psychotherapy, *Canad. Psychiat. Ass. J.*, 9: 140.

Burnham, W. H. (1924) *The Normal Mind*. New York, Appleton.

Cabanac, M. (1971) Physiological role of pleasure, *Science*, 173: 1103.

Campbell, B. A. and Church, R. M. (1969) *Punishment and Aversive Behavior*. New York, Appleton-Century-Crofts.

Campbell, D., Sanderson, R. E., and Laverty, S. G. (1964) Characteristics of a conditioned response in human subjects during extinction trials following a single traumatic conditioning trial, *J. Abn. Soc. Psychol.*, 68: 627.

Cautela, J. (1966) Treatment of compulsive behavior by covert sensitization, *Psychol. Rec.*, 16: 33.

Cautela, J. (1967) Covert sensitization, *Psychol. Rep.*, 20: 459.

Cautela, J. (1970) Covert reinforcement, *Behav. Ther.*, 1: 33–50.

Cautela, J. (1970a) Covert negative reinforcement, *J. Behav. Ther. Exp. Psychiat.*, 1: 273.

Cautela, J. R. and Kastenbaum, R. (1967) A reinforcement survey schedule for use in therapy, training, and research, *Psychol. Rep.*, 20: 1115.

Church, R. (1963) The varied effects of punishment, *Psychol. Rev.*, 70: 369.

Clark, D. E. (1963) The treatment of monosymptomatic phobia by systematic desensitization, *Behav. Res. Ther.*, 1: 63.

Cohen, R. and Dean, S. J. (1968) Group desensitization of test anxiety, *Proceed., 76th Ann. Conv. Amer. Psychol. Ass.*, 615.

Cooke, G. (1966) The efficacy of two desensitization procedures: An analogue study, *Behav. Res. Ther.*, 4: 17.

Cooper, A. J., Ismail, A., Smith, C. G., and Loraine, J. (1970) Androgen function in 'psychogenic' and 'constitutional' types of impotence, *Brit. Med. J.*, July 4.

Cooper, J. E. (1963) A study of behavior therapy, *Lancet*, 1: 411.

Costello, C. G. (1964) Lysergic acid diethylamide (LSD-25) and behavior therapy, *Behav. Res. Ther.*, 2: 117.

Costello, C. G. (1970) Dissimilarities between conditioned avoidance responses and phobias, *Psychol. Rev.*, 77: 250–254.

Dalton, K. (1964) *Pre-menstrual Syndrome*, Springfield, Illinois, Thomas Co.

Darwin, P. L. and McBrearty, J. F. (1969) The subject speaks up in desensitization. In R. D. Rubin and C. M. Franks (Eds.), *Advances in Behavior Therapy, 1968*, New York, Academic Press.

Davison, G. C. (1964) A social learning therapy programme with an autistic child, *Behav. Res. Ther.*, 2: 149.

Davison, G. C. (1965) The Influence of Systematic Desensitization, Relaxation and Graded Exposure to Imaginal Aversive Stimuli on the Modification of Phobic Behavior, Ph.D. Dissertation, Stanford Univ. Published (1968) under the title, Systematic desensitization as a counterconditioning process, *J. Abn. Psychol.*, **73**: 91.

Davison, G. C. (1967) The elimination of a sadistic fantasy by a client-controlled counterconditioning technique, *J. Abn. Psychol.*, **73**: 84.

Davison, G. C. and Wilson, G. T. (1972) Critique of 'desensitization: Social and cognitive factors underlying the effectiveness of Wolpe's procedure,' *Psychol. Bull.*, **78**: 28.

DeMoor, W. (1970) Systematic desensitization versus prolonged high intensity stimulation (flooding), *J. Behav. Ther. Exp. Psychiat.*, **1**: 45–52.

Dengrove, E. (1968) Personal communication.

Denholtz, M. (1971) The use of tape recordings between therapy sessions, *J. Behav. Ther. Exp. Psychiat.*, **1**: 139.

Destounis, N. (1963) Enuresis and imipramine, *Amer. J. Psychiat.*, **119**: 893.

Donner, L. (1970) Automated group desensitization: A follow-up report, *Behav. Res. Ther.*, **8**: 241.

Donner, L. and Guerney, B. G., Jr. (1969) Automated group desensitization for test anxiety, *Behav. Res. Ther.*, **7**: 1.

Drooby, A. S. (1964) A reliable truce with enuresis, *Dis. Nerv. Syst.*, **25**: 97.

Drooby, A. S. (1964) Personal communication.

Drvota, S. (1962) Personal communication.

Dunlap, K. (1932) *Habits: Their Making and Unmaking.* New York, Liveright.

Dworkin, S., Raginsky, B. B., and Bourne, W. (1937) Action of anesthetics and sedatives upon the inhibited nervous system, *Current Res. Anaesth.*, **16**: 283.

Edelman, R. I. (1971) Operant conditioning treatment of encopresis, *J. Behav. Ther. Exp. Psychiat.*, **1**: 71.

Edwards, N. B. (1972) Case conference: Assertive training in a case of homosexual pedophilia, *J. Behav. Ther. Exp. Psychiat.*, **3**: 55.

Efram, J. S. and Marcia, J. E. (1967) The treatment of fears by expectancy manipulation: An exploratory investigation, *Proceed., 75th Ann. Conv. Amer. Psychol. Ass.*, 239.

Ellis, A. (1958) Rational psychotherapy, *J. Gen. Psychol.*, **59**: 35–49.

Ellis, A. (1970) *Address to the 1970 Meeting of the Assoc. Adv. Behav. Ther.*, Miami, Fla.

Erwin, W. J. (1963) Confinement in the production of human neuroses: The barber's chair syndrome, *Behav. Res. Ther.*, **1**: 175.

Everaerd, W. (1970) Reading as the counterconditioning agent in a cardiac neurosis, *J. Behav. Ther. Exp. Psychiat.*, **1**: 165.

Eysenck, H. J. (1952) The effects of psychotherapy: An evaluation, *J. Consult. Psychol.*, **16**: 319.

Eysenck, H. J. (1953) *Uses and Abuses of Psychology.* London, Penguin Books.

Eysenck, H. J. (1957) *The Dynamics of Anxiety and Hysteria*, London, Routledge and Kegan Paul.

Eysenck, H. J. (1959) Learning theory and behavior therapy, *J. Ment. Sci.*, **105**: 61.

Eysenck, H. J. (1960) *Behavior Therapy and the Neuroses*, Oxford, Pergamon Press.

Eysenck, H. J. (1963) *Experiments with Drugs.* New York, Pergamon Press.

Eysenck, H. J. (1964) *Experiments in Behavior Therapy.* Oxford, Pergamon Press.

Eysenck, H. J. (1965) The effects of psychotherapy, *International J. Psychiat.*, **1**: 97.

Eysenck, H. J. (1970) The classification of depressive illness, *Brit. J. Psychiat.*, **117**: 241.

Farmer, R. G. and Wright, J. M. C. (1971) Muscular reactivity and systematic desensitization, *Behav. Ther.*, **2**: 1.

Farrar, C. H., Powell, B. J., and Martin, L. K. (1968) Punishment of alcohol consumption by apneic paralysis, *Behav. Res. Ther.*, 6: 13.

Feingold, L. (1966) Personal communication.

Feldman, M. P. and MacCulloch, M. J. (1965) The application of anticipatory avoidance learning to the treatment of homosexuality. I. Theory, technique and preliminary results, *Behav. Res. Ther.*, 2: 165.

Feldman, M. P. and MacCulloch, M. J. (1967) Aversion therapy in the management of homosexuals, *Brit. Med. J.*, 1: 594.

Feldman, M. P. and MacCulloch M. J. (1970) *Homosexual Behavior: Therapy and Assessment.* Oxford, Pergamon Press.

Flanagan, B., Goldiamond, I., and Azrin, N. (1958) Operant stuttering: The control of stuttering behavior through response-contingent consequences, *J. Exp. Anal. Behav.*, 1: 173.

Frank, J. D. (1961) *Persuasion and Healing.* New York, Shocken Books.

Frankl, V. (1960) Paradoxical intention: A logotherapeutic technique, *Amer. J. Psychother.*, 14: 520.

Franks, C. M. (1965) *Conditioning Techniques in Clinical Practice and Research.* New York, Springer.

Freeman, H. L. and Kendrick, D. C. (1960) A case of cat phobia: Treatment by a method derived from experimental psychology, *Brit. Med. J.*, 1: 497.

Freund, K. (1960) Some problems in the treatment of homosexuality. In H. J. Eysenck (Ed.), *Behavior Therapy and the Neuroses.* Oxford, Pergamon Press.

Friedman, D. E. (1966) A new technique for the systematic desensitization of phobic symptoms, *Behav. Res. Ther.*, 4: 139.

Friedman, D. E. and Silverstone, J. T. (1967) Treatment of phobic patients by systematic desensitization, *Lancet*, 1: 470.

Fry, W. H. (1962) The marital content of an anxiety syndrome, *Family Process*, 1: 245.

Garfield, Z. H., Darwin, P. L., Singer, B. A., and McBrearty, J. F. (1967) Effect of *in vivo* training on experimental desensitization of a phobia, *Psychol. Rep.*, 20: 515.

Gath, D. and Gelder, M. G. A. (1971) *Treatment of Phobias — Desensitization versus Flooding.* Paper delivered to Dept. Psychiatry, Temple Univ. Medical School., November 8, 1971.

Gaupp, L. A., Stern, R. M., and Galbraith, G. G. (1972) False heart rate feedback and reciprocal inhibition by aversion relief in the treatment of snake avoidance behavior, *Behav. Ther.*, 3: 7.

Gelder, M. G. and Marks, I. M. (1965) A controlled retrospective study of behavior therapy in phobic patients, *Brit. J. Psychiat.*, 111: 561.

Gelder, M. G. and Marks, I. M. (1968) Desensitization and phobias, a cross-over study, *Brit. J. Psychiat.*, 114: 223.

Gelder, M. G., Marks, I. M., Sakinovsky, I., and Wolff, H. H. (1964) Behavior therapy and psychotherapy for phobic disorders: Alternative or complementary procedures? Paper read at Sixth International Cong. of Psychother., London.

Gelder, M. G., Marks, I. M., and Wolff, H. H. (1967) Desensitization and psychotherapy in the treatment of phobic states: A controlled enquiry, *Brit, J. Psychiat.*, 113: 53.

Gellhorn, E. (1967) *Principles of Autonomic-Somatic Integrations.* Minneapolis, Univ. Minnesota Press.

Gershman, L. and Stedman, J. (1971) Oriental defense exercises as reciprocal inhibitors of anxiety, *J. Behav. Ther. Exp. Psychiat.*, 2: 117.

Gerz, H. O. (1966) Experience with the logotherapeutic technique of paradoxical intention in the treatment of phobic and obsessive-compulsive patients, *Amer. J. Psychiat.*, **123**: 548.

Getze, G. (1968) Adverse appeal to senses cuts smoking, *Los Angeles Times*. Reprinted by Z. Wanderer, Center for Behavior Therapy, Beverly Hills, Calif.

Glynn, J. D. and Harper, P. (1961) Behavior therapy in transvestism, *Lancet*, **1**: 619.

Gold, S. and Neufeld, I. (1965) A learning theory approach to the treatment of homosexuality, *Behav. Res. Ther.*, **2**: 201.

Goldberg, J. and D'Zurilla, T. J. (1968) A demonstration of slide projection as an alternative to imaginal stimulus presentation in systematic desensitization therapy, *Psychol. Reps.*, **23**: 527.

Goldiamond, I. (1965) Stuttering and fluency as manipulable operant response classes. In L. Krasner and L. P. Ullmann (Eds.), *Research in Behavior Modification*. New York, Holt, Rinehart & Winston.

Goldstein, A. (1972) Flooding versus extinction in the elimination of conditioned fear in cats. Unpublished Manu.

Goldstein, A., Serber, M., and Piaget, J. (1970) Induced anger as a reciprocal inhibitor of fear, *J. Behav. Ther. Exp. Psychiat.*, **1**: 67.

Goldstein, A. and Wolpe, J. (1971) Behavior therapy in groups. In H. I. Kaplan and B. J. Sadock (Eds.), *Comprehensive Group Psychotherapy*. Baltimore, Williams & Wilkins.

Gottlieb, J. S. and Frohman, C. E. (1972) *A Probable Biologic Mechanism in Schizophrenia*. Mimeo.

Gourevitch, M. (1968) Eloge de Francois Leuret, *Inform. Psychiat.*, **44**: 843.

Granville-Grossman, K. L. and Turner, P. (1966) The effect of propranolol on anxiety, *Lancet*, **1**: 788.

Gray, J. A. (1964) *Pavlov's Typology*. Oxford, Pergamon Press.

Grinker, R. R. and Spiegel, J. P. (1945) *War Neuroses*. Philadelphia, Blakiston.

Guthrie, E. R. (1935) *The Psychology of Human Learning*. New York, Harper & Bros.

Guttmacher, A. F. (1961) *Complete Book of Birth Control*. New York, Ballantine.

Hallsten, E. A. (1965) Adolescent anorexia nervosa treated by desensitization, *Behav. Res. Ther.*, **3**: 87.

Hamilton, D. M. and Wall, J. H. (1941) Hospital treatment of patients with psychosomatic disorders, *Amer. J. Psychiat.*, **98**: 551.

Herzberg, A. (1941) *Active Psychotherapy*. London, Research Books.

Hodgson, R., Rachman, S., and Marks, I. M. (1972) The treatment of chronic obsessive-compulsive neuroses: Follow-up and further findings, *Behav. Res. Ther.*, **10**: 181.

Homme, L. E. (1965) Perspectives in psychology — XXIV, Control of coverants, the operants of the mind, *The Psychol. Rec.*, **15**: 501.

Homme, L. E., Csanyi, A. P., Gonzales, M. A., and Rechs, J. R. (1971) *How to Use Contingency Contracting in the Classroom*. Champaign, Research Press Co.

Horsley, J. S. (1936) Narco-analysis: A new technique in shortcut psychotherapy, *Lancet*, **1**: 55.

Hull, C. L. (1943) *Principles of Behavior*. New York, Appleton-Century.

Hunter-Brown, M. and Lighthill, J. A. (1968) Selective anterior cingulotomy: A psychosurgical evaluation, *J. Neurosurg.*, **29**: 513.

Hussain, A. (1964) Behavior therapy using hypnosis. In J. Wolpe, A. Salter, and L. J. Reyna, *The Conditioning Therapies*. New York, Holt, Rinehart & Winston.

Hussain, M. Z. (1971) Desensitization and flooding (Implosion) in treatment of phobias, *Amer. J. Psychiat.*, **127**: 1509.

Ihli, K. L. and Garlington, W. K. (1969) A comparison of group versus individual desensitization of test anxiety, *Behav. Res. Ther.,* 7: 207.

Jacobson, E. (1938) *Progressive Relaxation.* Chicago, Univ. of Chicago Press.

Jacobson, E. (1939) Variation of blood pressure with skeletal muscle tension and relaxation, *Ann. Int. Med.,* 12: 1194.

Jacobson, E. (1940) Variation of pulse rate with skeletal muscle tension and relaxation, *Ann. Int. Med.,* 13: 1619.

Jacobson, E. (1964) *Anxiety and Tension Control,* Philadelphis, Lippincott.

James, B. (1962) Case of homosexuality treated by aversion therapy, *Brit. Med. J.,* 1: 768.

Jones, H. G. (1960) Continuation of Yates' treatment of a tiquer. In H. J. Eysenck (Ed.), *Behavior Therapy and the Neuroses.* Oxford, Pergamon Press.

Jones, H. G. (1960) The behavioral treatment of enuresis nocturna. In H. J. Eysenck (Ed.), *Behavior Therapy and the Neuroses,* Oxford, Pergamon Press.

Jones, M. C. (1924) Elimination of children's fears, *J. Exp. Psychol.,* 7: 382.

Jones, M. C. (1924) A laboratory study of fear. The case of Peter, *J. Genet. Psychol.,* 31: 308.

Kahn, M. and Baker, B. L. (1968) Desensitization with minimal therapist contact, *J. Abnorm. Psychol.,* 73: 198.

Kallman, F. (1952) Comparative twin studies on the genetic aspects of male homosexuality, *J. Nerv. Ment. Dis.,* 115: 283.

Kallman, F. (1953) *Heredity in Health and Mental Disorder.* New York, Norton.

Kanfer, F. H. and Phillips, J. S. (1970) *Learning Foundations of Behavior Therapy.* New York, Wiley.

Kantorovich, N. V. (1929) An attempt at associative reflex therapy in alcoholism, *Psychol. Abst.,* No. 4282. 1930.

Kelly, D. (1972) Physiological changes during operations on the limbic system in man, *Cond. Ref.,* 7: 127.

Kennedy, W. A. and Foreyt, J. (1968) Control of eating behavior in an obese patient by avoidance conditioning. *Psychol. Rep.,* 22: 571.

Kent, R. N., Wilson, G. T., and Nelson, R. (1972) Effects of false heart-rate feedback on avoidance behavior: An investigation of 'cognitive desensitization', *Behav. Ther.,* 3: 1.

Kimmel, H. D. (1967) Instrumental conditioning of autonomically mediated behavior, *Psychol. Bull,* 67: 337.

Kimmel, K. D. and Kimmel, E. (1970) An instrumental conditioning method for the treatment of enuresis, *J. Behav. Ther. Exp. Psychiat.,* 1: 121.

Knight, R. P. (1941) Evaluation of the results of psychoanalytic therapy, *Amer. J. Psychiat.,* 98: 434.

Kolvin, I. (1967) Aversive imagery treatment in adolescents, *Behav. Res. Ther.* 5: 245.

Kondas, O. (1965) The possibilities of applying experimentally created procedures when eliminating tics, *Studia Psychol.,* 7: 221.

Krasner, L. (1971) Behavior therapy, *Ann. Rev. Psychol.,* 22: 483.

Krasner, L. and Ullmann, L. P. (1965) *Research in Behavior Modification.* New York, Holt, Rinehart & Winston.

Krasnogorski, N. I. (1925) The conditioned reflexes and children's neuroses, *Amer J. Dis. Child.,* 30: 754.

Lader, M. H. and Mathews, A. M. (1968) A physiological model of phobic anxiety and desensitization, *Behav. Res. Ther.,* 6: 411.

Landis, C. (1937) A statistical evaluation of psychotherapeutic methods. In L. Hinsie, *Concepts and Problems of Psychotherapy.* New York, Columbia Univ. Press.

Lang, P. J. (1964) Experimental studies of desensitization psychotherapy. In J. Wolpe, A. Salter, and L. J. Reyna, *The Conditioning Therapies,* New York, Holt, Rinehart & Winston.

Lang, P. J. (1968) Appraisal of systematic desensitization techniques with children and adults. II. Process and mechanisms of change, theoretical analysis and implications for treatment and clinical research. In C. M. Franks (Ed.), *Assessment and Status of the Behavior Therapies and Associated Developments.* New York, McGraw-Hill.

Lang, P. J. and Lazovik, A. D. (1963) The experimental desensitization of a phobia, *J. Abn. Soc. Psychol.,* **66**: 519.

Lang, P. J., Lazovik, A. D., and Reynolds, D. (1965) Desensitization, suggestibility and pseudotherapy, *J. Abn. Psychol.,* **70**: 395.

Lang, P. J., Melamed, B. G., and Hart, J. (1970) A psychophysiological analysis of fear modification using an automated desensitization procedure, *J. Abn. Psychol.,* **76**: 221.

Langley, J. N. and Anderson, H. K. (1895) The innervation of the pelvic and adjoining viscera, *J. Physiol.,* **19**: 71.

Lathrop, R. G. (1964) Measurement of analog sequential dependency, *Human Factors*, **6**: 233.

LaVerne, A. A. (1953) Rapid coma technique of carbon dioxide inhalation therapy, *Dis. Nerv. Syst.,* **14**: 141.

Laverty, S. G. (1966) Aversion therapies in the treatment of alcoholism, *Psychosom. Med.,* **28**: 651.

Lavin, H. I., Thorpe, J. G., Baker, J. C., Blakemore, C. B., and Conway, D. G. (1961) Behavior therapy in a case of transvestism, *J. Nerv. Ment. Dis.,* **133**: 346.

Lazarus, A. A. and Abramovitz, A. (1962) The use of "emotive imagery" in the treatment of children's phobias, *J. Ment. Sci.,* **108**: 191.

Leach, E. (1969) Stuttering: Clinical application of response-contingent procedures. In B. B. Gray and G. England (Eds.), *Stuttering and The Conditioning Therapies.* California, Monterey Institute for Speech and Hearing.

Leaf, W. B. and Gaarder, K. R. (1971) A simplified electromyograph feedback apparatus for relaxation training, *J. Behav. Ther. Exp. Psychiat.,* **2**: 39.

Leahy, M. R. and Martin, I. C. A. (1967) Successful hypnotic abreaction after twenty years, *Brit. J. Psychiat.,* **113**: 383.

Leitenberg, H., Agras, W. S., Barlow, D. H., and Oliveau, D. C. (1969) Contribution of selective positive reinforcement and therapeutic instructions to systematic desensitization therapy, *J. Abnorm. Psychol.,* **74**: 113.

Lemere, F. and Voegtlin, W. L. (1950) An evaluation of the aversion treatment of alcoholism, *Qrt. J. Stud. Alcoh.,* **11**: 199.

Leschke, E. (1914) Quoted by J. G. Bebee-Center in *The Psychology of Pleasantness and Unpleasantness.* New York, Van Nostrand, 1932.

Leukel, F. and Quinton, E. (1964) Carbon dioxide effects on acquisition and extinction of avoidance behavior, *J. Comp. Physiol. Psychol.,* **57**: 267.

Leuret, F. (1846) *De Traitement Moral de la Folie.* Paris. Quoted by Stewart (1961).

Levis, D. J. and Carrera, R. N. (1967) Effects of ten hours of implosive therapy in the treatment of outpatients: A preliminary report, *J. Abn. Psychol.,* **72**: 504.

Lindsley, O. R. (1956) Operant conditioning methods applied to research in chronic schizophrenia, *Psychiat. Res. Rep.,* **5**: 118.

Little, J. C. and James, B. (1964) Abreaction of conditioned fear after eighteen years, *Behav. Res. Ther.*, 2: 59.

Locke, E. A. (1971) Is 'behavior therapy' behavioristic? An analysis of Wolpe's psychotherapeutic methods, *Psychol. Bull.*, 76: 318.

London, P. (1964) *The Modes and Morals of Psychotherapy.* New York, Holt, Rinehart & Winston.

Lovibond, S. H. (1963) The mechanism of conditioning treatment of enuresis, *Behav. Res. Ther.*, 1: 17.

Lublin, I. (1968) Aversive conditioning of cigarette addiction, *Paper read at 76th Meeting of American Psychological Ass.*, San Francisco.

Mack, K. (1970) Unpublished data.

MacVaugh, G. (1972) *Frigidity: Successful Treatment in One Hypnotic Imprint Session with the Oriental Relaxation Technique.* New York, Medcon Inc.

Madsen, C. H. (1965) Positive reinforcement in the toilet training of a normal child: A case report. In L. P. Ullmann and L. Krasner (Eds.), *Case Studies in Behavior Modification.* New York, Holt, Rinehart & Winston.

Maier, S. E., Seligman, M. E. P., and Solomon, R. L. (1970) Pavlovian fear conditioning and learned helplessness. In B. A. Campbell and R. M. Church (Eds.), *Punishment.* New York, Appleton-Century-Crofts.

Malleson, N. (1959) Panic and phobia, *Lancet*, 1: 225.

Marks, I. M. (1972) Flooding (Implosion) and allied treatments. In W. S. Agras (Ed.), *Learning Theory Application of Principles and Procedures to Psychiatry.* New York, Little, Brown.

Marquis, J. N. (1970) Orgasmic reconditioning: Changing sexual object choice through controlling masturbation fantasies, *J. Behav. Ther. Exp. Psychiat.*, 1: 263.

Masserman, J. H. (1943) *Behavior and Neurosis.* Chicago, Univ. of Chicago Press.

Masserman, J. H. (1963) Ethology, comparative biodynamics, and psychoanalytic research. In J. Scher, *Theories of the Mind.* New York, The Free Press.

Masserman, J. H. and Yum. K. S. (1946) An analysis of the influence of alcohol on the experimental neuroses in cats, *Psychosom. Med.*, 8: 36.

Masters, W. H. and Johnson, V. E. (1966) *Human Sexual Response.* Boston, Little, Brown.

Masters, W. H. and Johnson, V. E. (1970) *Human Sexual Inadequacy.* Boston, Little, Brown.

Mawson, A. B. (1970) Methohexitone-assisted desensitization in treatment of phobias, *Lancet*, 1: 1084.

Max, L. W. (1935) Breaking up a homosexual fixation by the conditioned reaction technique: A case study, *Psychol. Bull.*, 32: 734.

Maxwell, R. D. H. and Paterson, J. W. (1958) Meprobamate in the treatment of stuttering, *Brit. Med. J.*, 1: 873.

McConaghy, N. (1964) A year's experience with nonverbal psychotherapy, *Med. J. Austral.*, 1: 831.

McGlynn, F. D., Reynolds, E. J., and Linder, L. H. (1971) Systematic desensitization with pre-treatment and intra-treatment therapeutic instructions, *Behav. Res. Ther.*, 9: 57.

McGlynn, F. D. and Williams, C. W. (1970) Systematic desensitization of snake-avoidance under three conditions of suggestion, *J. Behav. Ther. Exp. Psychiat.*, 1: 97.

McGuire, R. J. and Vallance, M. (1964) Aversion therapy by electric shock: A simple technique, *Brit. Med. J.*, 1: 151.

Mealiea, W. L. and Nawas, M. M. (1971) The comparative effectiveness of systematic desensitization and implosive therapy in the treatment of snake phobia, *J. Behav. Ther. Exp. Psychiat.*, **2**: 85.

Meduna, L. J. (1947) *Carbon Dioxide Therapy.* Springfield, Ill., Charles C Thomas.

Mesmer, A. (1779). Quoted by C. L. Hull (1933) *Hypnosis and Suggestibility.* New York, Appleton-Century.

Meyer, V. (1957) The treatment of two phobic patients on the basis of learning principles, *J. Abn. Soc. Psychol.*, **58**: 259.

Meyer, V. (1963) Paper read at Behavior Therapy Seminar, University of London.

Meyer, V. (1966) Modifications of expectations in cases with obsessional rituals, *Behav. Res. Ther.*, **4**: 273.

Meyer, V. and Mair, J. M. (1963) A new technique to control stammering: A preliminary report, *Behav. Res. Ther.*, **1**: 251.

Migler, B. (1967) Personal communication.

Migler, B. and Wolpe, J. (1967) Automated desensitization: A case report, *Behav. Res. Ther.*, **5**: 133.

Miller, G. E. (1967) Personal communication.

Miller, N. E. and DiCara, L. V. (1968) Instrumental learning of vasomotor responses by rats: Learning to respond differentially in the two ears, *Science*, **159**: 1485.

Miller, N. E., Hubert, E., and Hamilton, J. (1938) Mental and behavioral changes following male hormone treatment of adult castration hypogonadism and psychic impotence, *Proc. Soc. Exp. Biol. Med.*, **38**: 538.

Miller, R. E., Murphy, J. V., and Mirsky, I. A. (1957) Persistent effects of chlorpromazine on extinction of an avoidance response, *Arch. Neurol, Psychiat.*, **78**: 526.

Moore, N. (1965) Behavior therapy in bronchial asthma: A controlled study, *J. Psychosom. Res.*, **9**: 257.

Morganstern, K. P. (1973) Implosive therapy and flooding procedures: A critical review, *Psychol. Bull.*, **79**: 318.

Morganstern, F. S., Pearce, J. F., and Rees, W. (1965) Predicting the outcome of behavior therapy by psychological tests, *Behav. Res. Ther.*, **2**: 191.

Mowrer, O. H. and Viek, P. (1948) Experimental analogue of fear from a sense of help-lessness, *J. Abn. Soc. Psychol.*, **43**: 193.

Murphy, I. C. (1964) Extinction of an incapacitating fear of earthworms, *J. Clin. Psychol.*, **20**: 396.

Napalkov, A. V. and Karas, A. Y. (1957) Elimination of pathological conditioned reflex connections in experimental hypertensive states, *Zh. Vyssh. Nerv. Deiat.*, **7**: 402.

Neale, D. H. (1963) Behavior therapy and encopresis in children, *Behav. Res. Ther.*, **1**: 139.

Oliveau, D. C., Agras, W. S., Leitenberg, H., Moore, R. C., and Wright, D. E. (1969) Systematic desensitization, therapeutically oriented instructions and selective positive reinforcement, *Behav. Res. Ther.*, **7**: 27.

Orwin, A. (1971) Respiratory relief: A new and rapid method for the treatment of phobic states, *Brit. J. Psychiat.*, **119**: 635.

Osgood, C. E. (1946) Meaningful similarity and interference in learning, *J. Exp. Psychol.*, **38**: 132.

Palmer, H. A. (1944) Military psychiatric casualties, *Lancet*, **2**: 492.

Patterson, G. R. and Gullion, M. E. (1968) *Living with Children: New Methods for Parents and Teachers.* Champaign, Research Press.

Paul, G. L. (1966) *Insight versus Desensitization in Psychotherapy.* Stanford, Stanford Univ. Press.

Paul, G. L. (1968) Two-year follow-up of systematic desensitization in therapy groups, *J. Abn. Psychol.*, **73**: 119.

Paul, G. L. (1969) Physiological effects of relaxation training and hypnotic suggestion, *J. Abnorm. Psychol.*, **74**: 425.

Paul, G. L. and Shannon, D. T. (1966) Treatment of anxiety through systematic desensitization in therapy groups, *J. Abn. Psychol.*, **71**: 124.

Pavlov, I. P. (1927) *Conditioned Reflexes*. Trans. by G. V. Anrep. New York, Liveright.

Pavlov, I. P. (1941) *Conditioned Reflexes and Psychiatry*. Trans. by W. H. Gantt. New York, International Publ.

Pearce, J. F. (1963) *Aspects of Transvestism*. M.D. Thesis, University of London.

Pecknold, J. C., Raeburn, J., and Poser, E. G. (1972) Intravenous Diazepam for facilitating relaxation for desensitization, *J. Behav. Ther. Exp. Psychiat.*, **3**: 39.

Phillips, L. W. (1971) Training of sensory and imaginal responses in behavior therapy. In R. D. Rubin, Fensterheim, H., Lazarus, A. A., and Franks, C. M. (Eds.), *Advances in Behavior Therapy*. New York, Academic Press.

Philpott, W. M. (1967) Personal communication.

Pitts, F. N. and McClure, J. (1967) Lactate metabolism in anxiety neurosis, *New Eng. J. Med.*, **277**: 1329.

Poppen, R. (1970) Counterconditioning of conditioned suppression in rats, *Psychol. Rep.*, **27**: 659.

Potter, S. (1971) *The Complete Upmanship*. New York, Holt, Rinehart & Winston.

Premack, D. (1965) Reinforcement theory. In D. Levine (Ed.), *Nebraska Symposium on Motivation*. Lincoln, Univ. Nebraska Press.

Rachman, S. (1961) Sexual disorders and behavior therapy, *Amer. J. Psychiat.*, **118**: 235.

Rachman, S. (1965) Studies in desensitization. I, The separate effects of relaxation and desensitization, *Behav. Res. Ther.*, **3**: 245.

Rachman, S. (1966) Studies in desensitization: III, Speed of generalization, *Behav. Res. Ther.*, **4**: 7.

Rachman, S. and Teasdale, J. D. (1968) Aversion therapy. In C. L. Franks (Ed.), *Assessment and Status of the Behavior Therapies and Associated Developments*. New York, McGraw-Hill.

Rachman, S. and Teasdale, J. (1969) *Aversion Therapy and Behavior Disorders*. London, Routledge and Kegan Paul.

Rafi, A. A. (1962) Learning theory and the treatment of tics, *J. Psychosom. Res.*, **6**: 71.

Rainey, C. A. (1972) An obsessive-compulsive neurosis treated by flooding in vivo, *J. Behav. Ther. Exp. Psychiat.*, **3**: 117.

Rathus, S. A. (1972) An experimental investigation of assertive training in a group setting, *J. Behav. Ther. Exp. Psychiat.*, **3**: 80.

Raymond, M. J. (1956) Case of fetishism treated by aversion therapy, *Brit. Med. J.*, **2**: 854.

Raymond, M. and O'Keefe, K. (1965) A case of pin-up fetishism treated by aversion conditioning, *Brit. J. Psychiat.*, **111**: 579.

Razani, J. (1972) Ejaculatory incompetence treated by deconditioning anxiety, *J. Behav. Ther. Exp. Psychiat.*, **3**: 65.

Reade, W. (1872) *The Martyrdom of Man*. London, Watts & Co. (1943).

Reed, J. L. (1966) Comments on the use of methohexitone sodium as a means of inducing relaxation, *Behav. Res. Ther.*, **4**: 323.

Reyna, L. J. (1964) Conditioning therapy, learning theories and research. In J. Wolpe, A. Salter and L. J. Reyna (Eds.), *Conditioning Therapies*. New York, Holt, Rinehart & Winston.

Ritter, B. J. (1968) The group treatment of children's snake phobias using vicarious and contact desensitization procedures, *Behav. Res. Ther.*, 6: 1.

Robinson, C. and Suinn, R. (1969) Group desensitization of a phobia in massed sessions, *Behav. Res. Ther.*, 7: 319.

Rothballer, A. B. (1959) The effects of catecholamines on the central nervous system, *Pharm. Rev.*, 11: 494.

Rubin, L. S. (1970) Pupillary reflexes as objective indices of autonomic dysfunction in the differential diagnosis of schizophrenic and neurotic behavior, *J. Behav. Ther. Exp. Psychiat.*, 1: 185.

Rubin, M. (1972) Verbally suggested responses as reciprocal inhibition of anxiety, *J. Behav. Ther. Exp. Psychiat.*, 3: 273.

Salter, A. (1949) *Conditioned Reflex Therapy*. New York, Creative Age.

Salter, A. (1952) *The Case Against Psychoanalysis*. New York, Holt, Rinehart & Winston.

Salzer, H. M. (1966) Relative hypoglycemia as a cause of neuropsychiatric illness, *J. Natn'l. Med. Ass'n.*, 58: 12.

Sanderson, R. E., Campbell, D., and Laverty, S. G. (1963) Traumatically conditioned responses acquired during respiratory paralysis, *Nature*, 196: 1235.

Sandison, R. A. (1954) Psychological aspects of the LSD treatment of the neuroses, *J. Ment. Sci.*, 100: 508.

Sargant, W. and Dally, P. (1962) The treatment of anxiety states by antidepressant drugs, *Brit. Med. J.*, 1: 6.

Schaefer, H. H. and Martin, P. L. (1969) *Behavioral Therapy*. New York, McGraw-Hill.

Schwitzgebel, R. R. and Kolb, D. A. (1964) Inducing behavior change in adolescent delinquents, *Behav. Res. Ther.*, 1: 297.

Scrignar, C. B. (1971) Food as the reinforcer in the outpatient treatment of anorexia nervosa, *J. Behav. Ther. Exp. Psychiat.*, 2: 31.

Semans, J. H. (1956) Premature ejaculation, a new approach, *South. Med. J.*, 49: 353.

Semans, J. H. (1962) Personal communication.

Serber, M. (1970) Shame aversion therapy, *J. Behav. Ther. Exp. Psychiat.*, 1: 213.

Shames, G. H. (1969) Verbal reinforcement during therapy interviews with stutterers. In B. B. Gray and G. England (Eds.), *Stuttering and The Conditioning Therapies*. California, Monterey Institute for Speech and Hearing.

Sherman, A. R. (1972) Real-life exposure as a primary therapeutic factor in the desensitization treatment of fear, *J. Abn. Psychol.*, 79: 19.

Shmavonian, B. M. and Wolpe, J. (1972) Unpublished data.

Shorvon, H. J. and Sargant, W. (1947) Excitatory abreaction with special reference to its mechanism and the use of ether, *J. Ment. Sci.*, 93: 709.

Siegel, G. M. and Martin, R. R. (1967) Verbal punishment of disfluencies during spontaneous speech, *Lang. & Speech*, 10: 244.

Simonov, P. V. (1962) Stanislavskii method and physiology of emotions, Mimeo.

Simonov, P. V. (1967) Studies of emotional behavior of humans and animals by Soviet physiologists. *Paper read at Conference on Experimental Approaches to the Study of Behavior*, New York.

Singh, H. (1963) Therapeutic use of thioridazine in premature ejaculation, *Amer. J. Psychiat.*, 119: 891.

Skinner, B. F. (1938) *The Behavior of Organisms*. New York, Appleton-Century-Crofts.

Skinner, B. F. (1953) *Science and Human Behavior*, New York, Macmillan.

Skinner, B. F. and Lindsley, O. R. (1954) Studies in behavior therapy. Status reports II and III, Office of Naval Research Contract N5 ori-7662.

Slater, S. L. and Leavy, A. (1966) The effects of inhaling a 35% carbon dioxide, 65% oxygen mixture upon anxiety level in neurotic patients, *Behav. Res. Ther.*, 4: 309.

Solomon, R. L. (1964) Punishment, *Amer. Psychol.*, 19: 239.

Solyom, L. (1969) A case of obsessive neurosis treated by aversion relief, *Canad. Psychiat. Assn. J.*, 14: 623.

Solyom, L. and Miller, S. (1965) A differential conditioning procedure as the initial phase of the behavior therapy of homosexuality, *Behav. Res. Ther.*, 3: 147.

Stampfl, T. G. (1964) Quoted by London (1964).

Stampfl, T. G. and Levis, D. J. (1967) Essentials of implosive therapy: A learning-theory-based psychodynamic behavioral therapy, *J. Abn. Psychol.*, 72: 496.

Stampfl, T. G. and Levis, D. J. (1968) Implosive therapy, a behavioral therapy, *Behav. Res. Ther.*, 6: 31.

Stetten, D. (1968) Basic Sciences in Medicine: The example of gout, *New Eng. J. Med.*, 278: 1333.

Stevens, S. S. (1957) On the psychophysical law, *Psychol. Rev.*, 64: 153.

Stevens, S. S. (1962) The surprising simplicity of sensory metrics, *Amer. Psychol.*, 17: 29.

Stevenson, I. and Wolpe, J. (1960) Recovery from sexual deviation through overcoming non-sexual neurotic responses, *Amer. J. Psychol.*, 116: 737.

Stewart, M. A. (1961) Psychotherapy by reciprocal inhibition, *Amer. J. Psychiat.*, 188: 175.

Stoffelmayr, B. E. (1970) The treatment of a retching response to dentures by counteractive reading aloud, *J. Behav. Ther. Exp. Psychiat.*, 1: 163.

Stuart, R. B. (1967) Behavioral control of overeating, *Behav. Res. Ther.*, 5: 357.

Stuart, R. B. (1969) Operant-interpersonal treatment for marital discord, *J. Consult. Clin. Psychol.*, 33: 675.

Stuart, R. and Davis, B. (1972) *Fat Chance in A Slim World*. Champaign, Research Press.

Sulzer, E. S. (1965) Behavior modification in psychiatric adult patients. In L. Ullmann and L. Krasner (Eds.), *Case Studies in Behavior Modification*. New York, Holt, Rinehart & Winston.

Sushinsky, L. W. and Bootzin, R. R. (1970) Cognitive desensitization as a model of systematic desensitization, *Behav. Res. Ther.*, 8: 29.

Suzman, M. M. (1968) Propanolol relieves anxiety symptoms, *Mod. Med.*, May: 36.

Taylor, J. G. (1955) Personal communication.

Taylor, J. G. (1959) Personal communication.

Taylor, J. G. (1963) A behavioral interpretation of obsessive compulsive neurosis, *Behav. Res. Ther.*, 1: 237.

Teplov, B. M. (1959) Some results of the study of strength of the nervous system in man. In B. M. Teplov (Ed.), *Typological Features of Higher Nervous Activity in Man*, Vol. 2. Moscow, Akad. Pedagog. Nauk. RSFSR.

Terhune, W. S. (1948) The phobic syndrome, *Arch. Neurol. Psychiat.*, 62: 162.

Thomas, E. J. (1968) Selected sociobehavioral techniques and principles: An approach to interpersonal helping, *Social Work*, 13: 12.

Thorpe, J. G., Schmidt, E., Brown, P. T., and Castell, D. (1964) Aversion relief therapy: A new method for general application, *Behav. Res. Ther.*, 2: 71.

Tomlinson, J. R. (1970) The treatment of bowel retention by operant procedures: A case study, *J. Behav. Ther. Exp. Psychiat.*, 1: 83.

Tursky, B., Watson, P. D., and O'Connell, D. N. (1965) A concentric shock electrode for pain stimulation, *Psychophysiol.*, 1: 296.

Ullmann, L. P. and Krasner, L. (1965) *Case Studies in Behavior Modification*. New York, Holt, Rinehart & Winston.

Ulrich, R., Stachnik, T., and Mabry, J. (1966) *Control of Human Behavior*. Glenview, Ill., Scott-Foresman.

Valins, S. and Ray, A. A. (1967) Effects of cognitive desensitization on avoidance behavior, *J. Pers. Soc. Psychol.*, 7: 345.

Van Egeren, L. F. (1970) Psychophysiology of systematic desensitization: The habituation model, *J. Behav. Ther. Exp. Psychiat.*, 1: 249.

Van Egeren, L. F., Feather, B. W., and Hein, P. L. (1971) Desensitization of phobias: Some psychophysiological propositions, *Psychophysiol.*, 8: 213.

Voegtlin, W. and Lemere, F. (1942) The treatment of alcohol addiction, *Qrt. J. Stud. Alcoh.*, 2: 717.

Wallace, R. K. (1970) Physiological effects of transcendental meditation, *Science*, 167: 1751.

Walton, D. (1964) Experimental psychology and the treatment of a tiquer, *J. Child Psychol. Psychiat.*, 2: 148.

Walton, D. and Mather, M. D. (1963) The application of learning principles to the treatment of obsessive-compulsive states in the acute and chronic phases of illness. In H. J. Eysenck (Ed.), *Experiments in Behavior Therapy*. New York, Pergamon Press.

Watson, J. B. and Rayner, P. (1920) Conditioned emotional reactions, *J. Exp. Psychol.*, 3: 1.

Weinreb, S. (1966) The effects of inhaling spirit of ammonia upon anxiety level in neurotic patients. Mimeo.

Wikler, A. (1948) Recent progress on research on the neurophysiological basis of morphine addiction. *Amer. J. Psychiat.*, 105: 329.

Wikler, A. (1972) Dynamics of drug dependence: Implications of a conditioning theory for research and treatment. Paper read at Eleventh Annual Meeting, American College of Neuropharmacology, San Juan, Puerto Rico.

Wilder, J. (1945) Facts and figures on psychotherapy, *J. Clin. Psychopath.*, 7: 311.

Wilkins, W. (1972) Desensitization: Getting it together with Davison and Wilson, *Psychol. Bull.*, 78: 32.

Williams, C. D. (1959) The elimination of tantrum behavior by extinction procedures: Case report, *J. Abn. Soc. Psychol.*, 59: 269.

Willis, R. W. and Edwards, J. A. (1969) A study of the comparative effectiveness of the systematic desensitization and implosive therapy, *Behav. Res. Ther.*, 7: 387.

Willoughby, R. R. (1934) Norms for the Clark-Thurston Inventory, *J. Soc. Psychol.*, 5: 91.

Winkelman, N. W. (1955) Chlorpromazine in the treatment of neuropsychiatric disorders, *J. A. M. A.*, 155: 18.

Wisocki, P. A. (1970) Treatment of obsessive-compulsive behavior by covert sensitization and covert reinforcement: A case report, *J. Behav. Ther. Exp. Psychiat.*, 1: 233.

Wohlgemuth, A. (1923) *A Critical Examination of Psychoanalysis*. London, Allen and Unwin.

Wolberg, L. (1948) *Medical Hypnosis*. New York, Grune & Stratton.

Wolpe, J. (1948) An Approach to the problem of neurosis based on the conditioned response. Unpublished manuscript, M. D. Thesis, Univ. of the Witwatersrand.

Wolpe, J. (1952) Objective psychotherapy of the neuroses, *S. A. Med. J.*, 26: 825.

Wolpe, J. (1952) Experimental neurosis as learned behavior, *Brit. J. Psychol.*, 43: 243. a

Wolpe, J. (1954) Reciprocal inhibition as the main basis of psychotherapeutic effects, *Arch. Neur. Psychiat.*, 72: 205.

Wolpe, J. (1956) Learning versus lesions as the basis of neurotic behavior, *Amer. J. Psychiat.*, 112: 923.

Wolpe, J. (1958) *Psychotherapy by Reciprocal Inhibition*. Stanford, Stanford Univ. Press.
Wolpe, J. (1960) Reciprocal inhibition as the main basis of psychotherapeutic effects. In H. J. Eysenck (Ed.) *Behavior Therapy and the Neuroses*. New York, Pergamon Press.
Wolpe, J. (1961) The systematic desensitization treatment of neuroses, *J. Nerv. Ment. Dis.* **112**: 189.
Wolpe, J. (1961) The prognosis in unpsychoanalyzed recovery from neurosis, *Amer. J. Psychiat.*, **118**: 35. a
Wolpe, J. (1962) Isolation of a conditioning procedure as the crucial psychotherapeutic factor, *J. Nerv. Ment. Dis.*, **134**: 316.
Wolpe, J. (1963) Quantitative relationships in the systematic desensitization of phobias, *Amer. J. Psychiat.*, **119**: 1062.
Wolpe, J. (1964) Behavior therapy in complex neurotic states, *Brit. J. Psychiat.*, **110**: 28.
Wolpe, J. (1964) Unpublished data. a
Wolpe, J. (1965) Conditioned inhibition of craving in drug addiction: A pilot experiment, *Behav. Res. Ther.*, **2**: 285.
Wolpe, J. (1969) Behavior therapy of stuttering: Deconditioning the emotional factor. In B. B. Gray and G. England (Eds.), *Stuttering and The Conditioning Therapies*. California, Monterey Institute for Speech and Stuttering.
Wolpe, J. (1969) How can 'cognitions' influence desensitization, *Behav. Res. Ther.*, **7**: 219. a
Wolpe, J. (1970) Emotional conditioning and cognitions: A rejoinder to Davison and Valins, *Behav. Res. Ther.*, **8**: 103.
Wolpe, J. (1970) The discontinuity of neurosis and schizophrenia, *Behav. Res. Ther.*, **8**: 179. a
Wolpe, J. (1970) The instigation of assertive behavior: Transcripts from two cases, *J. Behav. Ther. Exp. Psychiat.*, **1**: 145. b
Wolpe, J. and Flood, J. (1970) The effect of relaxation on the galvanic skin response to repeated phobic stimuli in ascending order, *J. Behav. Ther. Exp. Psychiat.*, **1**: 195.
Wolpe, J. and Fried, R. (1968) Psychophysiological correlates of imaginal presentations of hierarchical stimuli. I, The effect of relaxation. Unpublished manuscript.
Wolpe, J. and Lang. P. J. (1964) A fear survey schedule for use in behavior therapy, *Behav. Res. Ther.*, **2**: 27.
Wolpe, J. and Lang, P. J. (1969) *Fear Survey Schedule*, Educational and Industrial Testing Service, San Diego, Calif.
Wolpe, J. and Rachman, S. (1960) Psychoanalytic evidence: A critique based on Freud's case of little Hans, *J. Nerv. Ment. Dis.*, **131**: 135.
Wolpe, J. and Theriault, N. (1971) Francois Leuret: A progenitor of behavior therapy, *J. Behav. Ther. Exp. Psychiat.*, **2**: 19.
Wolpin, M. and Pearsall, L. (1965) Rapid deconditioning of a fear of snakes, *Behav. Res. Ther.*, **3**: 107.
Wolpin, M. and Raines, J. (1966) Visual imagery, expected roles and extinction as possible factors in reducing fear and avoidance behavior, *Behav. Res. Ther.*, **4**: 25.
Yamagami, T. (1971) The treatment of an obsession by thought-stopping, *J. Behav. Ther. Exp. Psychiat.*, **2**: 133.
Yates, A. J. (1958) The application of learning theory to the treatment of tics, *J. Abn. Soc. Psychol.*, **56**: 175.
Yeung, D. P. H. (1968) Diazepam for treatment of phobias, *Lancet*, **1**: 475.

Author Index

Subject Index

TITLES IN THE PERGAMON GENERAL PSYCHOLOGY SERIES